The Elusive Balance

This book was written under the auspices of
the Center of International Studies
at Princeton University

This book is a volume in the series

CORNELL STUDIES IN SECURITY AFFAIRS

edited by Robert J. Art, Robert Jervis,
and Stephen M. Walt

A complete listing appears at the end of the book.

The Elusive Balance

POWER AND PERCEPTIONS DURING THE COLD WAR

WILLIAM CURTI WOHLFORTH

Cornell University Press

ITHACA AND LONDON

First published 1993 by Cornell Univesity Press.

International Standard Book Number 0-8014-2822-X (cloth)
International Standard Book Number 0-8014-8149-X (paper)
Library of Congress Catalog Card Number 93-6857
Printed in the United States of America
Librarians: Library of Congress cataloging information
appears on the last page of the book.

㊀ The paper in this book meets the minimum requirements
of the American National Standard for Information Sciences—
Permanence of Paper for Printed Library Materials, ANSI Z39.48-1984.

Contents

Acknowledgments

I am grateful to Peter Hauslohner and Bruce Russett for the comments they offered on the earliest drafts of this book, and to Robert Jervis and George Breslauer for their comments on the latest.

Tom Banchoff, Paul Christensen, Forrest Colburn, Wolfgang Danspeckgruber, Aaron Friedberg, John Garofano, Peter Gelman, David Holloway, Atul Kohli, Gillian Paull, and H. Bradford Westerfield all read chapters along the way and provided helpful comments.

A great many colleagues and friends in Russia helped me on my numerous trips there. Aleksei E. Titkov of the Epokha Center for Humanities Research in Moscow was especially helpful in arranging two lengthy visits, in 1991 and 1992, and facilitating access to archives. I am also grateful to Vladimir Evstigneev and Igor Uriupin of the New Generation project, Konstantin Pleshakov of the Institute of the U.S.A. and Canada, El'giz Pozdniakov of the Institute of World Economy and International Relations, and Mikhail Zuev of the Military History Institute.

A fellowship from Stanford University's Center for International Security and Arms Control helped early writing and research. The costs of travel to Russia and other research activities were partially offset by grants from the Peter B. Lewis Fund and the Sumitomo Bank Fund, administered by Princeton's Center of International Studies.

This book is dedicated to my grandparents: Robert and Mildred Wohlforth and Merle E. Curti. They know why.

W. C. W.

Princeton, New Jersey

[vii]

Abbreviations

AAN	Arkhiv Akademii Nauk SSSR. Citations in following order: *fond/opis'/delo.*
AVP	Arkhiv Vneshnei Politiki SSSR; after January 1992, Arkhiv Vneshnei Politiki Rossii. Citations in following order: *fond/opis'/papka/delo.*
CDSP	*Current Digest of the Soviet Press.* Citations by volume, issue number, and page.
CIA	Central Intelligence Agency.
CPSU	Communist Party of the Soviet Union.
DDEL/JFD	Dwight D. Eisenhower Library, John Foster Dulles Files, Seeley G. Mudd Manuscript Library, Princeton University.
DDRS	*Declassified Documents Reference System.* To 1981: Washington, D.C.: Carrollton Press; post-1981: Woodbridge, Conn.: Research Publications. Citations by year (or RC, for Retrospective Collection)/document number/page.
DOS	Department of State.
EDC	European Defense Community.
EEC	European Economic Community.
FBIS-SOV	*Foreign Broadcast Information Service Daily Report: Soviet Union.*
FPD	Foreign Broadcast Information Service, *Foreign Press Digest.*
FRUS	*Foreign Relations of the United States.* Washington, D.C.: U.S. Government Printing Office.
GDR	German Democratic Republic.
Gorbachev	M. S. Gorbachev, *Izbrannye rechi i stat'i* [Selected speeches and articles], 8 vols. Moscow: Izdatel'stvo Politicheskoi Literatury, 1987–1991.
ICBM	Intercontinental ballistic missile.

IMEMO	Institut Mirovoi Ekonomiki i Mezhdunarodnykh Otnoshenii (Institute of World Economy and International Relations).
INF	Intermediate-range nuclear forces.
JCS	Joint Chiefs of Staff.
JFDP	John Foster Dulles Papers, Seeley G. Mudd Manuscript Library, Princeton University.
JIC	Joint Intelligence Committee.
JVFD	James V. Forrestal Diaries, Seeley G. Mudd Manuscript Library, Princeton University.
Lenin	V. I. Lenin, *Polnoe sobranie sochineniia* [Complete collected works], 5th ed., 55 vols. Moscow: Gosudarstvennoe Izdatel'stvo Politicheskoi Literatury, 1958–1965.
MAD	Mutual assured destruction.
MEiMO	*Mirovaia Ekonomika i Mezhdunarodnye Otnosheniia* (World economy and international relations).
MKhMP	*Mirovoe Khoziaistvo i Mirovaia Politika* (World economy and world politics).
NATO	North Atlantic Treaty Organization.
NEP	New Economic Policy.
NIE	National Intelligence Estimate.
NKVD	People's Commissariat of Internal Affairs (security police).
NSC	National Security Council.
OSS	Office of Strategic Services.
PRC	People's Republic of China.
PRM	Presidential review memorandum.
Stalin	I. V. Stalin, *Sochineniia* [Works], 16 vols. Vols. 1–13: Moscow: Gosudarstvennoe Izdatel'stvo Politicheskoi Literatury, 1946–1949. Vols. 14–16, ed. Robert H. McNeal: Stanford: Hoover Institution, 1967.
USIA	United States Information Agency.

The Elusive Balance

[1]

Power, Theory,
and Hindsight

This is a book about power in world politics in general and about the relationship between the Soviet Union and the balance of power during the Cold War in particular. Its empirical core is an investigation of how members of the Soviet political elite thought about the problem of power in world politics, mainly during the years between 1945 and 1989. I compare Soviet and American thinking at important periods of the Cold War in order to discern whether the two sides' views of power in world politics were related to the course of their prolonged mutual antagonism. In addition to seeking to know more about the Soviet Union and the Cold War, I aim to contribute to a better understanding of the nature and influence of power in world politics.

These motives, mixed as they may seem, are interdependent. To reflect upon the experience of individual states in world politics, we need international political theory, which generates expectations about the constraints states face. To reflect on international political theory, we must supplement abstract thinking with concrete research on individual states, political elites, and leaders. The rigid separation of the study of international politics from that of foreign policy may be useful for some purposes, but not for those of this book.

PERCEPTIONS OF POWER AND REALISM

This book investigates perceptions of power because other ways of conceptualizing power cannot be divorced from knowledge of the

[1]

outcomes one is seeking to explain. No concept is more central to international relations theory than power; and none is more elusive. The concept of power is so elusive that the prospects for a rigorous and testable balance-of-power theory that says anything substantial about world politics are exceedingly dim. But since scholars and statesmen consider power to be so important, no analysis of world politics is complete if it fails to treat the question of power. So power-centered analytical frameworks and working hypotheses are needed. The central argument here is that these frameworks will be improved with the accumulation of historical knowledge about how political elites have actually perceived power in various times and places.[1] The argument rests on a simple premise: If power influences the course of international politics, it must do so largely through the perceptions of the people who make decisions on behalf of states.

Before developing this argument, I ought to stress the modesty of the enterprise. As important as power is, it is only one of a large number of conceptual dilemmas lying athwart the course toward a powercentric theory of international politics deserving of the name. The realist approach, which has dominated the scholarly discourse on international relations since World War II, centers on a variety of concepts and propositions: the prevalence and permanence of conflict among the groups that act in world politics (city-states, empires, nation-states); the centrality of those groups; the concept of a rational strategic "interest"; and the vital importance of the distribution of power. The focus here is on the last of these realist concerns. The rest are almost as controversial.

One of the main ideas behind realist interpretations of international relations is that when human societies are organized into sovereign territorial units subject to no higher authority and relying for survival mainly on their own efforts, the distribution of power among these units will be the most important variable conditioning their behavior and the outcome of their interactions over the long run. Thucydides was the first to put the idea clearly in writing, half a millennium before Christ, but no doubt it predates him. Since the eighteenth century, theoretical thinking about international politics has been dominated by conceptions that attribute primary causal importance

---

[1] The major contemporary study of an individual state's perception of the balance of power is Aaron Friedberg, *The Weary Titan* (Princeton: Princeton University Press, 1988). For other studies of the perception of power before World War I, see W. C. Wohlforth, "The Perception of Power: Russia in the Pre-1914 Balance," *World Politics* 39 (April 1987): 353–81, and Risto Ropponen, *Die Kraft Russlands* (Helsinki: Historiallisia Tutkimiksia, 1968).

to the distribution of power. The exalted status of this one variable is due not only to tradition but to the fact that not just scholarly observers but also practitioners of diplomacy affirm its importance, publicly and privately, in office and in retirement.

Despite its centrality and longevity, balance-of-power theory has remained controversial, and for good reason. As Kenneth Waltz put it, "one cannot find a statement of the theory that is generally accepted."[2] That assessment is arguably only slightly less true today than it was when Waltz advanced it in 1979. Indeed, centuries of conceptual elaboration, political practice, and empirical research have done little to clarify perennial disputes about the balance of power.

One problem concerns the daunting ambiguity of the very term "balance of power." Does it mean a system or a condition, equilibrium or preponderance, a policy or an inevitable political law? Early postwar writers on the subject, notably Hans Morgenthau, were notoriously sloppy in their use of the term. But trenchant essays on the balance of power by the likes of Ernst Haas, Inis Claude, and Martin Wight and later works in the realist tradition by Waltz and Robert Gilpin have done much to clarify the language.[3] Attempts to quantify the balance of power in an effort to subject propositions to empirical testing, though they did not resolve the old debates, led to a much-needed clarification of terms and hypotheses.[4] It is difficult to read this literature without concluding that it represents a heartwarming case of genuine intellectual progress. Now scholars are much more careful to specify when they mean equilibrium, preponderance, or hegemony, and whether they are discussing a policy, an institution, a structure, an iron law, or a general tendency.

The same cannot be said of the elusive concept of power itself. The problem with power is not, as in the case of balance, primarily one of definition or terminology. Writings on power in world politics define it in two ways, and individual authors are usually clear and

[2] Kenneth Waltz, *Theory of International Politics* (Reading, Mass.: Addison-Wesley, 1979), 117.

[3] Hans J. Morgenthau, *Politics among Nations*, 5th ed. rev. (New York: Knopf, 1978), chaps. 11–14; Ernst B. Haas, "The Balance of Power: Prescription, Concept, or Propaganda?" *World Politics* 5 (July 1953): 442–71; Inis L. Claude, Jr., *Power and International Relations* (New York: Random House, 1962), chaps. 2–3; Martin Wight, *Power Politics*, ed. Hedley Bull and Carsten Holbraad (Leicester: Leicester University Press, 1978), chap. 16; Waltz, *Theory of International Relations*; Robert Gilpin, *War and Change in World Politics* (New York: Cambridge University Press, 1981).

[4] For instructive reviews of this literature, see Michael F. Sullivan, *Power in Contemporary International Relations* (Columbia: University of South Carolina Press, 1990); and Randolph Siverson and Michael Sullivan, "The Distribution of Power and the Onset of War," *Journal of Conflict Resolution* 27 (September 1983): 472–95.

consistent in their usage. A minority adopt a relational definition, most famously formulated by Robert Dahl as *"A's* ability to get *B* to do something it would not otherwise do."[5] By far the majority prefers a material definition of "power" as the capabilities or resources, mainly military, with which states can influence one another. Power, in this view, is the actual capacity to raise armies, deploy navies, occupy territory, and exert various forms of pressure against other states. Theorists in the realist or balance-of-power tradition are virtually unanimous in their insistence on defining power as capabilities.

Defining power as control (over other actors, outcomes, or the international system as a whole) leads almost inexorably to tautology, and hence is of little use for international political theory.[6] If one defines power as control, one must infer the relationship of power from outcomes. A relationship of power can never be known until after power is exercised. Under such a definition it is impossible to distinguish a given relationship of power from the outcome produced or influenced by that relationship, since the former will have to be inferred from the latter. Inferring the balance of power from outcomes and then using the balance of power to explain those outcomes appears to be a dubious analytical exercise.

The relational definition of power also presents the researcher with daunting empirical dilemmas, a deficiency recognized by Dahl and other contributors to the literature on "social power."[7] To assess the extent of *A's* power over *B*, the investigator must answer the counterfactual question: What would *B* have done in the absence

[5]Or, of course, *A's* ability to prevent *B* from doing something it would otherwise do. See Robert Dahl, "The Concept of Power," *Behavioral Science* 2 (July 1957): 202. See also Dahl, "Power," in *International Encyclopedia of the Social Sciences*, vol. 12 (New York: Free Press, 1968), and *Modern Political Analysis*, 4th ed. (Englewood Cliffs, N.J.: Prentice-Hall, 1984), esp. chap. 3. For the student of international relations, the best guide through this "social power" literature is David A. Baldwin, *Paradoxes of Power* (New York: Basil Blackwell, 1989), who makes the most compelling case for the application of the relational definition of power to international theory. In addition to "control over actors," other relational definitions include "control over outcomes" and "ability to prevail in conflict." See Jeffrey Hart, "Three Approaches to the Measurement of Power in International Relations," *International Organization* 30 (Spring 1976): 281–305; Karl Deutsch, *The Analysis of International Relations* (Englewood Cliffs, N.J.: Prentice-Hall, 1968), 22; Klaus Knorr, *The Power of Nations* (New York: Basic Books, 1975), 3–26. For a general discussion of various ways of conceptualizing power, see Bruce Russett and Harvey Starr, *World Politics: The Menu for Choice*, 3d ed. (San Francisco: W. H. Freeman, 1989), chap. 6.

[6]Waltz, *Theory of International Relations*, 191–92; Robert O. Keohane, ed., *Neorealism and Its Critics* (New York: Columbia University Press, 1986), 11. It is instructive to compare these statements with Dahl, *Modern Political Analysis*, chap. 3.

[7]See Dahl, "Concept of Power," 202, 214, and his *Modern Political Analysis*, 22–33.

of *A*'s exercise of power? Counterfactual analysis of that kind is an extraordinarily tricky business. The task is further complicated by Dahl's and his followers' insistence that any statement about power "verges on being meaningless" unless it clearly specifies domain (Over whom is power exercised? Who, exactly, is *B*?) and scope (the issues on which *A* can influence *B*).[8] The nature and measurement of power consequently shift with respect to an infinite number of actors and issues. This definition leaves the empirical researcher practically unable to distinguish power from politics as a whole.

A final reason scholars of international politics have tended to avoid the relational definition is conservative but nonetheless compelling. A term in the social sciences, or in any field of scholarly inquiry, ought to reflect common usage and intuitive understanding. Whatever the case may be with respect to the unmodified "power," by far the most common understanding of the venerable term "balance of power" refers not to the distribution of influence with respect to a particular issue but to the distribution of capabilities that may or may not be translated into influence over many issues.[9] Since this book is an inquiry into the utility of the balance-of-power framework, it must use the term "power" as it has been used in the hundreds of works treating this issue already standing on the shelves. To shift definitions now would be to risk adding to the already substantial semantic confusion that besets the analysis of power.[10]

The nearly unanimous affection of balance-of-power theorists for the power-as-capabilities definition has not spared them from their share of conceptual conundrums. These difficulties mainly concern the relationship between power (material capabilities or resources)

---

[8] Dahl, *Modern Political Analysis*, 27. Baldwin, *Paradoxes of Power*, makes the strongest case in favor of this proposition for international theory.

[9] Wight analyzes the use of the term through history in *Power Politics*, chap. 16. See also Haas, "Balance of Power."

[10] Some of the difference between those who favor the two basic definitions reflects an argument over the proper research agenda rather than the analysis of the concept of power itself. Realists are actually concerned with a limited domain: the leaderships of the great powers. The scope of their statements about the balance of power is usually limited to the issues of alignment, alliance, and war. They appear to be much more interested than the theorists of social power in the relationship between power resources and influence, or outcomes. They use the word "power" for Dahl's "power base" or "power resources," and "influence" or "prestige" for his "power." (See Dahl's discussion in *Modern Political Analysis*, 20–23.) Baldwin's discussion in *Paradoxes of Power*, for example, ignores the literature on power and war "in the context of [his] broader focus" (142). Further, it does not distinguish among "power," "influence," and "force" (7). As compelling as Baldwin's analysis is, it is hard to imagine a productive discussion of the balance of power in which distinctions of this sort are not made. Again, the real dispute is very largely over what the important issues are.

and influence or outcomes. Many authors assume that the balance of power is a real distribution of capabilities, to which states adjust or fail to adjust. The distribution of capabilities exists apart from the perceptions of statesmen, and influences (though no one goes so far as to say "determines") outcomes. Contemporary assessments will vary around the real distribution. Some leaderships will overestimate their power, others will underestimate it. Some will get the trends wrong. Bias and misperceptions will occur. The quality and quantity of evidence about power capabilities will naturally vary.

Scholars differ in the importance they attach to misperception, but most believe that a real, physical distribution of power exists out there, which people either perceive correctly or do not. The behavior of states may be affected by perceptions of power, most believe, but in the final analysis the outcomes of state interactions will be influenced by the real distribution of power. Kenneth Waltz's "structural realist" theory is merely the clearest and most rigorous presentation of this approach. Theorists from Jean-Jacques Rousseau and David Hume to A. J. P. Taylor, Arnold Toynbee, and Raymond Aron discuss the balance of power as an objective backdrop to international relations, conditioning the outcome of state interaction irrespective of the intentions, desires, or perceptions of statesmen.[11]

On the surface, the material definition appears to disentangle the balance of power from outcomes. It promises the benefit of distinguishing among "real" power, power as perceived by actors on the scene, and international outcomes, such as crises and wars. But this approach still begs the question how the analyst measures "real power," if not by reference to the outcomes he is explaining. What, if not hindsight, gives the scholar remote in place and time from the events she analyzes a special insight into the distribution of capabilities, not possessed by the participants themselves? Most works meas-

---

[11] See the quotations assembled in Wight, *Power Politics*, 178–79; Raymond Aron, *Peace and War*, trans. Richard Howard and Annette Baker Fox (New York: Doubleday, 1966), chap. 5. See also Hedley Bull's interesting formulation of the objective-subjective problem in *The Anarchical Society* (New York: Columbia University Press, 1977), chap. 5. For Bull, only objective balances of power have permanence and stability. Balances merely perceived are inherently unstable. Klaus Knorr, *The Power of Nations* (New York: Basic Books, 1975), treats perceptions as a "conversion process" linking real power capabilities and outcomes. The debate on U.S. decline and hegemonic stability theory in the 1980s did see increased attention to nonmaterial sources of power, such as "cultural," "structural," and "soft" power. See Bruce Russett, "The Mysterious Case of Vanishing Hegemony; or, Is Mark Twain Really Dead?" *International Organization* 39 (Spring 1985); Susan Strange, "The Persistent Myth of Lost Hegemony," *International Organization* 41 (Autumn 1987): 551–74; and Joseph P. Nye, *Bound to Lead: The Changing Nature of American Power* (New York: Basic Books, 1990).

ure power by reference to a very loose index of military, economic, and technical resources, plus population and territory. But combining such a large number of factors produces practically any distribution of power desired. This is as true of quantitative indicators of power as it is of the more impressionistic measures used by the classical realists. One can construct a plausible index of power capabilities that yields equilibria of power among states, hierarchies of power, unipolar distributions, and power transitions between states at practically any desired moment.[12]

Construction of a power index is further complicated by social, economic, and technological change over time, which may influence the sources of power.[13] The size of a state's population, for example, may have had more bearing on its power position in the nineteenth century than in the eighteenth. Individual states may thus gain or lose comparative advantage over time. Geographical position and social, economic, and political organization confer on different states different power conversion ratios. One state may be twice as efficient at converting resources into effective power as its neighbor. Germany, centrally located and highly efficient, is often cited as a state with a relatively high power conversion ratio in comparison with its great-power competitors. All of these influences are usually matters of speculation and dispute at any given time but become clear with hindsight as the outcomes of rivalries and wars provide evidence about effective power.

A material definition of power is at best a weak defense against the hindsight problem. A measurement of the distribution of capabilities can never be entirely divorced from the requirements of the theory concerned and knowledge of the history the theory is employed to explain or against which it is being tested. Such measurement problems confront even Waltz's structural theory, which requires limited precision in measuring the distribution of capabilities. The theory

[12]See Deutsch, *Analysis of International Relations*, 22; A. K. F. Organski and Jacek Kugler, *The War Ledger* (Chicago: University of Chicago Press, 1980), 19; and George Modelski and William R. Thompson, *Sea Power in Global Politics since 1494* (London: Macmillan, 1987), chap. 5, for measures that yield hierarchies. Jack Levy, "The Polarity of the System and International Stability: An Empirical Analysis," in *Polarity and War*, ed. Alan Ned Sabrosky (Boulder Colo.: Westview, 1985), finds extended periods of unipolarity in the history of the states system. The popular correlates-of-war indicators, as well as other broadly based indexes, tend to yield rough equilibria of power. For an assessment of these capabilities indexes in the case of World War I, see Wohlforth, "Perception of Power"; and, for the argument that reliable capabilities indexes can be constructed, Sullivan, *Power*, chap. 4.

[13]Stanley Hoffmann, "Notes on the Elusiveness of Modern Power," *International Journal* 30 (Spring 1975): 183–206; Nye, *Bound to Lead*.

[7]

draws inferences about the constraints imposed on states by different structures (distributions) of power: bipolar and multipolar. But the number of "poles" in a system depends on how one measures power. One analyst's unipolarity can be another's bipolarity.[14] The choice is determined by one's theoretical project coupled with knowledge of the outcomes one seeks to understand. This sequence calls into question the "prior" status of structure. The structure ("real" power) reveals itself in the course of diplomatic interaction, and then we employ that structure to explain the diplomacy. How does this approach differ from the relational definition's inference of a power relation on the basis of outcomes?

If "real" power is divorced from the actual calculations of statesmen and not driven by knowledge of outcomes, the idea is difficult to pin down. Some "classical" realists recognized this problem. Indeed, the elusiveness of power is one reason some early postwar realists, such as Martin Wight, Herbert Butterfield, and Edward Gulick, believed that a shared "moral" community of statesmen who also shared a single operational theory of the balance of power was a prerequisite for a functioning balance-of-power system.[15] If all the sovereigns agreed arbitrarily to assume that an equilibrium of power existed at some hypothetical initial point, and agreed further that power would be measured by a known formula, one can imagine a functioning balancing system, under which equilibrium would be maintained through alliance formation, compensation, and the adjustment of in-

[14]Most of the disagreement about polarity is the result of competing definitions of the term. For useful discussions, see Frank Whelon Wayman, "Polarity and War," *Journal of Peace Research* 21 (January 1984): 61–78; and J. D. Singer and Paul F. Diehl, eds., *Measuring the Correlates of War* (Ann Arbor: University of Michigan Press, 1990). However, scholars who define and measure polarity in an essentially identical manner can still perceive different structures in the same historical period. Compare, for example, Levy, "The Polarity of the System," with Ted Hopf, "Polarity, the Offense-Defense Balance, and War," *American Political Science Review* 85 (June 1991): 475–93. Or see the disputes over the polarity of the classical Greek system of city-states and the Congress of Vienna system in Richard Ned Lebow and Barry S. Strauss, eds., *Hegemonic Rivalry: From Thucydides to the Nuclear Age* (Boulder, Colo.: Westview, 1991); and the forum "Did the Vienna Settlement Rest on a Balance of Power?" in *American Historical Review* 97 (June 1992): 683–735. For earlier discussions of the concept of polarity, see Morton A. Kaplan, *System and Process in International Politics* (New York: Wiley, 1957), chap. 2; and Aron, *Peace and War*, chap. 5.

[15]Edward Vose Gulick, *Europe's Classical Balance of Power* (Ithaca: Cornell University Press, 1955), 24–29; the essays by Wight and Butterfield on the balance of power in *Diplomatic Investigations*, ed. Martin Wight and Herbert Butterfield (London: George Allen & Unwin, 1966); Butterfield, "The Balance of Power," in *Dictionary of the History of Ideas*, ed. Philip P. Wiener, 1:179–88 (New York: Scribner's, 1968); Morgenthau, *Politics among Nations*, adapts this position briefly (227), though he maintains elsewhere that the power balancing is inevitable (174) and impossible (215).

ternal military efforts. Under such conditions, power in world politics would begin to approximate money in economics because of shared assumptions about its value and fungibility.[16]

But the classical realists knew that such an ideal situation never obtained, even during the heyday of the balance of power in the eighteenth and nineteenth centuries. Because they believed that even within Christian Europe competition among states was intense, they knew that sovereigns would seek to deceive each other about the extent of their power, and would ignore any power-calculation formula if they thought they could prevail in some quick military campaign. Furthermore, a plausible formula could not be devised, because the outcome of a war could not be predicted in advance. The early realists consequently subscribed to Francis Bacon's warning that "there is nothing among civil affairs more subject to error than the forming of a true and right valuation of the power and forces of an empire."[17] As Aaron Friedberg points out, however, though they recognize the difficulty of measuring power, "when it comes to explaining how statesmen actually do their difficult job, the classical realists appear to lose interest and move on to other, more tractable subjects."[18]

Many analysts recognize the apparent ambiguity of all power calculations, and seek to ground their definition of power in concrete historical outcomes. A venerable tradition in international theory and practice, followed by intellectuals as diverse as V. I. Lenin, A. J. P. Taylor, and Robert Gilpin, is to regard major war as the ultimate "test" of the distribution of capabilities.[19] In this view, war is functional precisely because it determines the hierarchy of states in the scales of power. War thus provides reality to the concept of power. But one can question how reliable war is as a test of power, for many wars are terminated by negotiations, not by the complete victory of one side, and thus many war outcomes reflect statesmen's perceptions of power and expectations about future trends. And though a major war may establish the relation of power between the victorious coalition of states and its vanquished adversaries, it may produce quite am-

---

[16] On the analogy between money and power, see Baldwin, *Paradoxes of Power*, chap. 2.

[17] Cited in Gulick, *Europe's Classical Balance of Power*, 49.

[18] Friedberg, *Weary Titan*, 11.

[19] Lenin, 21:242; A. J. P. Taylor, *The Struggle for Mastery of Europe* (London: Oxford University Press, 1957), xxix; Robert Gilpin, *U.S. Power and the Multinational Corporation* (New York: Basic Books, 1975), 24, and *War and Change*, 31–33. See also Geoffrey Blainey, *The Causes of Wars* (New York: Free Press, 1973), 113.

biguous evidence about the relation of power among the victor states themselves. So, though wars may lead to dramatic changes in perceptions of power, they may not vitiate Bacon's warning about the difficulty of coming to a "true valuation" of the power distribution.

THE UNREALITY OF POWER

All of the foregoing considerations call into question the very idea of "real" power. A truly conclusive test of power that would yield incontestable results is difficult to imagine, short of a general war that destroyed all but one member of the international system. For statesmen, accurate assessments of power are impossible. For scholars, accurate assessments practically mean a correct rendering of the perceptions that inform decisions. Of course, real material balances are related to these perceptions, but we do not know how closely. The power value of various measurable resources becomes clear only after the fact. To put it more accurately, the relevant actors' opinions about the power value of various resources are influenced by the outcomes they regard as important. How frequently such outcomes occur, how strongly they influence opinions, and how uniformly they influence different actors are all currently matters of speculation among scholars (if they are considered at all). One can imagine a process of rolling revisionism as the flow of events provides a steady stream of evidence for revising present (and past) power assessments, or a punctuated revisionism, in which assessments settle into a stable pattern until they are interrupted by dramatic events, such as wars.[20]

The unreality of power complicates matters for international relations scholars. Assessing foreign policy at anything but a descriptive level requires a general international political theory that generates expectations about the nature of the external environment. But confidence in any theory demands that it be testable. The unreality of power naturally renders balance-of-power theories hard to test satisfactorily, no matter how rigorously they are formulated. Because power relationships reveal themselves only in hindsight, and even then imperfectly, establishing their connection to behavior or outcomes is problematic. Even the roughest correlational plausibility checks on various postulates of balance-of-power theories are always subject to questions about the accuracy of the measure of power used.

---

[20] These categories correspond roughly to Friedberg's "calculative" and "perceptual" models of assessment and adjustment in *Weary Titan*, 12–17.

Power, Theory, and Hindsight

The elusiveness of power and the consequent difficulty of testing are at least part of the reason for the oft-lamented lack of cumulation in international theory. Numerous incompatible formulations and propositions coexist under the "realist" rubric. Many differences are methodological or epistemological: classical versus neorealist, quantitative versus rational-choice realist, and so on. Many disputes concern interests; whether states seek security, for example, or also seek power for its own sake, for glory, or for control over the states system. And some differences are more apparent than real, reflecting the ubiquitous scholarly tendency to use the same terms to discuss different things or different terms to discuss the same things. So some contradictory conceptualizations and measures of power are merely reflections of these other disputes. But some of the disputes reflect differences about power itself and derive from its elusiveness.

The balance-of-power concept has been called upon to do many things: to explain the long-term regularities of international politics; to explain war; to explain order, stability, and cooperation under anarchy; and to identify the constraints and inducements the international environment presents to states. Are states systems generally characterized by equal or concentrated distributions of power? Do wars arise when power becomes concentrated in one state or diffused among many? Is order based on hegemony or equilibrium? Are states rewarded or punished for expanding power and influence? These are classic questions about the distribution of power. Two intellectual approaches to the question of power and world politics suggest different answers to all of them.[21]

Arguably the dominant strain is the *equilibrium* conception of the balance of power.[22] In this view, a rough equilibrium of power tends to emerge in any states system. An equilibrium emerges in response to a threat of hegemony. Each state, seeking to preserve its own independence, acts in the final analysis so as to prevent any one state from dominating the system. Kenneth Waltz calls the emergence and reemergence of equilibria a "law," by which he means a repeated pattern or general tendency. Scholars who adopt this understanding may be more or less deterministic, but they agree that the important things that happen in world politics, such as wars, alliances and realignments, concerts of powers, and crises, are related to the establishment of an equilibrium of power or the failure to establish one.

[21] Richard Rosecrance points out the distinction between these two strains in *The Rise of the Trading State* (New York: Basic Books, 1986), 56–57.

[22] See George Liska, *International Equilibrium* (Cambridge: Harvard University Press, 1957), esp. chaps. 1–2.

The equilibrium approach dates from the period of Europe's classical balance of power in the eighteenth century and is supported by the European experience after the Peace of Westphalia.[23] For centuries each attempt to achieve dominance over the European states system was stymied by the counterbalancing action of other states. In addition, wars involving the major powers tended throughout most of this period to be long and sanguinary, suggesting that rough equilibria of power prevailed before hostilities in most cases.

The second strain focuses on *hierarchy*.[24] Power resources buy not only security from other states but influence over them. Even if an equilibrium of capabilities obtains, status is not distributed equally. Within the states system, as in any social system, a status hierarchy more or less clear to all members will always emerge. In most periods, one state or group of states will enjoy preeminence, or hegemony, which in the final analysis rests on power. The important things that happen in world politics revolve around the struggle for influence, occasionally called the struggle for power, or prestige. Rising powers desire more influence, declining powers have difficulty adjusting to reduced status. Hierarchy, hegemony, and wars resulting from power transitions are to writers in this tradition as much international-political "laws" as the emergence of equilibrium is to Waltz.[25]

The history of states systems also lends support to the propositions of the hierarchical view, especially if pre-Westphalian systems are included in the analysis. Citing examples such as the China of the Warring States, the Greco-Roman system, and ancient India, Martin Wight concluded that "most states systems have ended in universal empire, which has swallowed all the states of the system."[26] Adam

[23]David Hume maintained that equilibrium ideas date back to the classical period: "Of the Balance of Power," in *The Philosophical Works of David Hume*, 4 vols. (Edinburgh, 1826), 3:373–83. Butterfield, however, makes a good case against this contention in "Balance of Power," tracing their origins to the seventeenth century and their real development only to the eighteenth century.

[24]In addition to Gilpin's, notable works that focus on hierarchies of power include E. H. Carr, *The Twenty Years' Crisis, 1919–1939: An Introduction to the Study of International Relations* (London: Macmillan, 1951); A. F. K. Organski, *World Politics* (New York: Knopf, 1968); Deutsch, *Analysis*; Organski and Kugler, *War Ledger*; Michael Howard, *The Causes of Wars* (Cambridge: Harvard University Press, 1984), chap. 1.

[25]Robert Gilpin, "The Theory of Hegemonic War," *Journal of Interdisciplinary History* 18 (Spring 1988): 591–613; Organski, *World Politics*; George Modelski, *Long Cycles in World Politics* (Seattle: University of Washington Press, 1987). For an excellent intellectual history and comparison of cyclical theories of world politics, see Joshua Goldstein, *Long Cycles and War* (New Haven: Yale University Press, 1988).

[26]Martin Wight, *Systems of States*, ed. Hedley Bull (Leicester: Leicester University Press, 1977), 43.

Watson's extensive survey concludes that *all* systems of states, even those formally based on the principles of equilibrium and sovereignty, show a "gravitational pull towards hegemony."[27] Even in the post-Westphalian system in Europe, certain states enjoyed preeminence. If the Hapsburgs, France, and Germany eventually failed in bids for hegemony, the Hapsburgs enjoyed sucess for a time, and the Dutch and especially the British exercised predominant influence for prolonged periods. Certain states could achieve preeminent influence without sparking counterbalancing actions on the part of other states.

The equilibrium and hierarchical interpretations both easily fall within the ambit of "realist" thinking about international politics, but the contradictions between them are striking, and illustrate the ambiguity of the concept of power. To start with, adherents of the two understandings appear to perceive different distributions of power through long reaches of world history. For hegemony to obtain, power must be sufficiently concentrated in one state to permit it to "lay down the law" to others, a situation that violates the tendency toward equilibrium, and indeed contradicts many scholars' very definition of a balance-of-power system.[28] In the hierarchical view, most states systems include a very powerful state that the others do not counterbalance. Writers in that tradition portray states as routinely able to translate aggregate power resources into political preeminence, while writers in the equilibrium tradition argue that any such effort is doomed. One view sees concentrated or even hegemonic distributions of power as the norm, while the other posits more equal distributions as the usual case. In one interpretation, states tend to balance against superior power, in the other they reveal at least as strong a tendency to defer to it.

In the equilibrium view, an impending or actual preponderance of power in the hands of one state or coalition makes war likely, as other states gather forces to defend their independence and the general equilibrium. In the hegemonic view, preponderance leads to peace, as no challenger will unleash war against an obviously superior opponent. In the former view, the possibility that one state might be in a position to lay down the law is a threat to international order; in the latter view such a condition is a prerequisite of order and its absence a precondition of disorder. One interpretation describes major wars

[27] Adam Watson, *The Evolution of International Society: A Comparative Historical Analysis* (London and New York: Routledge, 1992), 314.

[28] Emmerich de Vattel defines the balance of power as "such a disposition of things as no power is able absolutely to predominate, or to prescribe laws to others": *The Law of Nations* (New York: Samuel Campbell, 1796), 380.

[13]

as antihegemonial struggles to rebalance the system, while the other portrays major wars as struggles for hegemony, arising from power transitions between a dominant state and a rising challenger. In one view war results in the reestablishment of equilibrium while in the other it leads to the establishment of hegemony.

As I noted earlier, some of these apparent differences are artificial, the result of confusing terminology. "Hegemony," for example, may really mean "preeminence." Further, many authors limit the scope of hegemony, usually to economic matters, and the domain to certain subsystems, as in Soviet "hegemony" over Eastern Europe.[29] But the two approaches do overlap; their interrelationship appears quite complex and has yet to be worked out in the literature. Differences persist in explanations for patterns of outcomes and behavior over long stretches of history. Take the Cold War, for example. Was it a hegemonic struggle between a rising Soviet challenger and a dominant United States? Or did it consist of two great states of roughly equal power balancing against each other? Was the "long peace" due to the bipolar structure of the system or to U.S. dominance? Was cooperation between the United States and the other industrialized countries the result of the former's hegemony or of the overarching need to counterbalance Soviet power? "Realism" offers no single answer to these questions.[30] And analogous questions persist about earlier periods of world history, from the Greek system of Thucydides' day to the international pattern established by the Congress of Vienna.

Determining the Elusiveness of Power

The discussion so far suggests that much hinges on the nature of perceptions of power. The more patterned the relationship between perceptions and measurable resources, the better the prospects for

---

[29] See the definitions in Gilpin, *War and Change*; Modelski, *Long Cycles*; Wight, *Systems of States*; Watson, *Evolution of International Society*; and Robert O. Keohane, *After Hegemony: Cooperation and Discord in the World Political Economy* (Princeton: Princeton University Press, 1984).

[30] Examples abound of the assumption that one "realist" proposition on such questions can be contrasted with other explanations. Keohane, for example, contrasts "realist" with "institutionalist" explanations for postwar cooperation among the industrialized market countries. "For Realists . . . the early postwar regimes rested on the *political hegemony* of the United States": *After Hegemony*, 9. But many realists would hardly explain intrawestern cooperation, military and economic, in isolation from the requirement to balance Soviet power. Would a "realist" predict a decline in cooperation after 1960? That depends on whether one focused on American hegemony, which seemed to decline, or on Soviet capabilities, which seemed to increase.

evaluating existing formulations and further developing theory. Of course, knowledge about how political elites actually think about power may not lead to answers to any of the major questions about the balance of power. Instead the conclusion may be that such questions cannot be answered; that power cannot be measured in the best of circumstances; that the variable is simply too imponderable to be of much utility for understanding international politics. To arrive at an initial position on the utility of the balance-of-power concept, we need to know more about power as it is perceived and conceptualized by historical actors in various periods.

The acquisition of such knowledge is the underlying objective of the detailed analysis of Soviet thinking about power and the comparisons with American views in the chapters that follow. No amount of knowledge about the Soviet Union, the United States, or the Cold War could put us in a position to render a conclusive judgment about the balance of power. A single case study, and one subject to limitiations on the availability of important data, does not permit such immodesty. In addition, the Cold War years may prove to be untypical in many respects. And it must be acknowledged at the outset that the probability of discovering conveniently neat perceptual patterns is low. When one indulges in an analysis of beliefs and ideas and conducts research responsibly, one immediately accepts a cruel but familiar trade-off of rigor and parsimony in favor of richness and detail.

The arguments for accepting this trade-off in the analysis of power in world politics are nonetheless compelling, perhaps enough so to induce general readers not directly concerned with the Cold War or the Soviet Union to plow into some of the details. Research on perceptions of power will help to erase the bias of hindsight and establish the nature of the connection between real resources and perceived power. Rough patterns may be discovered in the perceptual record to lend credence to some propositions about power over others, or conceivably to reconcile seemingly imcompatible interpretations. Solid analysis of perceptions of power will contribute to the historical scholarship of the period in a way that international relations scholars will find useful.

This kind of empirical approach is still new, and the body of existing scholarship on it is insignificant in comparison with the literatures that seek to quantify power or theorize abstractly about it. Empirical and conceptual work are interdependent. It would be inappropriate to claim a privileged status for either. But given the lack of cumulation over the preceding millennium, it is fair to question

[15]

whether new and more rigorous reformulations of balance-of-power theory will fare any better than their myraid predecessors in the absence of new thinking and empirical research on power. The aim of this investigation is to get a fresh grasp on a frustratingly elusive concept. It may be of use even to those who do not share its epistemological premises.

The approach employed here obviously does not lead to decisive judgments on all the major uses of the balance-of-power concept: explaining patterns, war, order, and the constraints imposed by the international system. This last task is where general theories or frameworks most closely intersect foreign policy, where they are on the weakest ground, and where this book has most to say. Although research on a period spanning a half-century may permit tentative generalizations about the larger theoretical projects, this book can speak more authoritatively about the relationship between power and the things that concern statesmen and diplomats constantly: influence or prestige, security, alignment, and cooperation.

Balance-of-power frameworks, in short, are flawed and ambiguous, but are also ubiquitous and necessary. The goal of this book is a better understanding of their strengths and limitations. It pursues that goal through the analysis of the latest period of world history, the Cold War, in terms of the balance of power. This book seeks historical rigor without being agnostic about theory. It strives to be true to historical sources while attempting to reach generalizations and add to our cumulative knowledge about world politics. It is an effort to subject important concepts to critical analysis through close and responsible historical research. It is based on the assumption that while theories do identify some important regularities of international politics, their actual nature has still to be determined. It further assumes that of all the biases that beset the systematic analysis of world politics, none is more important or pervasive than hindsight. It represents a major effort to reduce this bias in the analysis of Soviet policy and the Cold War. As shall become evident, confronting the hindsight bias is extraordinarily difficult to do. Indeed, had I known what it required beforehand, I would never have undertaken the project in the first place.

Now that the most general objectives of the project are established, the next task is the transition from general concepts to the case at hand, the techniques used, the shortcuts taken. Such transitions are never as smooth as one would wish, for there is always something of a gap between general frameworks and specific cases, between the balance of power and the experience of individual states in concrete circumstances. The best way to make the transition from the concepts to the case is to confront the literature lying between studies of the nature and influence of power on the world scene and those that focus on individual states, in this case the Soviet Union. This book needs to be located in the universe of its Sovietological comrades.

[2]

Balance-of-Power Theory
and Soviet Foreign Policy

Our conceptual and empirical grasp on power in world politics is more tenuous than is generally recognized. Even when blessed with hindsight, shared definitions, and very loose requirements for accuracy, scholars and statesmen may discover different balances of power at the same time. Indeed, contradictory assessments of and beliefs about the balance of power can coexist in the mind of an individual statesman or scholar. Whether one adopts the common capabilities definition of "power," as here, or favors the relational definition of the term, it is difficult to escape the perennial problems of hindsight and tautology.

The connection between these general points and the hands-on analysis of foreign policy is much more intimate than it may appear at first glance. Establishing this connection ultimately requires further empirical documentation of the nature of power. Here we can spell out the connection only in general terms. Much of what is said here applies equally to the study of the foreign policy of any great power, but for simplicity's sake, and because of the important role the Soviet Union played in the Cold War, the focus is on that country.

THE SEARCH FOR A STANDARD

The way one looks at foreign policy depends on how one thinks the world works. Consequently, disputes about Soviet foreign policy are in part disputes about international politics. Studies of Soviet foreign policy include one or (more commonly) several of the following procedures: description of events; identification of long-term pattern (e.g., change vs. continuity); characterization of the pattern (e.g., expansion vs. defense); explanation (e.g., internal vs. external causality); evaluation (e.g., success vs. failure). The analyst's understanding of international politics influences her intellectual approach to any of these scholarly activities, in ascending order of importance (from description to evaluation). It follows that the state of our "science" of international politics is of vital importance for the study of Soviet (or any other) foreign policy. The issue would be trivial if there were general agreement on the basics of international political theory. But of course there is no such agreement, nor has there ever been.

Intellectual Background

The most venerable explanatory debate in the field concerns the primacy of external versus internal influences on Soviet behavior. George Kennan opened the debate in the postwar period, arguing in 1947 that Soviet behavior was "founded not in the realities of foreign antagonism but in the necessity of explaining away the maintenance of dictatorial authority at home."[1] A half-decade later, Barrington Moore, Jr., weighed in with the opposite assessment. "Sooner or later," he wrote, "the Soviets danced the power political quadrille. . . . The choice of antagonist or allies has been determined not primarily by ideological factors, but by the structure of the balance-of-power system itself."[2] That perennial debate lasted as long as the Soviet Union did, and analogous literatures debating the same question exist for every other great power that ever had its day in the sun.

The Kennan/Moore debate illustrates the common tendency of scholars to contrast the internally generated impulses of the Soviet polity with the requirements of the international system as if the latter were easily knowable, generally known, and widely agreed upon. But in any given period the requirements of the balance of power—or, to use more careful language, the incentives it creates—are matters of dispute among scholars. Neither Kennan nor Moore, nor indeed

---

[1] George F. Kennan ("X"), "The Sources of Soviet Conduct," *Foreign Affairs* 25 (July 1947): 570.
[2] Barrington Moore, Jr., *Soviet Politics—the Dilemma of Power: The Role of Ideas in Social Change* (Cambridge: Harvard University Press, 1950), 383. Also see Marshall Shulman, *Stalin's Foreign Policy Reappraised* (Cambridge: Harvard University Press, 1963), who argues for the "largely rational responsiveness of Soviet policy to changes in the world environment, and particularly to changes in power relationships" (3). Both works reach this conclusion about Soviet policy under Stalin.

scores of their colleagues who wrote in the ideology-versus-balance-of-power vein, spelled out very clearly any balance-of-power theory in any but the crudest terms. They wrote as if the difference between "ideology" and "the balance of power" were self-evident. When one reads these treatises, however, it is obvious that it is not. Soviet actions that Kennan thought had nothing whatever to do with the requirements of survival in a balance-of-power system, including prominently the establishment of hegemony over Eastern Europe, were explained by Moore as rational reactions to that system. An unrecognized part of the dispute concerned the balance of power, and not the Soviet Union. And what is true of Kennan and Moore is true of many other analysts who addressed their topic.

This analysis should not be stretched too far and too indiscriminately. Not all studies of Soviet foreign policy address the external-internal debate, and not all studies that do address that debate phrase it in terms of the balance of power. Many analysts are concerned merely with assessing competing domestic sources of Soviet behavior: conflict among Soviet leaders, the personalities of Soviet dictators, bureaucratic and institutional politics, and so on. Ultimately, one could argue that establishing a privileged domestic cause is only half the battle; that factor must then be compared with the international level of analysis. But, to paraphrase Keynes, ultimately everyone is dead. One cannot expect every scholar to test rigorously his or her explanation against every imaginable competing one. Some studies do address the internal-external debate, but not in terms of the balance of power, focusing instead on imperatives created by nuclear weapons, the scientific-technical revolution, global interdependence, or other international factors.

Two further caveats about earlier works are in order, both of which are central to the intellectual tradition to which this investigation belongs. First, as the field of international relations developed in the postwar years, a number of Sovietologists carefully and explicitly incorporated international political theory into their work. The debate clearly progressed from the days of Kennan and Moore. In addition, many scholars went beyond the crude external-internal dichotomy, seeking nuanced *interactive* explanations for change in Soviet behavior. Most important, they began to pose the issue not as "ideology *versus* the balance of power" but rather as "ideology *and* the balance of power." Ideology, or perceptions, began to be treated as an *intervening variable* lying between the international and domestic political systems.

The outstanding example of this approach is William Zimmerman's pathbreaking *Soviet Perspectives on International Relations,* published in 1969, which directly inspired this investigation. Zimmerman studied the publications of Soviet international relations specialists according to theoretically derived criteria (the major actors, the balance of power, etc.) Soviet perceptions were a kind of yardstick, a way of measuring the country's adaptation to the international system. Did the closed and authoritarian nature of the Soviet Union render it relatively impermeable to outside influences? Zimmerman found increasing intellectual adaptation on the part of the Khrushchev-era political elite to the realities of the international system. Despite its domestic peculiarities, the Soviet Union seemed capable of learning from its interaction with the outside world.[3]

With all its innovativeness, Zimmerman's work did not escape from the dilemma posed at the outset of this section. To what international system was the Soviet Union adapting? For Zimmerman, it was the international system as seen from the vantage of mid-1960s social science orthodoxy—an orthodoxy fiercely disputed even as he wrote his book. Should Moscow see a bipolar or multipolar distribution of power? That depended on whether the Soviets consulted Kenneth Waltz or Stanley Hoffmann. Should the Soviets think bipolarity or multipolarity was more stable? Again, that depended on whether they read Waltz, Richard Rosecrance, or J. D. Singer and Karl Deutsch.[4] Were states the main actors? Had nuclear weapons fundamentally altered international politics? The story was the same. The nature of the international system was contested in the 1960s, as it has always been.

Recent Efforts

The problem that dogged Kennan, Moore, and Zimmerman is still with us. Like their predecessors, the latest approaches to Soviet for-

[3]William Zimmerman, *Soviet Perspectives on International Relations* (Princeton: Princeton University Press, 1969). Excellent later works, which are more various than their titles suggest, include Charles A. Lynch, *The Soviet Study of International Relations* (Cambridge: Cambridge University Press, 1987); Margot Light, *The Soviet Theory of International Relations* (New York: St. Martin's Press, 1988); and Vendulka Kubálková and A. A. Cruikshank, *Marxism-Leninism and Theory of International Relations* (London: Routledge & Kegan Paul, 1980).

[4]See the selections by Waltz, Deutsch and Singer, and Rosecrance in *International Politics and Foreign Policy,* ed. James Rosenau, rev. ed. (New York: Free Press, 1969); Stanley Hoffmann, "Over There," *New York Times,* March 6 and 7, 1972, quoted in Kenneth Waltz, *Theory of International Politics* (Reading, Mass.: Addison-Wesley, 1979), 48.

eign policy require some judgment about the nature of the international environment. The discussion of foreign policy learning, for example, has doubtless become much more nuanced since the 1960s, particularly concerning the definition of the central term.[5] No exponent of the approach, however, has found a satisfactory answer to the epistemological dilemma Zimmerman faced.[6] Any retrospective assessment of a historical actor's learning capacity presupposes some understanding of the environment the actor was supposed to learn about. After all, the nature of the environment should determine the standards we use to assess learning.[7] If world politics is essentially an unpredictable, capricious, and uncertain realm, our expectations about any government's capacity for foreign policy learning will differ from those we would have if world politics were a realm governed by regular and known laws.

Most analysts of foreign policy learning believe that the international realm is subject to certain regularities about which states ought to learn.[8] As a rule, they see strong incentives for cooperation in international relations, and they assess the behavior and beliefs of historical actors accordingly. Some do not conceal the normative origins of their definitions of learning. Their own understanding of the international realities of the Cold War period suggests to them that cooperation was the unambiguously preferred strategy. Failure on the part of the superpowers to cooperate must have reflected a learning disability of some kind.[9]

[5]An early and very sophisticated treatment of learning in Soviet policy is Franklyn J. C. Griffiths, "Images, Politics, and Learning in Soviet Behavior toward the United States" (Ph.D. diss., Columbia University, 1972). George Breslauer and Philip Tetlock, eds., *Learning in U.S. and Soviet Foreign Policy* (Boulder, Colo.: Westview, 1991), is an important later collection.

[6]For a thoughtful critique of the learning model, see Matthew Evangelista, "Sources of Moderation in Soviet Security Policy," in *Behavior, Society and Nuclear War*, ed. Robert Jervis et al. (New York: Oxford University Press, 1991), esp. 266–75. Advocates of the learning approach do recognize the problem. See Philip Tetlock, "Learning in U.S. and Soviet Foreign Policy: In Search of an Elusive Concept," in Breslauer and Tetlock, *Learning*.

[7]See Kenneth Boulding, "The Learning and Reality Testing Process in the International System," in *Image and Reality in World Politics*, ed. John C. Farrell and Asa P. Smith (New York: Columbia University Press, 1967).

[8]For exceptions, see the chapters on arms control by Stephen Weber and Robert Levine in Breslauer and Tetlock, *Learning*.

[9]Breslauer, for example, treats "learning as any reevaluation of the goals and philosophical assumptions built into cold war paradigms, if the reevaluation undercuts unilateral approaches to ensuring national security in favor of cooperative approaches. This may be an arbitrary or normative choice, *but it is no more arbitrary than any approach that seeks to employ in the analysis of international relations the everyday usage of the learning*

The best traditions of social science, however, demand that the scholar define the historical environment in nonsubjective terms. Hence the appeal to theory. Analysts of foreign policy have found Kenneth Waltz's writings most useful in this regard. They focus on two propositions in particular. First is the idea that over time states learn about the structure of the international system.[10] Despite their ideological differences, the United States and the Soviet Union faced the same constraints and inducements associated with bipolarity. Their political elites might be expected to learn about and accommodate these constraints over time. The second crucial proposition is Waltz's formulation of the law of equilibrium: Equilibria inevitably emerge as states balance against threats to preserve their security; the preservation of security under anarchy leads to counterbalancing, which in turn defeats any state's aggressive search for security. Consequently, as Waltz puts it, "balancing, not bandwagoning, is the behavior induced by the system."[11] It follows that a state ought to learn over time that counterbalancing is inevitable and offensive searches for security counterproductive.

Today's scholars are armed not only with such theoretical insights but also with historical hindsight. Many of the policies the Soviet leaders followed now appear to have failed utterly. The ideas they professed now seem absurd and even logically inconsistent. The notion that the pitiably poor Soviet Union could compete with the United States and its wealthy allies for world leadership strikes today's onlooker as ridiculous. The question for modern scholarship becomes: How do we explain these ideas and associated policies that contradict the known laws of international politics and furthermore were totally counterproductive? The debate is between two broad approaches: a cognitive explanation (including the learning approach) that focuses on limitations on the human mind's capacity to process incoming information and on decision makers' use of simplified rules and inappropriate lessons from past experience; and a domestic political approach that focuses on the distorting effects of leadership competition or domestic political institutions narrowly self-interested in offensive foreign policies.[12]

---

construct": "What Have We Learned about Learning?" in Breslauer and Tetlock, *Learning*, 830; emphasis added.

[10] They "socialize," according to Waltz, *Theory*, 173.

[11] ibid., 126.

[12] For a sampling, see Robert Jervis and Jack Snyder, eds., *Dominoes and Bandwagons: Strategic Beliefs and Great Power Competition in the Eurasian Rimland* (New York: Oxford

Both of these approaches run up against the problem we started with: balance-of-power theory has not identified uncontested "laws" of international life. Waltz's treatise on the balance of power is ambiguous on this score. States ought to "socialize" to a given structure of power; but because they are so secure, "strong states . . . can afford not to learn."[13] Waltz argues that a bipolar structure yields less ambiguous feedback about its operation than a multipolar one simply because the number of relevant actors is small; yet the two superpowers in a bipolar structure are by definition unusually powerful and secure and consequently face only weak incentives to learn. The treatise is similarly ambiguous on the question of balancing. Equilibria may well be inevitable, but the international system may also reward offensive searches for security. As Jack Snyder observes, Waltz "has a foot in both camps" on the question whether offensive strategies can pay in world politics.[14]

So the researcher in search of theoretically derived laws of the balance of power must choose between various theoretical camps. Snyder prefers the "defensive Realism" of Stephen Walt to the "aggressive Realism" with which he associates John Mearsheimer.[15] But these two camps exist not within realism as a whole but within one strain of thinking called "neorealism." In short, it is a dispute among followers of Waltz. This is but a subsection of balance-of-power theory. The hierarchical understanding of the balance of power, as I noted earlier, highlights a different set of laws and regularities in world politics: concentrated, hegemonic distributions rather than equilibria; the possibility of translating power into political preeminence; a greater tendency to bandwagon; and an eternal struggle among the leading states for control over the international system.

Suppose for a moment that the studies cited above shared the hierarchical understanding of the balance of power. Suppose they used Robert Gilpin's hegemonic framework rather than Kenneth Waltz's

---

University Press, 1991). The premier example of the "political-institutional" approach is Jack Snyder, *Myths of Empire: Domestic Politics and International Ambition* (Ithaca: Cornell University Press, 1991). The Soviet case is only one of five that Snyder considers in this work, and by no means the most important. For a stronger statement of his argument on the Soviet Union, see "The Gorbachev Revolution: A Waning of Soviet Expansionism?" *International Security* 12 (Winter 1987–88): 93–131. For an effort to combine political and learning approaches, see George Breslauer, "Explaining Soviet Policy Changes: The Interaction of Politics and Learning," in *Soviet Policy in Africa: From the Old to the New Thinking*, ed. Breslauer (Berkeley: Berkeley-Stanford Program in Soviet Studies, 1992).

[13] Waltz, *Theory*, 173, 195.
[14] Snyder, *Myths of Empire*, 12, n. 36.
[15] Ibid.

equilibrium theory as their support.[16] The Cold War distribution of power would then be seen more as an American hegemony than as a bipolar equilibrium. As the challenger, the Soviet Union would be expected to perceive a tendency of states to bandwagon with the superior power of the United States. Furthermore, as contenders for hegemony, the two superpowers would be expected to be concerned with goals other than simple security. They would be expected, like all their predecessors since Athens and Sparta, to compete vigorously for influence over the international system. Indeed, even Waltz would affirm that their great-power advantage over all other states would afford them this indulgence. Their strategic perspectives would not be expected to converge.[17] Quite the contrary, each side's strategy would seek to undercut the other's by highlighting its own strengths and the adversary's weakness. Convergence would be strategic idiocy. As long as they occupied the positions of hegemon and challenger, each side would experience strong incentives to fashion its strategy in almost dialectical opposition to the other.[18] In each capital, the goal of security would compete with the goal of influence. Thus the analyst could not expect that cooperation would always be the preferred strategy, even if it would unambiguously enhance security, because cooperation might be available only at the price of a loss of influence.

What is learning and what is not, what is risky and what is prudent, what is success and what is failure, and what is bias and what is sound strategy all depend on one's view of the balance of power.[19] To assess Soviet foreign policy in the Cold War we need a solid grasp of the nature of power in world politics. If it is elusive, we need to know how elusive and in what ways. If it is characterized by uncer-

---

[16] Robert Gilpin, *War and Change in World Politics* (Cambridge: Cambridge University Press, 1981).

[17] Cf. Weber, in Breslauer and Tetlock, *Learning.*

[18] See Edward L. Luttwack, *Strategy: The Logic of War and Peace* (Cambridge: Belknap/Harvard University Press, 1987). This tendency would especially characterize declaratory doctrine, which the rivals would be likely to use to signal their confidence in their own power to their allies and to each other. Relevant here is Robert Jervis, *The Logic of Images in International Relations* (New York: Columbia University Press, 1989), esp. chap. 8.

[19] See Robert Jervis, *Perception and Misperception in International Politics* (Princeton: Princeton University Press, 1976), chap. 7; Robert Jervis, Richard Ned Lebow, and Janice Gross Stein, *Psychology and Deterrence* (Baltimore: Johns Hopkins University Press, 1985), chap. 1; and Jack Snyder, *Ideology of the Offensive* (Ithaca: Cornell University Press, 1984), 35–38., for analyses of ways to analyze bias in historical cases. On the difficulties of establishing the case for bias in uncertain circumstances, see George W. Downs, "The Lessons of Intervention Failure: Bias or Uncertainty?" in A. Levite et al., *Protracted Military Interventions: From Commitments to Disengagement* (New York: Columbia University Press, 1991).

tainty, we need to know how much. If it has laws, we need to know how severe the penalties for violation are in comparison with the illicit temptations it also offers. Only then can we begin to answer the questions so long and insistently asked by students of Soviet foreign policy. Only then can we know whether these questions are even answerable. Realist theories reflect the elusiveness of their subject matter. Theory cannot substitute for close historical research in establishing the degree of ambiguity inherent in the balance of power.

Before turning to that research, we must address the nuts-and-bolts issues of how it was conducted, how findings were organized, and how the investigation is structured.

Unpacking "the Balance of Power"

The first requirement is a working definition of the balance of power that is consistent with the macroanalytical frameworks under consideration here. A concept so malleable that it permits such contradictory understandings to coexist for so long requires careful treatment. I disaggregate the concepts of "power" and "balance of power" into the following four aspects:

1. The *elements* of power. What do people think power is? What elements combine to constitute national power? What resources matter in world politics? How important are military capabilities as opposed to economic or other resources? How important are forces-in-being in comparison with potential? How do observers rank sea power versus land power? Do nuclear weapons supersede all other elements of power? Judgments about the elements of power clearly reflect judgments about other aspects of world politics, such as the probability of war, the utility of various kinds of threats, and the fungibility of different kinds of resources.

2. The *distribution* of power. How does one's country rank against the other great powers? Which states are great powers? Did observers ever perceive bipolarity, and if so, when? How did they see underlying changes in the distribution of power? Who was gaining and who was falling behind? The concern here is not merely with the U.S.-Soviet balance but with the intrawestern distribution of power and the overall dispersion of power.

3. The *mechanics* of power. How does the balance of power work? What is the relationship between power and state behavior? How will an increase in A's power affect the behavior of B, C, and D? International relations theorists make much of the distinction between beliefs

[26]

in "bandwagoning" (states tend to ally with the stronger power) and "balancing" (states tend to balance against increasing power). Do decision makers believe that an increase in their country's power will attract other states or dislodge members from an opposing alliance?

The behavior that statesmen care about may be much more subtle than an outright change of alliance.[20] They may be concerned with the alignment of states lying outside any formal alliance. Will an increase in our power cause them to align with us? They may care most about the *attitude* of states within an opposing alliance.[21] Perhaps one of two states that oppose us appears more favorably inclined toward our view of things than the other. How will its attitude be influenced by changes in the distribution of power?

In practice, distinguishing between balancing and bandwagoning turns out to be extraordinarily complex. Consider a Soviet diplomat in Paris pondering this question sometime in the mid-1950s. France is firmly in the American camp. But is France bandwagoning with overwhelming U.S. capabilities or balancing against the Soviet Union? If the former is the case, increased Soviet power might weaken France's ties to Washington; if the latter is true, the opposite effect may be expected. If the United States becomes weaker with respect to France, will France seek more independence or nuzzle even closer to the Americans? Is American hegemony over France in the final analysis a source of stability or instability? Do French offers of improved relations with Moscow reflect a genuine desire to reduce dependence on Washington, or are they merely bargaining ploys to get more from the rich American uncle? Which groups within France are more favorable to a pro-Soviet policy and what actions on Moscow's part could strengthen them?

An assessment of the likely effect of increased Soviet power required an assessment of the sources of cooperation and conflict within the Western camp. This is where Soviet views of the balance of power closely intersected their views of intercapitalist politico-economic relations. To understand how Soviet observers thought

[20] In his important study of alliances, Stephen Walt makes no distinction between alliances and alignments: *The Origins of Alliances* (Ithaca: Cornell University Press, 1987), chap. 1; on "balancing vs. bandwagoning," chap. 2. On the difficulty of discerning the two in practice see Glenn H. Snyder, "Alliances, Balance, and Stability," *International Organization* 45 (Winter 1991): 121–42; Robert Jervis, "Domino Beliefs and Strategic Behavior," in Jervis and Snyder, *Dominoes and Bandwagons*.

[21] Examples would be cases in which increased power led to détente. Walt addresses this issue in "Alliance Formation in Southwest Asia," in Jervis and Snyder, *Dominoes and Bandwagons*. As we shall see, distinguishing between détente and bandwagoning is not easy in practice.

[27]

about balancing and bandwagoning, it is vitally necessary to understand their conceptual perspectives on imperialism, deriving in one way or another from Lenin's famous treatise of that name.

4. *Prestige.* What is the present hierarchy of prestige? That is, who has the most diplomatic weight? the greatest influence over global politics? How is the hierarchy changing? Most important, what is the relationship between power and prestige? Is a particular element of power, such as military capabilities, *fungible?* That is, which capabilities translate into prestige? Will an increase in power lead to greater weight in diplomatic councils?

The prestige concept not only is a central element in hierarchical understandings of power politics but is also, in Gilpin's words, the "everyday currency of international relations."[22] Statesmen are attentive to the way others perceive their power and prestige because a favorable impression abroad will increase the likelihood of successful diplomacy. The fundamental criterion of diplomacy is often taken to be the acquisition of allies, or, at the very least, the avoidance of counteralliances. But a statesman who already faces an opposing alliance may plausibly prefer to gain prestige or diplomatic favors from the leader of the opposing alliance rather than weaken the cohesion of that alliance. The hypothetical Soviet diplomat in Paris, for example, could submit an attractive plan for a rapprochement with France at Washington's expense only to find the leadership rejecting it because it would jeopardize a planned demarche to the United States.

Sources and Methodological Dilemmas

My main empirical objective is to describe changes in Soviet elite perspectives on one specific aspect of international relations, the balance of power, in the years since World War II. To provide historical background and the important comparison between multipolar and bipolar systems, we shall begin with prewar Soviet perspectives. To provide comparison and context, we must also examine American assessments.

For the American comparisons the sources are quite good, at least up until the mid-1960s. On the Soviet side, the situation is far better than it used to be but still requires special attention. I do make use of archival materials made available by the Soviet and Russian authorities after 1989. These documents, primarily from the Ministry

---

[22]Gilpin, *War and Change,* 30; on prestige, see 30–33.

of Foreign Affairs, cover the postwar years until the late 1950s. In addition, all who travel to Russia know that the atmosphere for conducting interviews improved dramatically as official suspicion of foreigners waned. The research presented here benefited from numerous interviews with ex-diplomats, scholars, and experts who occupied anterooms to the Kremlin's corridors of power. Memoirs, newspaper interviews with former policy makers and leaders, archive-based historical accounts by Russian scholars—all these sources increased in quality and quantity after 1989.

The welcome change in the quality of evidence on Soviet history in no way obviates the need for what is often dismissively or derisively called "Kremlinology." The researcher who wades into archives with scant knowledge of the public "party line" is committing a cardinal methodological error. As we shall see, the existence of a party line on most matters did not prevent discussion of policy options, but, as all those who once worked in the party-state apparatus attest, it nonetheless provided the most important context for all political communication in the old Soviet Union. Although the situation has changed radically and for the better, those who devoted years to acquiring the tools of old-fashioned Sovietology have not wasted their efforts.

Open sources still constitute the bulk of the material we shall consider. They constitute the typical array long available to students of Soviet politics: existing Western scholarship; Soviet newspapers, speeches, journals, party documents, which bear reading and rereading; the memoirs of leaders, advisers, and diplomats; and contemporary Soviet scholarly and expert publications. Interpretation of all textual material, whether open or classified, presents numerous methodological problems, familiar to scholars. One is faced with the classical questions of textual analysis: Does text represent belief? Is action based on belief? These kinds of questions are exceedingly difficult—if not impossible—to answer to everyone's complete satisfaction. Nevertheless, especially when dealing with public political sources, one must at least try to address the implications. Without trying to uncover the sources of belief or attempting to unveil in each case opportunistic beliefs versus beliefs of conviction, the analyst of public political texts must address a practical question, which is particularly acute in the Soviet case: Is the view expressed in the text a deliberate attempt to mislead the reader?

For most of the years covered by this investigation, Soviet sources were subject to explicit central censorship and pervasive self-censorship. They were characterized by an unusually high degree of conscious propaganda. The element of ritual was arguably higher in Soviet political communications than in those of other societies (though this would be difficult to measure). Words and phrases often took on an operational meaning—clear to politically relevant layers of the society—radically at variance with their literal meaning. And, as scholars began to discover after the collapse of the Soviet Union brought the slow opening of archives, government documents were by no means free from these disabilities. All bureaucracies have their codes and conventions for internal communications, but deciphering the operational meaning of Soviet documents is doubly difficult, for Russian and foreign scholar alike. The proportion of instrumental articulations in Soviet sources was, in short, much higher than that encountered in most others.

Despite some efforts to apply quantified techniques of content analysis to Soviet sources,[23] most scholars have found more flexible interpretive methods most applicable to the analysis of Soviet textual materials. In sorting out opportunistic from more genuine articulations, the analyst must consult as wide an array of sources as possible to control for propaganda targeted at specific audiences, and must above all seek to place each text in its historical and political context.[24] Only then can the analyst answer the question: What does the author of this text have an interest in manipulating? In the best of circumstances, one can discover indicators of beliefs over which the author has no conscious control or has no interest in manipulating.[25]

Each text must be judged in accordance with its polemical and tactical context. What is the party's general line at the time? What image is the leadership trying to convey? What is the foreign and domestic political conjuncture? To what events could the author be reacting? To whom may he wish to communicate? By extending the analysis over a long period of time, one can further identify those ways of thinking that, though they may initially have been advanced publicly for tactical reasons, nevertheless come to dominate and con-

[23] William Zimmerman and Robert Axelrod, "The 'Lessons' of Vietnam, and Soviet Foreign Policy," *World Politics* 43 (Ocober 1981): 1–24. See also Jack Snyder, "Science and Sovietology," *World Politics*, January 1988, 188–90.

[24] See Deborah Welch Larson's very informative discussion of these issues: "Problems of Content Analysis in Foreign Policy Research: Notes from the Study of the Origins of the Cold War Belief Systems," *International Studies Quarterly* 32 (1988): 241–55; also Richard Herrmann, "The Empirical Challenge of the Cognitive Revolution: A Strategy for Drawing Inferences about Perceptions," ibid., 173–203.

[25] Larson, "Problems of Content Analysis," 249.

strain the political discourse and thus have political effects.[26] In the end, the methodological problems are serious but surmountable when the focus is on long-term patterns.

As I noted earlier, it would be foolish to deny that a certain analytical tension characterizes any effort to combine general concepts and specific cases in concrete historical circumstances. We begin with questions about power in world politics and end up facing detailed questions about Soviet politics. Or our wish to understand Soviet behavior leads us far afield into balance-of-power theory. On the one hand lies the momentous and intricate Soviet experience of war, revolution, totalitarianism, great power, and sudden decline. On the other hand lie the general questions to which one suspects this tragic history holds at least some of the answers. The struggle to reconcile the two imperatives of fealty to historical accuracy and the search for large-scale and long-term patterns is reflected in the pages that follow. At its most general level, the argument presented here is that this struggle is a necessary and inevitable one for students of world politics.

[26] Zimmerman, *Soviet Perspectives*, 13. Beliefs may not be articulated purely for propagandistic reasons; they may be conjured up to support a decision imposed by particular circumstances. The beliefs may then go on to influence later decisions made in a different context. See Deborah Welch Larson, *Origins of Containment* (Princeton: Princeton University Press, 1985), 348–49.

[3]

The Origins of Old Thinking

When Mikhail Gorbachev and his fellow reformers began to reorient the foreign affairs of their country in the years after 1985, among the obstacles they perceived in their path were "stereotyped" ways of thinking about world politics in the Soviet Union and the West. Though a good portion of Gorbachev's "new political thinking" was intended as an answer to such nettlesome Western ideas as deterrence and containment, its main purpose was to replace traditional Soviet thinking about international politics. "Old thinking," to be found in any speech by Leonid Brezhnev, Iurii Andropov, or Konstantin Chernenko about the international situation, postulated the basic hostility of the capitalist West and the consequent primacy of military power in Soviet security. It was the intellectual bulwark of Gorbachev's more conservative colleagues. It formed the architecture of post–World War II Soviet strategic discourse. Hence we need to know the origins and contours of prewar Soviet thinking to interpret postwar views accurately.

Nowhere in his voluminous speeches and writings on the matter did Gorbachev subject the old thinking to rigorous analysis. Had he done so, he might have found the experience disquieting, for many of the basic postulates about world politics that he and his aides tried to consign to the dustbin of intellectual history originated not with Brezhnev but with the Old Bolsheviks, in the 1920s. Old thinking was not a product of the Soviet Union's experience in World War II or even something Stalin dreamed up to rationalize his dictatorial rule. It was the common reaction of Bolshevik Marxists to the failure of the German revolution after 1917 and the consequent need to build "socialism in one country." The old thinking about international relations was much more deeply intertwined with the whole Soviet command-administrative system than Gorbachev may initially have supposed.

Soviet old thinking represented learning about the multipolar power configuration in which Soviet Russia came of age as a state. The Bolsheviks revised prerevolutionary postulates on the basis of their early experience in world affairs and arrived at their basic model of world politics in the 1920s. Subsequent events fitted it as well as or better than contemporary Western models. This fact alone is of no small importance. A particular model's hold on people's minds is strengthened when momentous events appear to confirm it. By 1925, the basics of old thinking were accepted by the majority of active Bolshevik leaders: Stalin, Nikolai Bukharin, Grigorii Zinoviev, and even, in large part, the diplomats Georgii Chicherin and Maksim Litvinov. Then came the Wall Street crash of 1929, global depression, fascism, world war. For Soviets of the Khrushchev-Brezhnev-Gromyko generation, these were the formative international events in their lives. First the model, then the events. This sequence goes a long way toward explaining the long life of Soviet old thinking about world politics.[1]

THE PREWAR LEGACY: CONTEXTUAL FACTORS

Two contextual factors have to be kept in mind when we consider the evolution of Soviet perspectives on power in world politics. First, the Bolsheviks had no coherent theory of international relations before they seized power, and had to develop one as they went along. Soviet articulations about the international situation were consequently of a practical nature, and the meanings of terms and concepts were determined by the issue at hand. Only rarely did debates among Bolshevik leaders or theoreticians directly concern anything we would call balance-of-power theory. Instead, assumptions about power in international politics were implicit in Soviet debates about other things. The second factor is less often noted by students of Soviet history, but may be the most important: Soviet thought on the balance of power evolved in a multipolar context. And it was not

---

[1] As Robert Jervis puts it: "If a set of basic theories—what Kuhn calls a paradigm—has been able to account for a mass of data, it should not be lightly trifled with": "Hypotheses on Misperception," in *International Politics*, ed. Robert Art and Robert Jervis, 2d ed. (Boston: Little, Brown, 1985), 511.

just any multipolar configuration, but the singularly crisis-ridden and unstable interwar period, which E. H. Carr aptly termed the "twenty years' crisis."[2]

The Bolsheviks' prerevolutionary intellectual background contained bodies of theory that could be applied to international relations in support of either class confrontation or balancing among states. Marxists, and most particularly Soviet Marxists, strongly resisted seeing any contradiction between the two bodies of thought, but in non-Marxist eyes the distinction is hard to deny. On the one hand, a whole series of precepts emerged from the basic Marxist contention that class struggle was the taproot of history and from the dialectical tendency to see the historical process as a struggle of opposites. It followed from those precepts that should a proletarian party find itself holding state power in a world still populated by bourgeois states, its policy ought to be geared toward mobilizing the world proletariat to overthrow the world bourgeoisie. World politics would consist in a struggle between two camps: the proletarian party and all its internal and international allies, and the bourgeoisie, with its state apparatuses and class allies. The hostility of the two camps was presumed. For lack of a better term, scholars normally call this a "leftist" or "class-struggle" view.

On the other hand lay a body of Marxist thinking about the dynamics of relations among capitalist states, and here the most important work was Lenin's theory of imperialism. In his 1916 treatise *Imperialism as the Highest Stage of Capitalism*, Lenin argued that industry and capital had become so concentrated that it was possible to speak of monopolies acting at the level of the state.[3] That is, the capitalist state was now a prisoner of the logic of monopoly, which for Lenin was synonymous with aggression. Within capitalist states, competition was dying out—a development unknown in the capitalism Marx knew. Among capitalist states, however, competition was intensifying. Monopolies suffered from overproduction and continually needed new markets for their surplus product. Capitalist states, acting naturally and inevitably in the interests of "their" monopolies, were driven to compete with each other to obtain spheres of economic (and political-military) interest in various regions. The specific nature of this aggressive competition was determined, according to Lenin, by "the law of the uneven development of capitalism." Because capitalist

---

[2] E. H. Carr, *The Twenty Years' Crisis, 1919–1939: An Introduction to the Study of International Relations* (London: Macmillan, 1951).

[3] Lenin, 27:299–426.

states developed at different rates, no equilibrium among those states could be stable: any distribution of power, colonies, and market spheres soon felt pressure as formerly weak states became stronger and demanded more.

The theory portrayed international relations as an aggressive competition for markets and spheres of influence which combined economic with politico-military strategy. When a disjuncture between the formal distribution of market spheres and the underlying military-economic distribution of power occurred, the only way for the capitalist countries to redistribute the goods, in the final analysis, was through war. Although a long period of dynamic political disequilibrium and shifting alignments could precede such a war, war was inevitable because it was the only way states could "test" the distribution of power and hence agree on a division of the world's spoils.[4] The parallels between Lenin's framework and hegemonic realist theory are numerous and obvious.[5] To a certain extent, this Leninist framework did lend itself to classical diplomatic calculations of shifts in the balance of power. It also, however, involved assessments of market conditions, since the capacity for domestic absorption would influence the acuteness of the external search for markets. In an economic downturn, a capitalist state would redouble its aggressive search for foreign markets and spheres of influence. A worldwide recession or depression would intensify all contradictions among imperialist states. Sovietologists have tended to call the relative focus on maneuvering among interimperialist contradictions a more "rightist" line, for such maneuvering often called for prolonged collaboration with a bourgeois regime or imperialist bloc, and the consequent practical need to downplay revolutionary goals.

Armed only with basic balance-of-power theory and the knowledge that these two bodies of thought existed in Soviet Russia, any student of international relations would predict that experience would soon cause class-struggle notions to be pushed aside in favor of the more statist conceptions of Lenin's *Imperialism*. That is essentially what happened, with one important qualification: class-struggle precepts did not make a clean exit from the scene, but rather lingered backstage, ready to make an appearance if the Bolsheviks perceived a "revolutionary situation." Lenin and his followers believed that revolutions

[4] "There is and can be no way of testing the real might of a capitalist state other than by war": Lenin, 21:242.

[5] For a comparison, see Robert Gilpin, *War and Change in World Politics* (New York: Cambridge University Press, 1981), 93–95.

did not emerge inexorably from changes in basic economic relations. Instead, revolutions became possible only when the existing political regime underwent a deep crisis that shattered the habitual allegiances of the masses.[6] As in Russia in 1905 and 1917, such crises were often brought about by war. In a revolutionary situation, political forces polarized, class loyalties asserted themselves, and the dictates of the class struggle were the order of the day.

THE OCTOBER REVOLUTION AND INTERNATIONAL POLITICS

The period from 1917 to 1921 was the most genuinely leftist in the history of Soviet foreign policy, yet even in those years significant undercurrents of a rightist balance-of-power approach can be found. Lenin and other Bolshevik leaders thought that the World War in conjunction with their own example was producing at least the makings of a pan-European revolutionary situation.[7] They were desperately concerned to keep the Western governments from class cooperation against the revolutionary threat, and sought energetically to keep them at odds with each other. So the longings and fears produced by their revolutionary ardor eventually induced the Bolsheviks to apply diplomatic divide-and-rule tactics with great vigor. But the need for maneuvering diplomacy was not immediately obvious to all the revolutionary leaders. It became so only after the Germans delivered the Bolsheviks their first simple lesson in international politics.

For the first weeks after October 1917, the Bolsheviks' predisposition was to treat all the capitalist states equally as class enemies. Upon seizing power, they were not inclined to analyze world politics in terms of Lenin's *Imperialism*. That theory had applied to the functioning of the imperialist world system in normal, nonrevolutionary times. In the revolutionary situation they believed they faced, the Bolsheviks saw their task as the mobilization of the world proletariat to overthrow the imperialist regimes. Collusion with one imperialist grouping against the other might discredit the revolutionary republic in the eyes of the toiling masses and quench their revolutionary fire.

---

[6] For a brief outline of Lenin's views on revolutionary situations, see Wolfgang Leonhard, *Three Faces of Marxism*, trans. Ewald Osers (New York: Paragon, 1979), 67–68.

[7] See George Kennan, *Russia and the West under Lenin and Stalin* (New York: Little, Brown, 1961); E. H. Carr, *The Bolshevik Revolution*, vol. 3 (New York: Norton, 1981); and, for an analysis of Bolshevik concepts, N. V. Zagladin, *Istoriia uspekhov i neudach sovetskoi diplomatii* (Moscow: Mezhdunarodnye Otnosheniia, 1990).

This principle was at issue in the debates over the signing of the Brest-Litovsk peace treaty with Germany in early 1918.

When their revolution did not spark an immediate uprising in Germany, the Bolsheviks faced a contradiction between their promise of peace and their desire for world revolution. Peace required negotiation with Germany, which could compromise further revolution. In the spring of 1918 Germany forced the issue by conducting a series of offensives against practically nonexistent Russian resistance. The Bolsheviks split into factions, Bukharin and the left advocating a revolutionary war and Lenin and the right opting for an immediate "annexationist" peace.[8] Lenin's arguments were simple: Germany was too strong, too far from revolution, and the Bolshevik party too weak for any course other than capitulation. The "correlation of forces," encompassing both military and class elements, dictated acceptance of Germany's terms without delay.

The Brest-Litovsk peace that Lenin finally got the party to accept marks a turning point, insofar as it reflected what he called a "hard but necessary lesson": the need to distinguish among adversary states (as well as the need for an effective military force). And when the negotiations with the Germans took a turn for the worse, the Bolsheviks made some attempts to apply the principle more widely in order to gain time. Foreign Commissar Lev Trotsky first endeavored to play the Entente powers against Germany, then Germany against the Entente, and later, when the Allied powers began their intervention in the Russian Civil War, to play the United States against Britain and France. But all these maneuvers were conditioned by the expectation of a relatively short period of coexistence, which seems to have been but a few months even for the "statist" Lenin.

Trotsky's tentative diplomatic forays notwithstanding, the period between 1918 and 1921 was one of more or less consistent leftism, sustained by the revolutions of 1919, the Soviet-Polish War, and the formation of the German Communist Party and the revolutionary Third International (the Comintern). In the face of the hostility of all

---

[8] For accounts, see Richard Pipes, *The Russian Revolution* (New York: Knopf, 1990), chap. 13; Leonard Schapiro, *The Origins of the Communist Autocracy* (London: G. Bell, 1955), chap. 6, and his *Communist Party of the Soviet Union*, 2d ed. (New York: Vintage, 1971), 82–89. Soviet accounts focusing on Lenin's role include A. O. Chubarian, *V. I. Lenin i formirovanie sovetskoi vneshnei politiki* (Moscow: Nauka, 1972). For Lenin's argument, see *Lenin o vneshnei politike sovetskogo gosudarstva* (Moscow: Gosudarstvennoe Izdatel'stvo Politicheskoi Literatury, 1960), 120; and V. I. Lenin, *Izbrannye proizvedeniia*, 3 vols. (Moscow: Izdatel'stvo Politicheskoi Literatury, 1969), 2:482–89. For Bukharin's rejoinder, see Stephen Cohen, *Bukharin and the Bolshevik Revolution* (New York: Oxford University Press, 1971), 66, 68.

the capitalist powers, Bolshevik thinking gravitated toward the leftist, class-struggle theme. Although the immediate actors were states, their actions were dictated by class interests. Revolution would take place not only as a result of struggle within the capitalist states but also in the course of wars between those states and revolutionary Russia, which would have to prepare itself for the coming clashes. Ridiculing Karl Kautsky's accusation that the Bolsheviks were "building militarism, not socialism," Lenin outlined his view at the Eighth Party Congress in 1919: "As if there was ever a major revolution in history that wasn't connected to war! Of course not! We are living not merely in a state, but in *a system of states;* and it is inconceivable that the Soviet republic should continue to exist for a long period side by side with the imperialist states. Ultimately one or the other must conquer."[9]

Even during this most leftist phase of Soviet diplomacy, class confrontation coexisted with maneuvering diplomacy designed to weaken the cohesion of the opposing camp. A second stream of evidence competed with the inflow of information about workers' unrest, general strikes, revolutionary coups, and Western collaboration against Soviet Russia. With time Lenin and his colleagues learned, to their apparent surprise, that interimperialist rivalry continued apace, despite the increasing consolidation of the revolution in Russia. The British, French, Americans, and Japanese never entirely succeeded in cooperating effectively, pursued conflicting aims throughout their intervention, and withdrew from the scene with the apparent defeat of the White armies.

A confluence of events in late 1920 and 1921 marked the end of the leftist phase. On the domestic front, sailors revolted against the Bolshevik regime in the Kronstadt uprising, famine swept the countryside, and the leadership was forced to replace war communism with the New Economic Policy (NEP). On the world scene, the German revolutions failed, the foreign intervention and the Polish and Civil wars ended, Europe stabilized and began to recover, and Moscow reached a trade agreement with London. Lenin first spoke of a "certain equilibrium" between the two camps, and then he and the other Soviet leaders began to elaborate a balancing policy based on an undefined period of "peaceful cohabitation" with the capitalist states. The Bolsheviks' willingness to accept the trade-offs implicit in playing the balance-of-power game was made unambiguously clear in 1922, when Lenin and his foreign commissar, Chicherin, suc-

[9]Lenin, 38:139.

ceeded in weaning Germany from the Western camp in the Rapallo agreement.

Speeches and reports of the day still claimed that the world was divided into bourgeois and proletarian camps, but the focus was on manipulating the contradictions rending the capitalist states. Naturally, with hindsight, the Bolsheviks stressed continuity with the old policy, which lay in the fact that only these "interimperialist contradictions" had saved the revolution. But the time horizon was now much longer, imparting a measurably more traditional balance-of-power cast to the policy and its supporting analysis. As Lenin stated the basic principles late in 1920: "So long as we remain, from the economic and military standpoint, weaker than the capitalist world, so long we must stick to the rule: we must be clever enough to utilize the contradictions and oppositions among the imperialists."[10]

Only in the years after 1921 did the Bolsheviks seriously begin to analyze the world situation in the comparatively statist terms of the theory of imperialism. Clearly, in retrospect, they had overestimated the effect of their revolution on the world situation. The two post-1917 surprises—the failure of world revolution and the failure of the imperialists to unite against the Bolshevik regime—were linked. Had the world really been in as revolutionary a state as the Bolsheviks originally thought, the bourgeoisie would have sensed the threat and papered over its national differences long enough to try to eliminate the Red threat. But it was now evident that the dynamic of international politics would go on in more or less the same vein as before October 1917. Capitalist states would seek markets, they would grow at uneven rates, they would enter into arms races and diplomatic struggles. They would go to war.

Lesson number one for the Bolsheviks was that they had misread the revolutionary timetable. The Red train was due in some years rather than some weeks or months. That lesson took three years to learn, and the Bolsheviks were quite ready to unlearn it, as they did briefly in 1923, when Germany yet again seemed ready for revolution. This episode of Soviet learning is well known; what is much less well known is what happened next. Lenin's *Imperialism* was adapted, willy-nilly, to the international situation of the Soviet Union in the 1920s. The 1920s, which play such an important role in all debates about the internal development of the Soviet Union, were also the most

[10] Quoted in Carr, *Bolshevik Revolution*, 3:276.

important period in the evolution of old Soviet thinking about international relations.[11]

Though the Bolsheviks began to adapt themselves to a nonrevolutionary international situation after the events of 1921 and the introduction of NEP, it was not until 1924, after the final failure of the German revolution, that they seriously addressed the issue of capitalist "stabilization." In June of that year, Bukharin spoke to the Thirteenth Party Congress about a "certain stabilization of internal capitalist relations."[12] In 1924 and 1925, "stabilization" became the basic line of the Stalin/Bukharin leadership, along with its internal twin, "socialism in one country."[13] Naturally, if capitalism was not on the verge of revolution, the Soviets had to address the question whether a socialist alternative to capitalism could be constructed in the Soviet Union. Bukharin (hesitantly) and Stalin (wholeheartedly) answered this question in the affirmative. Calculating (wrongly) that this issue could be used to discredit the Stalin/Bukharin "duumvirate," Trotsky instigated a scholastic debate on socialism in one country. In his day-to-day analyses of the world situation, Trotsky never disputed the essentials of the original stabilization thesis or its corollary, that the Soviet Union would have to maneuver among the capitalist powers for years to come.[14]

Acceptance of the reality of capitalist stabilization vastly increased

---

[11] Scholars have as yet produced little research on the evolution of Soviet perspectives in these years. Valuable exceptions are Richard B. Day, *The "Crisis" and the "Crash": Soviet Studies of the West, 1917–1939* (London: New Left Books, 1981); Manfred von Boetticher's excellent *Industrialisierungspolitik und Verteidigungskonzeptionen der UdSSR, 1926–1930: Herausbildung des Stalinismus und "äußere Bedrohung"* (Düsseldorf: Droste, 1979); John Erickson, "Threat Identification and Strategic Appraisal by the Soviet Union, 1930–41," in *Knowing One's Enemies: Intelligence Assessment before the Two World Wars*, ed. Ernest R. May (Princeton: Princeton University Press, 1984); and Zagladin, *Istoriia uspekhov i neudach*, chaps. 1–2.

[12] *Trinadtsatyi s"ezd Rossiiskoi Kommunisticheskoi Partii (Bol'shevikov): Stenograficheskii otchet* (Moscow, 1924), 318, quoted in Day, "Crisis" and "Crash," 78.

[13] E. H. Carr, *Socialism in One Country, 1924–1926*, 3 vols. (New York: Macmillan, 1964), 1: chap. 30; Cohen, *Bukharin*, 148, 187.

[14] Later, in exile, Trotsky retrospectively sought to portray himself as the avitar of world revolution in this period. This inaccurate picture still influences many secondary accounts. For a convincing case study, see Robert Kelner, "Leon Trotsky and the Politics of Maneuver" (senior thesis, Princeton University, 1989). Also Day, "Crisis" and "Crash" and *Leon Trotsky and the Politics of Economic Isolation* (New York: Verso, 1977).

the salience of the state in Bolshevik assessments of the international situation. Increasingly, but gradually and never completely, Soviets began thinking of their country not mainly as a source of revolutionary inspiration and ferment but as a great power that could achieve security by the traditional means of statecraft. On the diplomatic front, this change found reflection in the "wave of recognitions" by other great powers, beginning in 1924 and ending only in 1933–34 with recognition by the United States and entry into the League of Nations. Theoretically, of course, economically defined classes remained the main actors, but the essential indicator of the condition of the class struggle on the world scene was state behavior. State action thus influenced Moscow's analysis of the international situation to a much greater degree than a literal reading of Lenin's theories would suggest.

Just as Marx had accorded practical primacy to the state in his political writings (e.g., *The Eighteenth Brumaire*), so did Lenin, Trotsky, Bukharin, and Stalin in their day-to-day polemics and treatises. Reading the speeches and articles of these and other protagonists in the Soviet debates, one immediately realizes that one is dealing with very hardheaded realpolitik. But it was a realpolitik of a type different from Western versions of that time or today: one that combined politico-military with economic assessments; one that would assign overarching strategic meaning to something like the Wall Street crash of 1929; and one that apparently explained the international politics of the multipolar interwar years quite satisfactorily, from the point of view of most relevant Soviets.

A corollary to the shift toward according primacy to states in international politics concerned the calculation of power. The military and economic power of states gained in importance over the influence of various substate forces such as communist parties, though the latter continued to be referred to in many discussions. Brest-Litovsk and the Civil and Soviet-Polish wars had demonstrated the indispensability of well-trained armed forces and an economy to supply them. For a large cadre of party officials, including Stalin, war was a formative experience.[15] The wars further generated a number of military experts and theoreticians of "total war," who were to argue throughout the

---

[15] Robert Tucker, *Stalin as Revolutionary* (New York: Norton, 1973), 402; Cohen, *Bukharin*, 313. For a view skeptical of the war's impact, see Sheila Fitzpatrick, "The Civil War as a Formative Experience," in *Bolshevik Culture*, ed. Abbott Gleason, Peter Kenez, and Richard Stites (Bloomington: Indiana University Press, 1985).

1920s for the unavoidable necessity of preparing the entire Soviet state and society for war.[16]

So by 1924 and 1925, the Bolsheviks recognized the primacy of the state in world politics for the policy-relevant future. As a matter of course, they had to address key questions about the nature of inter-state relations. What determined alignment behavior? How change-able were interstate configurations? How likely was war and what would be its character? Could it be prevented or only staved off, and if so, for how long? These questions were not subjects of debate. The most one finds is tendencies. Soviet diplomats, like their European contemporaries, discounted the threat of war (not surprising). The head of the Comintern still talked of revolution in more immediate terms (also predictable). Bukharin and Stalin played up the war threat to discredit the left opposition. But all would have subscribed to four basic postulates about international politics:

1. *Interimperialist contradictions provide diplomatic opportunities for the Soviet Union.* This proposition, based on Lenin's *Imperialism,* was the alpha and omega of Soviet views on international relations until the mid-1980s. The failure of the Allied intervention in the Russian Civil War had shown that the capitalists' class enmity toward the Bolshevik regime was attenuated by their mutual antagonisms. Lenin stressed this lesson in practically every speech on the international situation after 1921. The opportunistic process by which recognition of the stability of capitalism leads inexorably to focus on interimperialist contradictions is exemplified by Stalin's speech to the Moscow party organization in January 1925. Stalin lists the "allies of the revolution," beginning with the proletariat in the Western countries (for the mo-ment able to offer only moral help) and the oppressed peoples of the colonies (they currently lack the power to offer material aid), and resting finally on "the conflicts and contradictions between the capi-talist countries, which undoubtedly are the greatest support for our power and our revolution. It may seem strange, comrades, but it is a fact."[17]

For the half-decade after late 1921, Soviet policy was based on ex-

---

[16]John Erickson, *The Soviet High Command* (New York: St. Martin's, 1962), 289; Condo-leezza Rice, "The Making of Soviet Strategy," in *The Makers of Modern Strategy,* ed. Peter Paret (Princeton: Princeton University Press, 1986), 661: Michael Checinsky, "The Economics of Defence in the USSR," *Survey* 29 (Spring 1985): 59–78. On the militariza-tion of Soviet society in general: Mark von Hagen, *Soldiers in the Proletarian Dictatorship: The Red Army and the Soviet Socialist State, 1917–1930* (Ithaca: Cornell University Press, 1990).
[17]Stalin, 7:25–28.

ploiting the essential contradiction between Germany and the victori-ous Versailles powers. Moscow used this contradiction to secure valuable military and economic cooperation from the Germans, be-ginning with the Rapallo treaty in 1922. In addition, there was no shortage of examples of interimperialist squabbling over trade rights and concessions in the Soviet Union. So not only could the main contradiction among the imperialists be used, but various secondary contradictions (France vs. Britain, Europe vs. America, America vs. Japan, etc.) could also be turned to Soviet economic and political gain. Throughout the period, though the Soviets recognized the world as formally divided into two class-based camps, their discourse focused on exploiting contradictions and balancing among the powers.

Lenin's "law of uneven development" determined the specific na-ture of the interimperialist rivalries. Soviets expected relative changes in economic and military power (as well as changing economic condi-tions within individual capitalist states) to lead to dynamic shifts in alignments. It was at this level that complex debates about Soviet diplomacy took place. Speeches and articles by Bukharin, Trotsky, Zinoviev, Karl Radek, and Chicherin contained conflicting analyses of the implications of American recovery, Dawes Plan loans to Germany, Anglo-American alliance versus rivalry, and so forth. As intense as the disagreements among these Bolshevik luminaries appeared on the surface, they all shared the assumption that international align-ments and alliances were inherently dynamic and unstable. No Bol-shevik was fooled by the bucolic external appearance of 1920s diplomacy. No Kellogg-Briand pacts lulled them into complacency. Indeed, in their eyes the line between shifting alignments and inter-state war was thin indeed.

2. *Interimperialist contradictions inevitably lead to war.* Unlike the first postulate, the inevitability-of-war thesis did not need to await Gorba-chev's arrival before being revised. Nikita Khrushchev annulled it in 1956. But if anyone in Moscow in the 1920s believed that the major powers could adjust to shifting underlying balances without eventu-ally going to war, he kept his views to himself. Anyone so much as hinting that the imperialists could stabilize their mutual relations on any lasting basis was taking the route of the "renegade" social demo-crat Karl Kautsky and consigning himself to instant political obliv-ion.[18] Bukharin's "stabilization thesis" never for a moment suggested that interimperialist relations would be stabilized "Absurd," said

---

[18]See Bukharin's vicious anti-Kautsky polemic: *Mezhdunarodnaia burzhuaziia i Karl Kautskii, ee apostol* (Moscow: Pravda, 1925), esp. chap. 9.

Bukharin to the Fifteenth Party Congress. "Quite the contrary." Internal stabilization led to "an intensification of rivalry, an intensification of conflicts, which leads absolutely inevitably to a *second round of wars.*"[19] Stalin, naturally, agreed.[20]

From 1925 onward, the Soviet leaders stressed again and again that war was inevitable. What was not clear was when and among whom it would occur. What was the relation between interimperialist war and war against the Soviet Union? What was the impact of the growing Soviet state on international alignments? How to factor revolutionary Russia into the framework of Lenin's *Imperialism?* These matters become clear only after one considers the remaining two old-thinking postulates about power in world politics.

3. *War is connected in revolution.* In 1919 Lenin scoffed at Kautsky's "silly notion" that a "major revolution" could take place without war. Although muted slightly for obvious reasons (no one wants to be seen as a warmonger), this connection was alive and well in the 1920s. Bukharin, in articulating the party's general line, claimed that the world had entered an "epoch of wars and revolutions."[21] How so, when capitalism was stabilizing internally? Again, internal stabilization exacerbated external contradictions, leading to disequilibrium and war. War, in turn, vastly accelerated the rate of historical development, weakening the bourgeois states and leading to proletarian revolutions. As in Russia in 1917, war would intensify the ripening contradictions of capitalism. It would be a repeat, though on a grander, European scale, of the World War, Russian Revolution, and Russian Civil War.

Who really believed in imminent revolution? Comintern cadres, naturally, professed to believe. Lower-level Comintern people, still alive in postperestroika Moscow, claim it was widely believed at operational levels. It is hard to say what Stalin "really" thought, though his speeches suggest he was less ardent a believer in revolution than his ally Bukharin. More important than this guessing game were the implications of the war-revolution connection in the system of Soviet thought of those days. These implications concerned both domestic and international politics. For domestic affairs the implications of war and of revolution were similar. That is, for practical domestic purposes it mattered little whether interimperialist contradictions

[19] N. I. Bukharin, *Otchet delegatsii VKP (b) v IKKI XV s"ezdu VKP (b)* (Moscow/Leningrad: Gosudarstvennoe Izdatel'stvo, 1928), 25.

[20] See Stalin, 7:52–54, 91–93.

[21] Bukharin, *Capitalist Stabilization and Proletarian Revolution (Report to the VII Enlarged Plenum of the Executive Committee of the Comintern)* (Moscow, 1926), 42.

brought war with or without revolution. In either case the domestic imperative was to secure the home front. Frightful clashes with the bourgeois states were inevitable, and a Soviet victory would require an army, industry to supply it, and the elimination of domestic class elements that would form a fifth column for the enemy; namely, the kulaks, or rich peasants.[22]

As far as international relations was concerned, the connection between war and revolution inclined Bolsheviks to think of class struggle. If war implied revolution, revolution implied class struggle (not state balancing dynamics), and class struggle suggested that the imperialists would put aside their squabbles and collaborate to snuff out the socialist state. The association worked in reverse as well. When Soviets perceived that the great powers were collaborating, they smelled war in the air.

4. *The stronger the Soviet Union becomes, the more hostile the capitalists will become.* The mid-1920s was the period of the Locarno treaty and the westward drift in Germany's alignment. Though the concrete cooperation of Rapallo continued into the 1930s, its "spirit," the sense of the Soviet Union and Germany shoulder to shoulder against the Versailles powers, was progressively weakened. Consequently, for several years after 1925 the Western powers seemed less differentiated and more united against Moscow. Both Bukharin and Stalin noted in their speeches that despite the continued existence of intense contradictions among the Western powers, the "general tendency" at the moment was to cooperate against the Soviet Union.[23] A resolution of the Fifteenth Party Congress in December 1927 attributed this growing hostility to the successful development and "growing international-revolutionary influence of the USSR."[24] In portrayals of the day, the wily British were behind all schemes to unite the capitalist countries against the Soviet Union. London met with some success, Stalin explained, because of the Western countries' fear of weakening themselves in the face of Soviet power. They thus sought to "put off" and "paint over temporarily" their mutual contradictions and cooperate in an anti-Soviet direction.[25]

---

[22] These points were made in the editorial "Mezhdousobiia imperialistov i podgotovka voiny protiv SSSR," *Kommunisticheskii internatsional*, 1930, no. 4 (October 2), 3–11; quoted in Jonathan Haslam, *Soviet Foreign Policy, 1930–1933: The Impact of the Depression* (London: Macmillan, 1983), 25.

[23] Bukharin, *Capitalist Stabilization*; Stalin, 9:323–24.

[24] *Kommunisticheskaia Partiia Sovetskogo Soiuza v rezoliutsiiakh i resheniiakh* (Moscow: Gosudarstvennoe Izdatel'stvo Politicheskoi Literatury, 1953), 2:315.

[25] Stalin, 9:324.

The old class-struggle assumptions manifested themselves in the Bolsheviks' hypersensitivity to the prospect of the other powers' ganging up on them. The hostility thesis might be considered an echo of the Bolsheviks' earlier overestimation of the impact of their revolution on world politics.[26] At some point—never specified clearly—interimperialist contradictions could produce a crisis that the capitalists would seek to resolve through a joint endeavor against the Soviet Union. By the mid-1920s, Soviet analyses of the West were couched in terms of the "general crisis of capitalism."[27] This key term was the Bolshevik catchword describing the difference between capitalism before World War I and postwar capitalism. When the Western governments had decisively put out the revolutionary flames after the war, the Bolsheviks did not—or at least did not want to—believe that capitalism had returned to its nineteenth-century ways of relative stability and growth. Instead, they professed to believe that imperialism was even more crisis-prone and unstable in the postwar circumstances, and that it was due for another debilitating crisis, which would originate in the international sphere. Growing "socialist" economic and military power exacerbated the general crisis and brought capitalism nearer to its final apocalyptic end. Such thinking underlay much of the hostility thesis. The closer the final crisis comes, the more desperately the capitalists will put aside their mutual contradictions to snuff out the socialist republic. Thus Soviet growth in the mid-1920s coupled with apparent interimperialist collaboration could be portrayed as a prelude to war.

OLD THINKING AND THE WAR SCARE

The hostility thesis appears to be a predictable and relatively widely shared Soviet explanation for the post-Locarno phase of European

[26] Overestimation of one's own centrality in the calculations of others is not an unusual occurrence in politics, though these rate as egregious examples. See Robert Jervis, *Perception and Misperception in International Politics* (Princeton: Princeton University Press, 1976), chap. 9.

[27] M. M. Narinskii, "K voprosu ob obschchem krizise kapitalizma," *Novaia i noveishaia istoriia,* 1989, no. 3, 111–21. The term appears to have been coined by the Hungarian Comintern economist Eugen Varga in *Aufsteig oder Niedergang des Kapitalismus?* (Hamburg, 1925), 25. Among the very few Western anaysts who treat this concept are Franklyn Griffiths, "Attempted Learning: Soviet Policy toward the United States in the Brezhnev Years," in *Learning in U.S. and Soviet Foreign Policy,* ed. George Breslauer and Philip Tetlock (Boulder, Colo.: Westview, 1991); and Erik P. Hoffmann and Robbin Laird, *"The Scientific-Technological Revolution" and Soviet Foreign Policy* (New York: Perga-

diplomacy. Zinoviev, Lev Kamenev, Mikhail Frunze, and many other leading Soviet figures made reference to this thesis after 1925.[28] It gained the widest currency during the war scare of 1927–1929. Germany's relative shift westward, signified by the Dawes Plan and eventually the Locarno treaty, sparked a period of Soviet harping on the war threat. Always a theme in Soviet discourse, it increased dramatically in 1926 and reached war-scare proportions when Stalin secured his control over the regime. There can be little doubt that the Soviet leaders manipulated the war scare for factional and other instrumental reasons.[29] In this context, the hostility thesis, with its dire portrayals of an imperialist camp gathering its forces for an assault against the Soviet Union, was useful to the Soviet leaders.

The war scare and the hostility thesis, despite their later entanglement in factional fights and domestic politics, appear initially to have been genuine. The hostility thesis was a popular explanation for the post-1925 conjuncture. Talk of the inevitability of war long preceded the factional denouement of 1927–1929. All the protagonists, including the hapless Trotsky and Bukharin, subscribed to the inevitability-of-war thesis. It is quite likely that the alarmist public Soviet reaction to the relatively minor international alignment shift in the mid-1920s was mirrored, in less extreme degree, in internal assessments. These alarms were exaggerated publicly for propaganda purposes, to convince a relatively uneducated public in simple terms that further deprivations in the interests of building up the USSR's defense capacity were necessary.[30] Exaggeration also proved useful for factional reasons. But the Soviets were still learning about international politics. The theory of imperialism suggested that war was inevitable. What was not clear was the timetable. How long would it

mon, 1982), chap. 2. Both works deal with the concept mainly as it developed in the Brezhnev period.

[28] Carr, *Socialism in One Country*, 252–53.

[29] To members of the Soviet establishment just below the leadership level, this was abundantly evident. See Boetticher, *Industrialisierungspolitik,* esp. 301–11. For other analyses, see John P. Sontag, "The Soviet War Scare of 1927," *Russian Review* 34 (January 1975): 66–77; Alfred G. Meyer, "The War Scare of 1927," and Sheila Fitzpatrick, "The War Threat during the First Five-Year Plan," both in *Soviet Union/Union Soviétique* 5 (1978); Gabriel Gorodetsky, *The Precarious Truce: Anglo-Soviet Relations, 1924–1927* (Cambridge: Cambridge University Press, 1977), esp. 231–40. Von Hagen, *Soldiers in the Proletarian Dictatorship,* makes the important point that war scares were common throughout the 1920s and part of the Soviet "bellist" political culture.

[30] See Bukharin's tacit recognition of this purpose at the Sixth Comintern Congress: *Protokoll des 6. Weltkongresses der kommunistischen Internationale* (Hamburg/Berlin: Carl Hoym Nachfolger, 1928), 1:532.

take for shifts in the underlying distribution of power to erupt in war?

Because they were not clear about the timetable, and because they saw large changes in the underlying economic distribution of power among the key capitalist states, Soviets in this period in all likelihood tended to see the international system as more prone to war than Western statesmen did at the time. In addition, their economic determinism led the Soviet observers to exaggerate Anglo-American antagonisms. After all, an immense shift in underlying power in favor of the United States had occurred, yet Britain retained formal possession of vast spheres of influence and colonies. It appeared to men as intelligent as Trotsky, Radek, and Bukharin to be a recipe for intense rivalry, if not war.[31] This was one reason Moscow courted Washington so assiduously in the 1920s: America could counterbalance not only Japan in the East but Britain in the West. Only with experience in the 1930s did the lesson appear to have been learned that despite its immense economic power, the United States was politically capable of playing only a small world role.

In short, behind all the hullabaloo over the war scare, the Soviets most probably committed some errors of assessment in the 1920s along the lines suggested by their publicly expressed perceptions. Shifts in alignment that in hindsight seem trivial occasionally produced genuine concern in Moscow, where even level-headed observers doubtless thought the likelihood of war, perhaps with Poland, was higher than Westerners assumed at the time. The war-scare atmosphere also led to concrete results by forcing the regime to confront the issue of military power and its connection to industrialization. Apparently it was only in 1927 that the regime adopted contingency plans for war.[32] Military arguments figured prominently in the preparation of the First Five-Year Plan.[33] Councils and staffs for wartime contingencies were established, and a wartime version of the five-year plan was drawn up.[34] Technocratic military planners for total war, such as Chief of Staff Boris Shaposhnikov, gained influence.

Another manifestation of the war scare was the exacerbation of the

---

[31] See Bukharin, *Capitalist Stabilization*, 38; and, for Trotsky's views, K. K. Shirinin, "Trotskii i Komintern," *Novaia i noveishaia istoriia*, 1991, no. 8, and Carr, *Socialism in One Country*, 469–71.

[32] Erickson, *Soviet High Command*, 288.

[33] See, e.g., the resolution of the Fifteenth Congress (1927) on this score: *KPSS v rezoliutsiiakh i resheniiakh*, 332.

[34] E. H. Carr and R. W. Davies, *Foundations of a Planned Economy, 1926–1929* (London: Macmillan, 1969–1971), 1:428–29.

"grain crisis": peasants began hoarding grain, refusing to deliver it to the market and jeopardizing NEP. Stalin chose this moment to begin his move to oust Bukharin and the right-wing communists from the leadership and secure exclusive control over the regime.[35] Stalin's momentous "revolution from above," beginning with forcible collectivization of the peasantry in 1929, was not associated with some new model of world politics. It was justified rather on the basis of a "lurch to the left" by Stalin and a large part of the party. The degree to which this rising tide of revolutionary sentiment was genuine, as opposed to purely tactical, will be debated by historians. But the tactical utility of leftist sentiments for Stalin's drive against Bukharin is undeniable.

After 1927, Stalin began to assert that a revolutionary "class war" situation was developing within the country. Rightists who defended NEP were consequently traitors objectively in the bourgeois camp and had to be eliminated. In 1928, when Bukharin was already on his way out, Stalin and his many sympathizers began to assert that Europe, too, was entering a revolutionary situation. Coopting an analysis of the Comintern economist Eugen Varga, Stalin claimed that capitalism was entering the "third period" of its general crisis and that internal stabilization was coming to an end.[36] Thus "rightists" in the international communist movement had to be rooted out. This analysis implied revolution and war against the Soviet Union in the near term, and consequently the need to secure the home front via the "liquidation of the kulaks as a class" and vastly accelerated rates of industrial investment.[37]

The ultraleft phase, so useful to Stalin in cleansing the Soviet party and Comintern of Bukharinites, was given impetus by the Wall Street crash of 1929 and the ensuing world depression. Communist parties across Europe acted on the belief that the rise of fascism was only a brief prelude to revolution and concentrated their attacks on the near-

[35] See Robert Tucker, *Stalin in Power: The Revolution from Above, 1928–1941* (New York: Norton, 1990), chap. 4.

[36] See F. I. Firsov, "Stalin i Kommunisticheskii Internatsional," in *Istoriia i Stalinizm*, ed. A. N. Mertsalov (Moscow: Politizdat, 1991); and Ia. Pevzner, "Zhizn' i trudy E. S. Vargi v svete sovremennosti," *Mirovaia ekonomika i mezhdunarodnye otnosheniia*, 1988, no. 10, 18–22, for Russian accounts detailing Stalin's activities. For Stalin's argument: Stalin, 12:1–26.

[37] The connection between war and collectivization of the peasantry had been stressed as early as 1925: Checinsky, "Economics of Defence," 74 and n. 51. On the rise of "class struggle" thinking within the party in this period, see Hiroaki Kuromiya, *Stalin's Industrial Revolution: Politics and Workers, 1928–1932* (Cambridge: Cambridge University Press, 1988).

est enemy on the left, the Social Democrats. But already by 1934 Stalin, who claimed to have predicted the crash of 1929, once again appropriated an analysis first articulated by Varga and proclaimed that capitalism had weathered the worst phase of the current crisis.[38] He began to move away from ultraleft predictions of imminent revolution. More important, the ultraleft phase led to no substantial revision of the basic old-thinking model accepted by all in the mid- to late 1920s. Indeed, even during the ultraleft phase, when Stalin discussed Soviet foreign policy (as opposed to Comintern matters), he continued to articulate the basic precepts of the old view. The diplomats at the Commissariat of Foreign Affairs continued to implement the Rapallo line. The only amendment Stalin made to the basic old-thinking model, as we shall see, had rather sanguine implications for Soviet security. In short, Stalin's attack on NEP and Bukharin's defense of it did not involve competing models of world politics.

The plain fact is that Bukharin never developed an *international* corollary to NEP, and so was in a difficult position during the war scare and the onset of Stalin's revolution from above. Why did Bukharin harp on the war danger when he was at that very moment arguing for balanced Soviet industrialization? Why advance a line of analysis that inevitably played into Stalin's superindustrializing hands? Even as he distanced himself from Stalin on other questions, even as he elaborated his theory of "state capitalism," even as he articulated his theory of balanced industrialization for the USSR, he retained this focus on interimperialist rivalry and the inevitability of war.[39] Naturally, Bukharin feared being labeled as a "renegade" Social Democrat, preaching class peace. He needed to protect his left flank by forecasting revolution *somewhere*, if not within capitalism, then in its international relations. But, as his main Western biographer, Stephen Cohen, observes, Bukharin was not an opportunistic theorist like Stalin, switching theories as the factional situation demanded; he was a more genuine Marxist theorist. The main reason Bukharin did not develop a less threatening portrayal of international politics to complement his domestic arguments therefore appears to be genuine belief. Kautsky's notion of "ultraimperialism," that imperialism could somehow manage its external contradictions without war—an idea

[38] On Varga's role in this new assessment, see his letter to Stalin in AAN 1513/1/198 and "Vskryt' cheres 25 let," *Politicheskie issledovaniia*, 1991, no. 3, 156.

[39] See Cohen, *Bukharin*, 252–56; Bukharin, *Capitalist Stabilization*, 42–42, 59–60; *Mezhdunarodnaia burzhuaziia*; and *Otchet delegatsii VKP (b) v IKKI XV s"ezdu VKP(b)* (Moscow/Leningrad: Gosudarstvennoe Izdatel'stvo, 1928), 8–26.

Bukharin had vigorously polemicized against for a decade—was simply inconceivable to him.

Future Soviet reformers could always refer back to NEP as a more humane model of "socialism" than the one imposed on the USSR by the Party under Stalin. They could not, however, find a Bolshevik pedigree for a less alarmist analysis of international politics. The only Marxist alternative to the old thinking, Kautsky's ultraimperialism, had always been anathema to Bolsheviks and in any case was decisively discredited by the world crisis of the 1930s and the ensuing war. The lack of an international corollary was one of NEP's numerous shortcomings. It would perhaps be going too far to say that this shortcoming alone doomed Soviet "soft communism," but it certainly helped stack the deck against it.

A LEARNED AMENDMENT: THE CORRELATION-OF-FORCES THESIS

Stalin was not a theoretical innovator. He incorporated the ideas of his comrades. He adopted most of his ideas about international relations from Lenin and Bukharin, and, after he had liquidated more prestigious theoretical minds, the more pliant economist Evgenii Varga.[40] His public analyses of the international situation in the 1930s were largely direct continuations of 1920s modes of thinking, with one important exception. The hostility thesis, or at least the part of it that associated increased Soviet power with the temporary diminution of interimperialist rivalry, was soon pushed aside by events as sharp rivalries developed between Germany and Japan on the one hand and the Western powers on the other hand. Soviet discourse returned to intense focus on balance-of-power maneuvering. As Soviets had earlier portrayed Germany as the "least bad" capitalist country, so now they distinguished between the status-quo West and the revisionist Axis powers.

Stalin's report to the Sixteenth Party Congress in June 1930 contained the fundamental outlines of the balance-of-power model that would dominate the Soviet discourse for decades to come. After gloating about the discrediting of the "right deviationists'—liberal chatter about 'organized capitalism,'" Stalin analyzed the capitalist economic

---

[40]Dmitrii Volkogonov, *Triumf i tragediia: Politicheskii portret I. V. Stalina* (Moscow: Novosti, 1989), bk. 1, pt. 2, pp. 38–39; Pevzner, "Zhizn' i trudy." Even Stalin's truest admirer, Viacheslav Molotov, held this view: F. Chuev, *Sto sorok besed s Molotovym* (Moscow: Terra, 1991), 242.

crisis.[41] Intensified interimperialist contradictions implied a war threat to the USSR, he claimed, since the Western states and Japan might seek to resolve their antagonisms at the Soviet Union's expense. The hostility and war threat engendered by contradictions were one of two main tendencies Stalin identified in the capitalist countries' approach to the Soviet Union. The other tendency was toward the diplomatic settlement of disputes and mutually beneficial trade relations. If interimperialist contradictions explained the first tendency, what explained the second? Stalin answered: "Sympathy toward and support of the USSR on the part of workers in capitalist countries, the growth of the USSR's economic and political might; the increase in the USSR's defense capacity, the peace policy undeviatingly pursued by the Soviet regime."[42]

In short, the stronger the Soviet Union is, the better its relations with the essentially hostile West: "détente through strength," or what analysts have called the correlation-of-forces model.[43] This is the Soviet version of the well-known diplomatic affection for alliance-worthiness *(Allianzwürdigkeit; soiuzsposobnost')*: the more powerful a country is, the more inducements it can offer for an alliance and the more resources it can contribute, so the better able it is to play the balance-of-power game. In Soviet terms, it is better able to exploit interimperialist contradictions. International relations theorists would term this kind of thinking a belief that bandwagoning prevails in world politics. As the power of our state grows, others will be inclined to align with us or at least defer to us. This is the opposite of the notion of balancing: the stronger a state gets (or the more it is perceived as a threat), the more other states align (balance) against it. The idea of balancing seemed to be implicit in the hostility thesis of the late 1920s.[44] So the experience of a decade and a half of diplomacy suggested to Moscow that bandwagoning rather than balancing characterized alignment behavior.

Stalin's model of world politics contains two distinguishing ele-

---

[41]Stalin, 12:235–61.

[42]Ibid., 257.

[43]David Holloway, "Gorbachev's New Thinking," *Foreign Affairs* 68 (1988–1989): 66–81. Some Soviets had subscribed to this viewpoint all along. See, e.g., L. Ivanov, *SSR i imperialisticheskoe okruzhenie* (Moscow: Izdatel'stvo Kommunisticheskoi Akademii, 1928), 154. But the public discourse between 1925 and 1929 had clearly focused on the hostility thesis.

[44]Of course, there were major differences. The hostility thesis literally predicted temporary balancing against increased Soviet power, followed by revolution, and, presumably, the end of international relations as previously understood. But in the near term, at least, it assumed that increased Soviet power would unite the opposition.

ments. The first element describes the generalized security threat emanating from the nature of capitalism. The second, correlation-of-forces element suggests the degree to which this danger is alleviated by Soviet power. This basic two-tendencies framework would go through various adjustments over the next half-century—now one tendency predominating, then another—but it would remain essentially in place. The evidence is quite good that the first element of the model, focusing on the war threat, underwent substantial attack and revision throughout the postwar years. The evidence is less convincing that anyone before Gorbachev seriously questioned the second, peace-through-strength postulate.

In succeeding speeches, Stalin altered the war-threat side of his model to correspond to immediate needs and his reading of the international situation. The basic two-tendencies model, however, remained in place. Always it was the growing economic, political, and military might of the USSR that accounted for reasonableness on the part of the Western countries and Japan. In addition, Stalin continued to give varying degrees of emphasis to nonstate factors, such as the "sympathy" or "support" of masses of workers throughout the world. But the support of these substate forces, Stalin stressed at several junctures, was itself a function of the Soviet state's developmental successes.[45] So the international proletariat could never substitute for Soviet state power in preventing war and securing better international relations, but could act only as a dependent adjunct.

The events of the 1930s and the eventual world war fitted the Leninist-Stalinist apocalyptic-statist view of world affairs remarkably well. As Stalin explained in his report to the Eighteenth Party Congress in March 1939, the law of uneven growth had exerted increasing pressure on the "regime" imposed by the victorious states after the World War. These economic contradictions fed political antagonisms, which were expressed in the creation of hostile camps among the imperialist countries and the threat of a new "imperialist war."[46] The Soviets had the timing slightly off in the mid-to-late 1920s. They misread the minor realignments in that period. But the next decade proved the modified theory of imperialism and the correlation-of-forces, bandwagoning hypothesis correct in all their essentials. Throughout the 1930s, the stronger the Soviet Union became, the more seriously it appeared to be taken by the capitalist countries.

By the eve of World War II, Stalin thought he had achieved such a

[45] Stalin, 13:29–42, esp. 38–40; 161–215, esp. 170–71; 282–379, esp. 284–97, 299–302.
[46] Stalin, 14:327–45, esp. 334–41.

strong position that the other major powers were vying for his favors. Indeed, the Hitler-Stalin pact of August 1939 ratified the classic old-thinking precepts about bandwagoning from two sides. On the one side, the fact that London and Berlin were competing for Moscow's allegiance was proof of the contention that stronger states make more attractive allies. On the other side, Stalin himself chose to bandwagon with Nazi power rather than balance against it via an agreement with the French and British. Stalin may not have known how other leaders felt when they were confronted by his power, but he knew his own feelings when he was faced with Hitler's power.[47]

There was ample evidence here to support Stalin's oft-expressed contention that "the weak are beaten, only the strong are respected." Nothing, of course, ratified these propositions more completely than the experience of World War II. Once the war got under way, Soviet influence over other actors in international relations correlated precisely with Soviet military power. The Western allies were never more obsequious than when they were at a palpable power disadvantage. They became notably more assertive after they deployed forces on the Continent and after the United States developed the atomic bomb.

OLD THINKING AND THE MECHANICS OF POWER

The main lesson to be drawn from the Soviet Union's interaction with power politics in the interwar years is the difficulty of learning about the balance of power. The concepts scholars study turn out to be quite relevant to the experience of historical actors, but the fine distinctions they make are hard to find in practice. Uncertainty and ambiguity are inherent in strategic situations. Consequently Bolshevik ideas about world politics which may seem ludicrous today could appear entirely plausible at the time.

International relations theorists who adhere to the equilibrium view contend that the constraints and inducements offered to individual states by a multipolar structure (consisting of three or more great powers) are different from those presented by a bipolar structure (only two great powers, as was the case after World War II). The main problem with a multipolar structure, in the influential view of Kenneth Waltz, is uncertainty.[48] When states form alliances against

[47] He is reported to have told Nikolai Ezhov, "We must come to terms with a superior power like Nazi Germany": Erickson, "Threat Identification," 402, n. 43.

[48] Kenneth Waltz, *Theory of International Politics* (Reading, Mass.: Addison-Wesley, 1979), 163–70.

perceived threats, none can ever be sure that its alliance partners will fulfill commitments at the crucial moment. All worry that someone will cut a side deal with the state that is perceived as a threat, or will defect and give some unfortunate state the "honor" of defending the status quo on its own. This inherent uncertainty suggests that the feedback individual states receive from the international system may be more ambiguous in a multipolar structure than in a bipolar structure. That is, as states monitor the effects of their policies, it will be less easy to tell whether policy based on a certain strategic belief is meeting with success.

The historical evidence from the years leading up to both world wars supports the contention that the uncertainty of multipolar structures also applies to the issue of balancing versus bandwagoning. In the years before 1914, the nations that sought to balance Germany suffered from uncertainties typical of alliances in multipolar structures, and their indecisiveness gave the Germans the impression that further forceful diplomacy could extract further concessions from them, if not lead them to break up their alliance. Before the July crisis, Berlin had won a series of easy diplomatic victories. The situation changed suddenly in that crisis—something that would have been hard to predict in advance. The coalition that opposed Germany in 1914—England, France, and Russia—was in all probability militarily the weaker. It thus took several years of warfare before the real anti-German coalition took shape with the addition of Italy and especially the United States. If one views the problem of uncertainty in alliance management from the other side—that is, from the side of the revisionist power—the result is ambiguity about whether bandwagoning or balancing really characterizes the situation. The context was even more uncertain in the years before World War II, when the states opposing Nazi Germany engaged in egregious buck-passing, and the real anti-Hitler coalition was not formed until 1941, two years after the war began.

This is the first consideration to keep in mind when we evaluate the evolution of Soviet perspectives on the balance of power in the interwar period. Soviet views did change, and "learning" may be as good a word to describe this change as any other. Within weeks of seizing power, the Bolsheviks were beginning to absorb the basic rules of the balance-of-power game. Soviet thinking became more complex as a result of experience. Though ultimate goals may not have been modified, by the mid-1920s immediate and even medium-term ones were. But Moscow was learning about a balance-of-power configuration rife with uncertainty, where "Keep your powder dry" may well have been the most fail-safe rule. It was not a simple matter to discern whether balancing or bandwagoning really prevailed. The ambiguity inherent in this situation helps to explain the seeming unevenness of Soviet views about the balance of power, particularly the adoption of the hostility (quasi-balancing) thesis in the mid-1920s and its replacement with the correlation-of-forces (quasi-bandwagoning) thesis in the 1930s.

A second important consideration concerns the perception of threat. Stephen Walt makes an important addendum to the theory of alliances by showing that states tend to balance against perceived threat rather than perceived power (though these two variables might be expected to covary in most cases).[49] This is an extremely important revision of the theory, for it introduces an inherently perceptual phenomenon, threat, into the calculation. If a state feels threatened, it will not be included to think in terms of balance of power at all, but will value all increases in its power. Any increase in capabilities, from whatever source, will be viewed as improving its diplomatic and security position. A state that feels threatened will view its policy in terms of balancing, regardless of what other states may think at the time or what we may think with hindsight.

Whether one is engaged in balancing or bandwagoning therefore depends on one's perception. In this context, it is doubtful whether it is entirely fair to characterize the interwar Soviet correlation-of-forces thesis as a bandwagoning notion. For many reasons, the Bolsheviks thought of the other great powers as inherently threatening. Doubtless they were ideologically predisposed to overperceive the threat. They were, as diplomatic histories always point out and as all Soviet sources indicate, hypersensitive to the possibility that the other powers would gang up on them. But they did have sound reasons for these suspicions. Soviet Russia did have to wage a war for its existence; it did have to fight for recognition. Only after it had substantially increased its power was it accepted as a diplomatic partner by the other states. In short, the Bolsheviks saw themselves balancing against the "imperialist threat." The stronger they got, the more seri-

---

[49] Stephen Walt, *The Origins of Alliances* (Ithaca: Cornell University Press, 1987). Distinguishing between threat and power may not be as straightforward as Walt implies. If "power" is measured by material indices and compared with "threat," one may discover discrepancies. Walt, for example, expects *imbalances* of power to form against threatening states. Given our earlier discussion of power in chap. 1, however, it is difficult to know what any discrepancy between threat and material power indices might mean. A comparison of perceived power and threat would be likely to discover close correspondence.

ously they would be taken by the other powers, and the better their security situation would be. And, as we have seen, the evidence generated by the Soviet Union's interaction with the other great powers supported this contention throughout its formative years. No doubt it was hard for Soviet leaders to imagine having too much power.

The ambiguity of evidence in the interwar multipolar structure and the problem of threat perception go a long way toward explaining the context of the evolution of Soviet perspectives on the balance of power. In the 1920s and 1930s, the Soviet diplomatic experience consisted of winning a place as a great power in an international context viewed as highly threatening. This experience captured a combination of bandwagoning and balancing elements. Bandwagoning is relevant because the experience of winning a place as a great power is essentially a tale of increasing power bringing increased prestige and allies in its wake. Russia had lost its status as a great power not only by virtue of having been weakened by war and revolution but also because it had become ideologically unattractive. The Bolsheviks had to work hard to overcome these debits. Thus, in the Moscow perspective of the time, prestige and recognition were things one fought and struggled for; respect for other states had to be *compelled* by the logic of power. All of these perceptions were captured in the correlation-of-forces side of Stalin's Sixteenth Congress model of world politics.

The balancing element is captured by the other side of that model: the presumed threat emanating from the "imperialist camp." Much of the harping on the war threat was doubtless instrumental, but it is unlikely that the Soviets and even Stalin himself completely discounted their own ideological notion of the "general crisis of capitalism." This view held that the imperialist states could engage in irrationally violent action when the system's internal and external contradictions generated a major crisis. Despite the near-term importance of interimperialist squabbling, Soviets always entertained a lurking suspicion that a generalized crisis could goad the other powers into jointly lashing out against the Soviet Union. The sense of threat increased the likelihood that accretions of Soviet power would be seen in terms of balancing.

The major lesson the Soviet Union learned in its interaction with the balance of power in these years was to value state military power, as opposed to less tangible elements of influence, such as the symbolic prestige conferred by revolutionary purity. Military power balanced against the potential "imperialist" threat. Military power made you more attractive as an ally. Military power won the war when diplomacy failed, and a place among the great powers when the war ended. This is the intellectual baggage Soviets carried with them as they regarded the post-1945 international configuration.

[4]

Confronting the Postwar
System, 1945–1953

Postwar periods are special for realist theories of international politics. For those realists who think in terms of hierarchy and hegemony, a major war reveals the true distribution of power, establishing a new hierarchy among the great powers upon which a new international order is based. The postwar years constitute a unique period in which states know where they stand in the scales of world power and cooperate or acquiesce in establishing the new order preferred by the most powerful state. In the equilibrium approach, major wars can lead to fundamental changes in the distribution of capabilities, to which states will have to adjust in the postwar period. The case of World War II is particularly dramatic, for it leads to a shift from multipolarity to bipolarity.

The gist of most retrospective analyses of the distribution of power immediately after the war and four years later is captured in Table 1.[1] For someone with no knowledge of what happened after 1946, these figures for that year do not speak for themselves. One could construct a case for American hegemony (especially if the U.S. atomic monopoly is also considered), U.S.-Soviet bipolarity, or a tripolar distribution including Great Britain.

Observers in 1946 knew that power balances were deranged by the recent war, with abnormally large numbers of men under arms in some countries and industrial production virtually destroyed in many others. Consequently, their expectations about trends in the power

[1] For discussions of variable selection and data collection, see the chapters by James Lee Ray and J. David Singer in *Measuring the Correlates of War*, ed. Singer and Paul R. Diehl (Ann Arbor: University of Michigan Press, 1990).

Table 1. Share of world power and of industrial-economic and military strength held by four countries, 1946 and 1950 (percent)

Country	World power[a]		Industrial-economic strength[b]		Military strength[c]	
	1946	1950	1946	1950	1946	1950
United States	36%	28%	71%	50%	38%	23%
Soviet Union	16	18	13	15	38	35
Great Britain	11	6	12	9	17	4
France	3	3	3	4	6	4

SOURCE: Major Power Capabilities Index, Correlates of War Project, University of Michigan; made available through the Interuniversity Consortium on Social and Political Research.
[a] Military expenditures, military personnel, total population, urban population, steel production, and consumption of industrial fuels.
[b] Steel production and fuel consumption.
[c] Military personnel and military expenditures.

relationship would play an important role in their assessments. A comparison of figures for 1946 and 1950 yields a simple, retrospective portrait of trends in postwar relationships, with the cases for American hegemony and tripolarity looking weaker over time.

In hindsight, the figures strongly suggest U.S.-Soviet bipolarity. People on the ground in 1946, however, had no idea what the precise configuration of power would look like. The vast majority of them thought in terms of multipolarity, with the wartime "Big Three" retaining their preeminence over the rest. After all, bipolarity as Kenneth Waltz defines it had never before existed in the history of the states system.[2] The terms "superpower" and "bipolarity" were not in general use in the immediate postwar period. True, "superpower" was coined by William T. R. Fox in 1944, but it had not yet been picked up by diplomats and journalists, and in any case Fox believed the United States, the Soviet Union, and Great Britain all qualified as superpowers.[3]

In took a full decade after the war's end for international relations theorists to begin to debate the distinction between bipolar and multipolar systems. Over a decade after that, Kenneth Waltz began to develop his argument that bipolar systems were inherently more

[2] Kenneth Waltz, *Theory of International Politics* (Reading, Mass.: Addison-Wesley, 1979).
[3] William T. R. Fox, *The Super-powers: The United States, Britain, and the Soviet Union—Their Responsibility for Peace* (New York: Harcourt Brace, 1944).

[60]

stable than multipolar ones. This argument reached full flower in Waltz's *Theory of International Politics*. By the 1980s, after thirty-five years' experience of stable bipolarity, it became the dominant position among those who regarded polarity as an important variable. The power of Waltz's deductive logic doubtless contributed to his theory's persuasiveness, but induction based on the experience of three diplomatic generations certainly did not hurt.

This combination of experience and theory contributes to a powerful tendency to assess the strategies and policies of post-1945 actors according to our contemporary understanding of the mechanics of bipolarity. But the intellectual history of the bipolarity idea should give us pause: first experience, then elegant theory. However, unambiguous the post-1945 strategic situation may appear to us now, the only way to establish the degree of ambiguity that truly characterized the situation is by close historical research. We must establish what contemporary observers thought or assumed about the nature of the distribution of power and the mechanics of the postwar balance of power, and how their views changed over time.

In the Soviet Union of the Stalin era, all political discourse, down to the level of private conversations among any but close friends and family members, was governed more by the party's general line than by any other factor. The pervasiveness of totalitarian constraints on the natural evolution of political thought distinguishes the Soviet Union from the other great powers of the period. Because all discourse had to be conducted in terms compatible with the general line, an exegesis of that line is an inevitable first step in any analysis of Soviet perspectives in the pre-Gorbachev era.

The analysis cannot end with an investigation of the general line, however, as it sometimes did in classical works of Kremlinology. The general line was itself fluctuating and shot through with contradictions. The leadership used its official media to try to communicate several things to several audiences. Stalin himself was no doubt uncertain about the precise direction events would take, and thus did not always wish to make unambiguous pronouncements. Further, Stalin was at the peak of his power, so secure in the wake of the great victory that he could afford not to make the general line as clear as it had been in the 1930s. His pronouncements were rare, and they generally took the form of interviews with newspaper correspondents, a method of communication much less authoritative than a speech to a party assemblage. Yawning gaps in logic and coherence opened up, into which both internal and public "expert" discussion could intrude.

The war's end brought forth a question, unarticulated but nonetheless detectable between the lines of the Stalinist discourse of the day: Would the great victory bring, at long last, a "return to normalcy," a relaxation of the harsh regime of the 1930s?[4] Would cooperation with the democratic powers and the defeat of fascism bring an end to the constant war scares, draconian social controls, unending purges, gigantic forced-labor camps, and material hardships? Stalin's negative answer to this question was made evident to the Soviet people soon after the conclusion of hostilities. In explaining to the people the continued need for the prewar Stalinist system, the leadership resuscitated much of the prewar class-struggle ideology, including its international aspect. Cognition of the postwar international realities had to take place in the context of a general line that reasserted the continued relevance of the prewar verities. As self-evidently false as some of these Stalin-era propositions about international politics may appear to today's observer, they seemed to many Russians in 1946 to be vindicated by the most dramatic events of their own lives and that of their country.

Stalin indicated the general nature of the postwar line in a speech to 4,000 party members at Moscow's Bolshoi Theater in February 1946. The speech, which ostensibly was part of the "election" campaign to the completely powerless and ceremonial Supreme Soviet, was the second-to-last speech the despot made to a large audience (the last one being his short introductory remarks to the Nineteenth Party Congress in 1953). Stalin first stressed that the recent war had been the inevitable result of the dynamics of the capitalist system. Since imperialism still existed, the forces that gave rise to World War II could give rise to a new war. He then argued at length that the war had tested the organization of the Soviet state, economy, and army, and proved them superior to all nonsocialist methods of organization. The war, furthermore, vindicated the prewar policies of forced industrialization and collectivization, which, he claimed, had transformed the Soviet Union from an agricultural to an industrial country in thirteen years. Stalin then gave specific industrial targets the Soviet

[4]Sheila Fitzpatrick, "Postwar Soviet Society: The 'Return to Normalcy,' 1945–53," in *The Impact of World War II on the Soviet Union*, ed. Susan J. Linz, 129–56 (Totowa, N.J.: Rowman & Allanheld, 1985).

economy had to meet, for "only under these circumstances will our Motherland be guaranteed against any eventuality." This mighty up-surge in industrial output would require three five-year plans, "if not more."[5]

To anyone schooled in the ideology of the day, the speech could hardly have been clearer. The Leader simply said that the war had not changed the basic dynamics of international relations. Despite the recent close Soviet collaboration with the Western powers, they were still part of an imperialist system that would inevitably give rise to wars. The postwar period, as Robert Tucker puts it, was now a new prewar period.[6] The lessons of the interwar years were still relevant. As in the 1930s, the Soviet Union would have to exert maximum effort to be ready for anything. In many respects, this was a return to the line of the Sixteenth and Seventeenth Party Congresses. There would be no return to normalcy.

The speech was a bombshell in the context of early 1946.[7] For four years the general line had not dared even to employ the word "capitalism" for fear of offending the Western allies. It had portrayed the struggle as one of the closely collaborating democratic states against the fascists and militarists. The new line brought back into currency not only "capitalism" but the much more nefarious "imperialism." The war, though it contained an antifascist component, was now portrayed in terms of Lenin's theory of imperialism and its inexorable law of uneven growth. Stalin's speech had an immediate effect on Soviet discourse. It ended all talk of continued cooperation with the Western allies in anything like the wartime intimacy. It ended discussion of the possibility of a warless world. From February 1946 onward, any analysis of the international situation had to be couched in terms of the Stalinized theory of imperialism.[8]

[5]Stalin, 16:1–22.
[6]Robert Tucker, *The Soviet Political Mind: Stalinism and Post-Stalin Change*, rev. ed. (New York: Norton, 1971), 91.
[7]For other interpretations, see ibid., 90–91; George Kennan to DOS, 2 December 1946, in *FRUS*, 1946, 6:694–96; William Taubman, *Stalin's American Policy* (New York: Norton, 1982), 135–36; Hugh Thomas, *Armed Truce: The Beginnings of the Cold War, 1945–46* (New York: Atheneum, 1987), chap. 1; William O. McCagg, *Stalin Embattled* (Detroit: Wayne State University Press, 1978), esp. 217–37.
[8]Cf., e.g., Petr Fedoseev, "Marksizm-Leninizm ob istochnikakh i kharaktere voin," *Bol'shevik*, 1945, no. 16, 31–59 (hinting at a conciliatory policy) with his "Bor'ba partii bol'shevikov za prevrashchenie nashei strany v peredovuiu, moguchuiu derzhavu," *Bol'shevik*, 1946, no. 9 (May), 12–31 (stressing past efforts to industrialize to build up the war power of the state), and "Sovremennaia burzhuaznaia sotsiologiia o problemakh voiny i mira," *Bol'shevik*, 1946, no. 22 (November), 31–51 (elaborating Stalin's speech on the true causes of World War II).

Though Stalin used the speech to reassert in broad terms the pre-war ways of thinking about international relations, this performance can hardly be compared with his prewar appearances before party gatherings. Then his reports were long and detailed, containing exhaustive analyses of trends in the capitalist world, the prospects for revolution in various parts of the globe, strategy and tactics for the international communist movement, and a justification for Soviet diplomatic moves couched in terms of an analysis of "interimperialist contradictions." All of these elements were missing from the 1946 speech. Of the four basic postulates of the old thinking, Stalin concentrated on one: imperialist contradictions mean war. He made no mention of contradictions as diplomatic opportunities, or of the connection between war and revolution, or of the old class-struggle suspicion that the capitalist powers would gang up on the Soviet Union, or even of the bandwagoning notion that increased Soviet power would lead to diplomatic triumphs. He left it to members of his circle, such as Molotov, Georgii Malenkov, and Andrei Zhdanov, as well as lower-level officials and ideologists, to work out how to apply the other three old-thinking postulates to the postwar realities.

After 1946, the general line repeated the pattern of the 1925–29 period. Just as Germany's drift away from the Rapallo spirit in the mid-1920s sparked Bolshevik fears of a joint imperialist endeavor against the Soviet Union, postwar Western efforts at cooperation, such as the Marshall Plan and eventually the Atlantic Alliance, played into a new bout of Soviet war-scare mongering. Just as in the 1920s, publicists in the postwar years portrayed the cooperation among the capitalists as inherently fragile and contingent upon shared anti-Sovietism. They claimed that the "general crisis of capitalism" had now reached its "second stage" as a result of socialism's gains and imperialism's losses in the war. The "second stage of the general crisis of capitalism" was simply a postwar version of the Comintern's old "third period" line, which Stalin had used in 1927 to purge the Soviet and other communist parties of Burkharinite right-wingers. They claimed that post–World War II capitalism would be even more unstable, crisis-ridden, and prone to irrational violence than its prewar predecessor. Anyone familiar with the prewar old thinking immediately recognizes all these and many more parallels between the rhetoric of Stalin's "second revolution" from above in the late 1920s and his postwar reassertion of orthodoxy. Publicly, at least, official Moscow was replaying old scenarios at slightly different speeds.

Though the line exhibited a secular trend toward greater dogmatism, more emphasis on the war threat, and heightened focus on class struggle, there were important variations and stages. The most important developments, from the perspective of analyzing the discourse on the structure of power, were Zhdanov's "two camps" speech in September 1947, the reassertion of the hostility thesis in the early 1950s, and the publication of Stalin's pamphlet *Economic Problems of Socialism in the USSR* in 1952. These events provided the context for the discussion of the postwar world among diplomats, economists, and other experts.[9]

FROM TRIPOLARITY TO TENUOUS ALLIANCE BIPOLARITY

In the immediate aftermath of the war, all Soviet observers agreed that the Big Three of Britain, the USSR, and the United States were the only remaining great powers. The Big Three were not equal, however, for in the West the underlying distribution of power had shifted in the United States' favor. According to the theory of imperialism, then, there was an objective contradiction between the United States and Britain, which gave rise to the following set of questions: How would the two countries readjust their spheres of influence to correspond to the new correlation of forces between them? Could their wartime cooperation continue despite the immense contradictions? Who was the main enemy? Should Soviet policy favor status-quo Britain, to help it defend its position against the American assault, or would it be better to favor revisionist America, to draw British power away from the Soviet periphery? How could Soviet policy profit from Anglo-American contradictions without entirely alienating either power? Should Moscow welcome or be alarmed by the prospect of America's return to isolationism? These were the burning questions, and at their root lay the question of the underlying structure of power.

One can discern two main arguments in Soviet sources before the end of 1947. Stalin's preelection speech, with its reassertion of Lenin's theory of imperialism, had the effect of silencing arguments that further Big Three cooperation in anything like its wartime intimacy was possible. The relationship would be some form of cooperation and

[9]For attempts to decipher these materials, which reach differing conclusions, see McCagg, *Stalin Embattled;* Taubman, *Stalin's American Policy;* Marshall Shulman, *Stalin's Foreign Policy Reappraised* (Cambridge: Harvard University Press, 1963); Werner Hahn, *Postwar Soviet Politics: The Fall of Zhdanov and the Defeat of Moderation* (Ithaca: Cornell University Press, 1982); Gavriel Ra'anan, *International Policy Formation in the USSR: Factional "Debates" during the Zhdanovshchina* (Hamden, Conn.: Archer, 1983).

competition with the other great powers. The only arguments remaining were, first, that Britain was the main threat, and policy must be directed against it; and second, the opposite view, that Britain must be pried away from the real threat, the United States. The two arguments shared both the realization that war between the Anglo-Saxon powers was out of the question and the assumption that fierce competition between them would inevitably come.

The anti-American position was efficiently expressed in "American Foreign Policy in the Postwar Period," a report prepared for Soviet diplomats at the Paris Peace conference in September 1946. Bearing the signature of Moscow's ambassador to the United States, Nikolai Novikov, the report was actually inspired and "coauthored" by Foreign Minister Molotov.[10] It portrayed a United States government completely under the sway of monopoly capital and bent on limiting the Soviet Union's postwar role as much as possible and intimidating it by fanning war psychosis. Fully half of it deals with Anglo-American contradictions. The American drive for global supremacy, the report states, is aided by a secret "understanding with England concerning the partial division of the world on the basis of mutual concessions"; London and Washington have agreed that China and Japan fall within the United States' sphere, while India, Indonesia, and other colonies in the Far East fall within Britain's; in the Near East the two countries have been unable to settle their differences; U.S. and U.K. military policies, as well as their line toward Eastern Europe, are closely coordinated; American penetration of important British possession and Britain's impending financial dependence are contradictions that place an unspecified limit on cooperation between the two powers; the United States is pursuing an anti-Soviet policy in Germany, but the report does not render an assessment of the extent of future U.S.-U.K. coordination on policy toward the western part of Europe.

What distinguishes this communication from contemporary public writings is its harsher, more pessimistic treatment of the United States. In this respect, it was approximately six months ahead of what would be said publicly. In all other respects, however, the document

---

[10] Novikov to Molotov, 26 September 1946; "Vneshniaia politika SShA v poslevoennyi period," AVP 06/8/45/759. Novikov's account, calling Molotov his "anonymous coauthor," is in N. V. Novikov, *Vospominaniia diplomata: Zapiski*, 1938–1947 (Moscow: Politizdat, 1989), 352. A translation of the report and discussion by historians are in "The Soviet Side of the Cold War: A Symposium," *Diplomatic History* 15 (Fall 1991): 523–64. The Russian historian Viktor Mal'kov, a contributor to the symposium, brought Novikov's memoirs to my attention.

is typical of open publications of the day. Its major point is that the United States is the main threat to Soviet security and influence in the postwar world. But the analysis also portrays Britain as a victim of the American assault, within, of course, the "imperialist" context. The analysis implies that Soviet policy might usefully take advantage of this contradiction, particularly in the Near East. Novikov's (and presumably Molotov's) focus on that region is worthy of note, for the report was written at precisely the moment when Stalin was bidding for a sphere of influence in northern Iran. On the USSR's eastern flank, the report saw no useful contradictions, and it was unclear on the situation to the west.

The Novikov-Molotov report reflects the tendency of Moscow observers to perceive the vast disparity in power between the Anglo-Saxon powers as a source of latent instability. As the international affairs expert Iosif M. Lemin put it, "The reduction of England to the position of a 'junior partner' in the Anglo-American bloc intensifies the struggle within the bloc and weakens its power."[11] This opinion reflected a view of the mechanics of power in which states of equal power are more capable of cooperation than unequal partners. Further, Britain was thought to be strong enough and potentially inclined to balance against, rather than bandwagon with, American power. Molotov, Novikov, Lemin, and many of their comrades appeared to share a belief expressed nearly two centuries early by Cardinal Richelieu, that "of two unequal powers, joined by a treaty, the greater power runs more risk of being abandoned than the other."[12] And in Soviet eyes the British compulsion to escape too tight an American embrace derived not only from such "subjective" factors as national pride and ambition but from fundamental economic forces. Leninism taught that capitalist economic power *repelled* rather than attracted other states. British capital would be harmed by American economic hegemony and would pressure the government for action. Thanks to

[11] I. M. Lemin, "Tridtsat' let bor'by SSSR za mir i bezopasnost'," *MKhMP*, 1947, no. 10 (October), 50. For Lemin's pro-Britain argument, see also "Mezhdunarodnye otnosheniia v 1945 godu," *MKhMP*, 1946, nos. 1–2, 20–34; *Anglo-amerikanskii blok i anglo-amerikanskie protivorechiia*, Stenogramma publichnoi lektsii (6 December 1946) (Moscow: Vsesoiuznoe Lektsionnoe Biuro, 1947); "Dva krizisa kapitalisticheskoi sistemy," *MKhMP*, 1946, nos. 4–5, 21; "K voprosu ob anglo-amerikanskikh otnosheniiakh," *MKhMP*, 1946, no. 12, 10; and "Vneshniaia politika SShA na sovremennom etape," *MKhMP*, 1947, no. 4, 3–19, esp. 12–16.

[12] Quoted in Robin Edmonds, *Setting the Mould: The United States and Britain, 1945–1950* (New York: Norton, 1986), 237. As Edmonds points out, British ministers also appeared to trust in this dictum until Suez.

[67]

the Soviet Union's increased power, it was now an attractive counter-weight to America.

A different interpretation of Russia's postwar position dated from the last year of the war, but coexisted with the anti-American assessment throughout 1946. This view was propounded by, among others, the prestigious economist Eugen Varga, who had been a player of no small consequence in domestic and Comintern struggles of the 1920s and 1930s. As we have seen, Varga had positioned himself with Stalin in the latter's struggle against Bukharin, originating the entire "third period" line for the Sixth Comintern Congress. He had also forecast the end of the worst phase of the Great Depression in 1933, a prediction Stalin himself appropriated. He advised the dictator on world economic matters throughout the 1930s and the war.[13] Consequently, his colleagues in Moscow and throughout the international communist movement considered him close to the Leader himself. Now the head of the Institute of World Economy and World Politics, he suggested that though America was the stronger of the two other great powers, Britain could be Moscow's more immediate adversary. In his *Changes in the Economy of Capitalism as a Result of the Second World War*, completed late in 1945, he predicted that Britain would fashion a "West European bloc" against both the Soviet Union and the United States, while the latter would maintain preeminence in Latin America and the Far East. "The Anglo-American contradiction will again be . . . the most important contradiction within the capitalist world."[14]

In Varga's view, Britain would, as it had done after World War I, stand behind various schemes to unite the Western powers and erect a cordon sanitaire around the Soviet Union. Britain had numerous assets respected by Soviets, over whom it had always cast an intimidating shadow in the interwar years: a vast network of military bases; an empire full of raw materials; diplomatic and intelligence acumen for putting together an anti-Soviet cordon; the ability (in the absence of effective Soviet countermeasures) to manipulate American policy; and finally, an asset to which Soviets increasingly referred only with sneering distaste, a "socialist" Labour government potentially capable of helping socialists in Europe to compete with communists

---

[13]See Iakov Pevzner, "Zhizn' i trudy E. S. Vargi v svete sovremennosti," *MEiMO*, 1989, no. 10, 16–33.

[14]E. S. Varga, *Izmeneniia v ekonomike kapitalizma v itoge vtoroi mirovoi voiny* (Moscow: Gospolizdat, 1946), 319.

for leftist hearts and minds.[15] Perhaps now, with the other powers reduced, the Anglo-American economic contradiction would at last produce political effects. The USSR, in Varga's version, would do well to adopt the classic checkerboard pattern of the balance of power: establish cordial relations with the power at your foe's rear; in this case, the United States.

Soviet propaganda and policy shifted between the anti-American and the anti-British lines. If we assume Stalin was in control of general policy, then it is safe to conclude that the dictator himself sided first with one and then the other. In 1945 and 1946, propaganda seemed to side with Varga as it viciously attacked the British while soft-pedaling differences with the Americans. Stalin's assumption at first seemed to be that the United States would probably return to a modified isolationism, defending its sphere in Latin America and its positions in the Far East, while Britain would seek, as it had done after World War I, to contain the Soviet Union. Provided the United States remained as peaceable as it had been in the interwar years, the Americans would make a perfect counterbalance to the wily British.

During much of the first year and a half after the war, incoming signals strongly indicated American disengagement. After Churchill's Fulton speech, for example, American Secretary of State James F. Byrnes stated that Washington was no more interested in an alliance with Britain against the Soviet Union than it was in an alliance with the Soviet Union against Britain.[16] Some of Stalin's conversations with Americans in this period suggest he was worried that the United States might become *too* isolationist, leaving him alone to deal with recalcitrant neighbors backed by Britain.

But the anti-American Novikov-Molotov report of late 1946 was, not surprisingly, prescient. Secretary Byrnes had taken a hard line toward Moscow at the Paris conference in September, Molotov had replied in kind, and a few months later Soviet propaganda shifted to a vitriolic anti-American line, coupled with relative friendliness to

---

[15] Varga stressed this point in "Anglo-American Partnership and Rivalry: A Marxist View," *Foreign Affairs* 25 (July 1947): 583–95. This article is in interesting contrast to Kennan's "X" piece, which appears in the same issue.

[16] Edmonds, *Setting the Mould*, 6. On 19 March 1946 the *Wall Street Journal* lamented that "the country's reaction to Mr. Churchill's speech must be convincing proof that the United States wants no alliance or anything that resembles an alliance" (quoted in ibid.). Belief in the United States' return to isolationism may also have been fed by the Soviet spies Donald Maclean and Kim Philby, who apparently underestimated Bevin's success in engaging the Americans in global affairs. See Anthony Verrier, *Through the Looking Glass: British Foreign Policy in an Age of Illusions* (New York: Norton, 1983), 59. I am indebted to David Holloway for this source.

Britain.[17] This campaign peaked in early 1947, when Stalin offered the British a treaty of military alliance outside the United Nations framework. It is not surprising that Stalin would maintain confidence in his ability to manipulate his former allies, given his wartime experience of dealing with Churchill and Roosevelt. On numerous occasions Stalin was presented with evidence of struggle between the two, and in particular of Churchill's commitment to the Empire and Roosevelt's disdainful attitude toward it. The overall pattern of Stalin's policy in this period—quiescent in the East, where there were no contradictions to exploit, and more forward in the Near East and West, where there were—is consistent with this interpretation.[18]

Abundant evidence flowed into Moscow to support Stalin's policy. British Foreign Minister Ernest Bevin's pro-American line was under strident attack from left and right. Fears of a Labour revolt against the policy mounted. The government and Foreign Office spoke of creating a Western European bloc as a "third force" between Soviet totalitarianism and rapacious American capitalism. The conditions on Washington's 1946 loan to Britain appeared draconian. As the *Economist* put it later in 1947, "not many people in this country believe the Communist thesis that it is the deliberate and conscious aim of American policy to ruin Britain and everything that Britain stands for in the world. But the evidence can certainly be read that way. [If Washington continues on its course] then the results will be what the Communists predict, whether or not it is what the Americans intend."[19] And the evidence did not emanate only from public sources. In January 1947 Prime Minister Clement Attlee circulated a memorandum questioning Bevin's pro-U.S. line: "I think that before being committed to this strategy we should seek to come to an agreement with the USSR after consideration with Stalin of all our points of conflict."[20] A dispatch to Molotov from London claimed "that the formation of a broad, practically national bloc for agreement with the

[17]For views of this shift from London, see Victor Rothwell, *Britain and the Cold War, 1941–1947* (London: Jonathan Cape, 1982); Edmonds, *Setting the Mould;* Elisabeth Barker, *The British between the Superpowers, 1945–1950* (Toronto: University of Toronto Press, 1983); and Fraser J. Harbutt, *The Iron Curtain: Churchill, America and the Origins of the Cold War* (New York: Oxford University Press, 1986). The periodization of Soviet policy in these accounts coincides exactly with mine.

[18]For more on Soviet assessments of the Far East, based on some archival materials, see L. Bazhanov, "Sovetsko-kitaiskie otnosheniia: Uroki istorii i sovremennosti," *Novaia i Noveishaia Istoriia,* 1989, no. 2, 3. Most sources agree that Stalin consigned China to the U.S. sphere.

[19]23 August 1947; quoted in Edmonds, *Setting the Mould,* 106.

[20]Ibid., 158. See also Barker, *British between the Superpowers,* chap. 3.

Soviet Union is possible." "Soviet diplomacy," Molotov was told, "has in England practically unlimited possibilities."[21]

The situation changed in 1947. Soviet efforts to play the Anglo-American contradiction produced meager results, while cooperation between the capitalist powers proceeded apace. In the wake of the annunciation of the Truman Doctrine, and more markedly after the Marshall Plan, Soviet commentary shifted from presuming some kind of tripolarity to perceiving an unstable bipolarity of alignments. To Soviet minds, the American loan to Britain and the Marshall Plan were redolent of the Dawes Plan and the Locarno era of perceived interimperialist collaboration in the mid-1920s. In place of the "Dawesification of Germany" was the "Marshallization of Europe." In addition to all the clear external evidence indicating the emergence of two basic alignments, Soviet observers also received some guidance from above in the fall of 1947 in the form of Andrei Zhdanov's speech to the founding meeting of the Communist Information Bureau, or Cominform.

Zhadnov's report "On the International Situation" is best known for its proclamation that the world was divided into two camps: the "imperialist and antidemocratic camp headed by the United States, and the anti-imperialist and democratic camp headed by the Soviet Union and the new democracies [of Eastern Europe]."[22] By conjuring up the two-camps imagery, Zhdanov resuscitated a concept that dated from the earliest days of the Bolshevik regime, when it was beset by internal and external class enemies in the Civil War, but the real analogy was to the Dawes Plan years of the 1920s.[23] The speech did recognize some differences from the 1920s. The American role was now much greater and more malignant. The Americans were not just "putting Germany on rations," as they had done a quarter-century earlier; now they were "enslaving" all of Europe.[24] Further, the report noted that the Soviet Union was much stronger than it had been before, and the communist parties of Europe were better organized and larger. Zhdanov gave the signals to these parties to fight the Marshall Plan tooth and nail.

[21] "Beseda t. Aleksandrova s Vernerom," 8 December 1946, AVP 06/08/45/760. Werner was a "sympathetic, well-connected" German journalist.
[22] A. Zhdanov, *O mezhdunarodnom polozhenii* (Moscow: OGIZ, Gospolizdat, 1947), 16.
[23] Stalin proclaimed the two-camps thesis in an *Izvestiia* article in 1919: "Dva lageria," in Stalin, 4:232–35. At that point the camps consisted of both states and class allies, and "the struggle between these two camps forms the axis of all contemporary life." See also his report on the Fourteenth Party Congress in December 1925 (ibid., 7:283–85) and his meeting with a delegation of American workers in 1927 (ibid., 10:135).
[24] Zhdanov, *O mezhdunarodnom polozhenii*, chap. 3.

[71]

Zhdanov's explanation for Western cooperation rest on three basic assumptions that few Soviets of that period thought or dared to question. First was the essentially violent and coercive nature of U.S. policy. Throughout his 1947 speech, Zhdanov had Washington "trampling," "forcing," "enslaving," and "quashing" European states and their basic sovereign rights. He portrayed Britain, France, the Netherlands, and other countries as chafing under the American yoke. The notion of interimperialist contradictions, especially surrounding the future of Germany, suffused the speech, even though it focused on the temporary unity of the Western camp. Second, Zhdanov assumed that the impetus for Washington's aggressive course was internal: the need to find markets for bloated war industries. The third assumption, which followed from the second, was that Western cooperation was unrelated to anything the Soviet Union did. No matter how peaceful and reasonable the Soviet Union was, Zhdanov argued, the West would always "slander" it as a threat in order to overcome internal contradictions.

The new line reflected a conviction that the Marshall Plan would fail to stabilize postwar capitalism. In an assessment for Molotov, Varga suggested that an impending recession in the United States would render it incapable of performing the stabilizing role envisioned in the plan. For the time being, though, Washington would seek to garner the maximum political advantage from exporting capital abroad, which was in its own economic interest in any case. The plan served as a mechanism for demonstrating American hegemony in Europe, Varga argued, as well as a lever for influencing events in Eastern Europe.[25] The new general line was meant not only to fight the Marshall Plan in Western Europe but to combat socialist forces, led by Britain's Labour party, who collaborated with the Americans and maintained contacts with Eastern European comrades. Hence the need to clarify the identities of friend and foe via the rigid two-camps delineation.

Zhdanov's Cominform speech put an authoritative end to notions of tripolarity. From that point onward, Soviet analyses assumed that an unstable bipolarity of alignments had taken shape whose Western half rested on the tenuous but nonetheless frightening foundations

[25]E. S. Varga, "Plan Marshalla i ekonomicheskoe polozhenie Soedinennykh Shtatov Ameriki," 24 June 1947, AVP 06/09/18/213. Molotov, according to his later recollections, at first proposed to the Central Committee that the Soviet Union participate in talks on the Marshall Plan, along with the Poles and Czechs, but quickly changed his mind, fearing "dependence" on the West. See Feliks Chuev, *Sto sorok besed s Molotovym* (Moscow: Terra, 1991), 88.

of increasing Western cooperation. That cooperation, in turn, produced in Moscow the classic set of Bolshevik reactions: Western unity was fragile, because strategic and economic contradictions, especially surrounding the future of Germany, lay just beneath the surface; but it was also threatening, because the imperialists could overcome their mutual contradictions only by uniting on an aggressive anti-Soviet platform. Both the vulnerability and the aggressiveness of the imperialist grouping remained themes throughout the Stalin years. The balance between the two in any given Soviet source depended on shifts in the general line and the particular purposes of the author.

The shift to a perception of tenuous alliance bipolarity occurred largely without any conceptual change. To most of Moscow's official minds, the evidence of the first two postwar years did not discredit old-thinking postulates about capitalism and balancing mechanics. They still thought that American hegemony was a latent source of instability.[26] What the evidence showed was how weak first Britain and then France really were in relation to the United States. The external and (especially in France's case) internal weakness of these countries explained their rulers' decisions to bandwagon with American power, despite the harm it did to their economic and political interests.[27] In most Soviet eyes, there was precious little Western "cooperation." Instead, there was a temporary transatlantic truce based on a series of humiliating British and French capitulations to America's onslaught. "Cooperation" resting on such foundations could not be long lived.

As always, the general line left many questions unanswered. In particular, it was difficult to interpret incoming evidence about policy conflicts among the Western powers. Reports from Soviet diplomats and journalists stationed abroad suggested that much of the apparent interimperialist conflict reflected cynical posturing on the part of London and Paris. The Soviet ambassador to France, for example, dismissed local opposition to American policy on the German question as "newspaper blathering" and mere "platonic expressions of dissatisfaction."[28] The French and British governments would go through the

[26] E.g., I. M. Lemin, "Ekonomicheskie protivorechiia i bor'ba mezhdu amerikanskimi i angliiskimi imperialistami," *Voprosy Ekonomiki,* 1949, no. 7, 61–82, esp. 81; V. Maslennikov, "Nekotorye cherty obostreniia obshchego krizisa kapitalizma," *Voprosy Ekonomiki,* 1948, no. 2, 67–80, esp. 79; A. Leont'ev, "Dal'neishee oslablenie kapitalisticheskoi sistemy," *Bol'shevik,* 1949, no. 20 (November), 74–90, esp. 85; V. Cheprakov, "Neravnomernost' razvitiia kapitalisticheskikh stran," *Bol'shevik,* 1952, no. 9 (May), 38–53.

[27] For such an analysis in the case of France, see "Godovoi otchet posol'stva SSSR vo Frantsii za 1949 g.," 20 February 1950, AVP 136/40a/1/255a, esp. p. 108.

[28] A. Bogomolov to A. Vyshinskii, 17 December 1948, AVP 136/32/5/216.

motions of opposing American plans in order to excuse themselves before their people while privately intending to follow in Washington's wake all along. In addition, they were not above playing the contradictions game themselves by pretending to be interested in a rapprochement with Moscow merely in order to win better terms from the United States and an improved political position within the Western bloc.[29]

What were Soviet policy makers to do? If Moscow did nothing, London and Paris might succeed in limiting their opposition to the United States to empty posturing. So it was necessary somehow to "expose" the real nature of intrawestern contradictions. But if the Soviet Union responded to British or French hints about improved relations, it could well end up playing the fool in a cynical intraimperialist game of maneuver. Uncertainty about how "ripe" interimperialist contradictions really were limited Moscow's ability to make concessions in order to get things moving. If the contradictions were not yet acute enough, Paris and London would gladly snap up any Soviet concessions and trumpet them as brilliant successes for their pro-American policy.

Similar difficulties surrounded efforts to decipher the impact of increased Soviet power on the Western alignment. Soviet power had to cast a large enough shadow over the Western governments to force them to take Moscow seriously. Otherwise, they would continue to implement policies inimical to Soviet interests without regard to Moscow's reactions. Increased Soviet power exposed and exacerbated Western contradictions by, among other things, undercutting the credibility of American military guarantees.[30] Yet everyone knew that the imperialists were able to unite mainly by adopting an anti-Soviet platform. The stronger the Soviet Union was, the more credible the "Red menace" argument would become.

In this light, Stalin's 1948 blockade of Berlin appears as a prudent compromise among several potential risks: that Western policy would succeed in forming a West German state; that the Western governments would merely exploit any preliminary Soviet concessions; and that the crisis might escalate. Subtle forms of pressure against Berlin

[29]See "Politicheskii otchet za 1948 g. vo Frantsii," 12 March 1949, AVP 136/39/4/216a, esp. pp. 118ff; "Otchet posol'stva SSSR v Velikobritanii za 1948 god," 26 March 1949, AVP 69/35/1/127, esp. pp. 136ff.
[30]See "Politicheskii otchet posol'stva SSSP v SShA za 1949 g.," 1 March 1950, AVP 129/33a/41/243: "Loss of the American monopoly on possession of atomic weaponry has strongly undermined the prestige of the United States in the eyes of its allies and sharpened contradictions in the Anglo-American imperialist camp" (14).

produced the expected results in the form of hints of concessions from the U.S. ambassador, and Stalin turned up the pressure by initiating the blockade in June. That move at first generated evidence that all three major Western capitals were inclined toward substantial compromise, but these indications slackened with the success of the Berlin airlift.[31] Soviet policy then laid low until Stalin again sought to prevent the next major Western move on Germany, this time rearmament. Stalin's note of March 1952 expressing willingness to negotiate terms for German reunification was a less risky endeavor to nudge Western differences into the open. The evidence generated by that episode again suggested that there was at present no low-risk way to exploit interimperialist contradictions. Moscow would have to risk either more substantive concessions or more dangerous escalation to discover the true depths of Western solidarity.

The evidence about the sources of Western solidarity was ambiguous enough to support different interpretations. Some articles in the official press stressed American domination and temporary imperialist unity while others portrayed potentially significant contradictions. Diplomats in London and Paris highlighted British and French dependence on Washington, while officials at the Ministry of Foreign Affairs in Moscow continually demanded more information on policy-relevant contradictions.[32] The whole "debate," if it deserves to be described as such, got buried in a new bout of war-scare propaganda after 1948, which cited agreement among the imperialists as a prelude to war against the Soviet Union. With no clear signal from above and no convincing evidence from abroad, Soviet articulations about the structure of power and balancing mechanics continued in the old-thinking vein throughout the remaining years of Stalin's reign. At the Nineteenth Party Congress in 1952, not long before Stalin's death, the dictator's heir apparent, Georgii Malenkov, restated the classic argument that American hegemony would induce the middle powers

---

[31] See esp. Hannes Adomeit, *Soviet Risk-Taking and Crisis Behavior* (London: George Allen & Unwin, 1982).

[32] See V. Trukhanovskii, "Annotatsii i zakliucheniia po otchetu posol'stva SSSR v Londone za 1947 g.," 1 June 1948, AVP 69/32/1/116; V. Pavlov to G. Zarubin, 5 April 1952, and Vyshinskii to Zarubin, 19 May 1952, AVP 69/39/13/155. Vyshinskii claimed that the London embassy underestimated Britain's world role and overestimated its dependence on the United States, believing that "we should deal exclusively with the USA on important political issues." That course, he wrote, "leads to mistaken conclusions for Soviet foreign policy." On France: "Zakliucheniia na politicheskii otchet posol'stva SSSR vo Frantsii za 1951 g.," 30 April 1952; Vyshinskii to V. Avilov, 10 September 1952; and M. Sergeev to V. Zorin, 11 June 1952, all in AVP 130/42/17/248.

to adopt "an independent peace policy," which "would meet complete understanding on the part of the peace-loving countries."[33]

After Zhdanov's 1947 speech, the next major change in the line came in 1949, as a frenetic war-scare campaign got under way. On the rise throughout 1949, the campaign reached hysterical proportions after the onset of the Korean War in 1950 and lasted until Stalin's death in 1953. The general line replayed the "second revolution" rhetoric of the 1927–32 period: forces were polarizing, the class struggle was intensifying, the capitalist crisis was deepening, and spies, wreckers, imperialist agents, and saboteurs were back on the scene. In this context, the hostility thesis of the 1920s naturally made its reappearance. As one Soviet ideologist expressed it: "The Soviet people know that the greater our successes, the more intense the hatred on the part of the bourgeoisie. . . . The bourgeoisie's hatred will increase in direct proportion to the growth of the forces of peace, democracy, and socialism; this hatred will drive it on to fresh adventures."[34]

The simplest way to navigate through postwar Soviet articulations about the international situation is to recognize the general line's close connections to its prewar predecessor. Stalin insisted that capitalism was due for another round of economic crisis, protectionism, and instability, which, coupled with the law of uneven development, would produce a new war in ten to fifteen years. Although the timing and initial stakes of the coming war might derive from within the capitalist camp, it would involve the Soviet Union just as World War II had done. This was the thrust of Stalin's message in February 1946, and he repeated it in greater detail in his pamphlet *Economic Problems of Socialism in the USSR*, published in 1952.[35]

This intellectual route was easy in ideological terms, for it required the least adjustment of accepted Soviet ideological positions. A new

---

[33] *Bol'shevik*, 1952, no. 19 (October), 1–8.

[34] D. Chesnokov, "Rech' I. V. Stalina na XIX s"ezde KPSS," *Kommunist*, 1953, no. 2, 22; quoted in Tucker, *Soviet Political Mind*, 98. Chesnokov outlines the history of this thesis fairly accurately, with numerous quotes from Lenin and Stalin (17–22). See Tucker, 95ff., for a discussion of the contradiction between stress on the improved correlation of forces and increased threat. For further examples of the thesis in action, see Lavrentii Beria's 1951 Revolution anniversary speech in *Pravda*, 7 November 1951, 2–4 (*CDSP* 3, no. 42: 5–7). Ambassadorial reports to Vyshinskii's foreign ministry began to stress the hostility thesis in 1950. See, e.g., Zarubin to Vyshinskii, 21 February 1950, AVP 69/37/11/136.

[35] Stalin, 16: 226–32. In private he told Milovan Djilas in 1945: "The war shall soon be over. We shall recover in fifteen or twenty years, and then we'll have another go at it": Djilas, *Conversations with Stalin* (New York: Harcourt Brace & World, 1962), 115. As shown below, fifteen to twenty years was also the Western estimate.

interpretation of the postwar balance of power would require shifts in accepted positions on other issues. Or a change of views about seemingly unrelated matters could influence one's views of the balance of power. This was the experience of Eugen Varga.

THE VARGA ALTERNATIVE

With hindsight, the general line looks as inevitable as it was wrong. In postwar Moscow there was every reason for organizing the postwar evidence according to the old-thinking framework. The old postulates had proved themselves correct in the past. The world had seemed stable in the 1920s, but the Bolsheviks had known better. The apparent unification of the imperialists then was just a prelude to a major bout of contradictions and war. Why would anyone volunteer for the position of the new Kautsky, postulating ultraimperialism in the 1940s? It seemed improbable that anyone would, especially when the old view appeared to meet with Stalin's approval.

Despite these long odds, someone did step forward with a sophisticated and complex revision of Stalinist ideology on the world economy, and hence on world politics and war. The writings of Eugen Varga, long a collaborator and confidant of Stalin, amounted to an alternative strategic assessment of the postwar world. Varga could voice such an alternative in Stalin's Soviet Union because of his great prestige, his earlier association with the dictator, and the ambiguities in the general line and consequent uncertainty about Stalin's exact preferences. Varga had, after all, gone against the apparently prevailing winds from the Kremlin several times in the past, had suffered attacks by powerful Stalinist functionaries, and had been rescued by Stalin personally.[36]

Before we examine Varga's position, it may be useful to ask what underlying logic supported Soviet postwar views of the balance of power. Why did Soviets profess to perceive the postwar alignment to be so unstable? How could they see American economic power as a force *repelling* other capitalist states? At root is Lenin's theory of imperialism with its "inside-out" analysis, its assumption that internal economic conditions within each capitalist state largely determine its external behavior. Soviets could not or did not want to see inter-

---

[36] For Varga's privately expressed account of his run-ins with the NKVD, Nikolai Voznesenskii, and Andrei Vyshinskii in 1937 and 1942, see "Vskryt' cheres 20 let," *Politicheskie issledovaniia*, 1991, no. 2, 175–83, and no. 3, 148–63.

capitalist relations in any but zero-sum terms. The capitalist state was a prisoner of its monopoly bourgeoisie, and it could not step above the most narrowly conceived and immediate economic interests of that bourgeoisie, even if those interests drove the state into irrational policies from the standpoint of the capitalist system as a whole. To revise one's view of the balancing behavior of states, one had to revise one's view of the state's independence of certain domestic groups.

So Eugen Varga did not notice all of a sudden that the evidence from abroad failed to correspond to the existing model of world politics and then revise that model. Instead, he had begun to revise his view of the bourgeois state back in the 1930s, and the evolution of this view eventually led him, in an inside-out fashion, to see the postwar structure as a stable bipolarity reflecting U.S. hegemony within the Western camp of states. When Varga cited evidence about the foreign behavior of capitalist states, it was in support of his analysis of their internal economic and political conditions. The feedback generated by Moscow's interaction with the balance of power in the postwar period did not compel Varga to change his views. Rather, that evidence confirmed views he had changed earlier for other reasons.

As a top Comintern official, Varga was responsible for elaborating the "popular front" line advanced at the organization's Seventh Congress, which instructed communist parties to collaborate with other left forces to influence state policy. In the course of elaborating this line and conducting analyses for Stalin on behalf of his institute, Varga began to see in Hitler's and Roosevelt's policies evidence of the relative autonomy of the bourgeois state. He considered his analysis vindicated by the measures taken by the belligerent states in war.[37] In his book on changes in the economy of capitalism as a result of the war, he maintained that the war had increased the role of the state permanently; that the state could engage in limited planning; that the state in time of crisis could reflect the wishes of the entire bourgeoisie, even overruling individual monopolies in the process. Capitalism was bad; it was aggressive; it would always be the adversary, *but it was capable of change and it had already changed* from the

[37]For prewar views, see Richard B. Day, *The "Crisis" and the "Crash": Soviet Studies of the West, 1917–1939* (London: New Left Books, 1981), chaps. 4–5; for Varga's wartime analyses, Manfred Kerner, *Staat, Krieg und Krise: Die Varga-Diskussion und die Rolle des Zweiten Weltkriegs in der kapitalistischen Entwicklung* (Cologne: Pahl-Rugenstein, 1981), 35–61. László M. Tikos, "Eugene Varga: A Reluctant Conformist," *Problems of Communism* 14 (January–February 1965): 71–74, reveals interesting details from Varga's pre-Soviet years, including his early fascination with the role of the bourgeois state in war.

monopoly capitalism Lenin and Varga himself had first analyzed before World War I.[38]

These propositions were so controversial in 1946 that the "Varga debate" burst forth as soon as his book was published.[39] The main issue in dispute was Varga's view of the capitalist state, but there was an important balance-of-power corollary that few analysts have noticed. As we have seen, at first Varga retained a Leninist view of world politics, assuming that the postwar system would operate like the prewar one. In this respect he resembled Bukharin, who had argued that capitalism was stabilizing internally, but not in its international relations. Throughout 1946 Varga, like other Soviet observers, became increasingly aware of the real distribution of power, and specifically of Britain's weakness. In his view, only Britain's economic and military relationship with its empire equated it in any way with the United States. In his articles and lectures in this period he seemed to set up tests that England had to pass in order to be considered a great power. England failed each of these tests, and, with the Marshall Plan, Varga concluded that Britain was no longer an independent force; it was becoming a U.S. satellite, a "49th, overseas state of America."[40]

The relative autonomy of the bourgeois state and a clear perception of hegemony were the first two ingredients of Varga's interpretation.

---

[38] In addition to Varga's *Izmeneniia*, esp. chaps. 1–2, see his "Osobennosti vnutrennei i vneshnei politiki kapitalisticheskikh stran v epokhy obshchego krizisa kapitalizma," *MKhMP*, 1946, no 6, 8–17, esp. 11–14; and "Sotsializm i kapitalizm za tridtsat' let," *MKhMP*, 1947, no. 3, 2–24, and nos. 3–4, 9.

[39] For Western accounts, see Franklyn J. C. Griffiths, "Images, Politics, and Learning in Soviet Behavior toward the United States" (Ph.D. diss., Columbia University, 1972); William Zimmerman, "Choices in the Postwar World: Containment and the Soviet Union," in *Caging the Bear*, ed. Charles Gati, 85–108 (Indianapolis: Bobbs-Merrill, 1974); Jerry Hough, "Debates about the Postwar World," in Linz, *Impact of World War II*; Frederick C. Barghoorn, "The Varga Discussion and Its Significance," *American Slavic and East European Review* 7 (October 1948): 214–36; Kerner, *Staat, Krieg und Krise*; László Tikos, *E. Vargas Tätigkeit als Wirtschaftsanalytiker und Publizist in der ungarischen Sozialdemokratie, in der Komintern, in der Akadamie der Wissenschaften der UdSSR* (Tübingen, 1965); and, for a very useful bibliography, Peter Knirsch, *Eugen Varga* (Berlin: Osteuropa-Institut, 1961).

[40] This evolution can be traced through the following articles and lectures: *Anglo-Amerikanskie ekonomicheskie otnosheniia*, Stenogramma publichnoi lektsii (Moscow, 1946); "Anglo-Amerikanskie ekonomicheskie otnosheniia," *Bol'shevik*, 1946, no. 3 (February), 50–62, esp. 60–62; "Osobennosti vnutrennei i vneshnei politiki kapitalisticheskikh stran v epokhy obshchego krizisa kapitalizma," *MKhMP*, 1946, no. 6 (July), 16–17; "SShA i Angliia: Bor'ba i Blok," *Novoe Vremia*, May 1947; "Bor'ba i sotrudnichestvo mezhdu SShA i Angliei," *MKhMP*, 1947, no. 8 (August), 3–13; "Plan Marshalla" i ekonomiki Angllii i SShA, Stenogramma publichnoi lektsii (Moscow, 1947). Varga's writings in more popular publications were more orthodox.

The third was the growth of Soviet and overall 'socialist" power. In combination these three elements led Varga to deemphasize the significance of interimperialist contradictions, though he never for a moment believed they would disappear or become completely irrelevant for Soviet policy. In Varga's view, given American hegemony, the other capitalist states had little choice but to accept the Marshall Plan, which itself would entrench U.S. dominance. One of the key reasons cooperation with the United States was the logical policy was the shift in the correlation of forces in favor of the Soviet Union, as well as in favor of workers' and national liberation movements as a whole. Interimperialist squabbling was irrational in view of the existence of a powerful Soviet-led bloc, an active labor movement, and aroused masses in the colonies. The Western states were not so closely controlled by the narrowest and most absurdly self-interested sectors of the bourgeoisie that they could not see the logic in this situation.

Varga clearly recognized that capitalist states would bandwagon with American economic power, and that they would cooperate in the face of Soviet power. But the stronger socialism was, in his view, the more rational and tractable the capitalist states would become. They would not fight against each other, since to do so would weaken them at a critical juncture, and they would certainly not fight the Soviet Union, which was far too powerful. Wars among the imperialists or against the Soviet Union should therefore not be considered inevitable. The bourgeoisie had learned in the two world wars that major wars weakened it. It was the shift in the correlation of forces that ensured that the growth in the autonomy of the state caused by World War II would remain. Because of the changed correlation, there was a danger clear and present enough for the state to step above its immediate base and take measures to save the system. Varga's view was thus a sophisticated restatement of the correlation-of-forces model: the stronger the Soviet bloc became, the more reasonable the West would become.

Varga had revised the theory of imperialism to account for the existence of a powerful Soviet Union. Soviet power ensured that the capitalist states would retain the relative autonomy they had won in the Depression and the war. Relative state autonomy in turn ensured rational state action to preserve the system, which in the concrete postwar circumstances required the middle powers to collaborate with the United States. Looking at the world in 1947, Varga saw comparatively stable American hegemony and U.S.-Soviet bipolarity. Quite bravely, the Hungarian professor brought all these points together in his presentation to a meeting of economists called in October 1948 expressly to denounce him.[41]

The striking differences between Varga's interpretation of postwar realities and the views generally expressed in 1948 can best be summarized by reference to the handwritten notes he prepared before the 1948 meeting. Couched at a practical rather than highly theoretical level, the notes concern Varga's predictions about "prospects for the development of capitalism over the next ten to fifteen years":

1. *"There will be no third world war between capitalism and socialism.* Under the existing equilibrium of forces, which is likely to shift toward a preponderance of the socialist world's forces in the next ten to fifteen years, the risk for the imperialists is very great; the potential winnings do not match the risk of the destruction of the entire capitalist system."

2. *"There will be no real peaceful coexistence, and no disarmament."* Varga believed that monopoly capitalism could not survive without military production.

3. *"The Cold War will continue,"* because it reflected the fundamental antagonism between the two social systems.

4. *"The capitalist world's production will grow at an approximate average rate of 1.5 percent a year."* He expected two world "reproduction crises" in the period, of lesser intensity than the 1929–1932 crisis.

5. The loss of Eastern Europe and some colonies had been a blow to capitalism, "but not a fatal one."

6. *"The imperialists' struggle for markets; interimperialist contradictions will sharpen."* U.S. hegemony over other capitalist states, however, would lessen only "slowly."[42]

The problem with Varga's position was that it was not revolutionary, and consequently, in many eyes, not Marxist. By 1948 Varga was being accused of "errors of a reformist character," and this accusation was correct. Varga's views *were* of a reformist character. He had taken over Bukharin's "organized capitalism" position, but Bukharin had retained the basic theory of imperialism, so he could at least retain some credibility by predicting massive interimperialist upheavals, wars, and revolutions. By revising the theory of imperialism, Varga had gone much further. He supplied Burkharin's arguments with their missing international twin. The capitalist state could "organize"

---

[41] "O nedostatkakh i zadachakh nauchno-issledovatel'skoi raboty v oblasti ekonomiki," *Voprosy Ekonomiki,* 1948, no. 8, 66–110; no. 9, 51–116 (Varga's presentation, 54–57).

[42] E. S. Varga, "Perspektivy razvitiia kapitalizma na blizhaiushchee 10–15 let," AAN 1513/1/79; emphasis in original.

not only its own economy but its foreign relations as well. Where did revolution fit in? Varga's only response was to focus on the revolutionary potential of the Third World. Varga was perilously close to a Kautskyist, Social Democratic position, and his opponents and allies knew it. What separated Varga from those "right wing" views was his continued assumption of capitalism's basic hostility and aggressiveness, and his consequent focus on Soviet power as a restraining force. Stalinist ideologues would roll over these fine theoretical distinctions just as they had rolled over Bukharin's.

The direction of the Kremlin breeze was already fairly clear in May 1947, when the economists gathered to discuss Varga's *Changes in the Economy of Capitalism.* After all, Stalin had highlighted the theory of imperialism in his election speech. Still, the tone of the discussion was fairly cordial. Varga had not fully worked out the international relations implications of his analysis. The discussion focused on his views of the state, planning, the colonial situation, and the place of the "new democracies" of Eastern Europe in the world economy. On international questions, Varga was critized for dowplaying the "struggle of the two systems" and "the Stalinist characterization of the general crisis of capitalism and the new correlation of forces between socialism and capitalism on the world scene."[43] Most of the participants repeated these criticisms, vacuous and inaccurate though they were. Far from underestimating the struggle between the two systems, Varga stressed it as much as anyone else, claiming that in the interests of this struggle capitalism had to reform itself or face defeat. Far from underestimating the shift in the correlation of forces, he stressed the shift more than anyone else, claiming that it reduced the salience of interimperialist contradictions. Only the accusation that Varga failed to give "due" attention to the new stage of the general crisis contained truth, for Varga did not accept the proposition implied by this formulation, that the shift in the correlation of forces made capitalism more unstable and aggressive.

By the end of 1947 not only the direction but the mounting force of the Kremlin breeze became apparent, and by then only Varga failed to adjust his nose accordingly. In September, Zhdanov delivered his leftist speech to the founding Cominform meeting, and the next month saw the appearance of a book on the Soviet wartime economy by the powerful Politburo member and Gosplan chief, Nikolai Voznesenskii. Both of these men harbored long-standing personal, ideologi-

---

[43] "Diskussiia po knige E. Varga *Izmeneniia v ekonomike kapitalizma v itoge mirovoi voiny,*" *MKhMP,* 1947, no. 11 (suppl.), 57.

cal, and bureaucratic-turf grudges against Varga. Voznesenskii's book, which was reviewed widely and favorably and was awarded the Stalin Prize, directly attacked Varga's formulations.[44] The transcript of the May discussion was published, and then Varga's institute was closed and merged into the Economics Institute. The October 1948 meeting of economists was a rougher affair for Varga than the gathering of the previous May, as he was now without allies and his critics denounced him more confidently and vigorously, occasionally descending into the barely concealed anti-Semitism and xenophobia characteristic of the "anticosmopolitan" campaign then getting under way.[45]

The old professor not only did not retreat but stated his positions even more forthrightly at this meeting. Indignant comments rained down upon him. Liberally quoting Voznesenskii and Zhdanov, the participants accused Varga of "playing into the hands of the Social Democrats," denounced his thesis that wars were no longer inevitable, and attacked him for paying insufficient attention to the new correlation of forces and the new stage of the general crisis of capitalism. Now that Varga's analysis of world politics was clearer, practically every speaker denounced him for "deviating from the Lenin-Stalin theory of imperialism." In addition, they vigorously attacked the hegemony thesis, accusing him of apologizing for the Marshall Plan, and asserting that U.S. dominance "inevitably sharpens interimperialist contradictions." According to Iosif Lemin, always intellectually attached to the theory of imperialism, Varga's approach, "regardless of its author's will, leads to slurring over the issue of contradictions in the imperialist camp. . . . Slurring over these contradictions in characterizing the contemporary situation would mean exaggerating the forces of capitalism and minimizing the forces of socialism and democracy."[46]

Five months later, in March 1949, Varga published an abject, self-critical retraction of most of his ideas.[47] That same month his most powerful critic, Voznesenskii, disappeared, eventually to be murdered by the MGB in the "Leningrad affair." For four months at the end of 1951 and the beginning of 1952, 400 economists gathered in

[44] Nikolai Voznesenskii, *Voennaia ekonomika SSSR v period Otechestvennoi Voiny* (Moscow: Gospolizdat, 1947), 32.

[45] See, e.g., the remarks of I. Gladkov (not included in the *Voprosy Ekonomiki* transcript of the meeting) reproduced in no. 30 of Roy Medvedev's *samizdat* journal, published as *Politicheskii Dnevnik*, 1964–1970 (Amsterdam: Alexander Herzen Foundation, 1972), 226, 230.

[46] *Voprosy Ekonomiki*, 1948, no. 8, 70–71, 87, 89; no. 9, 66–67, 99.

[47] E. S. Varga, "Protiv reformistkogo napravleniia v rabotakh po imperializmu," *Voprosy Ekonomiki*, 1949, no. 3, 79–88.

Moscow to discuss the draft of a new basic text on political economy.[48] The new text was to be for economics what the infamous *Short Course on the History of the CPSU(b)* was for history; namely, state dogma. The meeting, presided over by Malenkov, Iurii Zhdanov, and Mikhail Suslov, produced two documents: matters agreed upon and matters still under dispute. These documents were then submitted to Stalin personally for final judgment. Stalin issued his verdict in his final work, a pamphlet titled *Economic Problems of Socialism in the USSR*. The Nineteenth Party Congress voted to include Stalin's "work of genius" as part of the party platform.

Despite his earlier public recantation, Varga restated his by-then well-developed argument for overruling Lenin's inevitability-of-war thesis at the closed economists' meeting. His handwritten notes for the meeting make the following points: (1) The bourgeoisie has learned from World Wars I and II that wars cause revolution. (2) "The imperialist camp—despite the presence of acute contradictions—is increasingly turning into one *military alliance*" with a single joint command, maneuvers, and weapons development. (3) *"The mutual interest of the big bourgeoisie"* in defense and struggle against socialism is *"in this particular historical period stronger than its internal contradictions."* (4) "It is extremely difficult to *imagine concretely* a new war among the imperialists," since the U.S. is stronger than all the other capitalist countries put together and since it can achieve its goals without war. The United States would simply not allow interimperialist squabbling to get out of hand. "Abstractly and theoretically" one could imagine the law of uneven development giving rise to a new war as Germany and Japan recovered strength, but here Varga stressed the extent of U.S. hegemony: "The downfall of the entire imperialist system will occur earlier than uneven development could fundamentally alter the existing relationship of forces in the imperialist camp."[49]

According to Varga's account of the meeting, published in 1964, the majority of those present rejected his arguments. But, he maintained, that was "understandable: at that time dogmatism reigned and it was not considered permissible for anyone but Stalin to say anything new."[50] Varga's account has a genuine ring: the years between 1949 and 1953 were about the worst possible time to try to

---

[48] For Varga's own account of the meeting, see his *Ocherki po problemam politekonomii kapitalizma* (Moscow: Nauka, 1964), 78. See also Iakov Pevzner's account, "Zhizn' i trudy E. S. Vargi v svete sovremennosti," *MEiMO*, 1989, no. 10, 30–31.

[49] E. S. Varga, "Spornye voprosy dlia rassmotreniia TsK," n.d. [1950], AAN 1513/1/61; emphasis in original.

[50] Varga, *Ocherki po problemam politekonomii kapitalizma*, 78.

say anything innovative. Indeed, Varga might have added that Stalin himself was uninterested in saying anything new.

Stalin devoted a section of his pamphlet *Economic Problems* to Varga's "mistaken" position on the noninevitability of war (he also devoted a few paragraphs to countering the separate argument that the peace movement could prevent war). The essence of his argument was that no structural transformation had occurred in world politics. The same forces that gave rise to World War II were still operating, though "imperceptibly." American hegemony would ultimately produce centripetal forces and major realignments among the capitalist powers, leading to war. He said that "first capitalist Britain, then capitalist France will ultimately be forced to wrest themselves from the U.S.A.'s embrace and enter into conflict with the U.S.A."

As far as Germany and Japan were concerned, "To think that these countries will not attempt to rise to their feet again, smash the U.S. 'regime,' and break away on a path of independent development is to believe in miracles."[51] In this connection, Stalin noted that it took Germany only fifteen to twenty years to recover from World War I. This was, in essence, a restatement of his position in February 1946.

The key to the pattern of Stalin's statements and actions throughout this period is his desire to enforce the prewar Leninist understanding of world politics. Postwar world politics would be a grand, cataclysmic replay of prewar world politics. There was no room in this scheme for the idea that the growth of Soviet and American power had dramatically altered the basic operating principles of international relations. Varga tried to sustain his contention that the world was now safer because of the Soviet Union's improved position by claiming that the contradiction between "socialism" and "imperialism" now outweighed in importance the contradictions among imperialist states. According to this formulation, which became the party's general line under Khrushchev, the Soviet Union was powerful enough to prevent war. Stalin's pessimistic reply was that interimperialist contradictions, the fundamental source of war in the ideology of the day, still took precedence. Thus war would come no matter what Moscow did. Though the Soviet Union was stronger than it had been in the 1930s, it was still incapable of preventing war, and had no option but to prepare for it.[52]

---

[51] Stalin, 16:226–32.

[52] Cf. the interpretation of Shulman, *Stalin's Foreign Policy Reappraised*. Shulman maintains that Stalin's *Economic Problems* reflects the dictator's turn toward a "rightist," more cooperative policy in response to shifts of power on the world scene. My analysis of the Varga dispute, as well as developments in Soviet ideology after Stalin's death,

Stalin's rhetoric, as well as that of legions of publicists who followed the line closely, seemed designed precisely to counter the argument that Moscow could affect the hostility of the West and ease the war danger. Imperialism was united. Contradictions were on the rise, but they only made the imperialists all the more prone to lash out against the Soviet camp. The Soviet Union had nothing to do with existing Western unity. The Western alliance was entirely the result of a fragile American hegemony, which created pressures that would erupt into war in fifteen years or so. Neither Soviet strength nor Soviet policy could affect the situation to any substantial degree. The Soviet Union was left with only one policy option: increase its military strength, liquidate "rootless cosmopolitans" and other fifth columnists, continue with the frantic five-year plans, and so on. Indeed, the fact that Stalin was intensifying this whole portrayal in his final years supports the supposition of many historians that he was planning a major purge on the eve of his death.

Varga's analysis almost certainly corresponded in his and his opponents' minds with a different foreign policy than the one followed by Stalin.[53] This alternative policy would have resembled the one actually followed by Stalin in the 1930s and by Khrushchev in the late 1950s; that is, greater reliance on diplomacy and more cooperation with noncommunist leftist forces. It would have been more flexible in identifying potential allies in the Third World. It is further possible that in Varga's and his opponents' minds his ideas implied a different *domestic* policy. In his speech at the 1948 economists' meeting, Varga stressed over and over again the connection between events in the capitalist world and the situation within the USSR, and vice versa. He appeared to be saying that changes in the Soviet Union were calling forth changes in the nature of its adversaries, which in turn implied further change in the Soviet Union. In modern language, the security threat was not so dire, and therefore Moscow could relax somewhat at home.

Why did Stalin reject the alternative? There are too many answers. There is no reason, however, to reject the hypothesis that Stalin be-

---

supports Robert Tucker's interpretation of the same document as reflecting Stalin's preference for continuing the policy of confrontation. See Tucker, *Soviet Political Mind*, chap. 4. See also below, chap. 6, on the implications of post-Stalin ideological developments.

[53] For an analysis discounting the policy significance of this dispute, see Paul Marantz, "Soviet Foreign Policy Factionalism under Stalin?: A Case Study of the Inevitability of War Controversy," *Soviet Union* 3 (1976): 91–107. Marantz is doubtless right when he says that there were no foreign policy "factions" in Stalin's Soviet Union. But there were differences of opinion, and they were not unimportant.

lieved what he said. Stalin's expressed position fitted the instrumental needs of his personal dictatorship; it fitted what is known of Stalin's personality; and it fitted his experience. Evidence suggests that between 1949 and 1951 Stalin was stressing the likelihood of a major war in high-level internal Communist Party and Cominform contexts as well as publicly.[54] He probably subscribed to his version of the theory of imperialism; accepted its implications for the Soviet Union's external security; believed he was preparing his country for an inevitable war; and thought that any fleeting diplomatic gain that could conceivably be won by some peace policy directed at Washington, London, or Paris was not worth the risk that it would be interpreted abroad as weakness and at home as a sign of domestic relaxation. He may well have been *less* inclined than he was before World War II to trust in the correlation-of-forces thesis and his own diplomacy to prevent war. After all, he had tried that once, and the results were well known.

AMERICAN PERSPECTIVES

On the surface, American assessments bore a striking similarity to contemporary Soviet views in the first years after the conclusion of the war. Like their Soviet counterparts, American decision makers did not at first see a bipolar structure of the Waltzian type—that is, a structure formed by only two great powers. Rather, they saw a bipolarity of alignments emerging, with the United States supporting a balance of power based on Britain and France, buttressed by American aid. It was not just Stalin who perceived America's disengagement from Europe in 1945; so did the British and the Americans themselves. The trajectory of U.S.-British relations as seen from Moscow corresponds closely to Washington's and London's view of the situation: close wartime collaboration deteriorating from a high point in 1944 to a low in late 1945, and improving after that. Washington decision makers shifted from worrying that the wily British were roping them into power-political schemes to fretting about Britain's and Western Europe's "will to resist" Soviet and communist pressure. And finally, the post–World War I spiral of depression, protection,

[54] For tidbits on Stalin's assessment of the likelihood of war in this period see Aleksandr Nekrich and Mikhail Heller, *Utopia in Power*, trans. Phyllis Carlos (New York: Summit, 1982), 504–5; "Wollte Stalin Togliatti kaltstellen?" *Osteuropa-archiv*, 1970, no. 10 (October), 705, 709–10, 717; and George Kennan's analysis in his *Memoirs, 1950–1963* (New York: Pantheon, 1972), 94.

and war was not on Soviet minds alone. Avoiding a repetition of that sad history was the alpha and omega of postwar U.S. policy.

The differences were subtle but decisive. Americans did not perceive the economic hegemony of their country as destabilizing. They did not see capitalist economic relations in exclusively zero-sum terms. The essence of their approach was to stress the positive-sum benefits of economic cooperation. They thought that the weaker and poorer the middle powers were, the more inclined they would be to bandwagon with Soviet power, and the stronger they became, the more closely they could collaborate with the United States. Instead of being faced with resentment at overweening American power, as the Soviet account had it, Washington was beset with demands for greater American commitments. The upshot was that despite all the worries about possible economic downturns, interallied squabbles, and communist party bandwagons, the Americans rated the probability of successful stabilization much higher than Stalin appeared to do.[55] In short, Washington was much closer to Varga's position than to Stalin's general line.

American officials realized early on that the postwar configuration of power would coalesce into two blocs. Intelligence assessments in 1945 held that the development of two blocs was the "most likely" outcome. Ambassador Walter Bedell Smith cabled from Moscow in May 1946 that "we are about to be driven into a position—if we are not already there—where the facts of the situation compel us to view Europe not as a whole, but as divided essentially into two zones."[56] In his "long telegram," Kennan advocated a policy designed to bring about two opposed grouping of states. By 1947 the existence of the two alignments was recognized as a fact. In the words of a Joint Chiefs of Staff (JCS) memorandum: "Among numerous factors bearing on the short term course of world politics, the current political conflict between the Soviet bloc and the western democracies will dominate, establishing the frame-work within which other forces operate."[57]

This was a bipolarity of *alignments*, however, not of power distribution in the Waltzian sense. Until late in 1948, most U.S. policy makers saw the goal as the reconstruction of a European balance of power. With American aid, they thought, France, Britain, and eventually

---

[55] For an extremely well-documented account reaching broadly similar conclusions, see Melvyn P. Leffler, *A Preponderance of Power: National Security, the Truman Administration, and the Cold War* (Stanford: Stanford University Press, 1992).

[56] *FRUS* 1946, 6:758.

[57] JCS, Joint Strategic Plans Committee, "Report on the World Political Situation up to 1957," 11 December 1947, *DDRS*, 1975/75B/2.

some form of Germany would be capable of containing Soviet power at some point in the not too distant future. The direct application of U.S. military power was not thought necessary. According to a CIA review in September 1947, "stabilization and recovery of Europe and Asia would tend to redress the balance of power and thereby to restrain the U.S.S.R."[58] Neither the Soviets nor the Americans yet appeared to comprehend in this period the actual extent of the reduced status of the other great powers. The common Soviet view of American policy as a somewhat more engaged version of the 1920s Dawes Plan—the United States as the financier of European recovery—was not far from what the Americans themselves thought they were doing.

Financial backing for a balance of power seemed not only all that was necessary before 1949 but all that was possible. Indeed, getting the European Recovery Program legislation through Congress turned out to be a tough and prolonged battle.[59] Each new U.S. commitment required political struggle at home, justification, assurances of reversibility, and political "cover" in the form of initiatives emanating from Britain and France.[60] Worries over contradictions with and among allies never disappeared, though confidence grew with the initial implementation of the Marshall Plan. American observers were acutely aware, however, of the importance the Soviets attached to Anglo-American contradictions. It was not necessary to have a nuanced understanding of Lenin's theory of imperialism to grasp this essential point. In the words of a 1946 State Department report: "Finding only two powers remaining in the world which can possibly be considered a threat to Soviet security, Soviet policy quite naturally resorted to the classic device, in the application of which the Soviets have proved so adept, of splitting the opposition."[61]

The United States ambassador and officers in the Moscow embassy were much more emphatic on this point, for they read daily press analyses of interimperialist contradictions. At a meeting with Secretary of State Byrnes, Ambassador Averell Harriman maintained that

[58] CIA, "Review of the World Situation," 29 September 1947 (1), *DDRS*, 1977/179A/1.
[59] See Forrest C. Pogue, *George C. Marshall: Statesman, 1945–1959* (New York: Viking, 1987), chap. 15.
[60] Numerous secondary treatments, based on extensive research in U.S. and British archives, place great emphasis on Britain's and particularly Ernest Bevin's role in easing America into Europe. See Alan Bullock, *Ernest Bevin: Foreign Secretary, 1945–1951* (New York: Norton, 1984); Edmonds, *Setting the Mould*; Barker, *British between the Superpowers*; Pogue, *George C. Marshall*; and Harbutt, *Iron Curtain*.
[61] "Policy and Information Statement on U.S.–U.S.S.R. Relations," 15 May 1946, *DDRS*, 1975/135D.

"the Russians are more afraid of facing a united West than anything else. In this connection . . . our relations with the Soviet [sic] would be vastly improved if we could settle our differences with Great Britain and France."[62] Similarly, Kennan cabled that Soviet foreign policy was based on the "conviction that economic struggle between U.S. and Great Britain is bound to lead to acute political tension."[63] By scrutinizing the Soviet propaganda line, analyzing the academic discourse, and, most important, observing Soviet foreign policy behavior, American policy makers were able to note the Soviet shift from the anti-British to the anti-American line in late 1946.[64]

American discussion of interimperialist contradictions reached its peak as the Soviet effort to woo Britain climaxed in Stalin's offer of a bilateral military alliance to Field Marshal Montgomery in January 1947, but it never died out completely.[65] Indeed, diplomats on the scene in Moscow interpreted Stalin's 1952 work *Economic Problems of Socialism in the USSR* as an indication of the Soviets' continued interest in exploiting Western contradictions. Although Stalin nowhere in that pamphlet (or anywhere else in the postwar years, for that matter) mentioned imperialist contradictions as diplomatic opportunities— he focused on them exclusively as causes of war—U.S. Ambassador Charles Bohlen and other diplomats still expressed concern that the dictator's real intent was to signal the return of *divide et impera* tactics.[66] The embassy continually warned Washington not to feed Soviet illusions in this regard.

The documents suggest that after their turn toward an active approach in 1946, the Americans tended to have a more robust view of Anglo-U.S. relations than the Soviets, or than the British themselves.[67] Washington and London saw Russia and its aims in remarkably similar terms, differed noticeably but manageably on Germany, and genuinely parted ways when it came to the Middle or Far East.

[62] Secretary of State Staff Committee minutes, 20 April 1945, *FRUS*, 1945, 5:840. At a dinner with American officials, Anthony Eden "expressed the belief that the chief pivot of Russian policy was an effort to drive a wedge between England and the United States": 20 April 1945, JVFD, box 1, 1: 310. See also 25 January 1946, box 3, 6: 1350.

[63] Kennan to Secretary of State, 29 January 1946, *FRUS*, 1946, 6:684.

[64] See telegram, Walter Bedell Smith to Secretary of State, 23 July 1946, ibid., 768–70; and memo of Francis B. Stevens to Llewellyn E. Thompson, 26 July 1946, ibid., 770–71.

[65] Smith to Marshall, 14 January 1947, *FRUS*, 1947, 6:517–18.

[66] See Bohlen to DOS, 7 July 1953, *FRUS*, 1952–1954, 8:1194; and U.S. Ambassador in France to DOS, 6 October 1952, ibid., 1056.

[67] British military officials were the most optimistic, having cooperated closely with their U.S. counterparts in the war. Civilian officials expressed more doubts. See the

Officials in Washington worried most about the effect of allied wrangling on Soviet intentions. They were concerned lest any diplomatic bungling or lack of coordination lead the Soviets to misinterpret the solidity of the Anglo-American relationship. They knew that the Soviets were hypercognizant of any differences between the two western powers. Should Stalin or his entourage become convinced of the utility of playing on interimperialist contradictions, Moscow could become less tractable in negotiations. Soviet splitting tactics would be a nuisance, not a danger. It was a question more of appearance than of reality.

The Czech coup, the Berlin blockade, the Soviet atom bomb test, the Chinese Revolution, and eventually the Korean War set in motion and solidified a distinct change in American perspectives on the balance of power. American decision makers became increasingly concerned about Soviet military capabilities. As we shall see, Washington began the Cold War focused mainly on the political and economic stabilization of Western Europe. With the passage of time, however, stabilization seemed increasingly to require a formal military alliance. The more important military power became, the more important direct American military involvement in the defense of Europe became.

Before 1949, American discussions revolved around restoring a balance of power based on Britain, France, and eventually some reconstituted Germany and Japan. All of these states were thought of as weakened versions of their prewar selves. The more Americans perceived the need for direct participation in establishing what they thought was a counterbalancing alliance, the more clearly they perceived the concentration of real power in their own and Soviet hands. As a 1949 CIA "Review of the World Situation" put it, "a bipolar power situation" had arisen: "At the present time, the distribution of power in the world is such that the U.S. and the USSR are alone capable of developing and maintaining modern power structures."[68] Americans genuinely hoped and perhaps expected the direct involvement of U.S. forces to be a temporary measure, but substantial and intricate involvement in the Western alliance was assumed from 1949 onward.

The late 1940s shift in the U.S. assessment of world power relation-

---

analysis and documents cited in Barker, *British between the Superpowers*; and Edmonds, *Setting the Mould*.

[68] CIA 0-49, 19 January 1949, *DDRS*, 1977/181D. The British understandably did not agree. They continued to see the British Empire as one of the three great powers. See Edmonds, *Setting the Mould*, 207–8.

ships produced an important change in the American discourse, both within the government and in public communications. The change concerned the salience of military power. The argument for the creation of NATO was that even if the Soviets were not ready for war and did not intend it in the near future, the economic, social, and political recovery of Europe required the sense of security and confidence in the future that only firm military guarantees could provide.[69] In the absence of such guarantees, stabilization could break down, and either pro-Soviet or chronically weak governments could be the result. American policy was governed at least partly by the assumption that weak states were more likely than strong ones to appease the Soviet Union or its agents, the communist parties.[70]

Obsessive American fears of what later came to be (somewhat inaccurately) called "Finlandization" have their origins in this early period of the Cold War. Europe needed to be "stiffened" against the communist threat. Stiffening required economic stabilization. Economic stabilization eventually appeared to require a military alliance. In short, Americans fretted that Soviet military power could translate into political influence. Weak states on the Soviet periphery could be induced to bandwagon with Soviet power. This fear worked its way into American discourse, which continually returned to the theme of Western Europe's "will to resist." When the Soviet Union began to make progress on its nuclear weapons program, and to build up a stockpile of the weapons, bandwagoning fears intensified. A CIA assessment of the allies' "will to resist" in early 1950 concluded that no NATO signatory would withdraw over the next few years, but that increasing Soviet atomic capabilities would translate into a reluctance on the part of allied governments to provoke Moscow in any way, such as by allowing high-profile U.S. military deployments on their territory.[71]

The German question captured the complex combination of bandwagoning worries and "interimperialist contradictions" which were the continual concern of Washington policymakers. Germany was thought to be particularly vulnerable to Soviet blandishments, for

[69] See John Lewis Gaddis, *Strategies of Containment* (New York: Oxford University Press, 1982), for this argument.

[70] For a discussion of "bandwagon images in American foreign policy" in this period, see the chapter of that title by Deborah Welch Larson in *Dominoes and Bandwagons: Strategic Beliefs and Great Power Competition in the Eurasian Rimland*, ed. Robert Jervis and Jack Snyder (New York: Oxford University Press, 1991). The chapter constitutes an argument for the plausibility of these beliefs in those circumstances.

[71] "Possible Political Developments of Strategic Significance between 1951 and 1954," 28 February 1950, *DDRS*, 1991/197/1–3.

three reasons. Germans correctly perceived their vulnerability to Soviet power, and hence were most concerned to avoid provoking the
Soviet Union. In addition, Moscow held decisive cards in the resolution of the national question. And West Germany's integration into
the Western system was blocked by European, particularly French,
fears of resurgent German power. If Germany was to be secured from
bandwagoning temptations, it would have to be brought into the
Western fold on a nondiscriminatory basis; but that move required
the "managing" of French fears. This would be the complex of policy
dilemmas confronting the United States for the next decade. It is no
surprise, then, that if one has to locate the moment at which American worries about the political utility of Soviet military power in Europe assumed their classic Cold War form, it would be Stalin's
blockade of Berlin in June 1948. Secretary of State George Marshall
expressed the common American view in a meeting with Truman in
July: ". . . we have the alternative of following a firm policy in Berlin
or accepting the consequences of the failure of the rest of our European policy."[72]

Soviets monitoring official statements and consuming intelligence
about discussions within the American government may well have
come away with the impression that their military power could indeed produce beneficial political effects on the world scene. After
all, here were responsible Americans saying they feared exactly this
outcome. Soviet beliefs about bandwagoning could easily be fed by
American rhetoric about the need to counter the Soviet "military
threat." Especially in regard to the German problem, Soviets had
good reason to believe that increased Russian power would exacerbate
rather than diminish interimperialist contradictions. The stronger the
Soviet Union was, the more the German government would seek to
reassure its people via closer association with the West, and the more
French-German antagonisms would be forced into the open.

Even if Stalin assumed that the Americans held most of the Western cards, pressure on Berlin and the ensuing intra-alliance wrangling could yield dividends. The Berlin complex of dilemmas caused
official Washington to vacillate between a conciliatory and a hard
line. In May 1948, in the weeks leading to the full blockade, U.S.
Ambassador Smith initiated conciliatory talks with Molotov without
consulting his allies. The Soviets leaked this news, causing a classic

---

[72]JVFD, box 5, 11/12:2369. Bevin put it even more dramatically: "The abandonment
of Berlin would mean the loss of western Europe" (quoted in Pogue, *George C. Marshall*,
308).

transatlantic row. Later, in October, with the blockade in force, Truman considered sending Supreme Court Chief Justice Fred Vinson to "plead with Stalin the aspirations of the American people for peace."[73] Marshall succeeded in scuttling the idea, but the signal had been sent. Such signals would complicate Stalin's task in monitoring the effects of his German policy. Even after winding the crisis down, Stalin could well have concluded that it had been close to success. Under a slightly different correlation of forces, a different outcome might be expected.

Soviet and U.S. bandwagoning beliefs parted ways, however, on the question of American hegemony in the non-Soviet world. Varga excepted, Soviets in this period saw overarching American economic and military power as a potentially destabilizing force. The greater the degree of U.S. hegemony, the more onerous the regime for the independent middle powers, the greater the incentive for them to seek to counterbalance American power, perhaps via Moscow. The stronger the Soviet Union was, the better counterbalance it would provide. Where Soviets saw American economic and military preeminence as destabilizing, Americans saw it as stabilizing. The more worried Americans became, the more they thought it necessary to apply their own power. The more direct power the United States applied, the more Stalin's Soviet Union appeared to perceive potential major instability, alliance shifts, and, eventually, war. Each side's beliefs found confirmation in the other side's rhetoric. Only time would reveal the extent of the contradiction.

Each superpower saw itself as reacting to moves by the other. In large part, each side perceived the emerging system of international politics as the result of concrete actions and preferences of the other side, rather then as an objective "structure" of power to which it was compelled to react. Nevertheless, the pattern of evidence is suggestive of a process of discovery on both sides as each became aware of its own and the other's centrality in the postwar balance. As Waltz's structural interpretation of realism suggests, the sheer concentration of capabilities in the two superpowers created realities to which they had to react. Patterns of thinking changed to account for those reali-

---

[73] Quoted in Edmonds, *Setting the Mould,* 179. Truman's motive may have had to do with domestic politics, but that would have been difficult to see from Moscow.

ties. On the American side, the intellectual accommodation to bipolarity seems to have been more pronounced, but the Soviets had to make adjustments as well. After 1949 the perceptual pattern begins to assume forms broadly familiar to anyone who was active politically during the Cold War.

Intellectual change on both sides can perhaps be described as "learning" if we define that term as "change in expressed beliefs toward what many now believe to have been the situation then." Soviet and U.S. thinking did not become more complex, nuanced, or scientific. It would be impossible to argue that they became less "ideological." Change was not neatly linear. Large contradictions persisted between the two sides' views, even if one prudently discounts much of the most extreme Soviet rhetoric. The Soviets began the postwar era with an expectation of a tripolar configuration consisting of three major world empires: the Soviet, the British, and the American. Washington began with an assumption of a bipolarity of alliances. When Moscow shifted to seeing a tenuous bipolarity of alliances, Washington arrived at something that at least began to resemble Waltzian power bipolarity. Both sides feared or anticipated some form of bandwagoning. Some Soviets hoped for positive political dividends from Moscow's military advantages; Americans feared them. Americans expected the middle powers to bandwagon with their economic superiority; most Soviets expected them eventually to balance against it. Americans saw the application of their military power to Europe as a precondition for middle-power balancing against the Soviet Union; Moscow saw the same capabilities as a precondition for middle-power balancing against the United States.

The Soviet evidence strongly suggests that Orwellian features of postwar Stalinism hindered the evolution of thinking. At each juncture Moscow seemed more reluctant than Washington to adjust prewar ways of thinking. The temptation is to attribute these lags to motivated bias on the Soviets' part. That is, the bizarre irrationalities of Soviet totalitarianism in other realms give rise to the suspicion that interpretation of international realities must have been influenced by Stalin's personal needs or the internal needs of his dictatorship. The existence of the Varga alternative, corresponding more closely to what we now think the real situation was, lends credence to this view. Further, a policy based on that alternative would most probably have met with greater comprehension in the United States, since the analysis of balance-of-power dynamics on which it was based was closer to the Americans' than the analysis favored by Stalin. Intellectually, Varga seemed a cut above his critics. He was a Marxist and a revolutionary but also an empiricist. The way he calculated the real extent of American hegemony and its likely longevity under a series of assumptions strikes today's reader as analytically sound and responsible. The case for bias looks strong, but it is complicated by two problems: overdetermination and the ambiguity of feedback.

There were too many reasons for the Soviets to be reluctant to jettison old-thinking postulates. Old thinking was a common Bolshevik intellectual response to the Soviet Union's international condition. In the interwar years, the amended theory of imperialism had adequately explained the international reality of a weak Soviet Union maneuvering within a system of powerful and mutually hostile capitalist states. France's effort to dominate Germany economically and politically had indeed led Germany to counterbalance through a rapprochement with the Soviet Union that included military and technical assistance badly needed by Moscow. Why wouldn't American efforts to dominate other capitalist great powers after World War II lead to analogous results? Similarly, in the 1930s and during the war, Western powers began to take the Soviet Union seriously as an ally *or* adversary only as it gained military power. Why wouldn't the USSR's military power produce a similarly forthcoming approach in the postwar situation?

The content of Stalin's rare interventions into the postwar Soviet discourse suggest that the dictator himself preferred to maintain as much of the traditional approach as possible. He even placed less emphasis on diplomacy and more on Soviet military power than he had in the 1930s. Stalin's preference for old thinking might have resulted from his perceived need to balance the image of a threatening external environmental to justify his dictatorship. Or he may have maintained his dictatorship to meet the requirements of an external environment he thought was threatening. Or he may have been reluctant to change his views because he was old and conservative, and had no wish to take risks with new approaches. He may have sensed the fragility of his empire and doubted its capacity to hold together in the face of alluring diplomatic and economic blandishments from the West.

Stalin had numerous reasons for rejecting Varga's alternative, some perhaps reflecting bias, some reflecting prudent conservatism. Meanwhile, the evidence generated by Moscow's interaction with the balance of power cut both ways. Recall that Varga arrived at his alternative only after a long intellectual process that began in the 1930s, before any postwar evidence about the balance of power was available. True, Varga had no difficulty demonstrating Britain's weakened position, and all were aware of the early failure of Soviet efforts to exploit Anglo-American contradictions. The harder task was to prove that the Western alignment based on U.S. hegemony was stable. Traditional thinkers could always cite new evidence of serious discord in the West. Much of this evidence was accurately reported in Moscow. Western governments were worried about effective cooperation, and not always convinced that all their balancing efforts would succeed. The stream of rhetoric from the authorities representing the other major states, one of the main pieces of evidence available to any government when it monitored the success of its policy, contained much that supported Soviet views of balancing behavior.

Evidence did not flow into Moscow in some neat, linear fashion, leading inexorably to the conclusion that bipolarity worked the way we now think it worked. Instead, patterns of evidence ebbed and flowed. U.S.-British cooperation sank from a high level in 1944 to a very low point by the end of 1945 and climbed fitfully after that. British power seemed much greater in 1945 than in the terrible winter of 1946–47, but then seemed to rebound rapidly in the ensuing year. The United States and Britain started out the period under the assumption that such a strong power as the Soviet Union had to be accommodated. Suddenly they shifted to the view that it had to be contained. Hints of concessions and deals mingled with the tough talk that stands out in retrospect.

Stalin's regime did not encourage innovation, to put it mildly. The dictator's 1946 speech, which stressed Lenin's theory of imperialism, appears to have inclined people to resist Varga's arguments. While steering a course close to the traditional view might not bring great rewards, it was obviously safer than propounding a new view that might turn out to be politically incorrect. On the other hand, Stalin's position was not entirely clear, and Varga was no neophyte in these kinds of debates. Players in the game could not be sure that Varga would not again come out on top, as he had managed to do consistently in the 1920s and 1930s. The writings of many of Varga's colleagues, such as Iosif Lemin, both before and after this period of high Stalinism, reflect genuine as opposed to instrumental intellectual differences. Some of Varga's opposition must therefore be explained by genuine as opposed to opportunistic resistance to his ideas.

In addition, it would be a mistake to overemphasize the differences between Varga and Stalin. Varga's alternative was an important revision, not a rejection, of Leninist-Stalinist thought. In truth, his views defy easy categorization. They were perhaps best described by the Russian historian Mikhail Gefter, who characterized them as "anti-dogmatic orthodoxy."[74] Varga retained a belief in the latent hostility and dangerousness of imperialism. He believed that Soviet socialism represented a more advanced and superior social system that would inevitably compete with capitalism. His alternative did not question the bandwagoning element of the Soviet belief system. On the contrary, Varga originated a much more sophisticated and nuanced version of the old correlation-of-forces logic under which Soviet power tamed the aggressive tendencies endemic to capitalism and rendered the imperialist adversary more rational and tractable. Varga, who believed that the twentieth century was capitalism's last, who was optimistic about the economic superiority of the Soviet command-administrative system, and who ended his days taking a decidedly Trotskyist view of his adopted country and its foreign policy, originated Khrushchev's general line, not Gorbachev's.[75]

The fact that the "reformist" Varga came eventually to a semi-Trotskyist analysis of the Soviet Union's cynical sellout of the revolution in pursuit of state interests raises the final objection to the bias argument. Varga's alternative was not alone in the postwar years. A left-revolutionary critique of Soviet foreign policy was on Moscow minds in Stalin's day and for decades after.[76] Never, in this view, had revolutionary prospects been so good as after World War II. Russia had been too weak to aid the revolutionary forces churned up by World War I, but now, despite its weaknesses, it was in an incomparably better position. Communist parties were strong and organized. Colonies were in turmoil. The bourgeoisie was tainted by its flirtation with fascism, while the Red partisans had valiantly fought the whole war through. But here was the timid, conservative Stalin vastly overestimating imperialism's power in China, and perhaps in Western Europe as well.

If we wish to indulge in counterfactuals, which the bias argument compels us to do, we must consider all of them. One alternative history would have a softer Soviet foreign policy, less control in Eastern Europe, and better relations with the West. Another alternative

---

[74] Mikhail Gefter, "Ia umru v pechali: Predsmertnye zapiski E. Vargi," *Politicheskie Issledovaniia*, 1991, no. 2, 178.

[75] For Varga's privately expressed views on the eve of his death in 1964, see "Vskryt' cheres 20 let,"*Politicheskie Issledovaniia*, 1991, nos. 2 and 3.

[76] The testimony of Georgii Arbatov, *Zatianuvsheesia vyzdorovlenie (1953–1985 gg.): Svidetel'stvo sovremennika* (Moscow: Mezhdunarodnye Otnosheniia, 1991), chap. 7, about the Soviet elite's "revolutionary inferiority complex," is telling on this score. For a semidissident Soviet left critique of Stalin's foreign policy, see Roy Medvedev, "Zametki po nekotorym voprosam vneshnei politiki SSSR" (April 1970), in *Politicheskii Dnevnik*, 670–90.

would portray a Stalin willing to take more risks, and the addition of highly organized and potentially rich Western countries to the social- ist fold. Which fantasy would have been more enticing to the political elite of Stalin's Russia? Which was more "realistic"? Honesty compels us to answer that we simply do not know.

The decisive years that set the Cold War mold were a time of tur- moil and extreme uncertainty. The feedback available to Moscow and Washington contained substantial ambiguity. Under uncertainty, many competing assessments will be generated, but choosing one becomes almost a matter of faith. It is necessary, therefore, to monitor the evidence over a longer run, as the relevant actors gain experience with the postwar international system. In addition, the story of the origins of the Cold War is still incomplete, for we have yet to address one of the most important questions: How were the composition of power and the hierarchy of prestige perceived?

[5]

War, Power, and the
Postwar Hierarchy, 1945–1953

War is the best test of the military power of a state. And a world
war, involving every major state, is the best test of the worldwide
distribution of power. The concentration of military capabilities in the
United States and the Soviet Union revealed by World War II was
unambiguous enough to be obvious at the time even if its implications
remained unclear. But of these two countries, which was the more
powerful? And if one was indeed more powerful, how much stronger
was it? After all, the two states had never fought each other. The
evidence produced by World War II was quite ambiguous on this
score. Moscow and Washington had different interpretations of the
war's results.

Differences between states' perceptions of power may be regarded
as inconsequential unless one takes seriously the realist proposition
that perceptions of power and diplomacy are intimately related. In
this view, parties to a negotiation frame their expectations and formu-
late their positions on the basis of, among other factors, their estima-
tions of their own and each other's capabilities. Capabilities may vary
with the issues, but most theorists of international relations place
particular emphasis on military power, since among states war is the
court of final appeal. If a state's behavior is indeed conditioned by its
perceptions of power, and if wars, even major wars, provide only
very imperfect tests of power, then we arrive at the unsettling conclusion that the influence of power on world politics may be substantial
but capricious. The less effectively war performs its testing function,
the less reality power possesses.

Even if Stalin, alone in his Kremlin office in 1947, had admitted that America had somehow emerged from the war in a preeminent position in the world, he would not necessarily have agreed with Washington about the exact degree of influence each enjoyed. Each state's degree of influence would become clear only over a period of diplomatic bargaining, maneuvering, and posturing. And this bargaining, if a substantial strain of realist thinking and diplomatic testimony is to be believed, had much to do with both sides' rough estimates of their relative power positions. Did they perceive a status hierarchy? Did they recognize a "hegemon"? And how did people on the scene understand the relationship between power and diplomatic influence? How important, in their eyes, were military capabilities, as opposed to economic, technical, cultural, and ideological elements of power?

THE GENERAL LINE ON WORLD POWER RELATIONSHIPS

The Soviet leadership's main message to its people and the world was that the Soviet Union had won a "world-historical" victory and no one should minimize its interests. In fact, the assertion of a fundamental shift in the correlation of forces in favor of socialism in general and the USSR in particular was a central part of the postwar ideological reformulation. This shift simultaneously justified the quick "Sovietization" of the Eastern European countries occupied by Soviet power,[1] supported the Soviets' argument for a large role in setting up the postwar arrangements among the great powers, and no doubt reflected a genuine assessment of the situation.

There was a secondary message, however. Stalin and his lieutenants were at pains to remind their people that a new war sometime in the future could not be ruled out, and the leadership had to be concerned with the military power of the Soviet state. This was the essence of Stalin's February 1946 "election" speech and many of his other official pronouncements. Needless to say, there was some contradiction between the focus on threat and the focus on increased

---

[1] With the exception of Yugoslavia, these countries did not experience real revolutions. To justify going ahead with revolutionary transformations anyway, Soviet ideologists referred to a *global* shift in the correlation of forces toward socialism, which was supposed to compensate for the unfavorable domestic class correlation in these countries. In practical terms, therefore, the Soviet Union could both defend these countries against "imperialism" and help domestic communist parties to thwart their organized class enemies.

Soviet and socialist power.[2] Stalin's sixteenth Party Congress model had asserted that a favorable shift in the correlation of forces made the Soviet Union's external position more secure. Incredibly, despite all the evidence of a vast improvement in the Soviet Union's security situation—evidence the leadership itself began by emphasizing—Stalin actually *decreased* the relative importance of the correlation-of-forces aspect of his basic model in his postwar public pronouncements. He was less inclined than before the war to suggest that Soviet power and policy could secure peace than to conjure up the war-scare imagery of the mid- to late 1920s. Gyrating between these two imperatives, the line first stressed increased power, then stressed threat, then tried to stress both simultaneously.

While most Western accounts of the immediate postwar period focus on Soviet weakness as a result of the war's devastation, the Soviets' contemporary public portrayal was intended to create an altogether different impression. Top Soviet leaders claimed that the war had vastly increased Soviet power and prestige. The gist of these statements was that the USSR was as strong as any other great state, and had to be treated by the other powers as an equal. This was, indeed, the message Soviet diplomats were delivering to their British and American counterparts in private discussions.[3] Foreign Minister Molotov articulated the line publicly in late 1945, spelling out in detail how the war had "shown all how our country grew and strengthened in the military-political sense."[4] Years later, in retirement, Molotov would proudly claim that territorial expansion had been his main goal as foreign minister.[5] Now he spoke as if that were the case, listing all the territorial acquisitions and political shifts that eventually became formalized in a list of specific changes referred to by all Soviet leaders as the "new correlation of forces."[6]

What was left out of the public presentation was an accounting of

---

[2] Robert Tucker, *The Soviet Political Mind: Stalinism and Post-Stalin Change*, rev. ed. (New York: Norton, 1971), 95–102, discusses this contradiction.

[3] See, e.g., memorandum of discussion between Deputy Foreign Minister Vyshinskii and Ambassador Smith: Smith to Director of Office of Eastern European Affairs, 16 January 1947, *FRUS*, 1947, 4:520; and Soviet memorandum to U.S. Secretary of State, 4 May 1948, *DDRS*, 1976/135E.

[4] V. M. Molotov, "28-aia godovshchina Velikoi Oktiabr'skoi Sotsialisticheskoi Revoliutsii," *Bol'shevik*, 1945, no. 21 (November), 8.

[5] Feliks Chuev, *Sto sorok besed s Molotovym* (Moscow: Terra, 1991), 14.

[6] The basic line was that "now our Fatherland is secure from German invasion in the west and Japanese invasion in the east": "Obrashchenie tsentral'nogo komiteta Vsesoiuznoi Kommunisticheskoi Partii (bol'shevikov)," *Pravda*, 2 February 1946, 1. For a typical editorial of the day touching on these issues: "Velikaia preobrazuiushchaia sila Leninizma," *Pravda*, 22 January 1946, 1.

the immense damage sustained by the Soviet Union in the war. Even as Molotov and others of Stalin's circle were extolling the Soviet Union's new status as a world power, the dictator was receiving detailed reports about destruction and deprivation in the areas formerly occupied by the Germans, as well as ongoing armed resistance to Soviet power by anticommunist partisans.[7] Nevertheless, it can hardly be doubted that these confident assertions about increased Soviet power reflected genuine beliefs. Who would deny that the war had left the Soviet Union in a more prominent place in world affairs than it had occupied previously? On the basis of these sources, however, it is impossible to state with complete confidence how Soviet leaders rated the Soviet Union in concrete comparison with the other great powers.[8] What the evidence does indicate is that they thought of power in military terms—which is hardly surprising, given their recent experience of an epochal military struggle.

While they abstained from concrete power comparisons, Soviet officials insisted in the immediate postwar years that the Soviet Union was more powerful than ever, and demanded influence over the international system equal to that of any other great power. Foreign Minister Molotov enunciated the line in his Supreme Soviet "election" speech in February 1946:

> The USSR now stands in the ranks of the most authoritative of world powers. Now it is impossible to resolve the important issues of international relations without the participation of the Soviet Union or without heeding the voice of our Motherland. The participation of Comrade Stalin is considered the best guarantee of the successful resolution of international problems.[9]

Practically every other Soviet notable repeated Molotov's words, or at least their gist, and editorials elaborated his points.[10] Naturally the

[7]See Dmitrii Volkogonov, *Triumf i tragediia* (Moscow: Novosti, 1990), bk. 2, pt. 2, pp. 23–29, 90. On the ensuing famine: Evgenii Aleksandrov, "Zhertvoiu pali . . . ," *Nezavisimaia Gazeta,* 16 April 1992, 5.

[8]During his anti-Britain phase, while he was trying to cozy up to Washington, Stalin did make some appreciative references to America's great power. See, e.g., Daniel Yergin, *Shattered Peace: The Origins of the Cold War and the National Security State* (Boston: Houghton Mifflin, 1977), 103–4.

[9]V. M. Molotov, *Voprosy vneshnei politiki* (Moscow: Gosudarstvennoe Izdatel'stvo Politicheskoi Literatury, 1948), 25.

[10]See, in particular, Malenkov's speech in *Pravda,* 8 February 1946, 2. Other top leaders used almost identical phrases; in *Pravda,* see, e.g., Zhdanov, 8 February 1946, 4, and Khrushchev, 29 March 1946, 2. For elaboration of Molotov's themes, see M. Kharlamov, "Ekspansionizm v poslevoennoi politike SShA i Anglii," *Bol'shevik,* 1946,

message got through to lower levels of the Soviet political system, which dutifully produced analyses stressing the vast increases in Soviet power.[11] This trend picked up when both Stalin and a member of his inner circle, Lazar Kaganovich, publicly called into question the old "capitalist encirclement" doctrine.[12] Stalin had last employed this doctrine in a domestic context. So long as the Soviet Union was surrounded by capitalist powers, he claimed in the purge year 1937, they would unleash spies, assassins, saboteurs, wreckers, and other agents against the socialist country.[13] This was a rationale for continual purges. Now, however, Soviet political analysts often cited Stalin's apparent revision to make the point that the United States and Britain lacked the power to effect a cordon sanitaire around the Soviet Union.[14]

The Soviet discourse on international affairs underwent a radical shift after Zhdanov's announcement of the two-camps doctrine at the founding meeting of the Cominform in September 1947. Zhdanov was at pains to stress above all the threat from imperialism and the consequent need to consolidate communist forces. After this speech, publicists made fewer triumphant references to the new correlation of forces. Instead, everyone followed Zhdanov's lead in concentrating on the threat from imperialism, now united under U.S. leadership, and the need to unite the "democratic camp" to withstand the assault. This shift is clearly revealed by a comparison of major leadership pronouncements before and after Zhdanov's speech.[15] The mass media fell in line and eliminated the contradiction between increased

---

nos. 17–18 (September), 38; F. Oleshchuk, "Sily demokratii i progressa v bor'be protiv fashizma i reaktsii," *Bol'shevik*, 1946, no. 15 (August), 33.

[11] See, e.g., the publicist F. Oleshchuk, of the Institute for World Economy and World Politics, quoted in Elbridge Durbrow, Chargé d'Affaires, to Secretary of State, 13 September 1946 (telegram), *FRUS*, 1946, 6:781–82; and S. Vishnev, "Ukreplenie oboronsposobnosti Sovetskogo Soiuza i ego mezhdunarodnoe znachenie," *MKhMP*, 1946, no. 11 (November), 40.

[12] See Kaganovich's speech to voters in Tashkent, *Pravda*, 8 February 1946, 4; and Stalin's interview with Alexander Werth, in Stalin, 16:64.

[13] Stalin, 13:195–97.

[14] Iosif Lemin, "Tridtsat' let bor'by SSSR za mir i bezopasnost'," *MKhMP*, 1947, no. 10 (October), 25–55, esp. 50.

[15] Cf. Molotov, "28-aia godovshchina," and Zhdanov in *Bol'shevik*, 1946, no. 21 (November), 1–17, with Molotov's two speeches on the anniversaries of the Bolshevik Revolution in 1947 and 1948: "Tridtsatiletie Velikoi Oktiabr'skoi Sotsialisticheskoi Revoliutsii," *MKhMP*, 1947, no. 11 (November), and *Bol'shevik*, 1948, no. 21 (15 November), 1–19.

power and increased threat by dropping all references to the correlation of forces.[16]

But the relatively pessimistic post-Cominform line did not last long. The Soviet atom bomb test and the Chinese Revolution in 1949 ushered in a new wave of optimism. Stalin's favorite lieutenant, Georgii Malenkov, spelled it out in a speech on the thirty-second anniversary of the revolution in 1949. He repeated the basic postwar "new correlation of forces" analysis but stressed that in recent years all aspects of the correlation (territorial, military, economic, "hearts and minds") had shifted even further in favor of socialism. The Western peace movement was mounting, the liberation struggle in the colonial world was gaining force, the socialist camp had been consolidated with the addition of the German Democratic Republic (GDR), and capitalism was due for a major economic crisis. In the struggle between socialism and capitalism, "the superiority of the socialist system is distinctly apparent."[17] A close reading of Malenkov's speech reveals the strong implication that "capitalist encirclement" was a thing of a past. And he was not alone, for both Stalin and Molotov called the encirclement into question, the latter going so far as to say that "since the creation of the firm anti-imperialistic alliance between the Soviet and Chinese peoples, between the two strongest states on earth, democracy and socialism have become a supreme force."[18] Commentators and analysts picked up the new line, talking of a "new stage" in international relations and penning new, optimistic formulations.[19]

Malenkov's speech, like a great many other public and internal assessments, was laced with quotations from within the capitalist camp acknowledging a shift in the balance of power. A continual refrain was that it was high time the Americans reassessed their postwar strategy, which was clearly beyond their real capabilities. Neither diplomats nor journalists stationed abroad had any difficulty

---

[16]The only optimistic-sounding formulation in use in the Soviet press of the day was directed at fraternal parties and intended to spur them to action. "In the current conditions the main danger to the working class is underestimation of its own forces and overestimation of the forces opposing it": P. Fedoseev in *Pravda*, 13 April 1948, 3.

[17]*Pravda*, 17 November 1949, as translated in *CDSP* 1, no. 43:3.

[18]*Pravda*, 11 March 1950, 2 (*CDSP* 2, no. 11: 7); emphasis added. Also see Molotov's comments, *CDSP* 1, no. 52: 9. For Stalin's statement: Stalin, 16:110. Further documentation is in Paul Marantz, "Soviet Foreign Policy Factionalism under Stalin? A Case Study of the Inevitability of War Controversy," *Soviet Union* 3 (1976): 91–107.

[19]See, e.g., Ilia Erenburg, "Perelom," *Kulturnaia Zhizn'*, 31 December 1950, 4 (*CDSP* 2, no. 52: 13); M. Tiurin in *Izvestiia*, 22 February 1949, 3 (*CDSP* 1, no. 8: 17); "Zashchita mira i bor'ba s podzhigateliami voiny," *Bol'shevik*, 1949, no. 22 (November), 7.

rounding up quotations from prestigious commentators, such as Walter Lippmann, arguing for a strategy of more modest objectives than those sought by Truman and Dean Acheson.[20]

In 1951, however, Stalin began to crack down on heretical notions that the threat from imperialism had begun to recede. As we saw in Chapter 4, in order to stress the threat of war despite their boasts of improvements in the correlation of forces, publicists brought the hostility thesis of 1925–1929 back into circulation.[21] The combination of great threat and more circumspection was captured by security chief Lavrentii Beria in his 1951 speech on the thirty-fourth anniversary of the revolution. He stated, for example, that the United States was "restoring the two seats of war, Germany and Japan," whose elimination was such an important part of the postwar correlation. The focus was on "the Marshallization of Europe" (its total subjugation to America) and the expansion of the West's military budgets, bases, and "war preparation."[22]

In the mass press, journalists filed away the optimistic formulations of the past two years for future use and harped on the unity of imperialism under the United States, its rising aggressiveness and military expansion, and the reality of the military threat emanating from the West. On the ideological front, back came the capitalist-encirclement doctrine, in the strongest reassertions of it since the end of the war.[23] Again and again these publicists stressed the thesis that the stronger socialism became, the more aggressive the imperialists became.

THE ELEMENTS OF POWER

The thrust of the general line was that the issue of the Soviet Union's basic security remained paramount. Since world politics, viewed through the prism of Stalin's general line, was mainly about great-power security, it followed that influence over security arrangements ought to be correlated with a state's military power. Given this official preoccupation with military security and the military power of the state, it is not surprising that Soviet discourse appeared to

[20] See, e.g., "Politicheskii otchet posol'stva SSSR v SShA za 1949 god," 1 March 1950, AVP 129/33a/041/243.
[21] See D. Chesnokov, "Rech' I. V. Stalina na XIX s"ezde KPSS," *Kommunist*, 1953, no. 2; and the discussion in Tucker, *Soviet Political Mind*, 95–98.
[22] *Pravda*, 7 November 1951, 2–4 (*CDSP* 3, no. 42: 5–7).
[23] V. Mikhneev, "O kapitalisticheskom okruzhenii," *Bol'shevik*, 1951, no. 16 (August), 58–62.

place even greater weight on the military power of the state than it had done before the war. In addition, military power itself continued to be thought of in classical terms.

Military Power

Every Soviet account of postwar military doctrine speaks of the mid-1950s as a period of "revolution in military affairs." Every shred of evidence available supports this version of events, which holds that the Soviet military did not seriously debate the influence of nuclear weapons on military affairs until that period. Though doubts were expressed privately, they could hardly overturn the influence of training, exercising, and planning based on the Stalinist norms.[24]

Stalinist military doctrine effectively implied throughout the 1945–1953 period that the USSR's large army made it supreme on the Eurasian landmass. It focused—perhaps predictably—on elements in which the Soviet Union enjoyed distinct advantages. In the dark days of 1942, Stalin formulated the five "permanently operative factors of war": (1) the stability of the rear; (2) the morale of the army; (3) the quality and quantity of divisions; (4) the armaments of the army; (5) the organization and ability of the command personnel.[25] Though this formulation clearly was of a morale-building nature, meant to contrapose the "permanent" factors that the USSR possessed against the "temporary" factors, such as surprise, which the Germans enjoyed, the entire experience of the war seemed to validate Stalin's focus on large armies. This doctrine became rigidified in the postwar period.[26] No serious examination of such new developments as long-range bombers and atomic bombs took place. The overall organization of the armed forces, the organization of the command staff, the course of training at the General Staff Academy—all retained the form developed during the war. Stalin was not interested in revising military doctrine and strategy.[27]

From 1945 through 1953 the Soviet military engaged in an intensive

[24] For ample evidence on this score, see Matthew Evangelista, *Innovation and the Arms Race* (Ithaca: Cornell University Press, 1988), chap. 5, esp. 157–62, 174, 177.

[25] Raymond Garthoff, *The Soviet Image of Future War* (Washington, D.C.: Public Affairs Press, 1959), 24–25.

[26] As one military editorial put it, Stalin's "permanently operative factors decide all problems of military theory": "Sovetskie vooruzhennye sily na strazhe gosudarstvennykh interesov nashei Rodiny," *Voennaia Mysl'*, 1949, no. 2, 13.

[27] Only two issues of the General Staff journal, *Voennaia Mysl'*, were found in Stalin's library after his death. See L. M. Spirin, "Stalin i voina," *Voprosy Istorii KPSS*, 1990, no. 5, 90–105.

and detailed examination of the lessons of the "Great Patriotic War" for doctrine, strategy, and the organization of the armed forces. Military sources in the open and closed press sought to demonstrate the superiority of the socialist system for mobilizing the resources of the nation for war. In his treatise on the economic aspects of modern war, Major General P. A. Belov analyzed quantitatively the contribution of the Allied powers to the destruction of fascism, demonstrating that despite an economy one-third the size of America's, the Soviet Union accounted for 80 percent of the war effort, even when Lend-Lease was taken into consideration.[28] Other analyses demonstrated the marginal role played by air power.[29] The upshot of all these analyses—none of them unsophisticated and some quite convincing—was that the Soviet Union's geographical position and especially its political-economic system gave it a comparative advantage in the production of military power. Stalin-style "socialism" allowed the country to devote a greater share of its resources to military production, and to obtain a greater increment of military power from each unit of economic resources expended, than the opposing capitalist system.

If mass armies and the ability to supply them are the main elements of the military power of a state, then the Soviet Union was obviously the primary military power in Europe and Asia. On the basis of these kinds of arguments, Soviet military authors essentially claimed military superiority over the United States, despite the latter's acknowledged economic advantages.[30] Though dark clouds could be seen on the military-political horizon, they could in no way be compared to the clear and immediate danger Germany and Japan had represented for Moscow throughout the 1930s. In both Europe and Asia, the land army threat, in the form of Germany and Japan, had been eliminated,

---

[28] P. A. Belov, *Voprosy ekonomiki v sovremennoi voine* (Moscow: Voenizdat, 1951), esp. chap. 6. For more figures on Soviet wartime military production, see A. I. Notkin, *Ocherki teorii sotsialisticheskogo vosproizvodstva* (Moscow: Gospolizdat, 1948), 272–73. Belov denounces Varga for suggesting the possibility of any economic planning under capitalism. Belov himself was criticized in a review for insufficient attention to the Stalinist military doctrine that "despite the sharp growth of military technology in the epoch of imperialism, man plays the decisive role in war": *Sovetskaia Kniga*, 1952, no. 9 (September), 95–98 (*CDSP* 4, no. 48: 8–9). The reviewer stressed masses and morale, two areas of assumed Soviet superiority.

[29] Col. A. Aleksandrov, "O strategicheskoi roli VVS SShA vo vtoroi mirovoi voine," *Voennaia Mysl'*, 1948, no. 7, 65–76. Circulation of this journal was restricted to general officers and admirals.

[30] For such arguments, see Maj. Gen. Talenskii, "Genial'nyi uklad v marksistko-leniniskoe uchenie o voine, voennuiu nauku," *Voennaia Mysl'*, 1952, no. 2, 15–37; Col. I. S. Baz', "Tvorcheskii metod sovetskoi voennoi nauki," *Voennaia Mysl*, 1949, no. 2, 14–34.

and as yet no land army had been formed to replace them. Despite the increase in the U.S. presence in these areas, no countervailing forces existed to oppose the vast Soviet Army. And the United States, though it was always said to be preparing for war and planning to unleash it soon, was always not quite prepared for it. Even low-level diplomatic reports arriving in Moscow reported American doubts "at the highest levels" about current military capabilities.[31]

As far as the atomic bomb was concerned, both the closed military press and open Soviet pronouncements consistently followed Stalin's public position that the bomb, powerful though it was, did not revolutionize tested theorems of military doctrine or traditional views of the determinants of state power, and in any case, the Soviet Union would soon possess its own. As Stalin put it to Alexander Werth of the London *Times*: "I do not consider the atomic bomb as serious a force as some political figures tend to do. Atomic bombs are intended for frightening the weak nerved, but they cannot decide the outcome of war, since for that there are absolutely not enough atomic bombs."[32] In private conversations, Stalin is reported to have expressed respect for the bomb's power and to have regarded it as something the Soviet Union had to possess, but never to have given any indication of re-thinking his approach to military affairs as a result of the new technology.[33] Knowing what we now know about the limitations on the United States' postwar atomic capability, Stalin's view seems much closer to the mark than popular contemporary Western notions about the "ultimate weapon."[34]

---

[31] Even hysterically anti-American war-scare reports acknowledged such doubts. See Tarasenko to Molotov, 6 October 1947, AVP 6/9/1041/67. American doubts about resorting to military force to break the Berlin blockade were accurately conveyed in V. Gorokhov, "Positsiia SShA v otnoshenii Otvetnoi Noty SSSR ot 14 iulia o polozhenii v Berline (spravka)," AVP 129/32/17/207.

[32] Furthermore, Stalin noted, "unilateral possession of the atom bomb cannot continue for long:" *Pravda*, 25 September 1946, 1. (I cite the *Pravda* version because the wording in Stalin, 16:56, has been altered.) Molotov reinforced this assertion a year later when he said that "the secret of the atom bomb . . . has long since ceased to exist": Molotov, "Tridtsatiletie," 13. Molotov based his assertion on the recent Soviet success in creating an atomic reactor: Volkogonov, *Triumf i tragediia*, bk. 2, pt. 2, p. 92.

[33] Milovan Djilas reports, for example, that in 1945 Stalin said of the atomic bomb: "That is a powerful thing. Pow-er-ful!": Djilas, *Conversations With Stalin* (New York: Harcourt Brace & World, 1962), 153. For more on Stalin's respect for the bomb, see David Holloway, *The Soviet Union and the Arms Race* (New Haven: Yale University Press, 1983), 29.

[34] The popular notion that Stalin somehow failed to grasp the bomb's significance has not stood up well under investigation. He was apparently well informed on the U.S. program and its limitations (aided by well-placed spies in the United States) and kept abreast of developments in the extensive Soviet program. See Molotov's comments on Stalin's "calm" attitude in Chuev, *Sto sorok besed*, 81–82.

Given this view, it comes as no surprise that commentary on the Soviet atom bomb test in 1949 was relatively restrained. Having downplayed the significance of the bomb for four years, Soviet commentators could hardly begin to tout the Soviet Union's possession of it now. None let slip any "superweapon" innuendo. The main point stressed in relation to the bomb was that, in Malenkov's words, "the American people are now beginning to realize that if the instigators of war organize a new slaughter of mankind, the sorrow of mothers, wives, sisters and children will visit the American continent, too."[35] This version of deterrence theory was expressed in practically every commentary on the bomb. In addition, as we saw in Chapter 4, commentators and analysts argued that Soviet atomic capabilities began to call into question the United States' strategic plans, diminishing its credibility and exacerbating inter-imperialist contradictions.

The assertion that the Americans were threatened by atomic weapons was somewhat fanciful in 1949, since the Soviets did not yet possess a transportable bomb, though their deployment of TU-4 bombers capable of reaching the United States was well under way. And in fact, in the period of optimism that ensued after 1949, much more frequent reference was made to the land army issue than to the bomb.[36] Soviet observers devoted considerable attention to Western efforts to deploy significant land forces in Western Europe, which they took as proof of the validity of their continued insistence on the decisiveness of a large land army.[37]

This pattern of discourse may have reflected a sophisticated deterrence strategy, whereby Stalin sought to represent his state as impervious to nuclear threats. Or it may have reflected genuine belief. In either case, the Soviet claim to equal status with the other great powers in world politics in 1946 was based primarily on conventional military power. When Soviet leaders and commentators discussed all other elements of power, such as economic development and technological level, they were honest enough to limit their claims to "catching up with and then surpassing" American levels at some

---

[35] Malenkov's speech on the anniversary of the revolution, *Pravda*, 7 November 1949, 2–4 (*CDSP* 1, no. 43: 7).

[36] See Stalin's comments on this issue quoted in "Bor'ba narodnykh mass za mir, protiv podzhigatelei novoi voiny," *Bol'shevik*, 1949, no. 8 (April), 3. For other analyses highlighting the land army issue, see E. Tarle, "K istorii anti-sovetskoi politiki amerikanskogo imperializma," *Bol'shevik*, 1951, no. 1 (January), 66; and B. L. Leont'ev, "The Struggle for Peace—Mighty Movement of Modern Times," *Voprosy Filosofii*, 1950, no. 1 (*CDSP* 2, no. 38: 6).

[37] M. Rubinshtein, "Proval atomnoi diplomatii amerikanskikh imperialistov," *Bol'shevik*, 1950, no. 6 (March), 47–49.

unspecified date in the future. Only on the scales of conventional military capabilities could and did the Soviets claim superiority.

Soviet commentary in the immediate postwar period did refer to other elements of power. Soviets spoke about the prospects for revolutions in Europe or in decolonizing areas of the globe. Success on that front would surely enhance the influence of the Soviet Union, the acknowledged leader of the world communist movement. On the economic front, Soviet experts calculated that their system would outperform Western economies in the years to come. And economists were constantly predicting a major economic crisis in the West, a development that would have to enhance the prospects of the USSR. These issues were given a substantial amount of attention, and no comprehensive internal assessment of the world situation would have failed to mention them, since they so clearly bore on the prospects for both security and influence. Although prospects for revolution, economic competition, and even a mass movement for peace in the West assumed importance in Soviet eyes and figured in Soviet policy, none possessed anything like the importance assigned to military power.

Prospects for Revolution

It would be a mistake to equate Soviet two-camp thinking with bipolarity, as the term is understood in the American literature. In most conceptualizations, states in a bipolar structure may tend to gravitate toward one or the other pole, but it is not an iron law that they do so. It is in the strict interpretation of the two-camp thesis, though; a state is either capitalist or socialist, and if it is capitalist, it is hostile. The only possibility for lasting gains in the international sphere—as opposed to temporary and conditional manipulation of interimperialist contradictions and successful internal socioeconomic development—is for additional countries to become socialist. It is easy to see here the confluence between two-camps thinking and a "left" revolutionary approach to foreign policy. At its extreme, two-camp thinking equates the fate of the correlation of forces with the fate of revolution worldwide.

In day-to-day discourse, Soviet observers occasionally recognized various shades and distinctions of alignments after the onset of the two-camps view in late 1947. Nevertheless, the two-camps view of the world held that all the capitalist countries, with all their colonies and all the Third World countries tied closely to imperialism, were "objectively" part of the imperialist camp. Even India, for which

Zhdanov had held out some hope in his 1947 Cominform speech, ended up classed in the capitalist camp once bourgeois rule had stabilized there. Eugen Varga tried to develop the thesis that a colony that had achieved independence by peaceful means and maintained economic ties to the metropole, as India had done, could pursue a relatively independent policy. Guardians of dogma vigorously denounced this thesis.[38] The bias was thus toward revolution as a means of advance, and this view raises the question of the extent to which Soviet observers may actually have expected revolutions in the Western metropoles or their colonies.

The leadership, for obvious reasons, had to tread carefully on this issue. But there is some evidence of optimism among scholars at the Institute of World Economy and World Politics in regard to the possibility of radical transformations in Western Europe in 1946 and 1947. Veterans of the era recall widespread revolutionary optimism, especially among former Comintern functionaries.[39] It is probable that some members of leadership circles shared this view, contributing to the general optimism. After all, there was much evidence of a move to the left across the globe as a result of the war. In Europe the Soviet Union's and the communist parties' roles in resisting fascism had served to erase the memories of the purges, show trials, and collaboration with Hitler of the 1930s. Europe was in dire economic straits, and it would not be surprising if a Marxist concluded that revolution was in the offing. It is impossible to say, however, whether Soviet perceptions were of a real "revolutionary situation" or whether the hope merely was that the strength of the leftist forces would thwart the realization of a seriously anti-Soviet line by the key continental European powers.

In the wake of Zhdanov's two-camps speech and the formation of the Cominform, Moscow incited the European communist parties to take a militant line against the Marshall Plan, including violent strikes and disruptions. Some of the revolutionary optimism emanating from Moscow may thus have been related to this policy; it would hardly have done to have important Soviet Communists discounting the prospects for revolutionary transformations just as European communists were being asked to go out on a limb. In private, people were

---

[38] See "Diskussiia po knige E. Varga *Izmeneniia v ekonomike kapitalizma v itoge mirovoi voiny*," *MKhMP*, 1947, no. 11 (November) (suppl.).

[39] See, e.g., Arbatov's interview with Iakov Pevzner in *Zatianuvsheesia vyzdorovlenie* (Moscow: Mezhdunarodnye Otnosheniia, 1991), 65.

toning down expectations.[40] In this light, the most one can say is that only in the immediate postwar period did Soviet observers appear to perceive the elements of a revolutionary situation in Western Europe. In later periods, Soviets expressed optimism about the peace movement and the potential for an economic crisis.

Scholars quickly perceived the "crisis of imperialism's rule" in the colonies as "one of the basic signs of the general crisis of capitalism, the deepening of its contradictions, [and] the weakening of the forces of the imperialist camp."[41] Several armed national liberation struggles were under way by 1947, and Soviet observers cited these struggles as grounds for optimism. In his 1947 speech, for example, Zhdanov noted that the Chinese Communists controlled territory containing 140 million people, and that the anti-imperialist forces in Indonesia had "liberated" areas containing 70 million inhabitants. But these developments received remarkably little coverage. Soviets analyzed the crisis in the European empires mainly in terms of the interimperialist struggle. The American assault against British, Dutch, and French possessions and spheres of influence increased contradictions and middle-power resentment against Washington, potentially weakening the Western bloc, particularly outside Europe. National liberation movements assumed importance through their influence on the major capitalist powers rather than in the direct sense of adding to the socialist camp.[42] The key ideological reformulations of the day focused not on the colonies but on the removal of Eastern European markets from the capitalist world system.

The real boost to serious attention to the Third World was clearly the success of the Chinese Revolution. There is much evidence that the speed of the Communists' victory took the top leadership by surprise.[43] But once the Communists were securely ensconced in

[40] In a closed speech to party international relations specialists in January 1948, for example, Varga suggested that a "temporary ebbing" of the revolutionary tide was taking place in Europe. His rank-ordering of revolutionary prospects was as follows: China, Greece, Italy, France; Germany was "either ours or theirs": "Uglublenie obshchego krizisa kapitalizma v resul'tate vtoroi mirovoi voiny," 13 January 1948, AAN 1513/1/54.

[41] M. Rubinshtein, "Bor'ba imperialisticheskogo i antiimperialisticheskogo lagerei," *MKhMP*, 1947, no. 11 (November), 90.

[42] See, e.g., diplomatic reports from Moscow's embassy in London. Zarubin to Vyshinskii, "Otchet za 1947 god," 28 April 1948, AVP 69/32/1/116, contains no report on national liberation movements in the British Empire. Future reports, after absorbing criticism from the ministry, include such a section, but couch it in terms of the Anglo-U.S. rivalry. See Zarubin to Vyshinskii, 21 February 1950, AVP 69/37/11/136.

[43] Many historians contend that Stalin feared U.S. intervention if the Communists looked like winning. See, e.g., E. P. Bazhanov, "Sovetsko-kitaiskie otnosheniia: Uroki proshlogo i sovremennost'," *Novaia i Noveishaia Istoriia*, 1989, no. 2 (March–April), 6.

Beijing, a great wave of optimism swept through the Soviet press and scholarly journals, as well as a noticeable and permanent increase in overall attention to national liberation movements.[44] People now expressed the expectation that the colonial crisis would churn up new members for the socialist camp. Molotov coined a formulation—repeated ad nauseam in the press—which placed the Chinese Revolution just after the Russian Revolution in overall importance (that is, above even the postwar Eastern European "revolutions").[45] Malenkov talked of a "new, considerably higher stage" of the liberation movement.[46] In this new stage, lower-level experts explained, some anticolonial movements could "go socialist," as China had done, and join the Soviet-led socialist camp of states.[47]

Revolution in a country as large and potentially powerful as China led to a kind of Soviet domino theory. It was assumed that victory in one country would morally and materially aid liberation struggles in neighboring states. As Malenkov noted in his report to the Nineteenth Party Congress in 1952, "The victory of the Chinese people still further revolutionized the East and stimulated the development of the liberation struggles of the peoples oppressed by imperialism."[48] Indeed, Asia was the focus of optimism in this period, as nationalist rebellions spread in Indonesia, Indochina, the Philippines, Burma, Malaysia, and Korea.

The new stage of the national liberation movement ushered in by the Chinese Revolution in 1949 was thus yet one more source of the optimism that began to be evident in that year. And the return to pessimistic portrayals of the overall correlation of forces and increased focus on threat in late 1951 was not accompanied by any reassessment of Third World struggles. The basic lines of the relatively optimistic view, focused on armed struggle by nationalist forces against the metropole, continued to dominate the remaining Stalin years. Because of the dominance of the two-camps view, the bias in Soviet

[44]The change was notable in diplomatic reporting. See Zarubin to Vyshinskii, "Otchet posol'stva SSSR v Velikobritanii za 1950 g.," 31 January 1951, AVP 69/38/9/145; and "Kolonial'naia politika Velikobritanii za 1950 g.," AVP 69/38/13/145, 20–125.

[45]"After the October Revolution in our country, the victory of the people's liberation movement in China is the greatest blow against the entire system of world imperialism and against all plans of imperialist aggression in our time": *Pravda*, 11 March 1950, 2 (*CDSP* 2, no. 11: 7).

[46]Malenkov's speech on the anniversary of the Revolution, *Pravda*, 7 November 1949, 2–4 (*CDSP* 1, no. 43: 9).

[47]E. Zhukov, "Problems of the National Colonial Struggle since the Second World War," *Voprosy Ekonomiki*, 1949, no. 9 (October) (*CDSP* 1, no. 49: 5).

[48]*CDSP* 4, no. 38: 3.

analyses of the Third World was toward movements led by communist parties. National liberation *had* to take the form of a "people's democracy"—that is, a government under Eastern European–style communist control—if a state was to be considered truly independent of imperialism. The criteria for enlarging the socialist camp and reducing the imperialist camp were thus stringent enough to limit the salience of the Third World in overall calculations of world influence in comparison with what it would become.

Economic Crisis and Competition

Like the potential for revolution, economic competition held out prospects for future gains but did not lie at the center of daily power comparisons. Soviet commentary assumed that the Soviet economy would grow faster than the capitalist economies, and that the socialist system of planning was superior for organizing the state for war. Though the leadership retained the goal of eventually catching up to and then surpassing the United States in per capita production, Soviet leaders and analysts alike placed great stress on the military aspects of the economy. In direct comparative analysis, they highlighted the Soviet Union's superior economic growth rates, stability, and lack of inflation and crises.[49] That the United States' economy was much more advanced and productive was so obvious as to require little mention. When Soviets discussed the national security implications of the economy, they inevitably argued that the system of central planning and collectivized agriculture allowed the Soviet Union to tap a greater percentage of its economic resources for a war effort than a capitalist state could do, thus implying that the Western economic advantage was not so decisive as the raw numbers implied.[50]

Economists were as sure in 1953 as they had been in 1949 that the capitalist economy would soon undergo a serious crisis. Economists argued with each other throughout the period—especially before 1949, when Varga was completely discredited—but never over the possibility of a postwar crisis of capitalist production. Their arguments—highly complex and abstract—were over the timing of the crisis and the nature of its causes.[51] After the war, Varga himself

[49]See, e.g., E. Manevich, "Dve sistemy—dva itoga poslevoennogo ekonomicheskogo razvitiia," *Voprosy Ekonomiki*, 1950, no. 2, 83–99, and Mikoyan's speech in *Pravda*, 11 March 1950, 2 (*CDSP* 2, no. 11: 12).

[50]See, e.g., Belov, *Voprosy ekonomiki*, and Nikolai Voznesenskii, *Voennaia ekonomika SSSR v period Otechestvennoi Voiny* (Moscow: Gospolizdat, 1947).

[51]I. Trakhtenberg, "Perekhod kapitalizma ot voennoi k mirnoi ekonomike," *MKhMP*, 1946, nos. 4–5 (April–May) (suppl.), saw a recession in the offing, but no major depres-

predicted a cyclical crisis of overproduction in two to three years (he was right), a much more muted boom than that of the 1920s, and then a major depression as serious as that of the 1930s.[52] After the Marshall Plan gathered steam, he revised his estimate, forecasting two major downturns in the coming decade, each of lesser magnitude than the Great Depression but large enough to keep overall growth down to 1.5 percent a year.[53] When Varga was criticized, it was not for his analysis of the capitalist crisis (although some rivals took the opportunity to advance their own pet theories on the capitalist cycle) but for his argument that the crisis could lead to some reform of capitalism.

On this issue Varga's critics charged that he overestimated imperialism's power. Planning implied to Soviet minds superior performance. Even the limited state planning of which Varga considered the capitalist state capable could alleviate the worst effects of the inevitable crisis and reinvigorate the capitalist economy relatively quickly. For these reasons, Varga's opponents accused him of "extolling capitalism's virtues." It is important to recognize, however, that no one, and certainly not Varga, was predicting crisis-free growth for capitalism, and all were confident of socialism's ability to grow faster and more consistently. In the self-critical, capitulatory article he finally had to write in 1949, Varga never even mentioned the issue of capitalism's economic crisis.[54]

---

sion until the 1950s; I. Kuzminov, "O krizisnom kharaktere ekonomicheskogo razvitiia SShA v poslevoennoe vremia," *Bol'shevik*, 1948, no. 23 (15 December), 42–53, denounced the thesis of "pent-up demand" propounded by Trakhtenberg and Varga, and thus held that the overproduction crisis was more imminent; V. Cheprakov, "Narastanie novogo ekonomicheskogo krizisa v kapitalisticheskom mire," *Bol'shevik*, 1948, no. 13 (July), 45–56, esp. 54–55, more urgently denounced other economists for accepting the possibility of any boom at all. Much of this "argument" was in fact posturing to adjust to the perceived general line. For a revealing discussion, see Aron Katseleninbogen, *Soviet Economic Thought and Political Power in the USSR* (New York: Pergamon, 1980), 132–45.

[52] E. S. Varga, *Izmeneniia v ekonomiki kapitalizma v itoge vtoroi mirovoi voiny* (Moscow: Gospolizdat, 1946), and Jerry Hough, *The Soviet Union and the Third World* (Washington, D.C.: Brookings Institution, 1986), 108, n. 10. A distinction that was very salient for the Soviet economists of this period, but one missed by many Western scholars, was that between cyclical crises and the major "crisis of the capitalist system of world economy," which led to wars. Conservative economists did take issue with Varga on the timing of the major crisis. On this distinction, see A. Shneerson, "Stalin o krizisakh kapitalisticheskoi sistemy mirovogo khoziaistva," *Voprosy Ekonomiki*, 1950, no. 1 (January), 53–66.

[53] E. S. "Perspectivy razvitiia kapitalizma na blizhaiushchee 10–15 let," AAN 1513/1/79.

[54] E. S. Varga, "Protiv reformistskogo napravleniia v rabotakh po imperializmu," *Voprosy Ekonomiki*, 1949, no. 3, 79–88. See also N. V. Zagladin, *Istoriia uspekhov i neudach sovetskoi diplomatii* (Moscow: Mezhdunarodnye Otnosheniia, 1990), 170–75.

Communists, of course, were not the only ones worrying about an economic crisis. Expectations of a postwar downturn in the United States after the wartime boom were widespread. And American economists, no less than Evgenii Varga, linked the recovery of the whole Western world with the United States' continued ability to provide capital and markets to war-devastated economies. Moscow analysts had to look no further than the pages of the Western business press to find evidence of bourgeois trepidation about the economic future. Naturally, communists operating under a revolutionary general line tended to be more alarmist than capitalist magnates—but not always. Stalin's interview with the Republican presidential hopeful Harold Stassen in April 1947 is revealing in this connection. Adopting Varga's analysis of the condition of the Western economies and the capacity of state policy to attenuate a recession, Stalin appeared more confident of the United States' ability to overcome a near-term overproduction crisis than did the representative of U.S. monopoly capital.[55]

Despite this intense attention to the state of the capitalist economy, Soviets did not portray the competition between the Soviet Union and the West, or even between the capitalist and socialist economic systems, primarily in economic terms. Discourse focused instead on the military-security aspects of the struggle. Consider Stalin's two-camps prediction as he enunciated it in 1927 and as he revised it for publication twenty years later. In both versions "two centers will form on a world scale, a socialist center, attracting to itself all the countries gravitating toward socialism, and a capitalist center, attracting all the countries gravitating toward capitalism." Then:

[Original] The struggle between these two centers over the possession of the world economy will decide the fate of capitalism and communism throughout the whole world, for the final defeat of world capitalism means the victory of socialism in the arena of world economy.

[1949 version] The struggle between these two camps will decide the fate of capitalism and socialism throughout the whole world.[56]

As Robert Tucker points out, Stalin's intent appears to have been to play up the politico-military element of the struggle and deemphasize

---

[55] The dictator appears to have been probing to see Stassen's reaction. See the excerpt in William Taubman, *Stalin's American Policy* (New York: Norton, 1982), 137–39.

[56] Stalin, 10:135; I. Stalin, *Beseda s pervoi amerikanskoi rabochei delegatsiei* (Moscow: Partizdat TsK VKP [b], 1937), 36; Tucker, *Soviet Political Mind*, 270–71.

the Bukharinist (and Khrushchevian) focus on economic competition. He wanted people to believe that in 1927 he had already foreseen the nature of the struggle as he viewed it in 1947.

Public economic assessments did undergo change. In 1950, as the general line as a whole began to shift, higher echelons orchestrated an abrupt end to the proliferation of competing hypotheses about capitalist crisis and imposed a clear line. Now economists' analyses were supposed to conclude that capitalism had entered a new phase characterized by absolute stagnation.[57] At the end of his reign Stalin was apparently preparing for another purge, and the stagnation thesis, with its prediction of an imminent "crisis of the imperialist system" (as opposed to a mere cyclical overproduction crisis), fitted perfectly the domestic need to crack down. It worked well in tandem with the hostility thesis, predicting that Soviet strength would provoke the capitalists to lash out against the Soviet Union. The entire thrust of Stalin's activity on the ideological front after 1950 was a reimposition of a new, quasi-third-period line. Focus on the imminent world capitalist crisis was consonant with this aim, as it harked back to the crisis of capitalism that preceded World War II.

The nature of the economic debate in the comparatively open atmosphere before 1947 indicates that Soviets who thought about economic matters believed their own theories. They expected that the West would go through a recession later or sooner, and that eventually it would be faced with a major economic crisis. They thus could be confident that long-term trends were even more favorable than the short-term trends of the postwar years, when the Western economies were growing as a result of the need to rebuild capital and infrastructure destroyed in the course of the war. It would be surprising indeed if top leaders, including Stalin, did not share these views at least in a general sense.

The Peace Movement

In addition to the potential for revolution and economic competition, the only other candidate for an important element of power in these years was the European peace movement, which was most active between 1949 and late 1951. At its peak in 1950, when a Soviet

---

[57] The discussion in "Za marksistko-leninistkuiu razrabotku teorii i istorii ekonomicheskikh krizisov," *Voprosy Ekonomiki,* 1950, no. 11, 85–111, marks the onset of neo-third-period dogmatism in economics.

authority claimed it had reached a "new stage,"[58] two or three lengthy articles on the peace movement were appearing every day in *Pravda* and at least one editorial or major article in each issue of the monthly scholarly journals. Diplomatic reports from Moscow's embassies in Europe contained lengthy and optimistic reports on the peace movement.[59] The mass movement for peace was a new yet transitory element in postwar analyses of the relationship of forces. In fact, it appears to have been one of the factors that contributed to optimistic portrayals of the world scene after 1949.

Soviet policy was to influence the peace movement to thwart American attempts to increase the conventional military power of the West by rearming Germany. Since for the moment the prospects for manipulating intrawestern contradictions seemed dim, the preservation of the favorable military balance after the war depended in large part on the peace movement. It was the peace movement, not inter-imperialist contradictions, that was cited most often and most emphatically in this connection. And in fact in 1950, and for a few years afterward, the movement did seem to be able to stall plans for the "remilitarization" of Germany. It was not until after Stalin's death that significant conventional military forces began to be built up on the western borders of the Soviet bloc. Still, the peace movement must have seemed a fragile basis on which to rest Soviet security.

Much of the expressed Soviet optimism on the peace movement, however, was doubtless related to the Soviet policy of influencing the movement. In other words, it could well have seemed unwise to express pessimism on the movement's potential while urging it forward. This certainly was the case on the inevitability-of-war question. During the period of optimism, many Soviet leaders, including Stalin and Malenkov, expressed optimism about the peace movement's ability to prevent war.[60] In October 1948, for example, Stalin told a *Pravda* correspondent that Soviet peace policy could "make unleashing a new aggression impossible, if not forever, then at least for a long time."[61] Things got so out of hand that in *Economic Problems* Stalin had to restate his view that the peace movement, while capable of

[58] V. Kremichev, "Dvizhenie storonnikov mira na novom etape," *Bol'shevik*, 1950, no. 7 (April), 34–40.

[59] In some reports the peace movement assumed a greater role in ensuring Soviet security than interimperialist contradictions (military power was always first): "Politicheskii otchet posol'stva SSSR v SShA za 1950 god," 8 March 1950, AVP 129/35/41/245; see also Zarubin to Vyshinskii, "Otchet . . . za 1950 g.," AVP 69/38/9/145.

[60] See Marantz, "Soviet Foreign Policy Factionalism under Stalin?"

[61] Quoted in "Sovetskie vooruzhennye sily na strazhe gosudarstvennykh interesov nashei Rodiny," *Voennaia Mysl'*, 1949, no. 2, 6.

preventing *particular* wars, could not eliminate the possibility of war altogether. It is likely that this same dynamic was at work in at least some of the cases of expressed Soviet optimism about the peace movement's ability to thwart Western policy. In any event, as the peace movement subsided in 1951, expressions of optimism about it dropped out of the discourse, and the capitalist-encirclement doctrine was again the order of the day.

The urgency of Stalin's across-the-board reassertion of capitalist encirclement and immediate threat indicates that the peace-movement stage may have given an opportunity to those who questioned Stalin's emphasis on the war threat and the military power of the state to make their point subtly. In any event, Stalin seemed to regard Varga's noninevitability argument as much more substantial than the expressions of faith in the peace movement. He devoted more space to dealing with Varga's detailed thesis than to refuting peace-movement advocates. And when Stalin's dogmas were overturned under Khrushchev, it was Varga's view that won out.

AMERICAN PERSPECTIVES

Americans did not accord extant military power the importance it seemed to enjoy in Soviet eyes. Although military power retained its background importance, in the immediate context the United States' primary asset was thought to be its economic capabilities, and the Soviet Union's main asset the strength of its communist allies in Western Europe and elsewhere. In addition, the atom bomb seemed to produce a somewhat greater impression on Americans, although most merely incorporated the bomb into views of the nature of war developed in the course of the recent conflict.

Americans agreed with the implied Soviet view that the USSR was now the supreme military power on the Eurasian landmass. They were confident in the Soviet economy's capacity to recover. They expected relative Russian power to increase as recovery got under way. They also expected the Soviets to develop the atomic bomb and the beginnings of a delivery capability within a half-decade.[62] They did not, however, expect the Soviet Union to expand beyond its contiguous security zone by force of arms, in part because they recognized

[62] Jack H. Nunn, *The Soviet First-Strike Threat: The U.S. Perspective* (New York: Praeger, 1982), 64–65; John Prados, *The Soviet Estimate: U.S. Intelligence Analysis and Soviet Strategic Forces* (Princeton: Princeton University Press, 1986), 18–19.

the extent of the damage the Soviet economy and society had suffered at the hands of the Germans. American analysts conceded that the Soviet Union possessed deployed military capability vastly superior to that of the United States, but they assumed that their country had superior war *potential*. The key was that since renewed hostilities were seen as unlikely, extant military power did not imply influence in the immediate context—yet the immediate context was no less important than the construction of the postwar international order.[63]

The first clue to American views is the dominant assessment that the USSR's current military power was superior to that of any other great power. Before hostilities had ceased in Europe, American intelligence observers concluded, in George Kennan's words, that at war's end "Russia will find herself, for the first time in her history, without a single great-power rival on the Eurasian landmass."[64] The British staff agreed that no group of Western European states could, with Britain's help, prevent the Russians from overrunning Europe.[65] A top-secret memorandum from the Office of Strategic Services (OSS) to the president in April 1945 summed up the situation as follows:

Russia will emerge from the present conflict as by far the strongest nation in Europe and Asia—strong enough, if the United States should stand aside, to dominate Europe and at the same time to establish her hegemony over Asia. Russia's natural resources and manpower are so great that within a relatively few years she can be much more powerful than either Germany or Japan has ever been. In the easily foreseeable

---

[63] Melvyn P. Leffler's major study of these years reaches fundamentally similar conclusions on the basis of an infinitely larger sampling of documents: *A Preponderance of Power: National Security, the Truman Administration, and the Cold War* (Stanford: Stanford University Press, 1992). A review of British diplomatic documents reveals general similarity between the views expressed in them and the essential American assessment. The Foreign Office saw Russia as dominant militarily but unlikely to risk war, animated by expansive great-power ambitions but containable by cooperative actions of the Western allies. See, e.g., Graham Ross, ed., *The Foreign Office and the Kremlin: British Documents on Anglo-Soviet Relations, 1941–1945* (Cambridge: Cambridge University Press, 1984), docs. 41–46; Sean Greenwood, "Frank Roberts and the Other 'Long Telegram': The View from the British Embassy in Moscow, March 1946," *Journal of Contemporary History* 25 (January 1990): 103–22; Victor Rothwell, *Britain and the Cold War, 1941–1947* (London: Jonathan Cape, 1982); Robin Edmonds, *Setting the Mould: The United States and Britain, 1945–1950* (New York: Norton, 1986); Elisabeth Barker, *The British between the Superpowers, 1945–1950* (Toronto: University of Toronto Press, 1983); Fraser J. Harbutt, *The Iron Curtain: Churchill, America, and the Origins of the Cold War* (New York: Oxford University Press, 1986); and Alan Bullock, *Ernest Bevin: Foreign Secretary, 1945–1951* (New York: Norton, 1984).

[64] U.S. Embassy, Moscow, to Secretary of State, n.d., *FRUS*, 1945; 5:854.

[65] Post-hostilities Planning Commission paper, July 1944, cited in Barker, *British between the Superpowers*, 13.

future, Russia may well outrank even the United States in military potential.[66]

Intelligence sources held that the Soviets could, if they chose, overrun Europe, Northern China, Korea, and much of the Near and Middle East, though they doubted the Soviets' capacity to hold on to such territory. At present the USSR had little capability to strike U.S. territory directly, although present programs indicated it would have such ability, as well as atomic bombs, within five to ten years.[67] Though the United States was invulnerable to Soviet power, it could not interpose an effective military barrier to the expansion of Soviet power in any direction. The key, according to a 1947 CIA assessment, was that because of the dramatic weakening of all the states on the Soviet periphery, "the balance of power which restrained the U.S.S.R. from 1921 to 1941 has ceased to exist. The only effective counterpoise to the power of the Soviet Union is that of the United States, which is both latent and remote. Consequently, the U.S.S.R., despite its present weaknesses, enjoys an overwhelming preponderance of power at every point within logistical reach of its land forces."[68]

The second clue to the American perspective is the decisive assumption that the Soviets would not use their great military power for direct conquest.[69] Once on firmly believes the adversary cannot or will not attack, the usefulness of his military power as an instrument of influence or coercion is largely vitiated. According to a memorandum that Kennan wrote after his transfer from the Moscow embassy to the Naval War College in April 1946, and that was shown to the president, the Soviets "do not have the preponderance of political power in the world today and therefore cannot risk a political showdown. They are equally conscious of the fact that they cannot afford a military showdown at this time."[70] The essence of Kennan's—

[66] OSS, "Problems and Objectives of United States Policy," 12 April 1945, *DDRS*, RC, 316D. The OSS was the predecessor of the CIA.

[67] See the report prepared for Truman by Clark Clifford, for which he sounded out the views of all the major bureaucracies: "American Relations with the Soviet Union," 26 September 1946, *DDRS*, 1975/139B.

[68] CIA, "Review of the World Situation," 26 September 1947, *DDRS*, 1977/179A.

[69] In addition to Leffler, *Preponderance of Power*, esp. 306, see the assessments reported by Navy and Defense Secretary James V. Forrestal in JVFD, 3 April 1946, box 2/4; 6 October 1946, box 3/5; 21 and 23 October and 23 November 1948, box 5/13–15. Also see quotations in Matthew A. Evangelista, "Stalin's Postwar Army Reappraised," *International Security* 7 (Winter 1982 – 83): 110–38. Evangelista effectively argues that Soviet capabilities were exaggerated. In the course of demonstrating this proposition, he reveals the depth and pervasiveness of this (apparently mistaken) perception.

[70] 30 October 1946, *DDRS*, 1980/18C.

and most American analysts'—assessment was that the balance of power was primarily psychological in nature: Soviet power was intimidating only if the key states—mainly in Western Europe—thought it so.[71] If the United States had the capacity to bolster these countries' confidence, it had the capacity to limit Soviet power to its Eastern sphere.

Americans based their assumption of the Soviets' unwillingness to advance by force on four assessments. First, the Soviets needed time to rebuild their war-devastated economy. As a memorandum of the Joint Intelligence Committee (JIC) put it in early 1945, the Soviet Union "will have neither the resources nor, so far as economic factors are governing, the inclination to embark on adventurist foreign policies which, in the opinion of the Soviet leaders, might involve the U.S.S.R. in a conflict or critical armament race with the great Western powers."[72] A 1945 OSS report claimed the USSR would not be ready for war for fifteen years; a study by the Joint Chiefs of Staff (JCS) in December 1947 put the figure at ten; in 1946 and 1947, the Moscow embassy picked up hints of the extent of damage from the Soviet press and from leaders' speeches.[73] The Soviets not only had to rebuild the economy; they were thought to face a formidable task in their efforts to subjugate the Eastern European peoples, the newly annexed areas, and even the Russians and other nationalities within the USSR. In Kennan's words, "further military advance west would only increase responsibilities already beyond Russia's capacity to meet."[74]

A second reason Americans regarded the Soviets as unlikely to use their military forces followed from the first; they believed that the Soviets expected their power to increase in relation to that of potential adversaries as they reconstructed their economy with the aid of reparations and looted hardware from Eastern Europe.[75] As Clark Clifford

[71] This argument is developed by John Lewis Gaddis, *Strategies of Containment* (New York: Oxford University Press, 1982).

[72] JIC 250/1, "Estimate of Postwar Soviet Capabilities and Intentions," 31 January 1945, *DDRS*, 1978/242D.

[73] OSS, "Problems and Objectives"; JCS, Joint Strategic Plans Committee, "Report on the World Political Situation up to 1957," 11 December 1947, *DDRS*, 1975/75B. For embassy reports, see Chargé d'Affaires to Secretary of State, 9 September 1946 (telegram), *FRUS*, 1946, 6:787; Walter Bedell Smith to Secretary of State, 13 January and 5 November 1947, *FRUS*, 1947, 4:515–17, 606–12. This increased knowledge of Soviet economic troubles had an immediate impact on Washington. See Central Intelligence Group, "Revised Soviet Tactics in International Affairs," 6 January 1947, *DDRS*, 1980/134C.

[74] Telegram from Moscow: "Russia's International Position at the Close of the War with Germany," *FRUS*, 1945, 5:859–60. Kennan believed that this factor could even ease Russian power eastward.

[75] See JIC 250/1, *DDRS*, 1978/242D.

put it in a memorandum on U.S.-Soviet relations prepared for the president: "Time is on the side of the Soviet Union, since population growth and economic development will, in the Soviet view, bring an increase in its relative strength."[76] In addition, the Americans believed that Moscow had high expectations of expanding in Western Europe, or at least of preventing a Western bloc, by non-military means; that is, by relying on communist parties. As one internal State Department memo put it, "the Soviets still do not want war, but believe that despite us they can gain their strategic objectives of control not only of the heartland of Europe and Asia, but actually of the shores of these continents."[77] Telegrams from the Moscow embassy were full of reports that "the Kremlin" believed it faced a "revolutionary situation" in Western Europe and the Far East.[78]

The final element—in many ways the most difficult to assess precisely—was the American belief in the ultimately superior economic and military potential of the West, and of the United States in particular. Kennan summed up that faith in his "long telegram" of February 1946, which was highly influential, at least at the operational levels of the U.S. government: "Gauged against the Western World as a whole, [the] Soviets are still by far the weaker force. Thus, their success will depend on [the] degree of cohesion, firmness and vigor which [the] Western World can muster."[79] According to a CIA assessment, "the persistent threat of Soviet military force *in being* will continue to be checked by U.S. power *potential.*"[80] "Potential" here seems to subsume two elements: the Americans' monopoly on the atomic bomb and their latent military-industrial capacity.[81]

Most intelligence assessments supposed that any war would be a prolonged affair characterized by initial Soviet advances. The United States would reply with atomic strikes designed to inhibit Soviet war production while it geared up for a major amphibious assault.[82] The atomic bomb was thus seen as an adjunct to latent U.S. military-industrial capabilities. Richard Betts observes: "During the brief period of effective nuclear monopoly, U.S. forces lacked what would

[76] *DDRS*, 1975/139B/6. See also JVFD, 28 April 1947, box 4/1–8, 1603.
[77] Harley Notter to Dean Rusk, 14 July 1947, *FRUS*, 1947, 4:578.
[78] See Smith to Secretary of State, 5 and 8 November 1947, *FRUS*, 1947, 4:606–12 (esp. 607), 614–15; and Durbrow to Secretary of State, 1 December 1947, ibid., 624–26.
[79] *FRUS*, 1945, 5:707.
[80] CIA, "Review of the World Situation," 16 December 1948, *DDRS*, 1977/181C; emphasis mine.
[81] Leffler, *Preponderance of Power*, 116.
[82] For this kind of analysis, see CIA, "Review of the World Situation," 26 September 1947.

now be called 'assured destruction' capability. Fission weapons were too few and too low in explosive power. The U.S. Strategic Air Command could have inflicted great destruction on the USSR, but there was grave doubt that U.S. atomic attacks could prevent the Soviet army from rolling to the English Channel and the Pyrenees."[83] Betts's observation, based on an extensive analysis of formerly top-secret intelligence documents, underlines what is often obscured in accounts of postwar international relations: that the "nuclear revolution" did not occur in 1945, but was a much slower process that perhaps really culminated only with the development of intercontinental and submarine-launched ballistic missiles in the early 1960s. Marc Trachtenberg summarizes the prevalent view within the U.S. government: "The atomic bomb, as important as it was, had not rendered the existing conceptual framework obsolete, and this was true even after the Soviet Union had begun in 1949 to amass atomic forces of its own."[84] In short, American officials privately shared Stalin's public assessment of the atomic bomb.

Still, at a less rigorous level, one can detect indications that many American officials saw the bomb as offsetting the Red Army *as a deterrent*. The documents are permeated by a general and diffused assumption that the Red Army, regarded as a potentially powerful instrument to be used only in the most extreme circumstances, was offset by the atomic bomb, similarly a terrible weapon whose credibility applied only to the most extreme cases.[85] James Forrestal summed up the relationship in December 1947: "As long as we can outproduce the world, can control the sea and can strike inland with the atomic bomb, we can assume certain risks otherwise unacceptable. . . . The years before any possible power can achieve the capability effectively to attack us with weapons of mass destruction are our years of opportunity."[86] The bomb did add yet one more element to the argument that the Soviets would not move forward by force. But it was only one element, and by no means the main one. The stress in the analyses is on the other factors.[87]

[83] Richard Betts, *Nuclear Blackmail and Nuclear Balance* (Washington, D.C.: Brookings Institution, 1987), 145.

[84] Marc Trachtenberg, "Strategic Thought in America," in *History and Strategy* (Princeton: Princeton University Press, 1991), 3. See also Leffler, *Preponderance of Power*, 11.

[85] This was essentially Marshall's view. See Forrest C. Pogue, *George C. Marshall: Statesman, 1945–1959* (New York: Viking, 1987), esp. 334.

[86] Quoted in Gaddis, *Strategies of Containment*, 62.

[87] Ambassador Smith constructed the Soviet view in a conversation with Forrestal: "The atomic bomb by itself will not be a deterrent to their making war. They count on their great diversification and vast areas": JVFD, 24 September 1948, box 5/12, 2519.

Kennan's belief of 1945, that the primary threat was political and psychological rather than military, was thus shared by the Washington establishment by 1947. A CIA report on the world situation in 1947 expressed the belief that "the greatest present danger to U.S. security lies, not in the military strength of the U.S.S.R. and the possibility of Soviet armed aggression, but in the possibility of the economic collapse of Western Europe and accession to power of elements subservient to the Kremlin."[88]

Americans were intensely concerned with two Soviet assets: the potential for an economic collapse in Europe and the potential for communist parties to capitalize on it on Moscow's behalf. American policy makers closely followed Soviet analyses of capitalism's economic situation. Because they did not grasp the distinction that Soviet analysts made between "crisis" (which often meant merely a typical recession in the business cycle) and "crisis of the world capitalist system" (a disaster on the order of the Great Depression), Americans on the scene believed that the Soviets had a higher expectation of a major depression in the West than in fact they did. Their concern may well have been the result of their own fear that a revolutionary situation was developing in Europe, for this fear underlay most policy papers of the day. Perhaps for this reason, contemporary Western analyses mistakenly thought the Varga debate centered on the issue of capitalism's economic crisis.

In any event, practically every policy analysis between 1945 and 1948 held that Soviet plans for expansion were based on the expectation of a crisis in Western Europe and a depression in the United States.[89] This perception was reinforced when the Soviets shifted their primary emphasis from splitting tactics to leftist activism in 1947. To the new ambassador in Moscow, Walter Bedell Smith, "the present reversion to aggressive tactics appears to be based on the belief that a so-called 'revolutionary situation' has developed which if taken advantage of will permit the Kremlin further to consolidate its World War II gains and extend its influence and control."[90] As far as the United States was concerned, another State Department memorandum observed, "the Soviets [incorrectly] believe that the United States will not be able, for reasons of anticipated economic weakness, political compulsions, and immediate military inadequacy, to interpose an effective obstacle to their broad strategic plan."[91]

[88] CIA, "Review of the World Situation," 26 September 1947.
[89] Ibid. is a good example.
[90] Smith to Secretary of State, 5 November 1947, *FRUS*, 1947, 4:606–7.
[91] Notter to Rusk, 14 July 1947, ibid., 578.

Americans thus tended to see the postwar contest between the United States and the Soviet Union as primarily economic, political, and psychological rather than military. The Soviet Union's ideological appeal and organized communist allies assumed a crucial role in this context. It was not so clear in 1947 and 1948 that communist influence was on the wane. The communist coup in Czechoslovakia in February 1948 seemed to underscore the value of this Russian asset. The communist parties appeared to represent an element of Soviet power that stretched far beyond the Red Army's most westward encampment, and it was an element that enjoyed immediate, tested credibility. It gave Soviet power a scope far greater than any reckoning of material indices would indicate. Dean Acheson recalled later that "the threat to Western Europe seemed to me singularly like that which Islam had posed several centuries before, with its combination of ideological zeal and fighting power."[92] In this context, America's economic wealth, immense markets, cultural ties to other Western countries, and political leadership were the main elements of its power.

The Czech coup, the Berlin blockade, the Soviet atom bomb test, the Chinese Revolution, and eventually the Korean War set in motion and solidified a distinct change in the American perspective on the balance of power. The view gained ground that the balance of power had shifted against the U.S.-led bloc, either in measurable terms or in the perceptions of key allied elites. In addition, the salience of military power grew notably, and the construction of a stable balance of power was seen increasingly in military terms.

The speed and intensity of the change varied with the level of the political establishment. Military planners, supported by Defense Secretary Forrestal, had long questioned the feasibility of creating a self-reliant Europe without American forces and of containing the Soviets without an increase in U.S. conventional capability, and so were less affected by the 1949 "shocks."[93] Other analysts, both within and outside of government, shared Kennan's view that "there is little justification for the impression that the 'cold war' . . . has suddenly taken some drastic turn to our disadvantage."[94] Many argued against assigning too much importance to the Soviet bomb test.[95]

[92] Dean Acheson, *Present at the Creation: My Years in the State Department* (New York: Norton, 1969), 376.

[93] NSC, n.d., notes and excerpts from Forrestal's diaries, *DDRC*, RC/304A. See also JVFD, 19 July 1948, box 5/11, 2369; and D. A. Rosenberg, "American Atomic Strategy and the Hydrogen Bomb Decision," *American Historical Review* 66 (June 1979): 62–87.

[94] Kennan to Secretary of State, 17 February 1950, *FRUS*, 1950, 1:160–67.

[95] For a full discussion, see Gaddis, *Strategies of Containment*, 89–126; and Leffler, *A Preponderance of Power*, 326–32. The British disagreed on two important points: they

Overall, however, the collective mood did shift in 1949, and the new mood was reflected, and arguably exaggerated, in the decisive policy statement of the period, NSC-68. In 1948 and 1949 the CIA continued to maintain that the aggregate Western position was improving, despite setbacks in China.[96] But by mid-1950, when the State Department's Policy Planning Staff under Paul Nitze was drafting NSC-68, the CIA's assessment had shifted. Now "the West has lagged behind the USSR in terms of total gain of political, economic, and military strength. . . . Soviet power has increased in relation to that of the Atlantic Treaty nations."[97] NSC-68 itself was a pessimistic document. Acheson later wrote that it was deliberately exaggerated in an effort to "bludgeon" the fractious policy establishment into sufficient order to permit Truman to adopt and implement a decision.[98] It concluded that "our military strength is becoming dangerously inadequate." It claimed that the Soviets' military and economic power was increasing in relation to the Americans', and that if present trends continued, they would achieve military superiority by 1954.[99] A vast increase in American defense expenditures and a commitment to develop the thermonuclear bomb were NSC-68's main policy recommendations.[100] If doubts about the president's ratification of the document were ever raised, North Korea's invasion of South Korea put an end to them and ensured wide acceptance of the document's propositions by American national security bureaucracies, the Congress, and the public as a whole.

Despite reservations held by important members of the political establishment, most of the essential propositions of NSC-68 were adopted by the various agencies and came to dominate public and internal administration discourse on national security matters. NSC-68 never maintained that the Soviet Union had achieved military superiority over the United States. Neither NSC-68 nor its supporting intelligence analyses saw a major war as imminent. Instead, all expressed concern about two likely developments: a proxy war (as hap-

---

thought the British Empire remained an independent great power, and that communism was not monolithic. See Edmonds, *Setting the Mould,* 207ff.

[96] CIA, "Review of the World Situation," 16 December 1948 and 20 April 1949, *DDRC,* 1977/101C and 281B.

[97] CIA, "Review of the World Situation," 1 April 1950, ibid., 283D.

[98] Acheson, *Present at the Creation,* 374.

[99] Prados, *Soviet Estimate,* 21–22, covers the range of estimates on this score.

[100] See *FRUS,* 1950, 1:235–92.

pened in Korea, and as had earlier been feared in Yugoslavia)[101] and a potential window of vulnerability in the mid-1950s.[102] These two fears, in addition to worries over the NATO states' resoluteness in the absence of concrete military guarantees, underlay the increased importance accorded to military capabilities. The document maintained that "we possess superior overall power in ourselves or in dependable combination with like-minded nations." Nevertheless, it did stress the adverse trends in the relationship, and follow-on assessments expressed more uncertainty about trends in the power relationship than had been the case before.[103]

War and the Elusiveness of Power

World War II proved a surprisingly poor test of world power relationships. That military struggle, as epochal as any in history, failed to remove daunting uncertainty from the distribution, elements, and mechanics of power. It even yielded conflicting signals on the hierarchy of prestige in the society of states. Significant asymmetries in perception of power persisted throughout the early Cold War period, and indeed contributed to the onset of the conflict. Let us briefly review the evidence on Soviet and American perspectives before we turn to the more general questions raised by this analysis.

The Elusive Balance and Superpower Perspectives

The major change in Soviet discourse on the international situation after World War II was the increased emphasis on military security and military power, especially after 1947. On reflection, the intensity of public Soviet concern over the threat of war bears little resemblance to what we now know to have been the real situation. Soviet authorities harped on the war threat in the peaceful 1920s, placed greater

[101] On the proxy-war issue, see Beatrice Heuser, "NSC-68 and the Soviet Threat: A New Perspective on Western Threat Perceptions and Policy-Making," *Review of International Studies* 17 (January 1991), 17–40.

[102] Prados, *Soviet Estimate.*

[103] See, e.g., CIA, "Probable Long-Term Development of the Soviet Bloc and Western Power Positions," July 1953, *DDRS*, 1989/1387. A White House memorandum of 18 March 1953, summarizing the views of the various national security bureaucracies, concluded that "time appears to be running *against* us": *DDRS*, 1988/565. As always, however, at any given moment the Soviet power position was viewed as inferior. See NSC minutes, April 1953, *DDRS*, 1991/187.

faith in diplomatic maneuver in, of all times, the late 1930s, and harped again on the war threat in the late 1940s. As tempting as it is to dismiss public expressions of concern over military security as meaningless or wholly propagandistic, in every case the Soviets had reasons—indeed, too many reasons—to focus on military power.

Although the language used was often hyperbolic, the entire elite discussion in the postwar period reflected an intense preoccupation with the military aspects of national power. Between 1945 and 1947, Soviet leaders and commentators focused on the military-territorial improvements in the Soviet Union's position. They then shifted attention to the military threat from imperialism. In public, at least, the Soviets considered military capabilities to be by far the most important component of national power. They framed economic issues in military terms. Soviet leaders, official spokesmen, experts, and academics of all stripes justified economic policies and priorities in terms of military necessity and stressed the virtues of socialist planning for mobilization.

Prudent conservatism suggested that war was possible, though probably, as Stalin said publicly and privately and as the Western governments estimated, not before ten to fifteen years had passed. It took no great strategic acumen to see that the coalition the Soviet Union would probably face would be superior economically and technically, though at a certain geographic disadvantage. Stalin's 1946 statement that the Soviet Union had to think, prepare, and sacrifice now in order to be in a position to field a technologically sophisticated force in ten to fifteen years' time would have made sense to any military man. In the meantime, a large force was needed to quiet domestic insurgencies and pacify the Eastern European security zone. Stalin's Leninist understanding of imperialism and world politics may well have inclined him to see the Western powers as inherently much more aggressive than they saw themselves or than we see them today. The experience of the war had hammered home every imaginable lesson about keeping powder dry and trusting in one's own power rather than in devious diplomacy. And if these arguments for valuing military power above all are not enough, one can toss in the added consideration that the sense of external threat helped maintain the disciplined totalitarianism at home that Stalin doubtless considered best suited to the task of reconstructing the devastated country while presenting an imposing, monolithic face abroad.

Mixed with all these concerns about a possible war in the future was consideration of the present diplomatic situation. If the West was too strong fifteen years hence, the Soviet Union could lose a war. If it was too strong now, the Soviet Union could lose the peace. According to Molotov, Stalin often lamented that old Russia could "win wars but didn't know how to exploit the fruits of victory."[104] The dictator and his foreign minister were determined to reverse the trend. Implicit and explicit in the Soviet discourse throughout the 1945–1953 period, but especially evident in the first two postwar years, was the argument that the Soviet Union had won a particular place in the postwar world by right of its performance in the war. Much Soviet commentary reflected a conviction that the USSR's wartime role should translate into influence over peacetime arrangements among the great powers.

The argument for great-power "equality" may well have reflected deep philosophical or ideological conviction, but it was more obviously related to diplomatic undertakings then under way: the occupation of Japan; the reconstruction of Western Europe; the future of Germany and the prospects for reparations; the distribution of colonial and other prizes and responsibilities in the Near and Far East. And though we may not know exactly what Stalin and Molotov expected from the postwar settlement, we do know what they and their minions said: that they got less than they expected, hoped for, and thought they deserved. Or, perhaps more accurately, they resented the price they had to pay for what they did get: American global dominance.

So, as important as military power was for long-term security, the Soviet leadership also sought to exploit it both rhetorically and politically for immediate purposes. Stalin and his circle talked and acted exactly as such realists as E. H. Carr, Ralph Hawtrey, Geoffrey Blainey, and Robert Gilpin would expect.[105] They seemed to recognize that the war would define world politics for some time to come, that the postwar situation was fluid, and that it was important to stake out as large a role as possible. Further, they claimed, as the authors just mentioned all do, that victory in war translates into prestige—that is, into power recognized by others—and that prestige leads to diplomatic influence, because statesmen recognize the background importance of war. And it is inconceivable that Stalin and Molotov would not have agreed heartily with Hawtrey's injunction that "in a diplomatic conflict the country which yields is likely to suffer in prestige because the fact of yielding is taken by the rest of the world to be

---

[104] Chuev, *Sto sorok besed*, 78.

[105] See the discussion and works cited in Robert Gilpin, *War and Change in World Politics* (New York: Cambridge University Press, 1981), 30–32.

evidence of conscious weakness."[106] So Stalin presented a face of implacable power to the rest of the world and preferred stalemates to substantive concessions.

The results of Stalin's efforts to translate military victory into political gain were mixed. On the one hand, Soviet military power did hold a territorial sphere and, coupled with organizational, police, intelligence, and propaganda assets, transform it into some kind of international-political entity. And military power together with international communist resources largely succeeded in putting the West on the defensive, although it made continuing diplomatic sallies at the East European sphere. In retirement, Molotov often expressed pride in what he and his boss had achieved.[107] On the other hand, the United States emerged from World War II and early postwar diplomacy as the undisputed hegemon of the non-Soviet world, possessing far greater diplomatic weight than the USSR. Washington's globe-girdling policy constrained Stalin's influence over diplomatic arrangements affecting Soviet security. America's ability to unite the other major powers, even if temporary, constricted Moscow's room to maneuver and vastly increased the West's bargaining power.

American policy was based on a different assessment of the operative balance of power than the one that probably prevailed in the Kremlin. In contrast to their Soviet counterparts, American decision makers tended to see the primary issue as the political and economic stabilization of the situation in Europe. Military power obviously retained its long-term and background importance, but in the immediate circumstances perceptual and psychological factors were more important. They feared Soviet military capabilities, especially when they anticipated the future, but thought that their psychological effects could be neutralized for the time being by largely nonmilitary resources. They saw economic crisis, political instability, and communist parties as Moscow's main assets. Thus U.S. economic power was regarded as most effective in the immediate circumstances. The role of the atomic weapon in both Soviet and American perspectives appears much smaller than it has often been portrayed. The real distinction was between the Soviets' focus on their current military power and the Americans' focus on overall potential and existing economic capabilities.

An additional critical factor in the American (as well as Soviet) view was a sense of urgency. All appeared to realize that the postwar

---

[106] Quoted in ibid.
[107] See Chuev, *Sto sorok besed,* 78.

situation was fluid and that the way the lines were drawn in the first crucial postwar years would determine future politics to a great extent. The picture from the American side is best summed up in a comment made by Forrestal to Marshall in April 1947. The United States, he told the secretary of state,

> had everything which the world needed to restore it to normal and the Russians had nothing—neither capital nor goods nor food. The only products that they could export were chaos and anarchy. I said that I was very glad that he was setting up this planning organization because in the use of our vast resources and present power, we were up against the factor of time which conversely was on the Russian side; that we *had* the ability to be a catalyst in the restoration of the world economy but it had to be done very fast and using all the talents in the country, which means business management as well as proper government policy.[108]

As Khrushchev and Brezhnev would discover, Forrestal's words were prophetic, for the international hierarchy that emerged in those critical postwar years proved extremely resistant to revision.

The Elusive Balance and the Onset of the Cold War

Underlying post-1945 diplomacy was a U.S.-Soviet argument over power and prestige. It would be inappropriate to force final conclusions at too early a stage in the analysis, but it is instructive to consider the elusive postwar balance in terms of the "unpacked" aspects of the balance of power spelled out in Chapter 2.

1. *The war as a test of the distribution of power.* The Russians made a very convincing case that theirs had been the decisive contribution to the overall victory, and indeed, the Western allies did not contest that basic point. Superficially, then, the war appeared to reveal quite clearly the real distribution of capabilities: the Soviet Union was the preeminent military power on the Eurasian landmass. In the rest of the world, including its oceans and much of its skies, the United States was the weightiest power. The British Empire, however, was seen in all major capitals as a player of the same essential rank as the United States and the Soviet Union until 1948. After that, London and Moscow only very slowly (and unevenly) revised downward their estimates of Britain's capabilities.

---

[108] JVFD, 28 April 1947, box 4/7, 1603. See also Leffler, *Preponderance of Power,* 2–3.

Bipolarity, which seems to salient in hindsight and in numerical representations of the balance of power (such as those in Table 1) came only very slowly and incompletely to the minds of postwar statesmen. Postwar diplomacy cannot be explained unless the difficulty of "discovering bipolarity" and its purported laws is taken into account. But the ambiguity left in the war's wake transcends that problem. The major uncertainty surrounded the implications of the revealed military distribution. Russia was temporarily weakened by the war, and America temporarily enjoyed something arguably close to hegemony. Further, Russia's major asset, military power, was temporarily devalued in comparison with the value it had possessed in the war and was expected to possess again in the near future. These contradictions turn out to have been crucial to the onset and course of the Cold War.

2. *The utility of elements of power.* Moscow highlighted military power. Americans acknowledged its background significance, but in the present circumstances they stressed economic, cultural, and organizational capabilities. The Cold War clash of these two perspectives yielded only partially conclusive results. Military capabilities won Stalin and Molotov a vastly improved position of status and security on the world scene. For men who started out as underground operatives in a tiny revolutionary band and who had doubted the advisability of taking power in 1917, this was a phenomenal transition indeed. But America, whose losses in the war were minimal, emerged enriched and threateningly dominant near most Soviet borders. Soviet efforts to thwart this American expansion by exploiting the psychological effect of military power and interimperialist contradictions were effectively countered by the United States' use of nonmilitary elements of power.

This episode illustrates the frustrating capriciousness of the balance of power. All the great powers acknowledge Russia's contribution to victory in the war. All agree that another war in the future is likely. All are engaged in negotiating postwar settlements that bear decisively on Moscow's security position. Yet Russia is denied a voice in those settlements commensurate with its demonstrated capacity to make war. In the immediate circumstances all are exhausted by war, resort to arms is unlikely, and consequently the utility of military power is temporarily devalued. But the immediate circumstances are no less consequential than the setting up of the whole postwar order.

3. *The mechanics of power.* Thus far, we see an argument over the degree of influence in the postwar world in which each side highlights its present advantages within and among all elements of power.

On military power, for example, Americans highlight air and sea power more than do the traditionally land-focused Russians. Americans, especially publicly, put more weight on atomic weapons than the Soviets do. Some of this stance is signaling to impress friend and foe, but some reflects long-standing traditions derived from geography and political culture. Overall, the Americans stress economic power and business capabilities; the Russians draw attention to the Red Army's undoubted prestige.

Each side's vision of its proper place in the world may well have been influenced by its understanding of balancing mechanics. Russians thought the United States' position was precarious and unsustainable because of contradictions inherent in capitalism; Americans saw their economic capabilities as a potent stabilizing force. The Soviets' compulsion to challenge the United States' world role and the Americans' commitment to defend it were related to each side's view of the robustness of the postwar settlement. Again, the temptation is to see much of both sides' views of balancing mechanics as purely derivative of their struggle for influence, but in both cases dominant views reflected deeply embedded ways of thinking: economic liberalism in the American case and Leninist Marxism in the Soviet.

4. *Prestige.* Prestige turns out to be the nub of the issue. It is in this connection that World War II performed its testing function particularly badly. The temporary weakening of Russia and strengthening of America coupled with the temporary devaluation of military power added up to a postwar settlement embodying from the first a classic contradiction between power and prestige. Soviet prestige did not correspond to the country's perceived military potential. Soviet influence over diplomatic arrangements that had implications for both security and the more ephemeral goal of control over the international system did not reflect Soviet power as demonstrated in the most recent and best test available, World War II.

The Soviet Union gained immensely in the postwar period, and in no way could it be called as dissatisfied a power as, say, post–World War I Germany. But unlike Germany, Russia was willing and inclined to struggle immediately for its "rightful place" in the society of nations. As a consequence, world politics assumed its classic prewar form. It polarized into two camps. In this view, the emergence of two tight alliances resulted not from the concentration of power in the hands of the Soviet Union and the United States but from their conflict over power and prestige.

The most general conclusion to which our analysis leads is that the problems of equilibrium and hegemonic rivalry are both essential to the Cold War case. States' efforts to secure themselves did lead to rough balancing of military potentials. Though the Americans tended to discount the likelihood of a major war in the near term, they agreed with the Soviets that in the future the chances of a new war would increase. So the possibility of war and the consequent importance of military capabilities remained influential background factors in world politics, just as realist interpretations suggest. The American decision makers saw themselves as attempting to forge an alignment of states that *eventually* would be able to deploy military forces to counter those of the Soviet Union. But in order to create the preconditions for balance on the military scale of power, American, British, and French leaders had to oversee the creation of U.S. preponderance on nonmilitary scales. And that preponderance, in turn, fostered in Moscow the classic combination of resentment and fear which lies behind hegemonic rivalry.

Much about the Cold War story appears unique to those circumstances, but elements common to other periods of international history are evident upon closer examination. These elements are best dealt with in a more comparative study, but two deserve mention here. Arguably, World War II was a poor test of power not because of factors that might be considered unique to that war, such as the development of atom bombs, but because of factors that characterized earlier world wars: the exhaustion of one side and, most important, the fact that the capabilities needed for winning the war are not identical with those useful for influencing the peace. Another historically common asymmetry underlying the Cold War rivalry is the problem of unequal conversion ratios between various elements of power. The Soviet Union, like Germany and revolutionary/Napoleonic France before it, enjoyed a comparative advantage in the production of military power. This advantage, which derived from geography as well as from the nature of the Soviet political and economic system, was made much of by Stalin and his generals. But it was a mixed blessing, for it meant that efforts to counter Soviet power would yield preponderant countercoalitions on nonmilitary scales of power.

Already by 1949 the classic challenger's argument was audible from Moscow. The temporarily deranged distribution of power, which had facilitated Washington's "hypertrophied" world role, had now shifted. The Soviet Union's acquisition of atomic capabilities, its economic recovery, the Chinese Revolution, the consolidation of the "socialist camp" (without Yugoslavia but including the new German Democratic Republic), all rendered America's globe-girdling strategy unsustainable. It was time for a revision. Interrupted by the Korean War and ensuing war-scare hysteria, and eventually by Stalin's death and the ensuing succession struggle, this argument lay below the surface waiting to be used. Khrushchev would pick it up and make it his own after 1956.

[6]

Perceived Power and the
Crisis Years, 1956–1962

The problem for anyone who wishes to dismiss the importance of power is that the evidence consistently indicates that statesmen attach immense importance to it. The problem for anyone who wishes to establish the importance of power is that the concept is ambiguous enough to support seemingly contradictory generalizations. Statesmen can perceive equilibrium and hegemony simultaneously. They may try to balance power while at the same time struggling to alter their status in the global hierarchy. The search for security becomes enmeshed in a struggle for influence and prestige. Consequently, distinctions that may be clear in theory and in hindsight are extraordinarily hard to make in practice: offense versus defense, balancing versus bandwagoning, deterrence versus the spiral model.

Time, it might reasonably be thought, should diminish the problems of discerning the operative dynamics of a given international system. By 1955, when Nikita Khrushchev achieved ascendancy in the Kremlin, the leaderships of the great powers had amassed a decade's experience with military bipolarity and American hegemony. Perhaps by then the constraints of the system had become clear? The problem statesmen faced when they had to decide how to adjust their policies has already been mentioned: the feedback generated by previous policies could be interpreted many ways. And this problem was compounded by another factor. Time brings experience, but it also brings change. Lessons learned from earlier periods may not apply to a new situation.

Table 2. Share of world power and of industrial-economic and military strength held by five countries, 1955 and 1960 (percent)

Country	World power[a]		Industrial-economic strength[b]		Military strength[c]	
	1955	1960	1955	1960	1955	1960
United States	26%	22%	39%	31%	28%	28%
Soviet Union	18	17	15	17	26	22
Great Britain	5	4	7	7	5	3
West Germany	4	4	6	7	1	2
France	3	3	4	4	5	4

SOURCE: Major Power Capabilities Index, Correlates of War Project, University of Michigan; made available through the Interuniversity Consortium on Social and Political Research.

[a] Military expenditures, military personnel, total population, urban population, steel production, and consumption of industrial fuels.

[b] Steel production and fuel consumption.

[c] Military personnel and military expenditures.

The figures in Table 2 capture one important source of change in world power relationships: the United States' "return to normalcy" as other countries recovered from the war's devastation. The America that commanded over half the world's economic production when it forged the international hierarchy in the immediate postwar years now accounted for less than a third. The rest of the figures tell a story of stable bipolarity. West Germany's economic recovery is well under way, and Britain and France appear just able to hold their own. The gap between the two superpowers and states of the next rank looks as great as ever.

What the numbers fail to capture is the dramatic rise in Soviet power which captivated the political world after 1955, providing the framework for the equally dramatic diplomacy of the "crisis years" between 1959 and 1962.[1] Khrushchev's Russia seemed to be posing a fundamental challenge to the West in all areas of competition, from nuclear weapons and the conquest of space to solutions to the basic problems of economic development and political organization. Coupled with hindsight, the figures tempt us to dismiss the importance of Khrushchev-era perceptions. Since we now know that Soviet-style socialism posed no real challenge to the American-led liberal camp,

[1] The source of this apt description is Michael R. Beschloss, *The Crisis Years: Kennedy and Khrushchev, 1960–1963* (New York: HarperCollins, 1991).

expressed beliefs to the contrary must reflect a bias of one kind or another. And it is true that both the Soviet and American political systems seemed to induce exaggeration of Soviet power gains. But that should not obscure what Cold War veterans on both sides of the old iron curtain affirm: that the rise in Soviet power seemed every bit as real in the late 1950s and early 1960s as its decline did thirty years later.

KHRUSHCHEV'S EXUBERANT GENERAL LINE

The most striking feature of the general line that rose and declined with the fortunes of N. S. Khrushchev was its all-encompassing optimism. Confidence bordering on swaggering boastfulness pervaded all corners of official Soviet life. Socialism could prevail peacefully and was already prevailing. The former colonies were all going to gravitate toward socialism. Life would be better for all Soviet people. The Soviet economy would continue to outperform capitalism in all respects. Soviet science had surpassed Western science in important areas. National differences among the Soviet peoples were a thing of the past. Members of the "socialist community" (as Stalin's "camp of peace" was now called) could go their own socialist ways without harming the world interests of socialism. And the balance of power, whether considered broadly as a correlation of all socialist versus imperialist forces or more narrowly as merely the military balance, had shifted radically in the Soviet Union's favor and would continue to do so.

Soviet citizens who were politically active in Khrushchev's time recall that those were optimistic days.[2] Many were convinced that the true potential of Soviet socialism had been held in check by Stalin's regime. They expected a powerful surge forward once the repressive Stalinist fetters were removed. And no one foresaw the future scientific and technological revolution in the West and Japan which was then just stirring. But public bullishness about the correlation of forces, and particularly about the military balance, also served Khrushchev's domestic and international purposes. Practically any

---

[2]See, e.g., Fedor Burlatskii, "Khrushchev: Shtrikhi k politicheskomu portretu," in *Nikita Sergeevich Khrushchev: Materialy k biografii* (Moscow: Izdatel'stvo Politicheskoi Literatury, 1989), 20–21, and *Vozhdia i sovetniki: O Khrushcheve, Andropove i ne tol'ko o nikh* (Moscow: Politizdat, 1990), 167–69; and Georgii Arbatov, *Zatianuvsheesia vyzdorovlenie (1953–1985 gg.): Svidetel'stvo sovremennika* (Moscow: Mezhdunarodnye Otnosheniia, 1991), 65–75.

domestic program other than a continuation of Stalinism required some taming of the military and heavy-industrial sector's demand for resources. The military-industrial complex's claim on resources was based on the perception of external threat. The more favorable the military balance, the less the external threat, and the more leeway the leadership would have to put a brake on military spending.

As for foreign affairs, it was axiomatic that the stronger the Soviet Union was, the more successful its diplomacy would be. If Moscow's negotiating partners, particularly the United States, perceived a shift in the distribution of power in favor of the Soviet Union, they would be more inclined to deal seriously with Soviet proposals. Indeed, the more Khrushchev could convince the West that he himself was firmly convinced of Soviet power, the stronger his hand would be. And success in diplomacy would not only be valuable in its own right, would not only reflect grandeur on Khrushchev himself, but would constitute concrete proof of Soviet security and consequently feed back into the domestic argument in favor of controlling military spending. So there were genuine reasons for optimism, buttressed by mutually reinforcing domestic and international incentives for ex- aggerating Soviet strength.[3] If these reasons for the marked optimism of the period are not enough, one could add Khrushchev's personal- ity; by all accounts he was congenitally optimistic and voluntaristic.

Cheery optimism about the international situation did not sound forth from the Kremlin immediately upon Stalin's death in March 1953. Instead, the public discourse exhibited a gradual retreat from the extreme gloom and pessimism of Stalin's last line. Whatever their differences, Stalin's successors appeared to agree that the quasi-third- period prognostications of imminent crisis, with all their portents of blood purges in the party, were counterproductive under the present circumstances. Some old-thinking postulates that had lain dormant since 1947 began to be heard again. For example, both Georgii Malen- kov, Stalin's successor as head of the Soviet government, and Foreign Minister Viacheslav Molotov made references to the notion that inter- imperialist contradictions provided opportunities for Soviet diplo- macy. The notorious hostility thesis was retired, to be replaced by its more outward-looking opposite, the correlation-of-forces bandwag- oning theme.

---

[3]The most impressive effort to piece together the complex interaction between for- eign policy and domestic leadership politics in this period is James Gerard Richter, "Action and Reaction in Khrushchev's Foreign Policy: How Leadership Politics Affect Soviet Responses to the International Environment" (Ph.D. diss., University of Califor- nia, Berkeley, 1989).

But Soviet politicians still kept within the bounds of Stalin's essential line: old thinking was still applied to the present world of nuclear weapons, bipolarity, and American hegemony in the Western camp; Varga's postwar theses were still out of bounds; the doctrines of two camps and the inevitability of war still remained in force. To revamp a general line that had been in force since 1947, and that Stalin himself had largely reaffirmed in 1953, required considerable authority within the party apparatus. It was precisely this authority that Beria, Malenkov, Molotov, and Khrushchev struggled over between 1953 and 1955.[4] It took considerable status in the ruling echelons to stand before a major party assemblage and declare fundamental doctrines associated with Stalin null and void. Only Khrushchev achieved such status.

Georgii Malenkov emerged as the leading figure after Stalin's death, though his power was steadily eroded by the rising Khrushchev. Only two weeks after Stalin's body was interred in the mausoleum next to Lenin, Khrushchev became de facto first (general) secretary of the party. By 1954 Khrushchev's name preceded Malenkov's in lists of Politburo members. In February 1955 Khrushchev had replaced Malenkov as the head of government, and in July he easily beat back a challenge by Molotov, removing Stalin's oldest comrade from his post as foreign minister.[5] By 1955, if not before, Khrushchev was considered to be the supreme leader, although Molotov and Malenkov remained in the party's executive body, the Presidium (later Politburo) until 1957.

The unlikely figure of Malenkov, a trusted Stalin lieutenant stained dark with purge blood, stepped forward in 1953 with a program stressing improvement of Soviet agriculture, consumer relief, and re-

[4]In addition to ibid. and Burlatskii, *Vozhdia i sovetniki*, chap. 8, important sources on these struggles include Iu. V. Aksiutin and O. V. Volobuev, *XX s"ezd KPSS: Novatsii i dogmy* (Moscow: Izdatel'stvo Politicheskoi Literatury, 1991), 7–65; Raymond Garthoff, "The Death of Stalin and the Birth of Mutual Deterrence," *Survey* 25 (Spring 1980); Carl Linden, *Khrushchev and the Soviet Leadership* (Baltimore: Johns Hopkins University Press, 1966); George Breslauer, *Khrushchev and Brezhnev as Leaders* (London: George Allen & Unwin, 1982); Michel Tatu, *Power in the Kremlin* (New York: Viking, 1968). For excellent documentation of the rhetorical manifestation of the struggle, see Paul Marantz, "Internal Politics and Soviet Foreign Policy: A Case Study," *Western Political Science Quarterly* 23 (March 1975), and Herbert S. Dinerstein, *War and the Soviet Union* (New York: Praeger, 1962), chaps. 4–5.

[5]On the dispute with Molotov and the Central Committee plenum in July, see Aksiutin and Volobuev, *XX s"ezd KPSS*, 63–65; Seweryn Bialer's testimony in Senate Committee on the Judiciary, *Scope of Soviet Activity in the United States*, 84th Cong., 2d sess., pt. 28, 6–7 June 1956, 1561–63; Uri Ra'anan, *The USSR Arms the Third World* (Cambridge: MIT Press, 1969), 86–129.

laxation of tensions abroad. In support of this position, Malenkov's speeches highlighted all the recent changes in the correlation of forces, and especially the Soviet test of a thermonuclear bomb. Taking a cue from Eisenhower's recent address to the United Nations, he advanced the claim that a nuclear war would end civilization (rather than the doctrinaire view that it would destroy only "imperialism"), suggesting that deterrence prevailed. In a speech to the Supreme Soviet in August 1953 he suggested that a more accommodating policy of peaceful coexistence directed toward the United States would isolate "aggressive circles" and exacerbate NATO contradictions.[6]

Malenkov's statements, especially concerning nuclear war, suggest an inclination to break out of hallowed old-thinking postulates and conceivably to pursue a détente policy vis-à-vis the West less challenging and bellicose than the one eventually followed by Khrushchev.[7] It is difficult to reach concrete conclusions on where Malenkov was headed when Khrushchev defeated him, for his speeches do not constitute an alternative analysis of international politics. Instead, they are firmly within the accepted old-thinking framework, though they include suggestive snippets and hints. In his August 1953 speech, for example, Malenkov also called for increased defense expenditures and restated the basic correlation-of-forces logic, claiming that increased Soviet power made U.S. acceptance of a peaceful-coexistence policy more likely.

In the 1953–1955 period, no one achieved the authority needed to articulate a real alternative line. Scholars and experts, cowed by their recent experience of Stalinism, would not venture anything without clearer guidance from above than was forthcoming. The leadership struggle did not churn up anything resembling the intellectual quality of Varga's postwar theses, or even of Stalin's prewar Congress reports. It is impossible, therefore, to speak of a "Malenkov alternative," much less of a "Malenkov model." There were instead Malenkov suggestions, just as there had been Beria suggestions in 1953, as the old NKVD henchman feverishly advanced radical proposals to alter his image as the toughest Stalinist of them all. Signals sent by politicians struggling for power may not be the best predictors of

---

[6] *Pravda*, 9 August 1953, 1–4 (*CDSP* 5, no. 30: 3–12).
[7] Jack Snyder, "The Gorbachev Revolution: A Waning of Soviet Expansionism?" *International Security* 12 (Winter 1987–88), 102–3, and *Myths of Empire: Domestic Politics and International Ambition* (Ithaca: Cornell University Press, 1991), chap. 5. Snyder observes that Malenkov's connections to Leningrad's military-industrial elite may have predisposed him to favor increases in military spending despite his occasional public hints to the contrary.

their behavior in office. Malenkov enjoyed preeminence within the leadership for too short a time to permit us to judge how he would have reacted to the situation Khrushchev later faced.[8]

With Malenkov's defeat and Khrushchev's ascendancy in the years after 1955, the basic message of the new general line became ever clearer: one could not be too bullish about the Soviet bloc's present power position or future prospects.[9] By the time he convened the Twentieth Party Congress in 1956, Khrushchev felt strong enough to denounce Stalin in his secret speech, and in his open report to pronounce authoritatively fundamental revisions in Soviet ideology. For the first time since the late 1920s, the party explicitly adopted new doctrines on international relations.

In his report to the Congress, Khrushchev declared Lenin's and Stalin's doctrine on the inevitability of war invalid. That doctrine, Khrushchev explained, was valid for a time when imperialism, with its economic laws leading to war, "determined the course of world events." In his *Economic Problems of Socialism in the USSR* Stalin had claimed that interimperialist contradictions, the fundamental source of war, took precedence over the contradiction between imperialism and socialism. Now, Khrushchev claimed, socialism had become so powerful that the axis of world development was the contradiction between imperialism and socialism. Before, the USSR was the helpless victim of the bellicose capitalist world system. Now it was powerful enough to change that system, to prevent it from generating war. Though war was still a possibility (because of imperialism's internal laws), it was "not a fatal inevitability."[10] With the announcement of the noninevitability of war, "peaceful coexistence of states with different social systems," which Stalin had referred to only in conversa-

---

[8]Some evidence on this score is contained in Malenkov's personal archive, analyzed in Elena Zubkova, "Malenkov, Khrushchev i 'ottepel,'" *Kommunist*, 1990, no. 14, 86–94, and "Lidery i sud'by: 'Posadnik' Georgiia Malenkova," *Politicheskie Issledovaniia*, 1991, no. 5, 182–88. Malenkov comes through as a more serious and learned Marxist than Khrushchev, less voluntaristic and more inclined toward rational, expert analysis. He was against dangerous military confrontation, but ruled out close cooperation with the West. In his private diary he denounced Khrushchev's dealings with the West as "opportunism" and a "betrayal" of the interests of the international revolutionary movement.

[9]Extensive documentation of these claims can be found in the pioneering work by William Zimmerman, *Soviet Perspectives on International Relations* (Princeton: Princeton University Press, 1969), chaps. 5 and 7; and Arnold Horelick and Myron Rush, *Strategic Power and Soviet Foreign Policy* (Chicago: University of Chicago Press, 1965).

[10]*XXs"ezd Kommunisticheskoi Partii Sovetskogo Soiuza: Stenograficheskii otchet* (Moscow: Izdatal'stvo Politicheskoi Literatury, 1956), 1:37. This doctrinal change calls into question the common Western interpretation of Stalin's *Economic Problems* as signifying a turn to a peaceful-coexistence policy. See chap. 4 above, n.52.

tions with Western reporters, became an ideological doctrine of Soviet foreign policy.

The fact that Khrushchev's revision validated Varga's earlier position does not mean that the analysis that undergirded it was identical to Varga's. By the time Varga presented his view to the 1951 economists' meeting, his argument was well developed and quite complex. Though focused on socialism's increased power, it also involved analyses of U.S. hegemony in the capitalist camp, the nature of the bourgeois state, the capacity of the bourgeoisie to learn from past experience, and so on. Khrushchev's argumentation was by no means so complex: it focused on the correlation of forces and the destructive nature of modern war only. These two interrelated elements were thus much more important to Khrushchev's argument than to Varga's more multicausal explanation.

A corollary to the revision on the inevitability of war was Khrushchev's second "innovation" (Varga had earlier implied much the same thing): the possibility of a peaceful transition to socialism. The "revolutionary transformation of capitalist society into socialist society" was not necessarily "associated with civil war under all circumstances," in part because "the forces of socialism have become stronger on a world scale, while those of capitalism have become weaker."[11] Socialist states could now aid revolutionary forces, even those that had achieved power via the ballot box, to overcome domestic enemies peacefully.

These two doctrinal revisions made a great deal of practical sense, for they were necessary to justify a policy of peaceful coexistence within the system of Soviet ideology, and a policy of peaceful coexistence is the sine qua non of survival in the nuclear age. If war is inevitable, any peaceful coexistence must be conditional and temporary. The same is true if revolutionary advance must be won by war alone. Such doctrines were clearly impractical in the nuclear age. But Khrushchev's revisions further entrenched the bandwagoning correlation-of-forces notion. As a result of the new doctrines, a policy of peaceful coexistence and a positive evaluation of the correlation of forces were linked, and anyone who defended the policy was led to present the correlation favorably. Policy demanded increased optimism about the correlation. Since imperialism was assumed to be aggressive, only a socialism equally strong or (better) stronger could counter its aggressive ways.

No element of the correlation of forces appeared more important

[11] Ibid., 38.

than nuclear weapons. After the announcement of the USSR's first ICBM test in August 1957, Soviet commentary on the international situation entered a new phase. From Khrushchev on down, the word now was that the West "had lost its former superiority in power."[12] Denial of Western superiority was the bellwether formulation in this period, but Soviet leaders added many others that signaled greater optimism about power relations. The old capitalist-encirclement doctrine, for example, was jettisoned, for, as Khrushchev asserted, it was "no longer clear who encircles whom."[13]

By 1958, ideologists were ready to proclaim that the "achievements of Soviet science [sputniks, ICBM test] have opened a new stage in the development of international relations."[14] In a few years the Soviet ideological apparatus transformed this "new stage," occasioned by Soviet missiles, into a full-blown "third stage" in the general crisis of capitalism.[15] Like both preceding stages (the first after World War I and the creation of the Soviet Union, the second after World War II and the formation of the Soviet bloc), this third stage was caused by a shift in the overall correlation of forces against capitalism. But the third stage was different in that it did not arise out of a war and it projected victory for communism without war. It was a Khrushchevian, nuclear-era stage, justifying the new policy of peaceful (but vigorous and sometimes bellicose) competition. In many ways, it formalized Varga's earlier contention that increased Soviet power weakened and tamed capitalism, pushing it toward socialism.

In fact, the whole declaration of the new stage was virtually required by ideology (just as the second stage had to be declared to justify the incorporation of Eastern Europe without real revolutions). After all, if the old hostile policy had been objectively correct, objec-

---

[12] *Pravda*, 26 January 1958, 1 (CDSP 10, no. 4:16); Iu. Zhukov, "Sorok let, reshivshie sud'bu kolonializma," *MEiMO*, 1957, no. 4, 67. For other formulations along these lines, see Nikolai Inozemtsev, "'Atomnaia diplomatiia' SShA: Proekty i deistvitel'nost,'" *MEiMO*, 1958, no. 3, 29–43, esp. 38.

[13] From an interview with *Figaro*, excerpted in *Pravda*, 27 March 1958, 1 (CDSP 10, no. 13: 28).

[14] "Uspekhi nauki i problemy mezhdunarodnykh otnoshenii," *Mezhdunarodnaia Zhizn'*, 1958, no. 3, 7. See also M. Marinin, "Nekotorye osobennosti nyneshego etapa mezhdunarodnykh otnoshenii," *MEiMO*, 1958, no. 6, 3.

[15] Referred to in articles from 1958 on, the third stage was first included in a major ideological document in the Statement of the Meeting of 81 Communist and Workers' Parties, which met in Moscow in November 1960: *World Marxist Review* 3 (December 1960): 15. It was also featured in the party's new program adopted in July 1961: *Program of the CPSU* (New York: International Publishers, 1963), 32. For a typical Khrushchev-era analysis of the third stage of the general crisis of capitalism, see E. S. Varga, *Kapitalizm XX veka* (1961), rpt. in Varga, *Izbrannye proizvedeniia: Kapitalizm posle vtoroi mirovoi voiny* (Moscow: Nauka, 1974), 130–44.

tive circumstances must have changed to require the new policy. Continual quantitative shifts in the correlation of forces, Khrushchev and his ideologists were saying, had led to a qualitatively new situation in which things formerly impossible were now possible. Soviet ideological tomes spelled out a long list of "cardinal" shifts in the correlation of forces as causes of the new stage: the economic successes of the Soviet bloc, advances of the anticolonial and national liberation movements, further congenital problems in the capitalist political economy, and so on. But every list included Soviet advances in nuclear weaponry, and it was indeed these advances that sparked the formulation of a new stage in the first place. It is difficult to avoid the conclusion that of all the changes leading to the third stage, none was more consequential in Soviet eyes than the reduction in the perceived American nuclear advantage.

One of the main problems of the international relations of the day—one cited again and again after 1955—was that "the leaders and ideologists of imperialism are proceeding from the deeply mistaken idea that the imperialist camp today is inarguably superior to the socialist camp in economic, military, and scientific-technical strength and can resolve world issues by its arbitrary power."[16] Article after article, report after report argued that this contradiction between the real correlation of forces and the Western governments' subjective perception of it was dangerous and had to be resolved. It was, in short, the classic challenger's argument: the balance of power has shifted since the period in which the hierarchy of prestige was established and the time has come for a revision.

Diplomatic reports from embassies abroad supplied evidence that though Westerners were still clinging to the old policies, they were becoming aware of the new power realities. Soviet diplomats larded their dispatches with quotations from the Western press, political figures, and even governmental officials questioning the sustainability of the present American "position of strength" policy given the new balance of forces. The upshot was that even "ruling circles of the U.S.A. are of the opinion that the East-West struggle has now entered a new phase, and that present U.S. policy . . . is unable to counter the Soviet Union's strengthened positions and its influence on the international scene."[17] The documents are suffused with the sense

[16] A. A. Galkin, V. I. Gantman, S. V. Datlin, I. I. Ermashev, A. I. Kalinin, S. A. Mikoian, G. A. Mirskii, S. M. Nesterov, and V. P. Nikhamin, "Tekushchie problemy mirovoi politiki," *MEiMO*, 1959, no. 7, 13.
[17] "Politicheskii otchet posol'stva SSSR v SShA za 1955 god," 3 March 1956, AVP 129/39a/1/287, 135. See in general pp. 115–56 and V. Bazykin, "O sostoianii vzaimootno-

that a major reconsideration of policy was in the offing in the Western capitals, owing in large part to increased Soviet power. As we shall see presently, these reports were not inaccurate.

Soviet boastfulness about the balance of power peaked in 1960–61, in the months surrounding Khrushchev's second Berlin ultimatum. In what was probably his most important speech on foreign and military policy, delivered to the Supreme Soviet in January 1960, Khrushchev said: "The balance of forces in the international arena is in favor of the peace-loving states."[18] He thus ushered in an era of almost two years' duration in which Soviet leaders and commentators commonly asserted that the Soviet bloc was superior in the scales of power. Major party documents and leaders' speeches made this claim. The party program, for example, speaks of socialism's "growing superiority over the forces of imperialism."[19] Khrushchev again, in his report to the Twenty-second Party Congress, stressed "the fact that the preponderance of power is on the side of the socialist commonwealth of peoples."[20] Soviet scholars naturally followed suit.[21]

Khrushchev doubtless believed broadly in what he said about the balance of power in those days, but as we know, there were powerful international, domestic, and psychological reasons for exaggeration. In addition, Khrushchev's foreign policy initiatives required optimism if the general line was to remain at all consistent with past positions. The brilliance of Varga's whole analysis of the 1940s was that it reconciled a policy of peaceful coexistence with fundamental Soviet ideological positions. The cleverness of Varga's bandwagoning notions lay in the fact that they equated increased Soviet power with increased prospects for détente. So neo-Stalinist left-wingers such as Molotov and the post-1955 Malenkov, and later Mao Zedong, could be accused

shenii mezhdu SSSR i SShA v period 1950–1054 gg. (kratkaia spravka)," AVP 129/39/15/287.

[18]*Pravda*, 15 January 1960, 1–5 (*CDSP* 12, no. 2: 10).

[19]*CDSP* 13, no. 29: 7.

[20]*XXXII s"ezd Kommunisticheskoi Partii Sovetskogo Soiuza: Stenograficheskii otchet* (Moscow: Izdatel'stvo Politicheskoi Literatury, 1962), 1:37. Khrushchev also made specific claims of military superiority (see ibid., 1:17), as did his defense minister, Rodion Malinovskii. See *Pravda*, 9 May and 24 January 1962 (*CDSP* 14, no. 4: 19): "I think the socialist camp is now stronger than these countries [NATO]." Malinovskii also implied superiority as early as May 1960, when he said, "The Soviet Union, despite its military superiority, does not threaten anyone": *Pravda*, 10 May 1960 (*CDSP* 12, no. 19: 20).

[21]Boasts are so ubiquitous in this period that virtually any foreign affairs article will contain several. For a survey, see Zimmerman, *Soviet Perspectives*, chap. 5.

of lack of faith in socialism and underestimation of socialist successes. Expressed optimism served to disarm these critics, least for a while.

DISTRIBUTION AND MECHANICS OF POWER

When Khrushchev announced at the Twentieth Congress that interimperialist contradictions were subordinate to the main rift between socialism and capitalism, he formally liberated the discourse from the old-thinking postulate that interimperialist contradictions lead to war (and war leads to revolution). Now people could contemplate changes in intrawestern and East-West power balances primarily in terms of their diplomatic implications for Moscow. Indeed, the trend was evident soon after Stalin's death, as the new leaders backed away from the neo-third-period "crisis" line that their former boss had approved over the previous three years. In both domestic and foreign affairs, many members of the elite felt that great things could be done with the legacies of the Stalin era if only more efficient and flexible policies were adopted. Not only the ebullient Malenkov but even dour, Stalinist Molotov suggested that the vastly increased power of the immense socialist bloc wedded to a more flexible diplomacy could yield dramatic results on the world scene. Scores of experts' articles and diplomats' reports buttressed this expectation.

Moscow's "new look" foreign policy consisted of two tracks: reduce tensions and exploit the ensuing interimperialist contradictions to achieve major policy goals. The policy was based on the idea, repeatedly stressed by Malenkov, that international tensions united the Western camp. A relaxation of tensions would complicate American propaganda about the "Soviet military threat" and render the pro-Washington policies of the French, British, and West German governments harder to justify. The new Soviet policy helped return great-power diplomacy to the world stage in the form of meetings of foreign ministers, the Korean armistice, the Geneva summit, and negotiations on Austrian neutrality. As valuable as these negotiations and meetings were in their own right, they were expected to facilitate even higher goals, primarily surrounding Germany, by bringing underlying contradictions to the fore. The view of balancing mechanics associated with this diplomacy was not new. It was a return to the kind of thinking that had prevailed before Zhdanov's leftist two-camps proclamation in 1947.

Moscow appeared to have a lot to work with after 1953. Diplomatic reports noted a series of potentially useful contradictions. Churchill and Anthony Eden seemed even more committed to a third-force role for Britain than the team of Clement Attlee and Ernest Bevin had been. Immediately after Stalin's death, Churchill vetted the idea of a summit with the new head of the Soviet state, Malenkov, to consider a range of Cold War issues. Eisenhower and Dulles opposed the idea from the start. British and American official minds had still not met on the issue of Britain's real status in world politics.[22] The French continued to be a thorn in the side of the United States in its efforts to rearm Germany via the European Defense Community (EDC). In bargaining with Washington over this issue, the French government maneuvered closer to London and raised the possibility of a more active Russian policy. The Soviet "peace policy" was complicating things for Paris, the Soviet embassy there reported, and "raised real prospects for improving relations between the USSR and France, weakening French dependence on the USA and raising its role in international affairs."[23] The French were still in a posturing mode, but the intensity of their maneuvers reflected the pressure the government was under.

The rise of West Germany naturally unsettled Russians, but it did have some positive effects by increasing contradictions with France and Britain. Furthermore, Bonn's latent capacity for independent action was a new and potentially troubling element for the Western bloc. The longer the German issue seemed stalled, the more likely the Federal Republic was to opt for direct negotiations with Moscow. The United States came under pressure to "do something" about the German issue, which in turn highlighted U.S.-French differences. Soviet nuclear deployment increased the vulnerability of Western European states, leading them to pressure Washington to soften the Eisenhower/Dulles "positions of strength" and "liberation" lines. This complex of pressures compelled even the Americans to adopt more flexible tactics.[24] And as optimistically phrased as reports from embassies abroad describing all these contradictions were, officials in Moscow wanted still more—more detail on policy rifts, factions within

[22] Belokhvostinikov to Molotov, "Otchet posol'stva SSSR v Anglii za 1953 god," 15 February 1954, AVP 69/41/14/167, 1–90, esp. 26–27 and 50–51.
[23] "Otchet posol'stva SSSR vo Frantsii za 1954 god," 28 February 1955, AVP 136/45/12/266, 60; see also report for 1953, dated 18 February 1954, AVP 136/44/16/260.
[24] For reports covering these points, see V. Bazykin, "O sostoianii vzaimootnoshenii mezhdu SSSR i SShA v period 1950–1954 gg.," 20 January 1955, AVP 129/39/15/287; A. Dobrynin, "Polititotchet posol'stva SSSR v SShA za 1953 g.," 14 February 1954, AVP 129/37/14/265, esp. 75–83; and "Otchet za 1955 g.," 13 March 1956, AVP 129/39a/1/287, esp. 115–90.

governments and oppositions, influential business interests, and so forth.[25]

Despite high initial expectations, the evidence generated by the new Soviet policy was mixed, and disappointments had steadily accumulated by 1955. The European Defense Community initiative did fail to get through the French Assembly, but as a result Britain took the lead in managing German rearmament. In 1955 the French ratified the Paris agreements, bringing Germany into NATO and nullifying the 1944 Franco-Soviet treaty of alliance. Diplomatic reports noted that the outcome could well end up worse than the EDC would have been, as Germany might now have a freer military reign.[26] At a more general level, Soviet observers began to sense that the ripeness of imperialist contradictions had been overestimated yet again in the post-1953 period. The Western powers were banding together even under the more rosy international conditions signified by the "spirit of Geneva."[27]

The change in 1955, however, was of the typically tentative kind, based on the typically ambiguous evidence flowing in from the West in that year. What really influenced the discussion was the much more dramatic Suez crisis in 1956, in which the United States easily demonstrated its command of Western affairs. Soviet commentary predictably focused on the relative increase of U.S. power. A decade had passed since the end of the war, and Stalin's prediction that America's allies would "break away" seemed as distant as ever. The new foreign minister, Dmitrii Shepilov, noted that "the domination of the United States is increasing [while] the international positions of Great Britain and France are weakening sharply."[28] An international affairs expert claimed that "1956, unquestionably, increased the already decisive superiority of the U.S.A. in the correlation of forces within the imperialist camp."[29]

With hindsight, it appears that it was not American capabilities

[25]See, e.g., N. Solodovnik to N. V. Slavin, "Zamechaniia po politicheskomu otchetu posol'stva SSSR v Anglii za 1953 g.," 2 April 1954, and V. Kuznetsov to Ia. A. Malik, 19 April 1954, both in AVP 69/41/14/167.

[26]"Otchet posol'stva SSSR vo Frantsii za 1955 god," 19 March 1956, AVP 136/46/9/269; G. Tsyganova, "Proval 'Evropeiskogo oboronitel'nogo soobshchestva' i novye plany perevooruzheniia Zapadnoi Germanii," 29 April 1955, AVP 129/39/15/287, 79–101.

[27]See, e.g., "Tematicheskie obzory: Prilozhenie k polotchetu posol'stva za 1954 god," 28 February 1955, AVP 69/42/22/174.

[28]*Pravda*, 2 February 1957, 3 (*CDSP* 9, no. 11: 7). Shepilov also cited relative increases in German and Japanese power.

[29]M. Marinin, "Nekotorye uroki i vyvody," *Mezhdunarodnaia Zhizn'*, 1957, no. 1, 113. Also see in the same issue the editorial "Novyi etap bor'by za mir," 3–9.

that increased in 1956, but merely Soviet (and British and French) perceptions of them. For Moscow observers, the relationship of forces within the Western camp had never been clearer. The basic facts, the size of the American economy and armed forces in relation to those of its allies, had been known since 1945. What had never been entirely clear was the precise implications of these observed relationships. Suez, coupled with the results of the "new look" diplomacy already logged in by the end of 1955, seemed to clear things considerably. America now looked stronger, the middle powers weaker, and the pro-U.S. bandwagon more robust.

The post-1953 diplomatic experience and the "lessons of Suez" were part of a gradual sea-change in Soviet perspectives on the distribution and mechanics of power. Soviet political minds fitfully and unevenly began to grasp the sheer magnitude of American hegemony in the Western camp, the relative weakness of the middle powers, and consequently the relative stability of their pro-American bandwagon. For some, such as Varga, the change occurred well before the mid-1950s; others took much longer to adjust. For most the shift was not a sudden realization but a slow accommodation. But the center of gravity had clearly shifted by the middle of the 1950s toward the view of American hegemony that Varga first articulated in 1948. Whereas early postwar writings assumed that American superiority was a factor of instability, now they held that only American predominance facilitated intrawestern cooperation. Before, Soviets assumed that capitalist states of equal power were more likely to cooperate. Now they thought that the more equal the various Western powers became, the less likely they were to cooperate successfully.

On the surface, this change looks like substantial learning about what we now regard to have been the dynamics of bipolarity. The shift did reflect ten years' experience with the basic postwar configuration of power, during which numerous policies had been tried, from total confrontation to more forthcoming accommodation. Substantially decreasing the cohesion of the opposing alliance or even defeating Western collaborative efforts that seemed to threaten Soviet objectives proved no easy task. Soviets had to accommodate this evidence. In doing so, they began to accept the underlying premise that international alignments were more stable than they had been in the multipolar configuration under which the Soviet Union had matured as a state.

Figure 1 categorizes various viewpoints about the likely effects on Western cohesion of U.S. hegemony in the capitalist camp and increases in Soviet power. Over the decade after the war's end people

Perceived Power and the Crisis Years

Figure 1. Shifting Soviet perspectives on balancing mechanics

	Soviet power unites West	Soviet power decouples West
U.S. dominance unites West	Varga, 1948	Khrushchev era, post-1956
U.S. dominance decouples West	Late Stalin hostility thesis	Stalin era

could, and did, rationally adopt any combination of beliefs about the effects of Soviet and American power. Indeed, individuals could shift from one box to another or even occupy more than one box at the same time.

The key to interpreting what would happen in later years, however, is that this sea-change in Soviet perspectives occurred largely *in the absence of conceptual change.* The basic conceptual framework, the modified theory of imperialism, remained in place. The new view of American hegemony reflected a shifting of categories within the old framework. Whereas in the immediate postwar period Moscow observers viewed the United States as the rising and dynamic capitalist challenger to dominant Britain, over time and especially in the years after Suez they began to cast the United States in the role of dominant power and the middle European powers individually or collectively as rising challengers. That is why America's great capabilities were seen in 1946 as destabilizing and in 1956 as stabilizing in the interimperialist context. In the former case, U.S. power *challenged* the existing distribution of markets and spheres of influence; in the latter case American power was already largely *defending* an established order. In the first case, the larger the power disparity in Washington's favor, the more acute the underlying contradictions and the more unstable the interimperialist order; in the second case, the greater the U.S. advantage, the more stable the order.

Most Soviet analysts did not trouble to ask how the United States had managed to make the transition from imperialist challenger to hegemon without generating much instability in the process. They were concerned with day-to-day and month-to-month policy analysis, and theoretical consistency was not their main concern. Part of the explanation, as Varga had already suggested, was increased socialist power, which created incentives for the imperialists to arrange their mutual affairs without giving revolutionary forces an opening. In retrospect, however, people stressed the temporarily weakened state

[153]

of the European powers and Japan after the war. American capital deviously exploited the deranged postwar correlation of forces to establish its dominance. The same extraordinary postwar circumstances that had permitted the Americans to limit Moscow's world role so successfully also facilitated their subordination of the other capitalist countries.

The new view appeared to clear some of the fog surrounding balancing mechanics. In particular, it reflected a secular decrease in expectations of shifts in alignment or alliance in the policy-relevant future. Since the essential conceptual framework remained unchanged, however, all it took was a new assessment of the intrawestern power balance to bring back the old expectations of shifts in alignment or at least in attitude. And, as we have seen, perceptions of power can change suddenly and in ways that seem capricious in retrospect. It did not take long for further events on the international scene to obscure the clarity Suez had seemed to impose on the Western power relationship, especially for people intellectually and professionally wedded to Lenin's *Imperialism*. After harping on American hegemony in the Western camp in 1956 and 1957, Soviet political figures and commentators returned to stressing the more comfortable fact that, as Khrushchev put it, "the United States is no longer as great a country in the international arena as it used to be."[30] "American capitalism," he told the Twenty-second Party Congress, "has passed its zenith."[31]

The contours of the post-Suez discussions of interimperialist contradictions consequently assumed familiar lines. Some international affairs experts continued to put forward classic arguments for "reaching out" to selected middle powers. Though they recognized that the United States was the clear hegemon of the Western bloc, they stressed America's dependence on particular assets possessed by its allies, such as Britain's network of military bases.[32] Others, more propagandistically inclined, continued the late-Stalin-era focus on the anti-Soviet unity of the West and the continued threat.[33] Academics

---

[30] *Pravda*, 21 October 1960, 2 (*CDSP* 12, no. 39: 5); A Manukian, "Oslableniie pozitsii SShA v kapitalisticheskoi ekonomike," *MEiMO*, 1961, no. 4; and Iosif Lemin, "'Evropeiskaia integratsiia': Nekotorye itogi i perspektivy," *MEiMO*, 1962, no. 5, 42–55.

[31] *XXII s"ezd Kommunisticheskoi Partii*, 160.

[32] See, e.g., I. Lemin, "Angliia posle suetskogo krizisa," *MEiMO*, 1957, no. 1, 21–36, and "K voprosu protivorechii mezhdu kapitalisticheskimi stranami," *MEiMO*, 1960, no. 8, 25–40.

[33] Most examples of this kind of thinking are found in the Foreign Ministry's journal *Mezhdunarodnaia Zhizn'*. See, e.g., M. L'vov and V. Grigor'ev, "Super-NATO?" 1959, no. 6, 50–57.

began their long fascination with European integration, just getting under way in this period, which held out the theoretical prospect of a "power center" capable of balancing against America.[34] Most, including the ever-empirical Varga, argued that even if such integration were possible, it was a long way off.[35]

For veteran diplomats and "realistic" policy analysts of Khrushchev's party-state bureaucracy, major alliance shifts were not the stuff of sober assessments. They could perhaps be contemplated by lamplight over vodka, when comrades spun tales of future diplomatic triumphs. For the time being, the question was how to influence the attitude of the key Western governments. And on that front, the assumption still prevailed that increased Soviet power aided any policy that sought to use contradictions among adversaries. Western governments could not be prodded into action by the appeal of argument and the quality of diplomacy alone. The question was where to aim power and policy, how to proceed tactically. Was it best to influence Washington directly, or to seek to alter its policy by pressuring the United States' allies to force a change?

The most common intellectual reaction to the apparent lessons of the 1953–1955 diplomacy and the Suez crisis was to focus on competition and cooperation with the United States. This is the major lesson Khrushchev appears to have drawn, but he was far from alone.[36] A focus on the United States by no means meant that Western contradictions played no role. It simply reflected the conclusion that direct courting of the middle powers was not the best way to decrease the Western alliance's cohesion on major policies, especially on the German issue. On the contrary, the best way to wean away the middle powers was to bypass them and focus on the United States. In this view, U.S.-Soviet amity would threaten the independent role the middle powers, and especially De Gaulle's France, envisaged for themselves. Fearing superpower "condominium"—that is, the superpowers' resolution of major issues at their expense—they saw no way

---

[34] On "power centers" see "Ob imperialisticheskoi 'integratsii' v Zapadnoi Evrope," *MEiMO*, 1962, no. 9 (suppl.), 9. For a discussion by scholars representing numerous positions on European integration, see "Obshchii rynok i ego rol' v ekonomike i politike sovremennogo imperializma," *MEiMO*, 1959, no. 7, 108–16; no. 8, 104–17; no. 9, 86–106; no. 10, 73–83.

[35] See E. S. Varga in "Obshchii rynok i ego rol'," *MEiMO*, 1959, no. 7, 110–12; Varga, "Kapitalizm dvadtsatogo veka," *MEiMO*, 1960, no. 1, 34–59, esp. 50–51; and "Teoreticheskie problemy ekonomiki 'Obshchego rynka,'" in *Ocherki po problemam politekonomii kapitalizma* (Moscow: Izdatel'stvo Politicheskoi Literatury, 1964), 308–28, esp. 309–12.

[36] Richter, "Action and Reaction," chap. 4.

to escape save by activating their Russian policy and, in effect, trumping U.S.-Soviet détente. Bilateral focus on Washington might thus actually decrease NATO's cohesion.[37]

Soviet observers remained Leninist enough to believe that the coercive and zero-sum content of intrawestern relations was large. Consequently, they still adhered to the view that the Western alliance was mainly a bandwagon on which the middle powers scrambled to join a self-interested and predatory America. Moscow officials were not about to buy arguments about disinterested American capitalism providing its allies with "public goods." Indeed, most were not willing to go as far as Varga had gone in 1948 in recognizing the relative autonomy of the bourgeois state. The middle powers were bandwagoning with the United States. The latter used every means to exert its influence over them. U.S. prestige was the glue that held the Western alliance together. If Washington's aura of hegemony could be weakened, perhaps these powers' deference to the United States would be decreased. America was powerful, and the middle powers deferred to it. If Russia were perceived to be equally powerful, would they not show it similar respect?

Post- 1956 Soviet diplomacy concentrated on the prestige struggle with America. For Khrushchev, the United States' relative decline in relation to its allies was merely part of his overall argument that America's influence far exceeded its real capabilities. He spoke often about U.S. economic decline and imperialist contradictions, but these were tactical forays meant to supplement the main line on the need for a revision of global prestige in Moscow's favor. Any datum that would support Khrushchev's argument that America's world role exceeded its real power was good enough for him. The essence of his approach was competition with the United States. Even if Khrushchev understood Varga's contention that increased Soviet power served to unite the opposition, he apparently believed that the diplomatic prizes he could win by convincing the world of the Soviet Union's increased strength outweighed any near-term cost in in-

[37]For analyses along these lines and approving responses from above, see Soviet Ambassador to France S. Vinogradov to Foreign Minister Gromyko, "O vneshnepoliticheskom kurse Frantsii," 20 August 1959; Zorin to Vinogradov, 7 September 1959; Vinogradov to Gromyko, "K predstoiashemu visitu N. S. Khrushcheva vo Frantsiiu"; Zorin to Vinogradov, 14 December 1959, all in AVP 136/49/2/279; and Vinogradov to Gromyko, "Doklad: Politicheskoe polozhenie vo Frantsii i rabota posol'stva," 8 January 1959, AVP 136/49/8/280. For earlier similar suggestions relating to Britain, with unfavorable responses from above, see Slavin to Molotov, 26 March 1955; Malik to Molotov, 28 May 1955; and Gromyko, Kuznetsov, and Zorin to Molotov, 2 June 1959, all in AVP 69/42/27/174.

creased Western unity. The prospect was not to be excluded, however, that after the Soviets had achieved a meeting of the minds with the U.S. leadership on the basis of a revised prestige hierarchy, the opposing coalition of states would lose much of its coherence.

ELEMENTS OF POWER AND PRESTIGE: MISSILE PRIMACY

If the extent of a state's influence over the international system is determined in the final analysis by its warmaking power, then two great powers in a condition of mutual deterrence ought to enjoy equal influence. If one takes seriously the proposition that military power is the source of a state's prestige, then all that was standing in the way of a larger political role for the Soviet Union in the world after World War II was America's monopoly on atomic weapons. In most other categories of military power, the Soviet Union was superior. The task for Moscow, then, was merely to catch up to the United States in nuclear weapons. If the Soviets could show that a new military relationship obtained in which the United States was no longer invulnerable to Soviet power, a new political relationship would surely follow. This was the argument Nikita Khrushchev propounded between 1957 and 1962. To make it more compelling, he tried to deceive the West about the extent of the Soviet Union's nuclear capabilities.

In Khrushchev's publicly expressed view, nuclear missiles were the primary elements of a state's military power; they reduced the importance of other categories of military capabilities; they were the main symbol of a state's technical prowess; they were so frightening that they would never actually be used; but, precisely because they were so frightening, they were useful for intimidating people and achieving relatively inexpensive diplomatic successes. In his speeches, in his writings, in his conversations with journalists, in his memoirs, in every forum both during his career and after it, Khrushchev expressed the opinion, as he put it to the January 1960 plenum, that "in our time a country's defense capacity is determined not by the number of soldiers it has under arms, the number of men in uniform. Aside from the general political and economic factors, . . . a country's defense capacity depends to a decisive extent on the firepower and means of delivery it has."[38] But on numerous occasions Khrushchev

---

[38] *Pravda*, 15 January 1960 (*CDSP* 12, no. 2: 10). See Nikita Khrushchev, *Khrushchev Remembers*, trans. and ed. Strobe Talbott (New York: Bantam, 1970), 260, 447, 519, 520,

opined that these weapons were so frightening they would never be used.[39]

While he may have believed they would never be used in war, Khrushchev's behavior indicates a belief that nuclear weapons did have a use. In a series of crises from 1956 to 1962 he tested the potentialities of the new weapons for redefining the Soviet-American relationship. Time after time he stressed the Soviets' capacity to destroy various Western countries with nuclear weapons. During the Suez crisis in 1956 he wrote to Eisenhower suggesting a joint undertaking against France and Britain, and then to the leaders of those two countries implying that they were reckless to attack Egypt when the Soviet Union had the power to annihilate them.[40] After *Sputnik* in 1957, Khrushchev seems to have concluded that now the USSR's perceived missile capability could be similarly useful against the United States itself. He initiated the missile deception, making extravagant claims about Soviet forces and capabilities.[41] During the Taiwan Straits crisis in 1958 he threatened to use nuclear weapons to support China if the United States attacked. He began the Berlin crisis in the same year, and throughout the three years of its duration he made repeated threats to various Americans. In June 1959 he told Averell Harriman:

> If you continue to operate from a position of strength, then you must decide for yourselves. We too are strong, and we will decide for ourselves. . . . Your generals talk of maintaining your position in Berlin with force. That is bluff. If you send in tanks, they will burn and make no mistake about it. If you want war, you can have it, and remember it will be your war. Our rockets will fly automatically.

Significantly, Khrushchev concluded: "We developed the hydrogen bomb before the United States. We have an intercontinental bomb while you have not. *Perhaps this is the crucial symbol of our position.* . . . Under these circumstances, it [is] unwise to threaten the Soviet Union."[42]

547, 567, 568; *The Last Testament*, trans. and ed. Strobe Talbott (Boston: Little, Brown, 1974), 20–21, 24, 28, 31, 35, 43, 53, 411, 498, 500 and esp. 535–37; and *Khrushchev Remembers: The Glasnost Tapes*, trans. and ed. Jerrold L. Shecter, with Vyacheslav V. Luchkov (Boston: Little, Brown, 1990), 148, 187, 192.

[39] Mohamed Heikal, *The Sphinx and the Commissar* (New York: Harper & Row, 1978), 129.

[40] Charles E. Bohlen, *Witness to History, 1929–1969* (New York: Norton, 1973), 432–33.

[41] The best source on Khrushchev's missile deception is Horelick and Rush, *Strategic Power*.

[42] DOS report, 23 June 1959, "Khrushchev Interview with Governor Harriman," *DDRS*, 1981, 223A; emphasis added.

In addition to such specific threats in crises, Soviet diplomacy in this period made more broad-based appeals for "equality" or "parity" with the United States in world affairs. Beginning in 1957, in the United Nations and other international organizations the Soviets demanded "parity"; that is, equal representation with the Western bloc. If this goal proved impossible to achieve, Soviet diplomats fell back to a request for equal representation for the Soviet bloc and the non-aligned states combined. In such forums, of course, the Soviets did not feel compelled to spell out precisely on what basis they made the claim of parity. When Khrushchev addressed the West or his own people on the topic of parity, he cited most frequently the military power of the Soviet state—apparently out of belief in the fungibility of military power. In 1961, for example, he told graduates of the Soviet military academies:

> Today it is acknowledged in the West that the forces of the Soviet Union and the other socialist countries are not inferior to the forces of the Western powers. However, the proper conclusions are not drawn from this fact: *where there are equal forces there must also be equal rights and opportunities.* Yet our partners, acknowledging that the correlation of forces has not shifted in their favor, nevertheless want to dominate in international agencies and impose their will there.[43]

Khrushchev's diplomacy and a large proportion of his public assertions about the correlation of forces were thus based in large part on an effort to capitalize on the partly real and partly imaginary shift in the strategic nuclear correlation. Khrushchev's optimistic general line coincided with the Soviets' brief superiority in missile technology and the ensuing missile deception. When the ruse was exposed, the line was revised. In other words, all of the other factors that Soviets included in the "correlation of forces" were not enough to sustain the optimistic general line once the missile deception collapsed.

At first blush, Khrushchev's "absolutization" of ballistic missiles may indeed seem like the "harebrained scheming" of which he was accused. After all, Stalin did have some good arguments. Even if declaratory military doctrine is thought of purely in terms of a rhetorical-political struggle with the West, a focus on ballistic missiles could appear unwise. The Soviet Union still possessed the geographical advantage that Stalinist doctrine had cited; it still had the centralized

---

[43] *Pravda*, 9 July 1961, quoted in Hannes Adomeit, *Soviet Risk-Taking and Crisis Behavior* (London: George Allen & Unwin, 1982), 251–52; emphasis added.

mobilization capacity, and the West still lacked a large land army. Most importantly, Khrushchev knew well that the real balance of nuclear power decisively favored the United States.

Nevertheless, the missile had a lot to recommend it as a device for increasing Soviet prestige. For one thing, it fitted Khrushchev's apparent perceived need to constrain the growth of defense spending, which would have been much larger in the case of a simultaneous nuclear/conventional modernization. Further, in spite of the deception, for several years the Soviets were ahead in this area. And focus on the missile undercut the importance of U.S. air bases around the USSR. Instead of buttresses against the Soviet land forces, these bases could now be portrayed as targets for Soviet missiles. Khrushchev's focus on missiles also undercut U.S. naval advantages. And the assumption that any war would inevitably be all-out and nuclear reduced the importance of overall Western economic predominance. Finally, the Soviet leaders learned from their experience under Stalin that conventional forces did not translate into world power. They may well have drawn the lesson that America now owed its central role to its superiority in nuclear technology, and thus sought to exploit the new relationship of forces in that area. If winning a war were really the aim, Khrushchev's doctrines might indeed have been reckless; but if the goal was greater prestige, they had merit, particularly since nuclear weapons and missiles were *new.* They were untested in both war and politics, so their effect would be governed by perceptions, which Khrushchev doubtless considered himself adept at manipulating.

It would be a mistake to see the Soviets' concentration on nuclear weapons in this period solely as a domestic and foreign policy tactic or as Khrushchev's personal doing. For even as Khrushchev was rattling missiles on the world stage, his defense establishment was formulating a new nuclear-centered military doctrine to replace Stalin's old "five permanently operative factors." And though military men never would have gone so far as Khrushchev did in discounting nonnuclear branches of the armed forces, their new military doctrine, which they discussed and worked out over the five years after 1955, assigned the central place in modern war to nuclear missiles. The Strategic Rocket Forces became a separate and prestigious service branch. Soviet military strategy became, essentially, a blueprint for nuclear-missile war. Though the Soviet Union did not yet possess the forces required for such a strategy, the new doctrine was meant to point the way for future procurement. It substantially complemented what Khrushchev and other civilian leaders were saying about the nature of power in the nuclear age.[44]

Although based in the main on military power and nuclear weaponry, Khrushchev's effort to increase Soviet prestige would be incomprehensible today without consideration of perceptions and expectations in regard to other elements of power. Especially in the years between 1957 and 1960, Khrushchev made his big push for diplomatic parity with the United States as the representative of a power that most observers, East and West, believed was rapidly on the rise. Khrushchev's apparent confidence that he could convince his diplomatic interlocutors of his country's newfound world status cannot be seen simply as a function of his personality, his domestic political needs, or a foreign policy ploy. In the middle of political elites round the world, the momentum was with Moscow in a series of crucial areas.

On the economic front, Soviets were convinced that their system would outperform capitalism, and thus close the gap with the West relatively quickly. Though they jettisoned Bolshevik dogma about the imminent collapse of imperialism and recognized that capitalism was essentially a stable socioeconomic formation for the foreseeable future, Soviets in the 1950s believed that their economy was poised to do what the Japanese and German economies actually did: catch up to the United States by the 1980s.[45] Privately, many economists were naturally skeptical of Khrushchev's most grandiose claims, and some were aware that Soviet economic statistics were being cooked with abandon, but many highly placed experts genuinely shared the leader's optimism. The Institute of World Economy and International Relations, whose main task was to analyze the economic competition between the two systems, was staffed at its highest levels with Comintern veterans infused with a basic faith in socialism's economic superiority. Its director, Anushavan Arzumanian, privately expressed the conviction in the late 1950s that Western Europe would achieve socialism within fifteen years. As one veteran of the era expressed it,

[44] Good sources on Soviet military doctrine in this period are Lt. Col. V. Kozlov, "The Development of Marxist-Leninist Teaching on War and the Army (A Survey of the Literature)," *Voennaia Mysl'*, 1968, no. 4 (FBIS, *Foreign Press Digest*, 27 May 1969, 85–95); Raymond L. Garthoff, *Soviet Strategy in the Nuclear Age* (New York: Praeger, 1962); Dinerstein, *War and the Soviet Union;* David Holloway, *The Soviet Union and the Arms Race,* (New Haven: Yale University Press, 1984), esp. 34–42.

[45] An editorial in the party's theoretical journal explicitly rejected the old "crisis" view in 1955: *Kommunist*, 1955, no. 14 (September) (*CDSP* 7, no. 38: 5). Both Khrushchev and Mikoyan repeated the rejection at the Twentieth Congress: *XX s"ezd Kommunisticheskoi Partii*, 15, 323.

the institute not only did not oppose Khrushchev's optimism, it actively contributed to it.[46]

The rehabilitated Varga noted in 1956 that socialism's growth rate was "two to three times" that of capitalism: "Now one can calculate with some accuracy when the USSR will overtake the leading capitalist countries economically. The correlation of forces of the two camps . . . is changing accordingly."[47] Soviet analysts admitted that Soviet output in 1958 was half the U.S. figure; that U.S. per capita output was over 2.5 times the Soviet; U.S. labor productivity over twice the Soviet; and so forth. But by extrapolating U.S. growth rates (averaging somewhere between 1.6 and 2.2 percent) and past Soviet growth rates (over 10 percent by their perhaps fanciful figures), they predicted that it would take ten years to reach the current U.S. level of production, twelve to thirteen years to surpass the United States in total production, and something like fifteen years to pass the American level of per capita production.[48] Further, the Soviet analysts explicitly rejected the "worm-eaten" argument that as levels of development rise, growth rates inevitably slow; that, they asserted, was true only of capitalism.[49] The Khrushchev leadership included these economic projections in major speeches and in the party's program.

Soviet projections were just as rosy for the competition over the Third World. Stalin and Zhdanov had maintained that countries recently freed from colonial rule were "objectively" part of the imperialist camp, unless a communist party won power. In his doctrinal revisions at the Twentieth Party Congress, Khrushchev shifted the line of demarcation to group the newly independent countries and the socialist camp in one "vast zone of peace, including the peace-loving states, both socialist and nonsocialist, of Europe and Asia." Thus, he proclaimed jubilantly, the zone of peace embraced "the majority of the population of the planet."[50] The new formulation clearly reflected optimism about the direction the countries of the Third

[46] Arbatov, *Zatianuvsheesia vyzdorovlenie*, 63–75; Burlatskii, *Vozhdia i sovetniki*, 167–68. On cooking statistics for the leadership, see Aksiutin and Volobuev, *XX s"ezd KPSS*, 130–32.

[47] "On the Economics of Postwar Capitalism," *Kommunist*, 1956, no. 4 (March), 13–32 (*CDSP* 8, no. 21: 3).

[48] A. Arzumanian, "Competition of the Two World Systems," *Pravda*, 9 July 1958 (*CDSP* 10, no. 27: 3–5). The Soviets were just as optimistic about the other socialist countries as they were about their own. D. Mel'nikov, "Novaia faza v otnosheniiakh mezhdu gosudartstvami," *MEiMO*, 1960, no. 5 (May), 22, had Czechoslovakia passing the United States in per capita production in 1965 and North Korea soon passing Japan!

[49] S. Strumilin, "Thoughts on the 7-Year Plan," *Literaturnaia Gazeta*, 2 December 1958, 1–2 (*CDSP* 10, no. 52: 3–4).

[50] *XX s"ezd Kommunisticheskoi Partii*, 22.

World would take. It also provided justification in Soviet ideological terms for a "forward" policy of competing with the West in these countries; such a policy is senseless if economic "laws" bind all former colonies to their former metropoles until they have undergone violent revolution. To a certain extent, then, the revision may be seen as flowing from a more confident view of Soviet capabilities.

After this doctrinal change, Soviet scholars began working through various analytical and classification schemes to group Third World countries.[51] The upshot of their analyses was a consensus, based partly on Moscow's heady early experience with Nasser's Egypt, that the latent antiwestern sentiment of much of the Third World would be expressed practically as pro-socialism and pro-Sovietism. As Khrushchev put it at the Twenty-second Party Congress: "In the present epoch almost any country, regardless of the level of development, can embark upon the path that leads to socialism."[52] He later asserted that all the countries of the Third World would eventually become socialist, "some sooner, some later"; that they already played "a progressive role in world affairs"; and that their "international role" as well as their overall number would "continue to grow."[53]

This concept of a steady process of decolonization, independence, socialist orientation, then socialism, with all its optimistic implications, was spelled out in an article in *Kommunist*, "The World 20 Years from Now," by the economist (and former Menshevik) Stanislav Strumilin. Strumilin extrapolated the postwar growth of socialism, prudently discounting the growth rate to allow for particularly favorable postwar conditions. His calculations yielded the forecast that 54 percent of the world's population would be socialist and only 16 percent imperialist by 1980. That increase was supposed to be accounted for almost exclusively by the Third World.[54]

Soviet optimism on the economic competition and the struggle for the Third World concerned trends, not current relationships. The new Khrushchevian outlook was much more expansive and inclusive than the narrow Stalinist view. It allowed a globe-girdling search for influence and allies. It contributed to the feeling that the Soviet Union was a rising power. But expectations about trends could not function as part of an argument for an *immediate* revision of the Soviet Union's

---

[51] For a fuller discussion of these developments, see Jerry Hough, *The Struggle for the Third World* (Washington, D.C.: Brookings Institution, 1986).

[52] *XXII s"ezd Kommunisticheskoi Partii*, 228.

[53] *Pravda*, 22 December 1963, 1–2 (*CDSP* 15, no. 51: 12, 16).

[54] S. Strumilin, "Mir cherez 20 let," *Kommunist*, 1961, no. 13 (September), 27 (*CDSP* 13, no. 38: 3–7).

diplomatic status vis-à-vis the United States, since Moscow was still so far behind in all nonmilitary indices, and since Washington seemed to respect military might most of all. Stalin's ideology in his latter years led to the conclusion that vast increases in Soviet influence would take place only in the context of major war and revolution. Khrushchev demilitarized expectations of future gains. But he did not demilitarize his actual diplomacy, which relied as much as ever on military power. Stalin tried to achieve political benefit from his conventional superiority. Khrushchev tried to do the same with his missiles.

With hindsight, it is easy to question the soundness of a policy of offensive détente based on the nuclear balance. At the time, however, there was no way the situation could be so clear. If war is unlikely, power is what people think it is. If Khrushchev could influence his adversaries' perceptions of power, he could win diplomatic victories on the cheap. Why spend such huge sums on military capabilities that might not be necessary? Was it harebrained to try to see what could be done with existing forces under existing circumstances?

When Khrushchev met John F. Kennedy in Vienna in June 1961, his prestige policy had been in place for four years, and it would have been hard to argue against the contention that it had so far met with success. Careful manipulation of threats and rewards in the Suez, Syria-Turkey, and Lebanon-Jordan crises had vastly increased the Soviets' sway in the Middle East. National liberation movements were bringing Moscow influence in Asia and Africa. Even in Latin America, Soviet policy was nudging U.S. interests by offers of aid to Bolivia and a building relationship with Castro's Cuba. After success elsewhere, Khrushchev transferred the strategy to Europe, issuing the first ultimatum on Berlin in late 1958. Although the demand for a revision in the status of West Berlin did not result in a substantial change in the Western position, it led to a prestigious summit at Camp David with Eisenhower in September 1959, with all the trappings of equality. The Eisenhower/Dulles team seemed ready to negotiate, contradictions among the Western powers appeared on the rise, and intelligence reports informed Moscow of the assessment common in Washington that the military position in Berlin was untenable.

Khrushchev arrived in Vienna to meet a man whose major presidential campaign theme was that a dangerous adverse shift in the balance of power had occurred under the Republican administration. Kennedy's campaign rhetoric had done more to advertise Khrushchev's claims to Western audiences than any amount of Soviet propaganda. All Khrushchev had to do now was translate the Americans' admission that the distribution of power had shifted in favor of the Soviet Union into some tangible recognition of Moscow's new status. The Soviet leader never defined exactly what he meant by superpower "equality" and "equal rights," and one can only speculate what action on the part of the United States would have met his requirements, to what extent parity was symbolic and to what extent it involved substantive concessions from the West. Available evidence suggests that Khrushchev may have been happy to get what Brezhnev got over a decade later: the West's recognition of the GDR and the whole postwar settlement.

Khrushchev's efforts to manipulate the metaphor of power, like Stalin's before him, were doubtless connected to concrete diplomatic and strategic objectives. The exodus of East Germans westward through Berlin was a threat to the German Democratic Republic. American talk of "rollback," coupled with talk of West Germany's acquisition of nuclear weapons, must have been frightening. A revision of Berlin's status, cutting off the exodus and symbolizing the West's acceptance of the Soviet sphere, would have disarmed skeptics in Moscow and Beijing. But the time, the place, and the immediate issues could easily have been different while the argument remained the same: The distribution of power has shifted, and the distribution of influence must follow suit.

Khrushchev naturally was aware of the risks he was running. He had to have known that Eisenhower and Kennedy had enough information to discount his most extreme boasts about Soviet power. Khrushchev and the General Staff eventually decided not to embark upon a full deployment of their first-generation intercontinental ballistic missile, the SS-6, whose success had sparked the onset of optimism in 1957, but to await a more capable follow-on. Though it succeeded in boosting the sputniks, the SS-6 was apparently too unreliable to function as a military booster. Major ICBM deployments had to await the follow-on missile. Thus, by 1960, Khrushchev was faced with a deteriorating strategic balance as U.S. deployments got under way. The situation was considerably worsened in the fall of 1961, when the Kennedy administration made public its reassessment of the "missile gap." On the basis of U-2 overflights and other sources of information, the new administration concluded that earlier estimates of a portending missile gap had been incorrect, that the USSR possessed only a "handful" of ICBMs, and that the United States was in a position of distinct strategic superiority.[55] U.S. policy had three

[55] See Horelick and Rush, *Strategic Power*, 88–90, on the U.S. reassessment.

components: first, the administration, in a series of speeches in the fall of 1961, publicized its finding; second, it began a doctrinal revision to account for the Soviets' eventual development of a significant ICBM capability—the doctrine of flexible response; and third, it embarked on a major military buildup.

The denouement of Khrushchev's strategy of redefining the balance of influence was the Cuban missile crisis. The deployment of missiles in Cuba now appears as a last-ditch effort to achieve what Khrushchev had been seeking all along: perceived parity with the United States. In the words of Fedor Burlatskii, one of Khrushchev's speech-writers, its main purpose was to "demonstrate Soviet might and create the conditions for political if not military parity" with the United States, which, in turn would "establish the possibility for achieving a compromise based on equal rights."[56] The former Central Committee official Georgii Shakhnazarov told a conference on the crisis: "The crisis between the United States and the Soviet Union on parity was inevitable . . . because it dealt with the correlation of forces, which was basic to superpower relations. It was very appropriate that it happened at this time and place, because at that time in the Soviet Union there was an opinion that we were strong enough to assert parity. It was a mistake, but our leadership believed it was so."[57]

Asserting parity was precisely what Khrushchev was seeking to do in the half-decade from 1957 to 1962, when the most optimistic characterizations of the correlation of forces dominated the Soviet scene. In the midst of international crises, Khrushchev and other Soviet spokesmen would make veiled nuclear threats. In more general contexts, they would base their assertions on deterrence-like arguments. Except for the initial period, when Khrushchev claimed that socialism would prevail in a nuclear war, and the brief period of proclaimed superiority, Khrushchev and others argued that mutual deterrence equalized the forces of the two sides, and thus demanded political parity. The "nuclear revolution," in other words, was supposed to deliver what World War II had left undone.

AMERICAN PERSPECTIVES

For decision makers in the United States, the Soviets' power was always increasing but it was never equal to the Americans'. The Sovi-

---

[56] Burlatskii, *Vozhdia i sovetniki*, 223–24.
[57] In *On the Brink: Americans and Soviets Reflect on the Cuban Missile Crisis*, ed. James G. Blight and David A. Welch (New York: Hill & Wang, 1989), 258.

ets never wanted a war now, but they were always more likely to want one in the future. The bipolar arrangement was inherently fragile and subject to future destabilization, but for now it was stable. NATO was always subject to disintegration, though for the time being it somehow held together. When we analyze American perspectives on the balance of power in the 1950s, as in other times, it is vital to maintain the distinction between expectations of future *trends* and perceptions of existing *relationships*. Apprehensions and expectations about future trends in the distribution of power are by nature impossible to subject to any empirical test. Or, to put it more accurately, expectations influence policy before they can be tested. And statesmen are no more inclined than scholars to verify the accuracy of their past prognostications.

Americans could hardly help but notice Khrushchev's loudly proclaimed optimism about the Soviet Union's power position. Indeed, on the surface they appeared to agree with much of what he and the Soviet propaganda machine were saying. Khrushchev would hardly have disagreed with the way Secretary of State Dulles described the situation in a private letter to Eisenhower in 1957:

> There is deterioration of the relative force equation between the Soviet Union and ourselves due to their accumulation of nuclear material and technical knowledge, particularly in the missiles field. This has certain repercussions, but I do not see how that kind of "deterioration" can be prevented. The West no longer possesses, and perhaps never again will possess, the monopoly of power which made it predominant in the world for so many centuries.[58]

The perceived rise in Soviet power brought visions of crumbling alliances, Third World bandwagoning with Moscow, Soviet technological and military superiority, massively increased diplomatic prestige for the Kremlin, and disorderly American withdrawals from positions so tenuously held since the conclusion of the war. Such was the perennial stuff of Washington nightmares, lurid scenes that found their way into the public prints as well as into confidential communications of American leaders, and, naturally, into Moscow-bound dispatches. These expressions of anxiety, however genuine, may well have obscured a more earthy reality: that at no time during the administration of Eisenhower or Kennedy did anyone doubt the United States' ultimate nuclear, overall technical, and economic supe-

---

[58] 17 October 1957, DDEL/JFD, White House Memoranda ser., box 5.

riority, and never did anyone conceive of the USSR as broadly equal in power to the United States. However anxious they were about the future, Americans based their policy on a robust view of their overall position vis-à-vis the Soviets. It is difficult in retrospect, and certainly would have been formidably so at the time, to distinguish fears of the future from assessments about the current state of things. This difficulty was increased by the fact that apprehensions figured more prominently in public statements than in classified assessments.

Evidence of increased Soviet self-confidence became manifest just as the U.S. intelligence community was expressing heightened concern about Soviet nuclear capabilities. As early as the summer of 1953, intelligence estimates were concluding that the United States "is losing, if it has not already lost, its long-standing invulnerability to crippling attack."[59] By 1956, as American fears about a "bomber gap" subsided, the "missile gap" intelligence was beginning to roll in.[60] The "Basic National Security Policy" statement of that year agreed with Khrushchev that the Soviets were "challeng[ing] the supremacy of western technology. . . . [They] have made remarkable technological progress in the last ten years, and are now expanding their scientific and technological resources more rapidly than the United States."[61] The document implicitly acknowledged the validity of Khrushchev's claim that an existential deterrence situation prevailed. Although the United States could still inflict a "decisive strike" against the USSR, by 1958 the Soviets would be able to respond with a "crippling blow." And the main concern was a disarming Soviet first strike, which, though difficult to coordinate, would multiply the effectiveness of the USSR's limited forces.[62] Further, by 1960 the Soviets would have a "significant" ICBM capability. Already somewhere between 20 and 30 million Americans would die in a Soviet retaliatory strike.[63] Thus the Soviet ICBM tests and sputnik launches in 1957, as well as the alarmist Gaither Committee report of late that year, merely

[59]"Probable Long-Term Development of Soviet Bloc and Western Power Positions," 8 July 1953, "Special Estimate," *FRUS*, 1952–1954, 8:1200. See also NSC 5440, 13 December 1954, *DDRS*, 1977/302G.

[60]See Lawrence Freedman, *U.S. Intelligence and the Soviet Strategic Threat*, 2d ed. (Princeton: Princeton University Press, 1986), 69–80.

[61]NSC 5602, 18 February 1956, *DDRS*, 1977/303A.

[62]Jack H. Nunn, *The Soviet First-Strike Threat* (New York: Praeger, 1982), 105–6.

[63]Richard K. Betts, *Nuclear Blackmail and Nuclear Balance* (Washington, D.C.: Brookings Institution, 1987), 153–54.

confirmed previous U.S. estimates, although they served to galvanize concern.[64]

Concern about Soviet bomber and missile development also prevailed outside the secretive corridors of the intelligence establishment. Influential legislators, notably Senators Stuart Symington and Lyndon Johnson, became increasingly alarmed about Soviet advances.[65] In reaction to *Sputnik,* Johnson organized hearings on U.S. missile readiness before the Armed Services Committee's Investigative Subcommittee on Preparedness. Influential industrialists and advisers to Eisenhower wrote the president to express their worries.[66] Democrats, loath to forget the damage caused by the "loss" of China, began early on to see a potential campaign issue in the perceived deterioration in the United States' position during the Republicans' watch. Each passing year saw mounting pressure on Eisenhower from within and outside of his own party to "do something" about the Russian challenge. The issue of "catching up" to the Russians and "regaining leadership" increasingly dogged the president, and only his great prestige on military issues and immense popularity permitted him to stem the tide of opinion in favor of large increases in defense and other government spending.[67]

Eisenhower's own perspective emerges clearly from the documents of his White House tenure. He discounted the likelihood of nuclear war because of its great destructiveness, yet maintained a robust view of deterrence because of the United States' clearly perceived superiority in retaliatory capabilities.[68] The president did not take seriously the worries over a potential Soviet surprise first strike, according to Jack Nunn, "not so much on political and risk grounds, but because of his belief that Soviet forces were no more prepared for war than U.S. forces."[69] Eisenhower's comparatively sanguine outlook resulted from faith in what John Lewis Gaddis calls his "asymmetrical strat-

---

[64] See Freedman, *U.S. Intelligence,* 69–70.

[65] John Prados, *The Soviet Estimate: U.S. Intelligence and Soviet Strategic Forces* (Princeton: Princeton University Press, 1982), 63–66.

[66] See, e.g., National Planning Association to the President, 8 and 15 October 1956, DDEL/JFD, White House Memoranda ser., box 5; and Richard S. Morse, president of National Research Corp., to the President, 1 November 1956, *DDRS,* 1976/256D.

[67] See Stephen E. Ambrose, *Eisenhower,* vol. 2, *The President* (New York: Simon & Shuster, 1984), esp. 566–79.

[68] For evidence, see ibid.; Betts, *Nuclear Blackmail,* 155; and David Allen Rosenberg, "The Origins of Overkill: Nuclear Weapons and American Strategy, 1945–1960," *International Security* 7 (Spring 1983): 28–44.

[69] Nunn, *Soviet First-Strike Threat,* 137.

egy," in which superior overall American retaliatory capacity was supposed to deter all levels of Soviet aggression.[70] The strategy, in Richard Betts's words, "bowed to the inevitability of growing U.S. vulnerability, but still took comfort from [the] persistence of greater Soviet vulnerability."[71] For the time being, he was impervious to Khrushchev's missile threats.[72]

In addition, Eisenhower maintained a healthy skepticism of intelligence projections, and both the bomber and missile gaps were *projected*, not existing gaps. All the alarmism of the period concerned trends, not existing force relationships, and thus diplomacy could still be based on the old assumption of superior nuclear capability. Eisenhower asserted repeatedly that the Russians understood the meaning of U.S. nuclear power, whatever they might say publicly. "They're not ready for war and they know it. They also know that if they go to war, they're going to end up losing everything they have."[73] On this issue the president's thinking coincided with that of his own national security bureaucracy, which also discounted any Soviet interest in war in the near term.[74]

But the set of concerns about the psychological "will to resist" of allied political elites which had surrounded the Marshall Plan and NATO decisions under Truman came back to haunt the Eisenhower team as Soviet nuclear capabilities surged forward. Dulles spelled out the worry in a "personal and private" letter to Eisenhower in September 1953, with which the president expressed general agreement.[75] The Soviets' development of atomic and nuclear "guided missiles," Dulles argued, called the whole NATO concept into question by undercutting U.S. atomic supremacy. Allied leaderships feared that the United States would stand aside if their territories came under attack, and Americans fretted that Europe would be reluctant to take risks if only U.S. security were threatened. Politically, Soviet nuclear power coupled with the already evident "peace offensive" could

[70] John Lewis Gaddis, *Strategies of Containment* (New York: Oxford University Press, 1982), 186–87. As Eisenhower put it in a memo to Dulles, "We must be constantly ready to inflict greater loss on the enemy than he could reasonably hope to inflict on us": 8 September 1953, DDEL/JFD, White House Memoranda ser., box 1.

[71] Betts, *Nuclear Blackmail*, 84.

[72] Ambrose, *Eisenhower*, 2:535.

[73] Diary entry by president's press secretary (James Hagerty), 8 February 1955, *FRUS*, 1955–1957, 24:24. See also Eisenhower to Churchill, 10 February 1955, DDEL, Dulles/Herter ser. (Whitman files), box 3, folder 16.

[74] See, e.g, comments by DOS Russian Desk officers, 3 March 1954, DDEL/JFD, White House Memoranda ser. box 1.

[75] Dulles to Eisenhower, 6 September 1953, and Eisenhower to Dulles, 8 September 1953, both in ibid.

prove a combination too tempting for Western Europe and Japan to resist. Six years later, under the pressure of Khrushchev's Berlin ultimatum, Dulles would express the same concerns even more stridently.[76] Official assessments by the intelligence agencies were permeated by the same worries.[77]

These fears produced two contradictory impulses. Sensing the vulnerability of the alliance, Americans groped for ways toward a negotiated easing of tension. In 1953, for example, Eisenhower concurred with Dulles's proposal for mutual withdrawals of Red Army and U.S. forces abroad. As Marc Trachtenberg documents, the two men similarly searched for some negotiated way out of the Berlin crisis six years later.[78] But the same sense of vulnerability led the Republicans, as it had their Democratic predecessors, to an almost obsessive concern with their prestige, or, as it came to be known in deterrence-theory parlance, their "credibility." Any American move that could be interpreted as a lack of resolve could feed the very fears among the allies Washington hoped to assuage. So any proposal to the Soviets had to be such as to leave no doubt about the United States' resolve to defend key interests. Hence the need to negotiate "from strength" and the formulation of proposals Moscow had a hard time accepting.[79]

Now we come to the nub of the issue, for Washington was usually confident enough in its power position at any given time not to give much away. Referring to the mutual withdrawal plan, for example, Dulles's 1953 memorandum asserts that "the present is a propitious time for such a move . . . because we will be speaking from strength rather than weakness." It is important to take note of *both* sides of the American reaction to rising Soviet power, for it is not inconceivable that Americans' fears of bandwagoning fed the Soviets' belief in the utility of military power for political gain. And the Soviets' expectation that increased power coupled with a "peace offensive" in

[76] See the document of 26 January 1959 cited by Marc Trachtenberg in *History and Strategy* (Princeton: Princeton University Press, 1991), 214. The discussion in this section benefited immensely from Trachtenberg's analysis and extensive archival research.

[77] See, e.g., National Intelligence Estimate (NIE), 7 June 1954, "Soviet Capabilities and Main Lines of Policy through Mid-1959," *FRUS*, 1952–1954, 8:1235–38, and Bohlen's objections, 1246–48. The Soviets' *Sputnik* and ICBM tests in 1957 accelerated concerns. See memorandum from Deputy Director of Intelligence and Research to Dulles, 14 November 1957, *FRUS*, 1955–1957, 24:183–84, and Ambassador Thompson's cable of 16 November 1957, 185–86; Office of Research and Intelligence, "World Opinion and the Soviet Satellite," 17 October 1957, *DDRS*, 1990/2388.

[78] Trachtenberg, *History and Strategy*, chap. 5.

[79] Trachtenberg demonstrates this brilliantly in the case of the Berlin crisis, but he accords less importance to the prestige factor than I do (ibid.).

Western Europe could prod the United States into concrete negotiations on matters of substance are more easily explicable if American reactions are taken into consideration.

Nuclear power was not the only area in which Washington saw significant Soviet advances. Americans were deeply impressed by what they thought was spectacular Soviet economic development. Intelligence assessments acknowledged that Soviet GNP was one-half the American, but noted that the Soviet economy was growing "faster than [that of] the U.S. or any other Western country."[80] Both the intelligence agencies and many individual observers, however, were remarkably sanguine about the long-term prospects. Most assumed that Soviet rates of growth would decline as the country industrialized further. The Soviet political and economic system, it was commonly thought, was unsuited to intensive economic growth.[81] More salient to Americans at the time was the impact of Soviet economic successes on worldwide perceptions of Soviet prestige. In the Third World particularly, capitalism was thought to face an uphill battle against state planning methods of development. Indeed, many prominent Americans believed that socialist systems were intrinsically superior at achieving the initial stages of extensive economic development.[82]

Diplomats on the scene furnished plenty of evidence on the way the Soviet leaders appeared to be assessing the new power relationship. In 1956 Ambassador Charles Bohlen alerted Dulles to what he called the "genuine as against assumed self-confidence of Soviet leaders. Ebullient personality of Khrushchev may account for some of the cruder manifestations of Soviet cockiness but this factor should not be overemphasized since from the Soviet point of view present domestic and foreign scene contain real elements for satisfaction."[83] Bohlen did refer to weapons modernization as one cause of optimism,

---

[80]NIE, 16 July 1953, "Soviet Bloc Capabilities through 1957," *FRUS*, 1952–1954, 8:1188. See also NSC 5440, 13 December 1954, *DDRS*, 1977/302G.

[81]See in particular the dispatches of Charles Bohlen, who frequently pointed out "the contradiction between the social and economic changes in the Soviet Union brought on by the process of industrialization and the antiquated forms of political rule which were devised and perfected in quite different circumstances": Bohlen to Deputy Director of Central Intelligence, 7 October 1957, *FRUS*, 1955–1957, 24:161.

[82]See Dulles's remarks to congressional leaders, 5 January 1958, JFDP, box 143; Secretary of Defense Charles Wilson's comments at 234th NSC meeting, 27 January 1955, *FRUS*, 1955–1957, 24:9, and at 398th NSC meeting, 5 April 1959, *DDRS*, 1990/1014; USIA, Office of Research and Analysis, "Free World Views of the U.S.-USSR Power Balance," 1960, *DDRS*, 1989/2845.

[83]Bohlen to Secretary of State, 27 January 1956, DDEL/JFD, Dulles/Herter ser., box 5, folder 4.

but he focused on a series of more general factors: the development of an exportable surplus of military and industrial goods for use in foreign policy; the Soviets' recognition of the "three camps," providing greater flexibility in diplomacy; and the elevation of the anticolonial policy from the party to the state level. Many reports from Moscow testified to the genuineness of Khrushchev's confidence: Khrushchev, Lewellyn Thompson reported, "exuded confidence and it was impossible not to be convinced that he genuinely believed what he was saying."[84]

Concern over Khrushchev's correlation-of-forces statements grew steadily over the period in both the legislative and executive branches, reaching a peak in 1959 in the wake of the renewed Berlin crisis. A Senate report in September 1959 observed: "Inherent in the . . . general observations by the Soviet Premier appears to be the belief that the 'Socialist camp' has now gained the upper hand in the power relationships presently prevailing in international politics."[85] A U.S. Information Agency survey of "free world views of the U.S.-USSR power balance," conducted in 1960, concluded: "The current consensus would appear to be that the USSR enjoys rough but effective equivalence in strength overall. Behind in some fields, ahead in others, the USSR is seen as capable of offering a credible competitive challenge to the U.S. in the major arenas of international rivalry."[86]

Khrushchev's none-too-veiled threats to Averell Harriman sparked great concern during the crisis when they were relayed to the State Department. Another development that brought the Soviets' claims to the fore was their new policy of demanding parity in the form of equal representation in all international organizations and negotiating forums. A State Department intelligence report observed: "Moscow's primary objective in demanding parity is to enhance the prestige of the bloc by presenting an image of a powerful and monolithic group of states which is at least equal to the Western powers in strength and with which the latter must accordingly negotiate on equal terms."[87]

Americans did not accept the Soviet argument for parity, even before the full extent of Khrushchev's missile deception became known.

[84]Thompson to Secretary of State, 6 September 1960, *DDRS*, 1984/002615. See also Thompson's telegram of 15 November 1957, *DDRS*, 1983/000496.
[85]U.S. Senate, *Khrushchev on the Shifting Balance of World Forces*, 86th Cong., 1st sess., 14 September 1959 (Washington, D.C.: U.S. Government Printing Office, 1959), 8.
[86]*DDRS*, 1989/2845.
[87]Bureau of Intelligence Research, "Intelligence Report," no. 8115, 24 September 1959, *DDRS*, 1981/223B.

The State Department's briefing papers for Eisenhower in preparation for Khrushchev's 1959 visit stressed that "the Soviets are dangerously misleading themselves if they think [the] world balance of power has shifted in favor of the Soviet bloc. . . . The Free World vastly exceeds [the] Communist Bloc in area, population, industrial and agricultural production, overall military potential and current military capacity." As far as Soviet parity arguments were concerned, the president was told, "there is no basis for equating the U.S. and its 57 sovereign allies with the 11 members of the Sino-Soviet bloc."[88]

The documents suggest that Americans generally refused to grant that the Soviets had achieved an equality of capabilities in *any* component of national power except for conventional ground forces. Each expression of concern about the Soviet power position concluded with a statement of faith in existing American economic, technological, and nuclear superiority. Most of the worry was over the perceptions of allied and Third World elites. They and the Soviets needed to be acquainted with the "real" situation. Before the Camp David summit, a State Department memorandum enjoined Eisenhower to "make Khrushchev understand that if the USSR continues to act on its view that the balance of power is shifting to the Soviet bloc and to attempt to force its will on non-Communist countries (Berlin and Laos are current examples), the risks of war will increase, as we intend to honor our commitments."[89]

Eisenhower, as we know, took comfort in the United States' superior nuclear strike capability. Both he and Dulles noted publicly and privately the superiority of the overall U.S. power position. In addition, the Soviet invasion of Hungary and Tito's independent course made them both acutely aware of intrinsic weaknesses in the Soviet alliance system. Dulles repeatedly expressed the belief that relaxation of tensions threatened unity in the East quite as much as in the West.[90] The president often expressed the view that Moscow's "satellite forces" were a liability rather than an asset.[91]

The evidence is sketchy and generally secondhand, but it indicates that Eisenhower did not directly attempt to "make Khrushchev

---

[88] "Major Themes of Khrushchev's Public and Private Statements and U.S. Counterarguments," DOS "Talking Paper," 8 September 1959, *DDRS*, 1983/000299.

[89] 18 September 1959, *DDRS*, 1983/000303.

[90] See memo of Dulles's conversation with Eisenhower on talks with Tito, 7 November 1955, DDEL/JFD, Dulles/Herter ser., box 3, folder 16. Tito gave Dulles background information on intersocialist contradictions in Europe and between the Soviet Union and China "better than any available to us."

[91] DDEL/JFD, White House Memoranda ser. box 1, Meetings with the President, August–December 1956, 6 November and 15 December 1956.

understand" that his correlation-of-forces thesis was mistaken. In his meetings with the Soviet leader, Eisenhower explicitly rejected a confrontational approach, and tried to focus on concrete issues.[92] He did tell Khrushchev that he would never give way on Berlin, and that the United States would honor all its commitments.[93] Both at an initial meeting in the Oval Office and later at Camp David, Khrushchev made a connection between the current Berlin crisis and the Soviet sense of having been denied a deserved role in world affairs after World War II. He claimed, for example, that the USSR would not move unilaterally in Berlin, even though the United States had done so after the war in Japan, "where we were deprived of rights we should have had."[94] Eisenhower dismissed the argument.[95]

Eisenhower spelled out the U.S. position: He was prepared to negotiate a solution to the Berlin problem, but not under the deadline ultimatum. Prestige concerns ruled out American concessions under threat. In the convivial summit atmosphere, Khrushchev relaxed the deadline. The Eisenhower team appeared intermittently to favor serious negotiations that would accommodate Soviet "defensive" concerns while codifying essential Western rights in West Berlin. The regime governing Berlin was seen as a nettlesome anomaly of the war, of no intrinsic strategic value. Indeed, many people in the administration admitted that the Soviets had legitimate concerns, some effective arguments, and indisputable local military superiority.[96]

Yet once again they felt their room to maneuver was limited by all the classic concerns over credibility. With the threat removed, there appeared to be little need to incur the political costs of making any major concessions. Khrushchev's frustration with this situation is clearly reflected in his diplomatic communications at the time and in his memoirs: Without the threat, the Americans don't do anything; with the threat, they make it a prestige issue, claiming their entire world position demands that they stand fast in Berlin. How can one deal with such people?

All the mixed signals about power and prestige came to a head in 1961. In his State of the Union message in January, President John F. Kennedy intoned: "Our problems are critical. The tide is unfavorable.

[92]Piers Brendon, *Ike: His Life and Times* (New York: Harper & Row, 1980), 799.

[93]Dwight David Eisenhower, *Waging Peace: The White House Years, 1956–1961* (Garden City, N.Y.: Doubleday, 1965), 441, 445.

[94]Peter Lyon, *Eisenhower: Portrait of the Hero* (Boston: Little, Brown, 1974), 801.

[95]Eisenhower, *Waging Peace*, 448.

[96]Trachtenberg, *History and Strategy*, chap. 5.

The news will be worse before it is better."[97] This was not mere political rhetoric. It was frank acknowledgment of the mood that animated the vast majority of the country's political elite. Kennedy was signaling to the political establishment that, unlike his predecessor, he was prepared to do something about adverse trends. The political mood in which Kennedy operated was well expressed by Henry Kissinger:

> The nature of the challenge can be stated as follows: the United States cannot afford another decline like that which has characterized the past decade and a half. Fifteen years more of a deterioration in our position in the world such as we have experienced since World War II would find us reduced to Fortress America in a world in which we had become largely irrelevant.[98]

Yet at that very moment a favorable intelligence reassessment of the overall strategic balance was under way. Nobody doubted that *trends* were a concern. But from 1960 on, confidence in the existing balance of forces increased steadily. Kennedy had exaggerated Soviet power and American weaknesses for political purposes. Further, everyone knew that Khrushchev had exaggerated Soviet nuclear missile capabilities. What became clear during 1961 was not the existence but the sheer extent of the Soviet deception. Khrushchev intensified his campaign over Berlin and his boasting about Soviet power just as Washington was becoming more bullish about its own position than at any time in the last half-decade.

The strategic reassessment was still under way in June 1961, when Kennedy consulted with Khrushchev in Vienna. Those "informal" talks revealed the differences over power and prestige which had underlain the U.S.-Soviet rivalry since 1945. Kennedy set out the American position clearly. The Soviet Union should be satisfied with the extent of influence it currently enjoyed over the international system, and should not seek to expand its sway. If Moscow would only accept the present distribution of political influence, all would be well: "You wish to destroy the influence of my country where it has traditionally been present."[99] The two most immediate manifestations of this problem were Laos and especially Berlin. Kennedy outlined the standard American credibility argument:

[97] Quoted in George C. Herring, *America's Longest War: America in Vietnam, 1950–1975* (New York: Knopf, 1986), 73.

[98] Henry Kissinger, *The Necessity for Choice* (New York: Harper & Row, 1960), p. 1.

[99] Beschloss, *Crisis Years*, 194. Beschloss's account of the meeting is based on the official memoranda of conversations, to which he obtained access after four years of appeal. Unless I indicate otherwise, quotations here are from this source.

If we were to leave West Berlin, Europe would be abandoned as well. So when we are talking about West Berlin, we are also talking about Western Europe. . . . it is not the right time now to change the situation in Berlin and the balance in general. [The Soviet Union] should not seek to change our position and thus disturb the balance of power.

Khrushchev dismissed any notion of freezing the status quo as impossible and insulting. If the Americans insisted on basing their policy on the preservation of the international status quo, then they must not want peaceful coexistence with the USSR. American policy suffered from delusions of grandeur: "The United States is so rich and powerful that it believes it has special rights and can afford not to recognize the rights of others." Khrushchev, who had been heating up his rhetoric on Berlin since January, issued a new ultimatum: an agreement by December, or Moscow would conclude its own treaty with the GDR. He repeated the argument he had made to Eisenhower, that the Soviet Union had been denied its rights in West Germany and Japan after World War II, despite its huge sacrifices in that conflict. After concluding a peace treaty, the Soviets would "never, under any conditions," accept special U.S. rights in Berlin. The final session ended with each leader attempting to place the burden of the initiative on the other.

Throughout his remarks, Khrushchev implied that the United States' predominance in world affairs was illegitimate. Its wartime role did not confer this position on it, and, as he had been saying since 1957, the current balance of power did not justify it. Kennedy poured fuel on this fire by saying unambiguously, "We regard . . . Sino-Soviet forces and the forces of the United States and Western Europe as being more or less in equilibrium."[100] This was no slip of the tongue, for he repeated the assessment several times during the summit. Khrushchev modestly responded that he was not sure "whether the balance of power was exact, but no matter; each side had enough power to destroy the other."[101] What Khrushchev would later call Kennedy's "admission," however, had a great impact on him. He cited it in numerous speeches and in his memoirs. Always he would ask, as he did in a letter to Kennedy on 27 October, during the missile crisis: "How then does the admission of our equal military

[100] Beschloss (ibid., 202) notes that Kennedy offered the same assessment to Eisenhower during their transition talks at Camp David.
[101] Arthur M. Schlesinger, Jr., *A Thousand Days* (Boston: Houghton Mifflin, 1965), 364.

capabilities tally with such unequal relations between our great states? They cannot be made to tally in any way."[102]

In the months after the summit, the American intelligence apparatus churned out a wholesale downward revision of Soviet capabilities. The CIA now realized that the Soviets had decided not to go ahead with full deployment of the cumbersome, liquid-fueled SS-6, and to wait for the second-generation ICBM to come on line. Accordingly, it concluded that "the USSR has been and is now conducting its foreign policy from a position of less strength in intercontinental striking power than the Soviet leaders have sought to imply."[103]

In October, Kennedy authorized Deputy Defense Secretary Roswell Gilpatric to go public with the information in a speech on the military balance and to provide more detailed briefings to allied governments known to be penetrated by Soviet intelligence.[104] The intent clearly was to communicate to the Soviets that the missile deception was blown, and thus to take wind from Khrushchev's sails on Berlin. The administration had even reassessed *conventional* Soviet capabilities in a favorable direction: whereas the earlier tendency was simply to tally up the ratio of divisions in Europe (something like 175 to 26), official assessments were now based on the realization that a Soviet division represented at best one-third the strength of a corresponding Western formation.

According to Gaddis, "The result of the recalculations of Soviet missile and manpower capabilities was to give the West, for the first time since 1945, a sense of overall military parity with the Soviet Union, possibly even superiority."[105] The upshot is that 1961 witnessed the greatest contradiction between Soviet representations about the existing distribution of military power and American beliefs. In American eyes, the situation was arguably better than it had been at any time since 1945. Although the evidence indicates that even in the absence of these reassessments the Americans would not have been amenable to Khrushchev's drive for parity, the new view laid to rest any possible doubts. After the construction of the Berlin Wall and the American rhetorical offensive on the balance of power, Khrushchev did slowly begin to back away from his more exposed positions. The Cuban missile crisis, of course, temporarily resolved

---

[102] *Problems of Communism* 41 (Spring 1992); 47. See also his speech during his May visit to Bulgaria, *Pravda*, 19 May 1962, 1 (*CDSP* 14, no. 20: 6), and to the World Peace Congress, *Pravda*, 11 July 1962, 2 (*CDSP* 14, no. 28: 3).

[103] CIA memo to General Taylor, 6 September 1961, *DDRS*, 1975/245A.

[104] Trachtenberg, *History and Strategy*, 221.

[105] Gaddis, *Strategies of Containment*, 207.

the contradiction between Washington's and Moscow's views of the balance of power.

The expanding historical record of the Cuban crisis indicates that all participants in the deliberations of the executive committee—indeed, everyone involved in the crisis on the American side—shared Kennedy's assumption that the United States had to force the Soviets to reverse their decision to deploy missiles in Cuba. The evidence further indicates that Kennedy's secretary of defense, Robert McNamara, had some grounds for his later contention that "parity," in the sense of mutual vulnerability to unacceptable damage, prevailed during the conflict. As Kennedy said of the Soviets at the outset of the crisis: "They've got enough to blow us up now anyway."[106]

Interestingly, the possibility of allowing the deployment to stand seems not to have been seriously considered.[107] The overwhelming majority of the deliberations during the crisis surrounded the question how best to reverse the Soviets' decision. Some assumed the deployment would materially improve the Soviets' military position in the wake of the public U.S. reassessment. The administration seems to have concluded that this was the primary motivation for the deployment in the first place.[108] Most worked on the assumption that a successful deployment would affect the perception of the balance of power more than it would alter the underlying strategic relationship. As Kennedy said after the crisis, a successful Soviet deployment "would have politically changed the balance of power; it would have appeared to [change it] and appearances contribute to reality."[109]

HEGEMONIC RIVALRY AND BIPOLAR STABILITY

The Kennedy administration's post-Vienna publicity blitz on the balance of power, its hard public line on Berlin, and its announcement of accelerated military programs caused a slow Soviet retreat from boastful optimism about the correlation of forces. Khrushchev appeared to realize the game was up—perhaps after the failure of the

[106]Betts, *Nuclear Balance*, 170. See also McNamara in Blight and Welch, *On the Brink*, 187–88. Kennedy's close adviser McGeorge Bundy also later claimed that the president believed by 1960 that MAD prevailed: "The Future of Strategic Deterrence," *Survival* 21 (November–December 1979): 269. In addition, see Trachtenberg, *History and Strategy*, chap. 6.

[107]Blight and Welch, *On the Brink*, 244–45.

[108]See memorandum from Roger Hilsman, 14 November 1962, *DDRS*, 1977/220D.

[109]Quoted in Arnold Horelick, "The Problem of Soviet Motivation," in *The Cuban Missile Crisis*, ed. Robert A. Devine (Chicago: Quandrangle, 1971), 137.

second Berlin ultimatum, definitely after the Cuban missile crisis. After the Gilpatric speech, Khrushchev subtly moderated his claim.[110] In the wake of the missile crisis, the Soviet discourse as a whole toned down portrayals of the balance of power. Khrushchev's successors banished the very term "correlation of forces" from their speeches, returning to the old "threat from imperialism" and "consolidation of forces."

Khrushchev's policy was based on the belief that the underlying distribution of power had shifted substantially enough to permit him to seek a revision of the Soviet Union's status in the international system. All political actors agreed that striking shifts in the power balance had taken place in the decade since the establishment of the essential international hierarchy in the aftermath of the war: China had joined the Soviet alignment, Western empires were crumbling, decolonization was proceeding rapidly, and the Soviet Union had achieved the nuclear capability to devastate Europe and, at the very least, lay waste to several American cities. The West seemed impressed by nuclear weapons, and the Soviet Union had certain advantages, so Khrushchev played them up. The strategy worked in the Near East and elsewhere in the Third World, and for a time in Europe. Since he believed that underlying trends were in his favor, Khrushchev doubtless concluded that any prestige gained by deception would not easily be lost, even if his deceit were discovered after the fact. He resembled someone who knows his or her salary will continue to increase in the future, and wants to begin enjoying the benefits of the coming wealth now.

Khrushchev's aim was, yet again, the "equality" he and many others in the Soviet elite felt they were denied in the aftermath of World War II. The term was not subject to precise definition or measurement, but seemed to imply a visible revision in the Soviet Union's status and a palpable change in the way the United States dealt with the country. Khrushchev and his comrades appeared to be animated by a desire for more influence and prestige for its own sake, but also because greater international status would add to their sense of security. "Equality" served also as an argument, an appeal, in their efforts to secure a favorable resolution of the Berlin crisis, while Berlin served as a symbol of equality.

---

[110] The major change was an end to claims of military superiority. Such claims in this period were of the "peace forces are stronger than war forces" variety. On military power, Khrushchev responded to the Gilpatric speech and other administration claims by reiterating Kennedy's Vienna assessment and arguing that the balance had not

It is easy to question the soundness of Khrushchev's strategy, and particularly his timing. Why not wait a few years until missiles really were coming out of Soviet factories "like sausages"? The timing would seem difficult to explain without reference to Khrushchev's impulsive personality. There is an uncanny resemblance between his domestic and international policies, both tending to rely on cost-saving panaceas—chemicals, corn, ICBMs. Many accounts focus on domestic leadership politics as the spur to Khrushchev's impatience. He needed quick and cheap international victories to keep his domestic program together. But of course the nature of his domestic policies and political travails was also a function of his personality. Purely international factors also help explain Khrushchev's impatience. Problems had been brewing with the Chinese since the Twentieth Party Congress in 1956. Perhaps it would be best to grab for as much prestige as possible now, while Beijing was still ostensibly on board?

If we pay heed to the elusiveness of power and to the capriciousness of perceptions of power, however, much of the timing puzzle vanishes. For it would be difficult to name a period when the dynamism of Soviet power so captured the world's political imagination. For the purposes of magnifying Moscow's capabilities, Khrushchev's Soviet Union captured the perfect combination of ideological movement and state power. Among the most important indicators of any country's power position are the statements and actions of the other major powers in the international system. If anyone in Moscow doubted that the Soviet Union was surging forward on all fronts, all he had to do was get access to Western and Third World commentary to lay any doubts to rest.[111]

Khrushchev's argument that equal military capabilities ought to translate into "equal rights and responsibilities" resembled those made by Stalin, Molotov, Vyshinskii, Zhdanov, and Khrushchev himself in the immediate aftermath of World War II. The difference this time was that "military power" meant something radically different than it had in 1946. It was now thought of primarily in terms of nuclear delivery capacity—almost a 180-degree turnaround from the view Stalin preferred the military to act upon. Other elements of military power were also important, but they appeared in both

---

changed since then. See, e.g., his speech to the World Peace Congress, *Pravda*, 11 July 1962, 2 (*CDSP* 14, no. 28: 3).

[111] Rand research corroborates the success the Soviets enjoyed in translating perceived trends into immediate power gains in the eyes of influential Westerners. See Herbert Goldhammer, "The U.S.-Soviet Strategic Balance as Seen from London and Paris," *Survival* 19 (September–October 1977): 202–7.

[181]

Khrushchev's expressed views and, to a lesser degree, the formal military strategy of the day as mere adjuncts to the rocket forces.

Evidence from the American side indicates that U.S. policy makers based their rejection of Soviet arguments for a revision of influence partly on their confidence in the West's ultimate superiority on all the main indices of power, with the exception, as always, of the conventional balance of forces in being. If they believed that a situation of mutual deterrence prevailed—and the evidence indicates that some people including President Kennedy, did—they did not think this "equalization" of the superpowers' military potentials implied any kind of equalization of their political influence.

The dramatic crisis years between 1959 and 1962 thus constitute the second cycle of the Cold War. Despite important differences, it had many features in common with the first: a perceived shift in power, publicly acknowledged by both sides; a new Soviet drive for increased prestige; positive early feedback on the policy; sharp crises that eventually revealed contradictions between the two sides' interpretations of the political implications of the power shift; a stalemate based on a temporary convergence of views on the balance of power and the prestige hierarchy. The balance-of-power concept provides a useful framework for explaining the diplomacy of the period. But it is important to bear in mind that the dramatic power shifts that were so real in the minds of leaders and elites, and that conditioned the international politics of the era, were largely ephemeral. They do not appear in broad-based measures of power. To put it another way: any measure of material power resources that captured the shift underlying the crisis years would fail to capture any other shift.

An important distinction between the two cycles concerns slowly changing beliefs about the stability of the postwar structure. International policies in the late 1950s and early 1960s would be incomprehensible without reference to the high degree of uncertainty surrounding the mechanics of power. American fears of bandwagoning, which earlier had focused on economic collapse, communist parties, and eventual Soviet superiority in conventional forces, were now given a boost by Soviet nuclear power. These fears, in turn, fed the Soviet perception that military power, and particularly nuclear weapons, possessed political utility that could be realized by means short of war. The Soviets might vastly improve their political and security situation if only they could break the psychological crutch of U.S. nuclear power on which the Western nations relied.

In both Washington and Moscow, however, the process of recognizing the essential stability of alignments was well under way by the

[182]

end of the 1950s. On the Soviet side, the ascendancy of many of Varga's theses about postwar capitalism opened up intellectual paths for a more forthright adjustment to the longevity of the existing international arrangement. As for the Americans, years of experience were leading them to recognize that interallied contradictions could redound to their favor as well as to Moscow's. Washington's sensitivity to the political vulnerabilities of various allied leaders was always high, but it diminished over the period, especially under Kennedy. Much of the sense of instability concerned trepidation or anticipation about future movement in great-power relations. Much of the bandwagon thinking really concerned not changes in alignment but the success or failure of individual policies in immediate circumstances. In *immediate* circumstances, official Washington and Moscow feared and anticipated *attitude* shifts among friends and foes. Actual changes in alliance were still on official minds, but they were matters for the future.

In short, major instability was even more a matter for the future in 1962 than it had been in 1956. Bandwagoning fears in 1962 concerned attitude rather than actual alignments to a greater extent in 1962 than in 1956. The acute struggle over power and prestige centering on Berlin resulted in a greater appreciation of the basic stability of the system.[112] The shift was subtle but noticeable in rhetoric and policy. Just as the postwar arrangement emerged as a result of U.S.-Soviet disagreement about power and prestige, it was reinforced and strengthened by an acute struggle over the same issues during Khrushchev's tenure. The symbiotic link between hegemonic rivalry and equilibrating tendencies in world politics was manifest yet again in the last series of superpower crises to occur in Europe.

[112] See Trachtenberg, *History and Strategy*, chap. 5, for evidence from the American side.

[7]

Détente and the Correlation
of Forces in the 1970s

Now that we know the Soviet Union's fate, it is tempting to read that destiny back into Soviet history. The totalitarian experiment was doomed from its start in 1917. Or its fate was sealed only when Stalin took over in the 1930s. Or its last hope was extinguished when Khrushchev set limits on his reformist thaw in the 1950s. By far the most popular interpretation is that the end began in the Brezhnev years, the "era of stagnation," as Mikhail Gorbachev began to call it early in his reform leadership. In terms of the balance of power, the case for Soviet decline is easy to make. By the measure used so far, the Soviet Union declined from 17 percent of "world power" in 1960 to 13 percent in 1970. The American rival, by contrast, held its own, going from 22 percent to 21 percent in the same period. According to figures used in the 1970s, the Soviet economy grew from just under to just over one-half the American over the decade, but growth rates were lower in the 1960s than in the 1950s, and were lower still in the 1970s.[1] There was no prospect of closing the gap. The economic figures for NATO and the Warsaw Pact nations were simply embarrassing. If one highlighted technological innovation or efficiency, the Soviet Union could easily be made to look like a pitiful giant and the United States like a flourishing, flexible technopower as of 1970.

But the picture that emerges most clearly when quantitative measures are applied in retrospect is an unexciting one titled "Bipolar Stability." All the essential balanced asymmetries that had characterized world politics in 1950 and 1960 were still firmly in place. The

[1] Ray S. S. Cline, *World Power Assessment: A Calculus of Strategic Drift* (Boulder, Colo.: Westview, 1975).

Soviet bloc was the weaker economically, but it still enjoyed its comparative advantage in military production. The Western alliance had modernized its conventional forces and built up its nuclear arsenal in the 1960s, but that move had been deftly checked by Brezhnev's own conventional and nuclear programs. The Soviets had matched and surpassed American nuclear deployments quantitatively (though not qualitatively) while retaining the perceived conventional edge they had enjoyed since 1945.

The picture requiring the most creative genius to paint would be "Dynamic Soviet Union Challenges America in Decline." Yet that was how power trends were perceived in the 1970s. And once again, it was not just Moscow's corps of spin managers who propagated the idea, but the highest U.S. officials, aided and abetted by academic experts and media pundits. Behind the rise and fall of détente in the 1970s, behind the Cold War's last, languid cycle, is a story of the Soviet political elite concluding not only that it had the power to achieve parity in prestige with the United States *but that it had actually done so.* The slow realization that that was not the case set the stage for the Gorbachev revolution in Soviet foreign policy and the end of the Cold War itself.

THE GENERAL LINE

In his Supreme Soviet election speech in 1974, Leonid I. Brezhnev observed: "After evaluating the general correlation of forces in the world, as far back as several years ago, we came to this conclusion: A real possibility exists for achieving a fundamental breakthrough in international affairs."[2] The breakthrough Brezhnev referred to was his détente policy, with its highly publicized summit meetings and international agreements. The image the general secretary sought to convey was that of a prudent and capable leader, furthering the interests of the Soviet state. First he reevaluated the correlation of forces. Then he concluded that the Soviet Union was sufficiently strong at long last to pursue its cherished goal of détente with the United States on the basis of political parity. And now he was reporting on the policy's great success to the assembled Soviet elite. Some members of that audience might have pondered the differences between this

---

[2]*Leninskim kursom: Reich i stat'i,* 9 vols. (Moscow: Izdatel'stvo Politicheskoi Literatury, 1970–1982), 5:76.

careful, can-do leader and the impetuous Khrushchev, whose boastful pronouncements had ultimately failed to achieve the same objectives.

But Brezhnev's speech, like that of many politicans, conveyed an oversimplified picture of the policy process, one that magnified the Soviet leadership's foresight. The process was by no means so simple and linear, proceeding from reassessment to new policy. Instead, the policy's success was part of the reassessment. A reassessment did take place in the late 1960s, after seven years of modesty and circumspection in discussions of the correlation of forces. But Brezhnev did not formalize the new, more optimistic view until he thought the policy based on that view was enjoying success. The policy's apparent success was the feedback that gave the Soviet leader the confidence to make his pronouncement to the Supreme Soviet. Here, in this careful policy style, lies the crucial difference between the détente policies of Khrushchev and Brezhnev. While the essential logic supporting the policies was practically the same, the Brezhnev regime had a higher standard for evaluating incoming evidence about its assessments. For the better part of a decade, these higher standards appeared to be met. As a result, retreat from this policy proved harder and ultimately more consequential than it had been two decades earlier, after the breakdown of Khrushchev's strategy.

A New Stage

By the middle of the 1970s it became accepted dogma that a fundamental turn in the correlation of forces had been achieved by the beginning of the decade. This was the fourth state in the development of international relations (1917, late 1940s, late 1950s).[3] It followed the pattern well worn by the second and third stages, proclaimed by Stalin- and Khrushchev-era ideologists in turn: a catalyzing event (the World War II victory in Stalin's case,; sputniks in the Khrushchev case, rough nuclear parity in Brezhnev's); increased optimism in the foreign affairs press; and then formalization by the CPSU's ideology specialists and official academics.

[3]See N. I. Lebedev (official chronicler of the fourth state), *Novyi etap mezhdunarodnykh otnoshenii* (Moscow: Mysl', 1976), esp. chap. 3. A concise but penetrating analysis is provided by N. V. Zagladin, *Istoriia uspekhov i neudach sovetskoi diplomatii* (Moscow: Mezhdunarodnye Otnosheniia, 1990), 200–213. Western analyses are numerous. Useful examples include Charles Allen Lynch, *The Soviet Study of International Relations* (Cambridge: Cambridge University Press, 1987), esp. 89–94; Robert Legvold, *The Concept of Power and Security in Soviet History*, Adelphi Paper no. 151 (London: International Institute of Strategic Studies, 1979); and Harry Gelman, *The Brezhnev Politburo and the Decline of Détente* (Ithaca: Cornell University Press, 1984), 26–31.

Our experience with postwar "stages" of the correlation of forces leads us to expect a new policy based on an optimistic assessment of the balance of power and a quest for a revision of the prestige hierarchy on the world scene. And such is indeed the case, though Brezhnev's stage was different. Khrushchev's third stage was formalized in the late 1950s, before he embarked on his intensive effort to redefine his relationship with the United States. Brezhnev's prudent ideological apparatus refrained from formalizing the new stage until after summits and arms-control agreements had already demonstrated the soundness of the analysis. Brezhnev's stage was also somewhat less grandiose than either Khrushchev's or Stalin's: this time no one proclaimed a new, fourth stage in capitalism's venerable general crisis.

Major party documents of the 1969–1971 period retained the restrained 1960s orthodoxy on the correlation of forces.[4] But in less formal circumstances, and especially after Moscow began claiming a "military strategic balance" between the USSR and the United States in 1970, Brezhnev began to use language reminiscent of Khrushchev's.[5] In Baku in October of that year, Brezhnev spoke of the "substantially strenghtened international position of the Soviet Union."[6] In March the general secretary consciously or unconsciously paraphrased Molotov's speech a quarter-century earlier when he declared: "At the present time no question of any importance in the world can be solved without our participation, without taking into account our economic and military might."[7] "Never before in its entire history," he proudly stated later, "has our country enjoyed such authority and influence in the world."[8]

The Twenty-Fourth Party Congress in 1971 put the official seal of approval on the optimistic mood. Echoing the words of Brezhnev the year before, Gromyko made his famous assertion that "today there is no question of any significance that can be decided without the Soviet Union or in opposition to it." Other Soviet leaders followed suit, and, for the first time since Khrushchev's days, the congress resolution

---

[4]Though Brezhnev's report to the meeting of communist parties in Moscow (7 June 1969) maintained restrained 1960s orthodoxy on all aspects of the correlation, later accounts cited it as signaling the new stage; see *Leninskim kursom*, 2:366–415, esp. 368, 369, 384–86, 393–94. So did journalistic analyses: M. Marinin and I. Sokolov, "Imperializm i revoliutsionnye sily na poroge 70-kh godov," *MEiMO*, 1969, no. 8, 3–16; V. V. Zagladin, "Revoliutsionnyi protsess i mezhdunarodnaia politika KPSS," *Kommunist*, 1971, no. 13 (September), 14–26.

[5]See the lead editorials in *Pravda*, 7 March and 9 June 1970 (*CDSP* 22, no. 23: 1–5).

[6]*Leninskim kursom*, 3:141.

[7]Quoted in Legvold, *Concept of Power and Security*, 9.

[8]*Leninskim kursom*, 6:245–46.

included ringing phrases about favorable shifts in the correlation of forces.[9] Arkady Shevchenko, at the time an adviser to Gromyko, observed in his memoirs that around the time of the congress, he "felt a clearcut revival of self-assurance in our leadership. After the many troubles of the 1960s, beginning with Berlin on through Czechoslovakia and our attempts to catch up with the United States in the arms race, the Soviet Union had recovered and was emerging as an even stronger U.S. rival."[10]

The congress set in motion a mood of official optimism that was detectable in all major party documents from 1971 onward.[11] Just before Nixon's visit to Moscow in the spring of 1972, Brezhnev delivered a report to a closed plenary session of the Central Committee spelling out the logic behind the détente policy. Shevchenko, who worked on the preparation of the report, said it stressed that the president's visit was "convincing proof" of the "powerful rise of Soviet influence throughout the world."[12] It was at this point that Brezhnev made explicit the connection between détente and the new correlation of forces.

Détente and the Correlation of Forces

In his election speech in June 1971 Brezhnev asked how it was that "disarmament is becoming increasingly possible in our era." His answer: "above all, the changes in the correlation of forces in the world—both sociopolitical and military forces."[13] Having lain dormant since the heady days of Khrushchev, the bandwagoning correlation-of-forces logic that Stalin had articulated four decades earlier at the Sixteenth Party Congress was back again. But the new-stage-equals-détente connection was more than a mere assertion about the correlation of forces to justify a new policy. It was more than a Khrushchevian doctrinal announcement. It was a well-worked-out

[9] *XXIV s"ezd Kommunisticheskoi Partii Sovetskogo Soiuza: Stenograficheskii otchet*, 2 vols. (Moscow: Izdatel'stvo Politicheskoi Literatury, 1971), 1:211, 482. See also Defense Minister Andrei Grechko's speech, 2:213.

[10] Arkady Shevchenko, *Breaking with Moscow* (New York: Ballantine, 1985), 267.

[11] See in *Pravda*, e.g., Brezhnev's and Kosygin's election speeches, 10 and 12 June 1971 (*CDSP* 23, no. 24: 1–4, 6–8); Viktor Grishin's speech on the anniversary of the revolution, 7 November 1971 (*CDSP* 23, no. 45: 6–9); and the resolution of the Supreme Soviet, 23 November 1971 (*CDSP* 23, no. 47: 2–3, 11).

[12] Shevchenko, *Breaking with Moscow*, 282. See also Georgii Arbatov, *Zatianuvsheesia vyzdorovlenie (1953–1985 gg.): Svidetel'stvo sovremennika* (Moscow: Mezhdunarodnye Otnosheniia, 1991), 212.

[13] *Pravda*, 12 June 1971, 1–3 (*CDSP* 23, no. 24: 6–8).

argument. Indeed, the argument was first spelled out publicly by analysts at the Institute of World Economy and International Relations (Institut Mirovoi Ekonomiki i Mezhdunarodnykh Otnoshenii, or IMEMO).[14]

Once Brezhnev stressed the new correlation/détente connection in his election speech, more detailed scholarly analyses followed. By mid-decade, every article touching on the overall situation had at least to mention the connection. One of the early formulators of the argument was Georgii Arbatov, director of the newly formed Institute of the United States and Canada. In a series of articles in the early 1970s, Arbatov set out the main lines of the analysis. In each article he implicitly contrasted the present détente argument from its Khrushchevian predecessor by pointing out "that the change in the balance of forces is not some kind of abstract formula but a tangible reality that is making the imperialist powers adapt to the situation."[15] In brief, the argument went as follows:

Nuclear parity has eliminated the United States' one major advantage, which earlier led U.S. leaders to believe they could negotiate "from a position of strength." The outcome of Vietnam shows the Americans that they cannot evade the logic of the strategic balance by engaging in "limited wars." The war has also galvanized mass movements in the West opposed to war and the arms race; it has created or strenghtened a "tendency" in the ruling elites of most Western countries to recognize the actual relation of forces and the futility of attempting to coerce the Soviet Union, and this "realistic tendency" is gaining influence in many countries. The West has been forced to address wrenching economic and resource problems and needs détente with the USSR to devote attention to their resolution. Further, the distribution of power in the world is becoming more polycentric and competition among the Western states more acute, causing some of them to seek good relations with the Soviet Union to secure a better position in the imperialist rivalry. Trends in the Third World, while not leading to any structural revision of the international system, as Khrushchev had believed, are favorable to the

---

[14]IMEMO experts were formulating "new stage" analyses as early as 1969, and the institute's journal adopted a more optimistic line even before the twenty-fourth Congress. See V. V. Zhurkin, "Budut li izvlecheny uroki?" *MEiMO*, 1969, no. 4, 17, 22; and the editorial "Na novykh istoricheskikh rubezhakh," *MEiMO*, 1971, no. 4, 3–14.

[15]Georgii Arbatov, "Strength of a Policy of Realism," *Izvestiia*, 22 June 1972 (*CDSP* 24, no. 25: 4–6). See also Arbatov, "American Imperialism and New World Realities," *Pravda*, 4 May 1971, 1–3 (*CDSP* 23, no. 18: 1–3); "Soviet-American Relations at a New Stage," *Pravda*, 22 July 1973, 4–5 (*CDSP* 25, no. 29: 1–5); "On Soviet-American Relations," *Kommunist*, 1973, no. 3 (February), 101–13 (*CDSP* 25, no. 15: 1–8).

USSR. The economic trends are also generally favorable. Thus a stabilization of the major strategic balance by no means implies a stabilization of the general correlation of forces, which continues to shift in favor of socialism.[16]

The correlation of forces was the objective background to the subjective element—the change in American (and Western European, especially German) policy. The way the Soviets introduced the "new stage" indicates that a reassessment of general correlation in the late 1960s led to the adoption of the "Peace Program" at the Twenty-fourth Congress in 1971. It also indicates that the European and American reactions to the new policy were themselves part of the reassessment. The policy and the analysis it was based on were intertwined and mutually supporting, but optimism about the correlation went beyond the necessity of supporting the détente policy. Even those who expressed skepticism about détente expressed optimism about the correlation.[17] Except for some arguments about the Third World, all policy arguments in the open sources were couched in terms of optimism. While one can find evidence to support the contention that some Soviets opposed détente, one cannot find evidence that anyone seriously questioned the notion of the new stage. A key question is: which of the changes Soviet analysts cited as leading to the new stage was the most decisive? Once again, a new correlation of nuclear forces was the determining factor that led to the new assessment.

For political analysts in the 1970s, the most important factor *leading* to the fourth stage was the Soviet Union's achievement of parity with the United States in nuclear weapons, but movement of the correlation *after* the onset of the new stage was entirely accounted for by nonmilitary factors. Once the Soviet Union achieved parity and was recognized to have done so by the West, Soviet leaders and political spokesmen began to evaluate the strategic equilibrium positively, and disclaimed any effort to shift it in their favor. Any further movement in the correlation, therefore, had to result from nonmilitary factors. For some spokespersons this was doubtless eyewash, for others a

---

[16] For an excellent and more detailed analysis of this Soviet view, see Coit D. Blacker, "The Kremlin and Détente," in *Managing U.S.-Soviet Relations,* ed. Alexander L. George (Boulder, Colo.: Westview, 1985), 119–37. Another very useful presentation is Raymond Garthoff, *Détente and Confrontation* (Washington, D.C.: Brookings Institution, 1985), 36–68.

[17] For books laced with skepticism about détente but littered with optimistic assertions about the correlation of forces, see Shalva P. Sanakoev and Nikolai K. Kapchenko, *Teoriia i praktika vneshnei politiki sotsializma* (Moscow: Mezhdunarodnye Otnosheniia, 1973); and German F. Vorontsov, *Voennye koalitsii i koalitsionnye voiny* (Moscow: Voennoe Izdatel'stvo, 1976), esp. 312–13.

reflection of genuine belief. The important thing is that this rhetorical maneuver permitted people publicly to downplay the importance of the military factor in the correlation while at the same time affirming the crucial role of Soviet military power in bringing about détente.

The proclamation of stages was a necessary part of the functioning of the Soviet political system before Gorbachev. The stages of the correlation of forces, it turns out, correspond to all sorts of other demarcations into stages. For example, Soviet accounts always divided American foreign policy into a series of stages. And, as might be expected, these stages corresponded to the overall stages of the correlation of forces.[18] The first stage, which lasted into the mid-1950s, was characterized by unrelieved U.S. "positions of strength" diplomacy; the second, which lasted until 1969, involved a greater emphasis on cooperation with a continued commitment to containment; the third stage was the stage of détente. Soviet discussions of U.S. diplomacy usually tied the various stages of U.S. diplomacy to the stages of the nuclear balance.[19] Further, each new stage of the strategic balance corresponded to the U.S. authorities' adoption of a new nuclear doctrine. In this way, public American nuclear doctrine practically served as an indicator of the whole correlation of forces.[20] Monitoring of American doctrine would give a Soviet observer clues about the real state of the balance of power. Since American doctrine seemed so sensitive to Soviet nuclear weapons, these weapons assumed a leading place in Soviet assessments. Public foreign policy analyses were honest enough to acknowledge the central role of the correlation of forces in bringing the West to reason and the central role of nuclear weapons in the correlation of forces. Arbatov recalled later, "We went no further than these arguments about the correlation of forces."[21] In a study of the role of military power in international

[18] See William V. Husband, "Soviet Perceptions of US 'Positions of Strength' Diplomacy in the 1970s," *World Politics* 31 (July 1979): 495–517; and Genrikh Trofimenko, *SShA: Politika, voina, ideologiia* (Moscow: Mysl', 1976).

[19] See (Man. Gen.) R. Simonian, "Strategicheskie pozitsii Pentagona i bezopasnost' narodov," *MEiMO*, 1978, no. 11, 16–26. Also, in the nuclear era the phases of the overall military situation correspond to the states of the nuclear balance: Col. E. Rybkin, "V. I. Lenin, KPSS ob imperializme kak postoiannom istochnike voennoi opasnosti," *Voenno-Istoricheskii Zhurnal*, 1983, no. 4, 3–10.

[20] See M. Mil'shtein, "Amerikanskie voennye doktriny: Preemstvennosti i modifikatsiia," *MEiMO*, 1971, no. 8, 30–41. Also Anatolii Gromyko, "American Theoreticians between 'Total War' and Peace," *Voennaia Mysl'*, 1969, no. 4 (*FPD*, 0004/70, 22 January 1970, 91–98), a review of Trofimenko's *Strategiia global'noi voiny* (Moscow: Mezhdunarodnye Otnosheniia, 1968), which follows in this vein of charting the United States' "adaptation" to the new correlation of forces via national security doctrines.

[21] Arbatov, *Zatianuvsheesia vyzdorovlenie*, 212.

relations, Colonel Vasilii M. Kulish (formerly on the General Staff, but at the time serving as the head of the military-political section at the IMEMO) asserted, "In the course of practically the whole postwar period, the most important element defining the condition of the military struggle between the two systems has been the strategic forces of the Soviet Union and the U.S.A."[22] Consequently, according to Deputy Foreign Minister Vladimir Petrovskii, "the nuclear equilibrium of the two powers forms the basis of the international equilibrium."[23]

The military balance, in particular the nuclear balance, formed the essence of the new stage and consequently lay at the root of Moscow's parity argument. In no other area of superpower competition could Soviet spokesmen credibly assert that onset of a qualitatively new stage. If the achievement of nuclear parity were left out of the picture, it looked considerably less rosy.

DISTRIBUTION AND MECHANICS OF POWER

Throughout the 1960s and 1970s the general line continued to stipulate that the contradiction between socialism and capitalism outweighed in importance the contradictions among capitalist states or between them and the developing countries. Representatives of the official line expressed the primacy of East-West relations by citing the ultimate decisiveness of the class struggle on the world scene, as reflected in the struggle between the U.S.- and Soviet-led alliance systems. In normal language, rivalry and cooperation with the United States would remain the lodestar of Soviet foreign policy, notwithstanding repeated efforts to woo this or that European power. As for scholars and commentators who occupied the political space below the party leadership, they analyzed (and advertised) the prospects for diplomatic wooing in the familiar terms of Lenin's *Imperialism.*

Two changes primarily distinguished this set of views from its Khrushchev-era predecessor.[24] First, Soviets at all levels appeared to perceive increased opportunities for diplomatic wooing even as they

---

[22] V. M. Kulish, ed., *Voennaia sila i mezhdunarodnye otnosheniia* (Moscow: Mezhdunarodnye Otnosheniia, 1972), 223.

[23] V. Petrovskii, "Novaia struktura mira: Formuly i real'nost'," *MEiMO*, 1977, no. 4, 18.

[24] For more evidence in support of both these changes, see Michael J. Sodaro, "Soviet Studies of the Western Alliance," in *Soviet Policy toward Western Europe: Implications for the Atlantic Alliance,* ed. Herbert Ellison (Seattle: University of Washington Press, 1983).

believed Soviet power on the rise. This combination of perceptions played well with the period's dominant bandwagoning notion about increased Soviet power leading to détente. It contradicted the "lessons" of the early postwar period and Khrushchev's years, which had seemed to vindicate Varga's contention that increased Soviet power united the opposition. This was a cause for optimism among members of the Soviet foreign policy establishment. The second difference was the continued maturation of the Soviets' intellectual rapprochement with the apparent stability of postwar great-power alignments. Even the official ideology, which in Khrushchev's day had continually speculated about future structural changes in world politics, through either "socialist" economic triumphs, advances in the Third World, or even revolutions in the West, now busied itself with glorifying the status quo as the best of all possible situations. Socialism in the USSR was "developed"; the two world economic systems would coexist indefinitely; Third World struggles would not lead to any structural shifts.

Soviet commentary on relations among the Western countries revolved around the theme of the "two tendencies within imperialism," originally identified by Lenin himself.[25] On the one hand was the unifying (or "centripetal") tendency and on the other was the "centrifugal" tendency toward contradictions. Soviet Westernologists held that these two tendencies interacted "dialectically." What exactly they meant was not always clear, for to say that two things interact "dialectically" is often to say nothing at all, or is a way of avoiding saying anything while appearing to say something profound. While analysts adopted this strategy of deliberate ambiguity in order to avoid antagonizing higher-ups, and others used "dialectical interaction" as a cover for muddled thinking and unprofessional scholarship, there were real differences among scholars as well as notable changes over time. The trend over the decade and a half after the Brezhnev-Kosygin team's accession to power in 1964 was toward increased emphasis on the Western contradictions, even though diplomatic activity, after some forays with France in the late 1960s, remained focused on Washington.

Throughout the 1960s a growing number of Soviet analysts wrote optimistically about the increasing polycentrism of the Western world. Scholars such as Iosif Lemin talked hopefully about the development of new "power centers" in international politics (Western Europe and Japan) and argued for a Soviet "peace policy" on Euro-

[25]Lenin, 36:332.

pean security directed at Western Europe.[26] Superficially, the argument had hardly changed since the days of Rapallo: Western European growth after World War II had exceeded the redivision of influence in the Western camp, leading to a major contradiction between the United States and its allies that Moscow could exploit for political and economic gain.[27] Analysts who were favorably disposed toward the new polycentrism were given a boost by France's defection from NATO's military wing in 1967 and the onset of British discussions about joining the EEC in 1967. Moscow's diplomatic activity in this period appeared to respond to the new opportunities by following Lemin's suggestion and seeking to engage Western European countries in the creation of a new security system to replace NATO. But Brezhnev and his leadership cohorts continued to uphold a general line that claimed that of the two tendencies that characterize imperialism, the centripetal, unifying tendency predominated.[28] Scholarly publications of the period were filled with debates about the real significance of changes in the intrawestern power balance.[29]

These scholars were opposed by others who hewed more closely to the general line. Their arguments, too, have a familiar ring, focusing on the essential class solidarity of the imperialists, no matter what market or trading arrangement they might come to in Western Europe.[30] Now, however, they expressed openly what had earlier been voiced only obliquely: A Western European "power center" might prove fatally attractive to Eastern Europe. After the events of the

[26]I. Lemin, "Velikaia Oktiabr'skaia Sotsialisticheskaia Revoliutsiia i mirovaia politika," *MEiMO*, 1967, no. 6, esp. 15.

[27]The Rapallo analogy was particularly stressed by such analysts as Margarita Bunkina, who focused on Germany. The evolution of her argument can be traced through her *Razvitie mezhimperialisticheskikh protivorechii v usloviiakh bor'by dvukh sistem* (Moscow: Izdatel'stvo Moskovskogo Universiteta, 1966); "Novyi etap mezhimperialisticheskogo sopernichestva," *MEiMO*, 1970, no. 9, 54–62; *Tsentry mirovogo imperializma: Itogi razvitiia i rasstanovka sil* (Moscow: Mysl', 1970).

[28]Brezhnev made this assertion in practically every major speech of the period, including his report to the Communist gathering in Moscow, 17 June 1969; see *Leninskim kursom*, 2:369.

[29]See in particular the report on an IMEMO conference on the fiftieth anniversary of the publication of Lenin's *Imperializm*: "Mezhdunarodnaia konferentsiia marksistov k 50 letiiu vykhod v svet knigi V. I Lenina 'Imperializm, kak vysshaia stadiia kapitalizma,'" *MEiMO*, 1967, no. 6, 58–106. The institute's director, Nikolai Inozemtsev, noted "differences" among the participants on "serious questions." Similarly, at a 1969 conference on international relations theory, a consensus on the importance of interimperialist contradictions still eluded scholars: "Kruglyi stol MEiMO: Problemy teorii mezhdunarodnykh otnoshenii," *MEiMO*, 1969, no. 9, 91.

[30]See, e.g., Oleg Bykov, "Evoliutsiia 'atlantisizma,'" *MEiMO*, 1969, no. 8, 28–36; and "Obshchaia strategiia imperializma, 'globalizm' i 'evrotsentrizm,'" ibid., no. 81–83.

Prague Spring in 1968, this was no paranoid fantasy.[31] Of the two (very broadly defined) groups of scholars, those who focused on Western polycentrism were more optimistic and confident about their country's international situation. They thought that a more flexible, 1920s-style diplomacy, which Iosif Lemin and others had advocated in the immediate postwar years, could be applied to the current bipolar situation to good effect. If Moscow were more sensitive to the resentments and economic interests of the middle powers of Europe, most especially Germany, it could obtain useful trade and financial cooperation while decreasing the cohesion of the opposing bloc of states. Two-camps scholars, on the other hand, wished to highlight the formidable power of the opposing alliance and consequent need for the Soviet Union to build up its forces. Their arguments combined Zhdanov's class-struggle rhetoric with Varga's practical assessments of the extent of American hegemony.

The course of events in the years after "normalization" in Czechoslovakia appeared to favor the advocates of polycentrism. Moscow's military answer to the Prague Spring not only kept Czechoslovakia firmly in the socialist fold, it not only put an end to West Germany's strategy of using its economic muscle to undercut solidarity of the Warsaw Pact nations, but it did nothing to undermine Western contradictions or the achievement of Soviet foreign policy goals in Western Europe. French independence continued to be a source of joy in Moscow, but the Social Democratic victory in West Germany, the onset of *Ostpolitik* under Chancellor Willy Brandt, and the ensuing series of treaties regulating the whole German question on terms acceptable to the Soviets (not to mention the beginnings of substantial German-Soviet trade) seemed to fulfill exactly the predictions of those scholars who had focused on interimperialist contradictions throughout the 1960s. Perhaps even more important in the Soviet context was the subtle shift in Brezhnev's prudently ambiguous general line.

At the Twenty-fourth Party Congress in 1971, Brezhnev proclaimed: "At the beginning of the 1970s, the basic centers of imperialist rivalry have become clearly defined: they are the U.S.A., Western Europe (above all, the Common Market countries), and Japan. Their economic and political competitive struggle is becoming increasingly acute."[32] Brezhnev offered no opinion about the real political significance of this development, nor did he openly revise the 1960s line

---

[31] Nikolai Inozemtsev, "Some Urgent Problems of European Security," *International Affairs*, 1968, no. 6, 68–71.
[32] *XXIV s'ezd Kommunisticheskoi Partii*, 1:38.

that the unifying tendency among the capitalist countries dominated. Nevertheless, for those attuned to such things, and by the standards of the day, this was a notable shift. Now advocates of polycentrism had a very authoritative Brezhnev quote to add to all those from Lenin's writings. Those who had focused all along on imperialist contradictions felt vindicated, and stated clearly what they had only implied before: that the "tendency toward the decoupling of the forces of imperialism is at the present stage more pronounced than the tendency toward their consolidation."[33]

In the years after the conclusion of the Warsaw and Moscow treaties with the two Germanys, evidence of European independence on foreign policy continued to accumulate. Britain entered the EEC, Kissinger's efforts to establish a "new Atlantic Charter" got nowhere with the Europeans, and in successive Middle East crises European countries exhibited a tendency to go it alone in defiance of stated American preferences. In the West, the talk was of the end of bipolarity, the beginning of a multipolar era, the primacy of economic concerns, the eternal "crisis of NATO." Soviet Westernologists never could agree on the precise dialectical combination of the centripetal and centrifugal trends, on the actual measurement of American hegemony, on the size of the lag between economic changes and political results, or on the question whether Western Europe could really become a "power center" (given the contradictions among its constituent countries).[34] But with all the mounting evidence of European independence in foreign policy, which seemed so dramatic at the time, it is hardly surprising that the experts' dialogue and even Brezhnev's vague general line assigned ever greater importance to inter-imperialist contradictions.

A puzzle nevertheless remains. Why all this talk of imperialist contradictions in the 1970s, when by all accounts Soviet diplomacy was transfixed by its détente relationship with Washington? Why, for that matter, were both the general line and the expert discussion more impressed by the West's "centripetal tendency" in the 1960s, when diplomacy seemed more geared toward courting Western Europe,

[33]M. K. Bunkina, "Protivorechiia atlanticheskogo partnerstva: Ekonomicheskii aspekt," *MEiMO*, 1972, no. 11, 65. Scholars such as Bunkina, who had concentrated on West Germany, felt particularly vindicated. See *SShA i Zapadnaia Evropa: Novye tendentsii v sopernichestve* (Moscow: Mysl', 1976), 174–75.

[34]On some of these questions, see Sodaro, "Soviet Studies of the Western Alliance"; and "Kruglyi stol MEiMO: Zadachi i perspektivy evropeiskoi bezopasnosti," *MEiMO*, 1972, no. 5, 84–102; Bunkina, *Tsentry mirovogo imperializma*, 104–9, and the review of the book by V. Motylev, "Uzly mezhimperialisticheskogo sopernichestva," *MEiMO*, 1972, no. 3, 143–44.

especially France? The answer is that most of the articles and speeches about imperialist contradictions were more or less straightforward, semijournalistic analyses of the potential for diplomatic maneuvering within the existing bipolar international situation. Soviets for the most part really believed in a "dialectical interaction" between American and European policies with respect to the USSR, so that it made sense to say that imperialist contradictions had increased and therefore the changes for a successful policy of détente with Washington were enhanced. The terms came from Lenin's *Imperialism,* and often made Soviet analyses sound much like those of the prewar years or the late 1940s. But in reality the subject matter was quite different. "Interimperialist contradictions" had by now metamorphosed from matters of life and death for the Soviet Union, from being the causes of wars, revolutions, and massive reorderings of the diplomatic scene, to a framework for discussing month-to-month diplomacy in a relatively stable bipolar world.

Like their counterparts in the West, Soviet scholars speculated about the changing nature of the international system (though, as a whole, they were less inclined to declare the end of bipolarity than some Western academics). And they doubtless thought the government's policy was misguided on this or that respect. Specialists on Europe often suggested that the government paid too much attention to the relationship with the United States. Specialists on France, Britain, and Germany quite naturally elevated the potential importance of those countries. But the disagreements were not large and did not concern the basic structure of world politics.

The very stability of the bipolar arrangement in these years actually facilitated experimentation with interimperialist contradictions. In the 1950s and 1960s revolts in Berlin, Poland, Hungary, and Czechoslovakia highlighted the fragility of Communist rule in Eastern Europe. In that context, notions of an independent West European "power center" seemed dangerous to many observers. But the situation in the 1970s appeared much more robust. Soviet writings suggest a greater confidence that the use of Western contradictions in pursuit of economic and political objectives posed no risk to Moscow's superpower role by undercutting the bipolarity on which it rested.

In light of these evident similarities between Soviet writings on the Western alliance and analogous Western writings of the day, it is fair to ask what remained of Lenin's *Imperialism* other than the rhetoric. Lenin's influence can be found in several assumptions shared by most Soviets professionally involved in international relations. Most important was the widespread belief that economic relations among capitalist countries were inherently conflictual. Soviet works assumed that the dynamics of monopoly capitalism forced states into rivalry and conflict. Since economic forces were in the final analysis determining, at some point changed economic balances must produce political effects. They assumed that economic forces led capitalist states to balance against each other. Specifically, Western European countries would individually or collectively seek to balance against American economic power either by mutual cooperation or by dealing with the Soviet bloc. Though the Soviets did not expect anything so dramatic as an alignment shift in the near future, certainly they foresaw great economic and political benefits for the Soviet Union along the lines of those it derived from its relationship with West Germany.

If economics on balance leads to Western contradictions, what explains Western unity? Here Soviets focused on American military power. The United States used its military preeminence to continue to extract political and economic benefits from its rivals even as its economic edge was diminishing. It provided a military service and took its payment in political and economic deference. In other words, the Western European states bandwagoned with U.S. military power, and this tendency overcame their natural inclination to balance against American economic power. This is where increases in Soviet military power paid their dividends. The Soviet's achievement of military parity vitiated the utility of American military power. Parity began to neutralize the previously ubiquitous psychological effect of America's nuclear umbrella on Western European minds. Thus the way lay open for the economic contradictions to come to the fore, pushing the Europeans away from the United States (and perhaps from each other as well). Once again, Soviets believed that their military power had great political utility precisely because it deprived America's military power of its political utility.

But the connections were even more ramified than that, for Soviets saw a more direct link between military power and Western contradictions. From Brezhnev on down, Soviets maintained that interimperialist contradictions ripened best in the warm sunshine of détente. Remove the tension, and contradictions come to the fore. This was precisely the line advanced by the hapless Malenkov in 1953. It reveals yet again the multifarious ways in which military power was seen to possess political utility. For it was military power, and particularly nuclear weapons, that brought the United States to détente, and détente that facilitated the emergence of economically and politically useful contradictions.

This set of views was yet another refinement over the cruder versions in vogue during Khruschchev's tenure. It was subtler and more complex, but the ideas were the same. The main difference was that in the earlier version military power induced political effects directly by affecting the perceptions of the key players. In the new version, military power brought political results indirectly, by undercutting the foundations of Western cohesion and allowing national political and economic forces to exert their natural fissiparous influence. Soviets were now much more confident that a détente policy would achieve good relations with the United States on the basis of equality *as well as* a diminution in the Western bloc's cohesion. They had much more evidence than in the 1950s that their policy was in fact becoming an important factor in intrawestern politics. The reason was parity. Parity cleared the decks for a real policy of exploiting interimperialist contradictions. A détente policy, the assumption was, can work only if it is backed up by the requisite forces. Events in the 1970s appeared to confirm this belief.

A final important effect of Leninist theory on Soviet views of the international situation in the 1970s was that it predisposed Soviets to be declinists. That is, it was axiomatic for many Soviet observers that the major source of international change would be American decline. This intellectual predisposition was no doubt buttressed by the impossibility of saying anything serious about the Soviet bloc itself in public. But Soviet declinists found ample support in the stream of Western writings on the same subject. The Western discourse, too, by and large assumed that the decline of the United States and the rise of Europe, Japan, China, and the South were the main wellsprings of international change.

If evidence from the West broadly supported Moscow's bandwagoning hypothesis and the modified theory of imperialism, data from the East made a mockery of official Soviet class-struggle ideology. The People's Republic of China, formally a "socialist" state, actively opposed the Soviet Union in the 1960s, and in the 1970s it began to align itself with the West.[35] If Yugoslavia, Hungary, Czechoslovakia, Romania, and Albania had not already done so, China completely discredited Moscow's statist two-camps thesis, which held that countries ruled by communist parties would stick together in international affairs. Conflicts with Czechoslovakia and China in 1968 and 1969 forced Brezhnev to acknowledge openly what most Soviets doubtless

---

[35] See Chief of Staff Marshal Viktor Kulikov's statements: "Development of Military Theory" (conference), *Voennaia Mysl'*, 1973, no. 2, 3–13 (FPD, 0045/73, 20 November 1973, 7).

knew already: that "objective contradictions" existed not only among capitalist states but among Soviet-type states as well.[36] Socialism, it turned out, was not immune to the law of uneven development.[37]

By the mid-1970s, China's behavior so blatantly contradicted Soviet ideological precepts that Moscow had to make an adjustment in the name of consistency. Acting in accordance with the dictates of the "class approach," the Brezhnev leadership sought to exclude China from the socialist camp altogether, claiming at the Twenty-Fifth Congress that relations with China were "special and separate" from intersocialist relations; that China was an "important reserve of imperialism"; and that Moscow was ready to normalize relations "on the basis of peaceful coexistence"—a term reserved for dealings with capitalist countries.[38]

When China was allied with Russia, Soviet leaders and commentators made much of its immense resources, often referring to it as a "great socialist power." The more closely Beijing aligned itself with Washington, and the more Washington talked about manipulating the U.S.-USSR-PRC strategic triangle, the more insistent Soviets became that China's power was only of regional significance and did not alter the essential bipolarity of world politics.[39] No Soviet discourse on the balance of power in this period was complete without the obligatory arguments against Nixon and Kissinger's "multiple centers of power" notions and Beijing's "three worlds" scheme. This partially explains the top leadership's wariness about "power centers" analysis and Brezhnev's refusal to let the general line go beyond mentioning the existence of the three imperialist centers. The confidence the Soviets displayed when they spoke of the robustness of Moscow's European position and their ability to play on capitalist contradictions without jeopardizing their superpower role was absent when they looked to the east.

Soviet views of power and alignment behavior in the Brezhnev years can accurately be described as centered on some concept of bipolarity, though the term was not understood in the Waltzian sense. Soviets held that the U.S.-Soviet relationship was the central one in

[36] See, e.g., Brezhnev's speech in Warsaw on 12 November 1968, after the Prague Spring, in which he spoke of "difficulties . . . of an objective character": *Leninskim kursom*, 2:326.

[37] A. Butenko, "Nekotorye teoreticheskie problemy razvitiia mirovoi sistemy sotsializma," *MEiMO*, 1971, no. 9, 99–108.

[38] *XXV s"ezd Kommunisitcheskoi Partii Sovetskogo Soiuza: Stenograficheskii otchet*, 3 vols. (Moscow: Politizdat, 1976), 1:33–34.

[39] For a scholar's analysis, see V. V. Zhurkin, "American-Chinese Relations: Concepts and Reality," *SShA*, 1973, no. 2, 12–23 (*CDSP* 25, no. 11: 1–7).

world politics; that U.S. hegemony was declining; and that Soviet military power opened the way for the emergence of significant, though not currently alliance-altering, intrawestern contradictions. For Soviet officials concerned with foreign affairs, the decade after 1965 was a heady series of victories in Europe and the West generally which ratified their basic framework for understanding world politics in all its essentials.

ELEMENTS OF POWER

The view of Brezhnev's détente policy and its supporting intellectual premises as a more sophisticated and ultimately more successful version of Khrushchev's efforts is buttressed by an examination of Brezhnev-era perspectives on the elements of power. Again and again, in realm after realm, Soviet military power turns out to be the necessary precondition for the operation of other factors in the ostensibly eclectic and multifaceted correlation of forces. And nuclear weapons, while not retaining quite the exalted status Khrushchev was wont to bestow upon them, nevertheless take the lead as the primary element of power.

Military Strategy and Military Power

Although the Soviets themselves did not begin to make the distinction until the late 1970s, it is nonetheless helpful to discuss Soviet military doctrine in terms of its sociopolitical versus military-technical aspects. During the Brezhnev years, the sociopolitical side of the doctrine, whose main aim was to prevent the unleashing of war against the Soviet Union, held that nuclear weapons were decisive in deterring any adversary from attack.[40] According to the military-technical side, whose aim was to prepare the country to fight any war that might nonetheless arise, nuclear weapons were the most powerful military means.[41] The central role of nuclear weapons in both aspects

[40] John Erickson, "The Soviet View of Deterrence: A General Survey," *Survival*, November–December 1982, 244. For a revealing Soviet discussion of parity and mutual deterrence, see Maj. Gen. M. Cherednichenko, "Military Strategy and Military Technology," *Voennaia Mysl'*, 1973, no. 4 (*FPD*, 0043/73, 12 November 1973, esp. 53).

[41] See, e.g., Col. V. Morozov and Col. S. Tiushkevich, "The Objective Laws of War and Their Reflection in Soviet Military Science," *Voennaia Mysl'*, 1974 no. 5 (*FPD*, 0016/74, 18 March 1974, 79); and Tiushkevich, "The Methodology for the Correlation of Forces in War," *Voennaia Mysl'*, 1969, no. 6 (*FPD*, 0008/70, 30 January 1970, 36).

of Soviet military thinking contributed to the notion that the existence of these weapons serves to equate otherwise unequal states in the general scales of global power. Khrushchev had employed such an argument in his offensive détente policy, but now nuclear parity really existed, a fact repeatedly recognized by the United States.

Soviet thinking about war did undergo changes in the years after the doctrinal consensus of the late Khrushchev era. Beginning in the late 1960s, Soviet analysts began to exhibit more uncertainty when they discussed the nature of future war. The doctrinal consensus of 1959–1960 had held that a future war would begin as a massive nuclear strike, which would be followed by retaliation and perhaps follow-on strikes. Ground forces would occupy territory, destroy enemy remnants, and defend against enemy ground attacks. The key military sources of the period held that a future East-West war would inevitably be nuclear. After 1968, however, many military sources in both the open and the restricted circulation press maintained that prolonged conventional or limited nuclear war was a possibility.[42]

Essentially, this doctrinal shift constituted a rejection of a single-variant view of future war. While the vast majority of military analysts had always rejected *single-weapon* theories of war (implied in Khrushchev's exclusive focus on nuclear missiles), the doctrinal consensus of the early 1960s came close to accepting a *single-variant* view of future war—it would inevitably be an all-out coalition war that began with deep nuclear strikes. After 1967, Soviet sources maintained that it was difficult to foresee precisely how the war might unfold, so it was necessary to prepare the people, the economy, and the military forces for all possible contingencies.[43]

This doctrinal shift is revealing on two counts. First, it is another example of American behavior serving the Soviets as an indicator of the correlation of forces. The key to the doctrinal shift was American military doctrine. When Soviet military analysts talked of the possibility of a nonnuclear phase, they explicitly referred to the new NATO doctrine of flexible response, which the Soviets saw as an "adaptation of American strategy to the new correlation of forces." As one classi-

---

[42] For Soviet considerations of the nature of future war, see (Col.) Mikhail M. Kir'ian, *Problemy voennoi teorii v sovetskikh nauchno-spravochnykh izdaniiakh* (Moscow: Nauka, 1985), 113.

[43] Western experts disagree on whether this change indicated that the Soviets now regarded containment of the conflict at the nuclear level as merely possible or actually desirable and achievable. Cf. Harriet F. Scott and William Fast Scott, *The Armed Forces of the USSR*, 3d ed. (Boulder, Colo.: Westview, 1984), with Michael MccGwire, *Military Objectives in Soviet Foreign Policy* (Washington, D.C.: Brookings Institution, 1987).

fied General Staff lecture explained, "Soviet successes in missile construction and nuclear weapons, superiority in conventional arms,
especially the ground forces, and the vulnerability of North America's
territory to Soviet strategic missiles . . . have forced the American
political and military leadership to seek a way out of the impasse."[44]
The increased American attention to the possibility of substantial
conventional warfare was, in Soviet eyes, a direct result of the improved Soviet position in the nuclear correlation of forces.

Second, the doctrinal shift had generally favorable implications for
Soviet military assessments of the correlation of forces, adding to the
period's general sense of security and comparative confidence. It is
true that the new NATO doctrine was accompanied by a significant
buildup of NATO ground forces, particularly of the West German
army. On the other hand, the shift in American doctrine was an
indicator that the Soviet Union itself could influence the nature of
a future war. The escalatory ladder was no longer the uncontested
possession of the United States. This feeling of control over one's
destiny must be considered an important element of power.

The Third World

If Brezhnev learned from Khrushchev to be careful when he made
pronouncements about overall power relationships, he learned to be
doubly cautious when he spoke about the Third World. Brezhnev and
the top leadership never included developments in the Third World
among the causes underlying the new stage of international relations
they made so much of. They waxed enthusiastic about "revolutionary" advances in the Third World only several years after they had
begun to express satisfaction with developments in other areas. Their
speeches in the 1969–1972 period, when they were beginning to project confidence about Soviet relations with the other great powers,
retain the 1960s scepticism about the Third World.[45] Only in mid-
decade, particularly at the Twenty-fifth Party Congress, did the top
leadership finally join with Moscow's revolutionary bureaucrats of the

---

[44] *Voennye doktriny glavneishikh kapitalisticheskikh gosudarstv (lektsiia)*," 1968, in personal
archive of Gen. Aleksei I. Radzievskii, former commander of the General Staff Academy
(courtesy of Aleksei E. Titkov). The main open source on American strategy at this
time was Genrikh Trofimenko's *Strategiia global'noi voiny* (Moscow: Mezhdunarodnye
Otnosheniia, 1968). The "correlation of forces" quote is from Anatolii Gromyko's review
of that book in *Voennaia Mysl'*, 1969, no. 4 (*FPD*, 0004/70, 22 January 1970, 92).

[45] Cf., for example, "Statement of the Conference of Communist and Workers' Parties
in Moscow," *International Affairs*, 1969, no. 8, 4–23, with Brezhnev's speech in *Leninskim
kursom*, 5:8.

international communist and worker's movement in celebrating anti-imperialist triumphs in the former colonial world.[46]

What can be discerned in the speeches of Brezhnev and other Polit-buro members in the years between 1972 and 1979 is a cautious expectation about two processes: the tendency for certain "nonaligned" nationalist Third World regimes to align themselves with Soviet positions in world affairs (essentially the line of the 1960s); and the increase in the number of "revolutionary" Third World states, the so-called countries of socialist orientation. The new element here was the expectation that political organization, in the form of Marxist-Leninist vanguard parties (as in Ethiopia, South Yemen, Afghanistan, Mozambique, Angola), could overcome economic backwardness and produce politically stable and reliable allies in distant areas of the world.[47] The most the Soviet leaders expressed was a certain optimism that relative gains could be made in the struggle with the West in the Third World. Never was there a hint that developments in the Third World would lead to any transformation in the nature of the system.

The Third World's importance did loom larger at other levels of the Soviet system. Scholarly/policy journals such as *International Affairs* and *World Economy and International Relations* not only exhibited high expectations about trends in the Third World but often expressed the view that these developments were of central importance in the overall correlation of forces. One *World Economy* editorial stated in 1974: "The development of the revolutionary process is leading to the transformation of socialism into the decisive factor of world development."[48] For old Comintern cadres such as the ideology chief Mikhail Suslov, Konstantin Zarodov, Boris Ponomarev, and other bureaucrats of the Central Committee's ideological and international communist affairs apparatuses, the struggle in the Third World was of primary importance, since the prospects for revolution anywhere else were so dim.

---

[46]See *XXV s"ezd Kommunisticheskoi Partii*, 1:34–39, and Joseph G. Whelan and Michael J. Dixon, *The Soviet Union and the Third World: Threat to Peace?* (Washington, D.C.: Pergamon-Brassey's, 1986), 25–27, for a useful comparison of Brezhnev's speeches to the twenty-fourth and twenty-fifth congresses as they relate to the Third World.

[47]See Francis Fukuyama, "Patterns of Third World Policy," *Problems of Communism*, September–October 1987, 1–13. Much Western scholarship exhibited a similar belief in the effectiveness of Marxist-Leninist vanguard parties in response to the dilemmas of modernization and dependency. See in particular Samuel P. Huntington, *Political Order in Changing Societies* (New Haven: Yale University Press, 1968), 334–43; and Kenneth Jowitt, *The Leninist Response to National Dependency* (Berkeley: Institute of International Studies, 1978).

[48]"Ob uglublenii obshchego krizisa kapitalizma," *MEiMO*, 1974, no. 9, 3.

A string of "victories" for pro-Soviet forces sustained this optimism. In a speech to a conference of ideological workers in October 1979, Ponomarev, the chief of the Central Committee's International Department (for liaison with foreign communist parties), listed these victories: Vietnam, Laos, Cambodia, Angola, Mozambique, Guinea-Bissau, Ethiopia, Nicaragua, and Afghanistan. "There is an inexorable process of replacing outmoded reactionary regimes with progressive regimes that are more and more of a socialist orientation."[49] Many articles that followed this line in discussing shifts in the correlation of forces paid almost exclusive attention to the "narrowing of the sphere of capitalist domination" by the national liberation movements.[50] In addition to clear victories for the "progressive forces," Soviets also cited defeats for the West as sources of optimism. The Iranian revolution, according to Foreign Minister Gromyko in an election speech in February 1980, left "a gaping hole in American foreign policy."[51]

The key event that sparked optimism about the competition for influence in the Third World was the war in Vietnam.[52] The war served as an indicator of the objective state of the correlation of the two sides' forces; it also contributed to an important American reassessment of the balance of power; and it independently sparked other, favorable changes.

It became routine for Soviet analysts to assert that the Americans failed "because the objective existing correlation of forces between socialism and imperialism on a global scale presented a limit to the

---

[49] Boris Ponomarev, "Vernost' idealam kommunizma," *Pravda*, 18 October 1979, 2, quoted in Aleksandr Nekrich and Mikhail Heller, *Utopia in Power*, trans. Phyllis B. Carlos (New York: Summit, 1986), 691.

[50] I. Gur'bev, "Osobennosti uglubleniia obshchego krizisa kapitalizma," *MEiMO*, 1981, no. 2, 14–17. In tracing the course of international change, Gur'bev simply counts the number of states and the percentage of world population "freed from imperialist domination."

[51] Andrei Gromyko, "Za mir i sotsial'nyi progress," *Pravda*, 19 February 1980.

[52] Cf. Ted Hopf's contributions to *Dominoes and Bandwagons: Strategic Beliefs and Great Power Competition in the Eurasian Rimland*, ed. Robert Jervis and Jack Snyder (New York: Oxford University Press, 1991), and *Learning in U.S. and Soviet Foreign Policy*, ed. George Breslauer and Philip Tetlock (Boulder, Colo.: Westview, 1991). Hopf agrees that the Soviet leadership accorded low salience to the Third World. He discounts the impact of Vietnam on Soviet assessments, however, finding that Brezhnev's "belief system" always held U.S. credibility in high regard. Hopf's content analysis may have been influenced by the general line's fundamental postulate that "imperialism's aggressive essence" was unchangeable. Focus on that de rigueur postulate might obscure the importance of its Brezhnev-era companion, the claim that the correlation of forces restrained imperialism *despite* its aggressive essence. Insofar as the Vietnam outcome awoke the U.S. elite to this fact, it overshadowed competition in the Third World in Soviet eyes.

military escalation that the U.S.A. carried out in Vietnam."[53] The outcome of the Vietnam conflict demonstrated that the "new correlation of forces" was more than just a generalized sense of equality connected to the nuclear equilibrium. It also had a dynamic aspect: the interrelation between the new correlation of forces and crisis outcomes in the Third World. Continuous favorable shifts in the correlation that led to a concomitant "reduction in the effectiveness of the forms, methods, and means of military struggle of the U.S.A. and the imperialist camp with world socialism."[54] Increased Soviet power enabled Moscow to aid Third World movements and deter the United States from escalating any resulting crisis.[55]

There is a direct analogy here to Soviet thinking about the connection between military parity and contradictions within the Western alliance. The Soviets' tendency to see economic relations among capitalist states as essentially conflictual carried over into many of their writings on relations between the industrialized and developing countries. As in the case of intrawestern relations, their modified Leninist perspective led Soviets to highlight military power in explaining continued Western influence in the Third World. To the extent that increased Soviet military capabilities, coupled with the growth of militarily strong pro-Soviet allies in the Third World, diminished the utility of American military power, the way would be cleared for the natural antagonisms between the Third World and the West to come to the fore. As in the case of Soviet views of the Western alliance, Soviets attached political utility to their military power at least partly because they thought it denied the West the ability to see its military power for political gains.

Confidence in their ability to contain escalation, which flowed from the Soviets' more robust assessment of their overall military posture, persuaded them that the Soviet Union need not fear military involvement in local conflicts. The outcomes of local wars could be influenced to Moscow's advantage without fear of escalation, as experience in Vietnam and later Angola and a series of other former colonial

[53] G. A. Trofimenko, "Uroki V'etnama," *SShA: Politika, Ideologiia, Ekonomika*, 1975, no. 6, 77.

[54] V. V. Zhurkin, *SShA i mezhdunarodnye konflikty* (Moscow: Nauka, 1975), 48. See also Zhurkin and E. M. Primakov, eds., *Mezhdunarodnye konflikty* (Moscow: Mezhdunarodnye Otnosheniia, 1972), 15.

[55] See Mark M. Katz, *The Third World In Soviet Military Thought* (Baltimore: Johns Hopkins University Press, 1982), 19, 38–39. For Soviet civilian and military expressions of this view, see G. Malinovskii, "Lokal'nye voiny v zone natsional'no-osvoboditel'nogo dvizheniia," *Voenno-istoricheskii Zhurnal*, 1974, no. 5, esp. 97; and Zhurkin and Primakov, *Mezhdunarodnye konflikty*, esp. 7–15.

possessions demonstrated.[56] Opponents of Soviet activism in the Third World in this period later acknowledged that they faced a problem when they argued against the policy: in the mid-1970s there was little evidence of active U.S. opposition to Soviet moves. As one such critic, Georgii Arbatov, observed, "A reduction in the level of trust is, after all, not so easy to notice immediately."[57] At the time, it seemed that the correlation of forces could shift, and Moscow could help it shift, in the Soviet Union's favor without threatening the military equilibrium between the two superpowers. The Soviet Union could simultaneously embrace a strategic equilibrium without embracing the international status quo or freezing the relationship of forces. It could be a risk-averse revolutionary power.

These limitations on the usefulness of Western military power in conflict situations contributed to the period's relative bullishness on competing for influence in the Third World. Underlying trends there were seen as favorable, and now it appeared that the West's ability to counter them by military means was severely constricted. This combination of basically favorable trends and a hamstrung West led to a rather optimistic prognosis. "The defeat in Vietnam," one article characteristically notes, "clearly reflects the unalterable fact that no reinforcement of imperialism in our time can lead to a change in its favor of the correlation of forces on the international scene, *or even to an interruption* of the people's liberation struggle in one or another region of the globe.[58]

The Vietnam War's importance for Soviet assessments was magnified by its evident effect on American perceptions. The U.S. defeat revealed the true state of the correlation of forces not only to the Soviets but to the American political elite as well. To take them at their word, Soviet analysts had long thought that U.S. leaders misestimated the correlation of forces. Khrushchev and his legions of foreign affairs commentators continuously argued that U.S. policy did not correspond to the "real" correlation of forces in the world. Soviet writings in the Brezhnev period expressed confidence that, at long last, events were showing the Americans the true limitations to their

---

[56] Lt. Gen. P. A. Zhilin and Maj. Gen. R.Briul', eds., *Voenno-blokovaia politika imperializma* (Moscow: Voennoe Izdatel'stvo Ministerstva Oborony SSSR, 1980), 329.

[57] Arbatov, *Zatianuvsheesia vyzdorovlenie*, 222–27. Arbatov relates this difficulty in arguing against aiding the People's Movement for the Liberation of Angola during an audience with Brezhnev.

[58] Oleg Bykov, "SShA i real'nosti mezhdunarodnoi razriadki," *MEiMO*, 1976, no. 8, 31; emphasis added. See also I. Gur'ev, "Obshchii krizis kapitalizma i ego dal'neishee uglublenie," *MEiMO*, 1975, no. 10, 36.

powers. Having predicted that the United States would fail in Vietnam (with some hedging during the years of heaviest involvement), and having spelled out in advance the "lessons" that Washington ought to learn from the experience, Moscow analysts were gratified when news from the United States suggested that the war indeed forced the American elite into an agonizing reappraisal.[59]

Soviet accounts suggested that a prerequisite of the "new stage" in world affairs was, in fact, the American ruling elite's subjective adjustment to the realities of the new correlation of forces. They never sorted out the question whether the Americans could yet again act in defiance of the new "realities" revealed by the war. Could Washington "unlearn" the lessons of Vietnam? No one asked this question. Soviets seemed to believe that the change in American perceptions was irreversible. Unlike the "new correlation" of the Khrushchev days, which consisted so largely of Soviet efforts to capitalize psychologically on global trends, the "new correlation" now was genuine— "objective," to use the popular Soviet term of the day. The war made the new state of affairs transparent: both Moscow and Washington now at last seemed to be seeing the same balance of power.

Soviet analysts also recognized discrete effects of the war on American decline and Soviet rise. The war mobilized and enlivened revolutionaries throughout the Third World; galvanized mass antiwar movements in the West; sapped Washington's military and economic reserves; exacerbated contradictions among the Western countries; and resulted in the emergence of a powerful state, Vietnam, which itself was able to render assistance to other liberation movements and act as a valuable strategic asset for Moscow.

The key here is that, as with Brezhnev's cautious correlation-leads-to-détente analysis, the outcome of Vietnam seemed to vindicate an earlier analysis of the correlation of forces. All of the various changes that made the U.S. defeat inevitable had occurred before the war. But it was "the victory of the Vietnamese people," Genrikh Trofimenko quoted Brezhnev as saying, that "showed 'how much the possibilities of imperialism have narrowed in our day.'"[60] The war's most profound influence was as an indicator of the overall correlation. In the words of one article in *World Economy and International Relations* in late 1969: "If the aggression in Vietnam was a kind of test of the real correlation

---

[59] V. V. Zhurkin, "Budut li izvlecheny uroki?" *MEiMO*, 1969, no. 4, 17.

[60] Genrikh Trofimenko, "Osnovnye postulaty vneshnei politiki SShA," *SShA: Politika, ideologiia, ekonomika*, 1981, no. 7, 6.

of forces in the world, its consequences have already demonstrated that this correlation is not to the advantage of imperialism."[61]

The Economic Competition

As in the case of competition in the Third World, Brezhnev-era optimism about economic rivalry was but a pale shadow of its exuberant Khruschevian predecessor. Economists did replace the line of the post-Khrushchev 1960s, which evinced profound respect for the economic potential of capitalism and acknowledged the secular increase in growth rates in the West, with the view that capitalism's currency crises, unemployment, inflation, and lower growth were incurable. But they advanced no argument that rivaled in boldness those of Khrushchev and such economists as Varga and Strumilin, who had made a case for the achievement of "preponderance" for the socialist world economy within a generation. Not only did analysts in the Brezhnev era jettison Strumilin's assumption of continued new additions to the socialist world, but they toned down considerably their projections for the economic growth of the existing socialist countries. They openly acknowledged the continued technical superiority of the Western economies. By the late 1960s, the Soviets essentially acknowledged that the two forms of economic organization—socialist and capitalist—would coexist indefinitely. Moscow's rumbling ideology machinery did not voice this recognition formally until the mid-1970s, when it replaced the old dialectical approach of two mutually antagonistic world economies struggling for world domination with the assertion of the prolonged interdependence of Western and Soviet-type economies.[62]

As in the case of the Third World, to make a qualitative distinction between the optimism of the Khrushchev era and that of the Brezhnev period is not to deny that optimism was greater in the mid-1970s than it had been a decade earlier. For, despite the decline in optimism about the performance of the socialist economy, the belief lingered that the relative position of the West, and particularly of the United States, was slipping in relation to both the socialist countries and the Third World. This view clearly had its origins in actual events, the first of which was the collapse of the postwar international monetary

[61] M. Marinin and I. Sokolov, "Imperializm i revoliutsionnye sily na poroge 70-kh godov," *MEiMO*, 1969, no. 8, 13.
[62] On this shift, see Elizabeth K. Valkenier, *The Soviet Union and the Third World: An Economic Bind* (New York: Praeger, 1983), 46.

order in the early years of the Nixon administration. In their election speeches in 1971, all the Soviet leaders took gleeful note of this development.[63] At the Twenty-fifth Party Congress, Brezhnev boldly proclaimed that the problem of recurring crises and periods of stagnation was beyond the capacity of "state-monopoly capitalism" to solve.[64]

But economic competition played an even less significant role than competition in the Third World. It had no "revolutionary" constituency. Aware of their own system's weaknesses, institute analysts would have been embarrassed by Khrushchevesque boasts. Soviets expressed confidence about economic rivalry only well after the onset of the "new stage" in international relations. It was clearly military power, not economic growth itself, that necessitated a détente based on parity. If negotiations were based on the relation of economic power, the West could still dictate terms.

The primary explanation for the shift on economic competition that eventually came is the course of actual events; namely, the severe recession and series of energy crises from 1975 onward. In 1974 IMEMO, whose task was to analyze the Western economies, was still hedging its bets on capitalism's prospects. Burned so often in the past by capitalism's resilience, institute analysts refrained from doomsaying, despite mounting evidence of serious problems.[65] By 1975, however, the institute's analysis had shifted. A worldwide crisis of the capitalist economy was under way, the worst in the postwar period. Some analysts stressed the extent to which the crisis represented an accumulation of cyclical phenomena, the implication being that these difficulties would prove temporary. Others focused on unique aspects of the crisis which could prove to be permanent. The consensus at the institute was that cyclical elements predominated, but that capitalism had entered a new and more troubled phase of its development.[66] Boris Ponomarev, of the Central Committee's International Department, was enthusiastic enough to proclaim "not simply a worsening but a definite qualitative shift in the general crisis of capitalism."[67]

[63]*CDSP* 23, no. 18: 1–3.
[64]*Leninskim kursom*, 9:479.
[65]See the summary by Nikolai Inozemtsev (director of IMEMO), "Capitalism in the 1970s: The Aggravation of Contradictions," *Pravda*, 20 August 1974, 4–5 (*CDSP* 26, no. 33: 3–5).
[66]"Ekonomicheskii krizis v mire kapitalizma," *MEiMO*, 1975, no. 4, 15–31, and no. 5, 61–82; "Kruglyi stul MEiMO: Infliatsiia—neot"emlimyi element kapitalisticheskoi ekonomiki," *MEiMO*, 1976, no. 1, 75–94; V. Martynov, "Uglublenie neustoichivosti ekonomicheskogo razvitiia kapitalizma," *MEiMO*, 1978, no. 7, 13–23.
[67]Boris Ponomarev, *Izbrannye rechi i stati* (Moscow: Politizdat, 1977), 535.

Brezhnev's report to the Twenty-fifth Party Congress in 1976 did take note of the crisis, observing that it was "a crisis whose sharpness and depth even bourgeois politicians admit can be compared only with the crisis of the early 1930s."[68] Still, the report devoted only one paragraph to the issue and made no reference even to a qualitative shift in the third stage of the general crisis.

In comparison with Khrushchev's drive for prestige, Brezhnev's effort enjoyed a considerably better military posture, not only on the nuclear front but in terms of conventional forces on the central front, naval and air forces, and power projection capabilities. By almost any reasonable measure, Brezhnev's USSR was a vastly more capable challenger to the United States than Khrushchev's had been. But psychologically the difference was even greater. Gone was the zeal, the boundless faith, the soaring confidence that Soviet state "socialism" had yet to reveal its true potential, the powerful feeling that things were developing rapidly. Brezhnev's government did have higher standards for assessing its prestige policy than Khrushchev's had had, and by these standards Brezhnev's policy was spectacularly more successful. Yet despite the Soviet Union's vastly greater resources, the mature Soviet political elite seemed to have lower expectations for "parity" with the United States than it had had in its adolescence under Khrushchev.

AMERICAN PERSPECTIVES

A brief look at the perspectives of top American decision makers yields two basic observations. First, Americans viewed increased Soviet military power as the main element that created a new situation in the 1970s. And second, the available evidence indicates that at no time did top American officials believe that increased Soviet military power necessarily translate into commensurate political influence. As in the immediate postwar period, the perception of equal military capabilities did not imply a belief in equal influence over the course of international relations. Because Americans now believed a situation of military parity existed, they explicitly referred to other elements of national power to explain the continued unique centrality of the United States in world politics.

In the 1970s, American officials saw the Soviet Union as a rising military power that presented a global challenge to U.S. policy. By the

---

[68] *XXV s"ezd Kommunisticheskoi Partii*, 51.

beginning of the decade, Washington assumed that the Soviets had achieved, or would soon achieve, essential strategic parity with the West. Most American analysts judged that American attempts to reverse the situation would be futile. Although U.S. policymakers perceived Soviet weakness in the economic competition, and even a reduction in the appeal of Soviet ideology, these weaknesses were in large part offset by newly perceived limits to American power in the wake of Vietnam. A sea-change in American confidence from the heady Kennedy days had taken place, and the whole debate was now over the limits to U.S. capabilities and the economic and political rise of the United States' allies. Further, American officials were clearly concerned, for at least the near and medium term, about the impact of the domestic situation on U.S. power. The post-Vietnam loss of a foreign policy consensus, the assertiveness of Congress, economic problems, and the "moral" crisis in American society all had their effects.

Top American policymakers had no doubts that the Soviet Union was seeking to redefine the terms of the superpower relationship on the basis of "parity." The Soviets made this point repeatedly on every front—diplomatic, military, and rhetorical. In 1970 they sought to test the relationship by attempting to set up a submarine base on Cuba, thus probing the limits of the 1962 understanding between Kennedy and Khrushchev. In 1971 and again in 1973, Soviet diplomats made strong bids for inclusion in the settlement of the Middle East issue. The Brezhnev team repeatedly sought implicit U.S. cooperation against China. The Soviets endeavored to counter each American naval deployment with a corresponding Soviet one, balancing, for example, U.S. forays into the Black Sea with their own excursions into the Caribbean. They sought formal declarations of equality in diplomatic documents. In practically all personal contacts with American leaders, Brezhnev and his Politburo comrades communicated, as President Nixon put it, "that they still crave to be respected as equals."[69]

The American side, despite recognition of Soviet strategic parity as well as reduced American global preeminence, once again rejected the Soviet bid. The underlying assumption of American diplomacy in the period—sometimes explicitly understood but most often implied by behavior—was that despite the new power relationship, the

[69] Richard M. Nixon, *RN: The Memoirs of Richard Nixon* (New York: Grosset & Dunlap, 1978), 619; see also 1035. And see Jimmy Carter, *Keeping Faith* (New York: Bantam, 1982), 247.

influence of the Soviet Union could be contained to the level of the 1950s or even earlier. Gains in some areas (such as Africa) were offset by losses in others (the Middle East). Détente was founded upon each side's belief that the other shared and accepted its assessment of the power and influence relationship. Détente unraveled as each side began to comprehend that the other had a rather different perspective on the balance of power and the hierarchy of prestige. To each side, the other's conception of its role, once it became evident, appeared as "pretension." Raymond Garthoff concludes: "Foremost among the causes of the ultimate failure of détente in the 1970s was a fatal difference in the conception of its basic role by the two sides."[70] While the Americans thought the Soviets might finally have recognized the legitimacy of the international order imposed after World War II, the Soviets believed the Americans had finally recognized the fundamental revision of that order.

The Nixon Doctrine and the "New Era"

There is a certain "Soviet" quality to the way Nixon and Kissinger articulated their foreign policy. In the typical Soviet way, upon arrival in power the administration claimed that a "new stage" had been reached which required a completely new policy. In the Soviet fashion, it buttressed its policy with a series of comprehensive and detailed reports, prepared by the NSC staff under Kissinger's direction, which spelled out the main assumptions and argumentation about the overall world scene underlying the new foreign policy. Finally, the Nixon White House at least tried to achieve Kremlin-like secrecy in the formation and implementation of its policy. The upshot is that the Nixon foreign policy reports, like the Kremlin's, provide a basic outline of the global analysis underlying the Nixon/Kissinger détente policy. Unlike most major Soviet policy statements, however, these reports strike one, even with almost two decades' hindsight, as unusually candid.[71]

The reports maintained that the postwar era had come to an end, a new era had arrived, and thus a new, flexible American policy was

---

[70] Raymond Garthoff, *Détente and Confrontation: American-Soviet Relations from Nixon to Reagan* (Washington, D.C.: Brookings Institution, 1985), 1069.
[71] This is how Kissinger himself (*White House Years* [Boston: Little, Brown, 1979], 159) and John Lewis Gaddis (*Strategies of Containment* [New York: Oxford University Press, 1982], 305) describe the annual reports. They can be found in *Public Papers of the Presidents of the United States: Richard Nixon* (Washington, D.C.: U.S. Government Printing Office, 1971–1974), 1970, 116–90; 1971, 219–345; 1972, 194–346; 1973, 348–518.

objectively necessary. They cited four essential changes in the world situation: Western Europe and Japan had risen to become independent power centers; the countries of the Third World had become more independent through the force of nationalism; the Soviet Union had achieved strategic parity; and "around the globe, East and West, the rigid bipolar world of the 1940s and 1950s has given way to the fluidity of a new era of multilateral diplomacy." The U.S. administration appeared to share the contemporary Soviet recognition of Japan and Western Europe as power centers, but predictably put more emphasis on the fact that the Soviet Union and the other socialist states "no longer present a solidly united front; we can now differentiate among them." The documents noted both implications of the decline of bipolarity: it implied, first, greater opportunities for diplomacy, but second, that "the era of American predominance is over. . . . In the new era, our friends are revitalized and increasingly self-reliant while the American domestic consensus has been strained by 25 years of global responsibilities." The major message to post-Vietnam America, then, was that the United States would henceforth rely on a greater degree on these revitalized local power centers and to a much lesser degree on its own forces.

A Soviet analyst could be excused for seeing in these and other public articulations of the Nixon/Kissinger foreign policy American ratification of the basic Moscow assessment of 1969, the kind of assessment that undergirded Brezhnev's détente policy. Here was the president of the United States solemnly proclaiming that "the postwar order of international relations," against which Moscow had chafed since 1947, "is gone."[72] Here was the American administration saying that the postwar era of U.S. hegemony was over, that now the Soviet Union possessed equal strength and the other major powers were more independent. The two superpowers were thus at least equals among these other states. But a closer reading of Nixon's and Kissinger's public articulations reveals something else entirely: the conviction that despite the new situation, the United States remained the key state and the Soviet Union could still be contained.

It is true that Kissinger, like many other American statesmen before him, was inclined to speak of the present distribution of overall power as an "equilibrium." But when he actually compared diplomatic weights, he maintained that "the United States remains the largest single factor in international affairs." Again and again Kissinger

---

[72] From Nixon's annual report on foreign policy, quoted in Deborah Welch Larson, "Learning in U.S.-Soviet Relations: The Nixon-Kissinger Structure of Peace," in Breslauer and Tetlock, *Learning,* 378.

maintained that though Soviet power had grown, it could be contained: "What is new today is the culmination of thirty years of postwar growth of Soviet industrial, technological and military power. No American policy caused this; no American policy could have prevented it. But American policy can keep this power from being used to expand Soviet influence to our detriment."[73]

This confidence that the American position could be maintained rested on two assumptions. First, Kissinger rejected the assumption that military power was "fungible," or easily translated into political influence, which is so common in international relations theory and so central to the Soviet perspective. "For centuries it was axiomatic that increases in military power could be translated into almost immediate political advantage. It is now clear that new increments of strategic weapons do not automatically lead to either political or military gains." The second point followed from the first. If military power is not fungible, then there cannot be a single distribution of power. "It is wrong to speak of only one balance of power, for there are several which have to be related to each other."[74]

In the Nixon's administration's official schema, the United States and the Soviet Union formed the bipolar military balance; the United States, Soviet Union, and China formed the tripolar political balance; and the United States, Western Europe, and Japan formed the tripolar economic balance. Since the military balance was not decisive and since only the United States figured in all three balances, America was clearly a uniquely central state that could manipulate all the others in a way favorable to its world position. Not only was the United States, and not the Soviet Union, a central player in all three balances, but in general it maintained better relations with all the other "poles" than any of them had with any other. This is by no means a recognition of overall parity for the Soviet Union. Instead, the United States is seen as the central balancer in a complex global balance of power. As President Ford saw it, the result of this diplomacy "was a recognition in world capitals that the United States was again the master of the international scene."[75]

The U.S. Rejection of Parity

Despite Kissinger's elaborate argumentation, its implied assertion of continued U.S. preeminence is clear only in retrospect. At the time,

[73] See the speeches reprinted in Henry Kissinger, *American Foreign Policy*, 3d ed. (New York: Norton, 1977), 283, 303–5, 317.
[74] Ibid., 310, 128.
[75] Gerald Ford, *A Time to Heal* (New York: Harper & Row, 1979), 128.

what doubtless stood out was the stress on U.S.-Soviet parity, the limits on American power, and the fact that an increase in strategic nuclear capability would not bring the *United States* tangible political gain. Indeed, much of the American and Western European discussion of alliance and overall world affairs attributed potential political utility to Soviet military (especially nuclear) parity. The constant fears of "Finlandization," the fretting over the "credibility" of Washington's security guarantees, the perennial conferences on the "crisis in NATO" all fed Moscow's belief that removal of U.S. military advantages would produce political dividends.

Three further indicators reveal the official American viewpoint: underlying beliefs revealed in memoirs; assertions about the "proper" Soviet role in various regional disputes; and actual U.S. diplomatic behavior. As far as the basic American attitude is concerned, Kissinger again provides the most insight. Relating his first encounter with Brezhnev in his memoirs, Kissinger notes: "equality seemed to mean a great deal to Brezhnev. . . . [I]t was central." The secretary of state consoled Brezhnev on this score: "He expressed his pleasure when in my brief opening remarks I stated the obvious: that we were approaching the summit in a spirit of equality and reciprocity. What a more secure leader might have regarded as cliché or condescension, he treated as a welcome sign of seriousness."

An attitude that the USSR was not as strong as it appeared, and that the Soviet leaders knew it, pervades Kissinger's account: "While [Brezhnev] boasted of Soviet strength, one had the sense that he was not really all that sure of it. Having grown up in a backward society nearly overrun by Nazi invasion, he might know the statistics of relative power but seemed to feel in his bones the vulnerability of his system." The general secretary "seemed in awe of American technology; he backed off in a crisis whenever we confronted him unambiguously with American power." The reason for Kissinger's view, in addition to the basic weaknesses of the Soviet system, was that "geopolitically the Soviet Union, despite its seeming power, was in an uncomfortable position."[76]

Nixon, too, thought he and Kissinger "had made a good impression" in assuaging Soviet concerns about parity at the first summit.[77] Perhaps because of these assurances, the Soviets sought concrete results of the new relationship vis-à-vis China, in the Middle East, and,

---

[76]Kissinger, *White House Years*, 1141–42. His impression at other summits was similar. See his *Years of Upheaval* (Boston: Little, Brown, 1982), 231.

[77]Nixon, *RN*, 619 (from his diary entry during the Moscow summit).

in the words of an unnamed Soviet official, in the "equal right to meddle in third areas."[78] But in none of these areas were the American leaders inclined to grant anything like parity. In their memoirs, Nixon, Kissinger, and Carter bridle at Brezhnev's suggestion for a mutual nonaggression pact, claiming, in Nixon's words, that it "smacks of condominium in the most blatant sense."[79] In addition to China, the key Soviet concern was the Middle East. At every summit or foreign ministers' meeting, the Soviet side made proposals for joint efforts or complained about the Americans' unilateral approach. At each meeting the American side followed the tack of Nixon and Kissinger in 1971; they offered general assurances of working together, avoided any specifics, and continued to work out unilateral solutions. As Kissinger put it: "We were not willing to pay for détente in the coin of our geopolitical position."[80] As far as the "equal right to meddle in third areas" was concerned, the eventual American reaction to Soviet moves in Angola, the horn of Africa, and Afghanistan indicated that U.S. policy makers viewed the Soviets' use of force to expand their influence as fundamentally illegitimate, unacceptable, and inconsistent with détente.[81] The key to Kissinger's contemporary argument about Angola was that though the country was intrinsically of little strategic worth, the United States had to oppose Soviet moves in order to prevent a dangerous precedent from being met.[82] In other words, the Soviet Union did not have an equal right to meddle.

The official American view, which was more emphatically expressed as the contradiction between it and the Soviet view became clearer over time, was that détente implied the Soviets' acceptance of the existing distribution of global influence, which precluded parity for the Soviet Union. This view was perhaps most bluntly communicated to Brezhnev by President Carter at the Vienna summit. As his Democratic predecessor had done two decades earlier during another summit in the same city, Carter explained to the Soviet leader the

[78] Alexander Dallin, "The Road to Kabul: Soviet Perceptions of World Affairs and the Afghan Crisis," in Vernon Aspaturian, Alexander Dallin, and Jiri Valenta, *The Soviet Invasion of Afghanistan: Three Perspectives*, ACIS Working Paper no. 27 (Los Angeles: University of California at Los Angeles, Center for International and Strategic Affairs, September 1980), 57.

[79] Nixon, *RN*, 1030. See also Kissinger, *White House Years*, 548, 554–55; and Carter, *Keeping Faith*, 258–59.

[80] Kissinger, *Years of Upheaval*, 299. See also Nixon, *RN*, 574; Carter, *Keeping Faith*, 205, 242; Ford, *Time to Heal*, 183, 303; and Zbigniew Brzezinski, *Power and Principal* (New York: Farrar, Straus & Giroux, 1983), 165, 175.

[81] See Garthoff, *Détente and Confrontation*, 524–33; and Brzezinski, *Power and Principle*, 180–81, for his rejection of Gromyko's "condominium" offer on Angola.

[82] Kissinger, *American Foreign Policy*, 321.

need to accept the existing world distribution of influence: "The United States has the will and the capability to defend its interests and the interests of its allies, and our maximum strength will be used if necessary. We have certain areas of vital interest, and the Soviet Union must recognize these interests. One such area is in the Persian Gulf and the Arabian Peninsula. Restraint is essential on your part not to violate our national security interests."[83]

The Late-1970s Shift

An element of the American political elite had been alarmed about what National Security Adviser Zbigniew Brzezinski called the "Soviet thrust toward global preeminence" ever since the Soviets achieved parity in the early 1970s.[84] This view was represented in the Carter administration, as well as a more sanguine view of Soviet power. The key to the shift in American views in the late 1970s is that actions by the Soviets—primarily their activities in Africa and Afghanistan—helped shift the balance between the two factions in favor of those who advocated a more confrontational line based on a more alarming assessment of Soviet power and intentions.[85] Concern about rising Soviet power animated important elements of the administration from the outset. After his inauguration, Carter ordered a detailed analysis of the overall balance of power, including its strategic, economic, and political aspects. The document produced by this review, Presidential Review Memorandum 10, concluded that only on the military front did the trends favor the Soviet Union to any significant extent. According to Brzezinski, PRM-10 "was relatively sanguine about our overall ability to compete politically, economically, and ideologically with the Soviet Union."[86] Presidential Directive 18, based on the recommendations of PRM-10, called for increased military expenditures.

In addition to increased military outlays, which began to rise in earnest in 1979 and 1980, the major policy initiative of the period was the opening of diplomatic relations and increased cooperation with China. Again, although Brzezinski advocated cementing the China

---

[83] Carter, *Keeping Faith*, 254. He repeated essentially the same message in a toast at a diplomatic dinner with the Soviet leaders that evening: Brzezinski, *Power and Principle*, 343.

[84] Brzezinski, *Power and Principle*, 148.

[85] See Garthoff, *Détente and Confrontation*, 629, 691, 788–89 for an account of the shift.

[86] Brzezinski, *Power and Principle*, 177.

tie from the beginning of the administration, the perception of growing Soviet aggressiveness and capabilities in combination with prodding from an even more alarmed Chinese leadership affected both the pace and the nature of the relationship. The relationship took on a much more forthright anti-Soviet tone and included an increasing element of military cooperation, symbolized by the visit of Defense Secretary Harold Brown to China in January 1980. What more decisively shifted the balance in the American administration between those who advised against too close ties to China for fear of adversely affecting the U.S.-Soviet détente, such as Secretary of State Cyrus Vance, and those who advocated close ties to China to offset growing Soviet power, such as Brzezinski, was President Carter's increased perception of rising Soviet power and threat, fed by actual Soviet behavior. The president outlined his thinking in his instructions before Brzezinski's trip to Beijing:

> . . . you should . . . share with the Chinese my view of the Soviet threat. To state it most succinctly, my concern is that the combination of increasing Soviet military power and political shortsightedness, fed by big-power ambitions, might tempt the Soviet Union both to exploit local turbulence (especially in the Third World) and to intimidate our friends in order to seek political advantage and eventually even political preponderance.[87]

Throughout the period, the logic underlying PRM-10 seems to have prevailed. The main perceived threat was the Soviets' effort to translate their military power into political advantage, and not their economic power or ideological attractiveness. Indeed, with its human rights campaign, the administration considered it had seized the high ground in the ideological struggle. The United States was still perceived to possess the assets needed to contain the Soviet Union. Kissinger's underlying view of the continued centrality of the United States and the Soviets' inability to challenge it in political and economic terms still obtained. The Soviets were seen as capable only of playing a disruptive role. As Brzezinski put it, "The Soviet Union might hope to displace America from its leading role in the interna-

[87] Ibid., Annex 1, p. 2.

tional system, but it was too weak economically and too unappealing politically to assume that position."[88]

BREZHNEV'S TEST OF THE CORRELATION OF FORCES MODEL

The evidence from the years between the late 1940s and the 1970s indicates that, as the equilibrium understanding of world politics leads one to expect, rough military parity characterized the superpower relationship all along. In the early years, Soviet conventional advantages balanced American atomic ones. By the last third of the 1950s, an existential nuclear deterrence situation prevailed, and it became more robust with time. Each side took comfort in its advantages and, perhaps more important, in the belief that war was not imminent. If the available evidence is even roughly accurate, we can conclude that the prospect of war had more real and immediate impact for the war-devastated Soviet Union than for the United States.

But what the equilibrium understanding does not consider is the political meanings of various military postures. Soviet and American leaders worried about war in the future, but they also thought about politics now. Moscow's military postures before the 1970s did not have the degree of political utility Americans feared and Soviets hoped. Brezhnev's expensive military modernization program led to a situation qualitatively different from that of any earlier period of the Cold War. There can be little doubt that the Soviet generals breathed easier in the 1970s than they had before. But Moscow's new military capabilities also altered the political situation. Coupled with what Brezhnev and Gromyko doubtless considered wise and competent diplomacy, they facilitated the achievement of cherished Soviet goals in world politics.

The 1970s saw the Soviet Union's European situation stabilized in ways Khrushchev had only dreamed about. The German situation was regulated, the GDR was recognized and secure, the postwar border changes in Central Europe were formally accepted. The Helsinki Final Act put an international-legal imprimatur on Moscow's conquests and sphere of influence. Trade with the Western countries skyrocketed, and it was carried out on terms that posed no threat to the Soviet system of rule. The Soviet role in the Third World was substantial and growing. In short, an increase in the value of the independent variable in the correlation-of-forces model, military

---

[88] Ibid., 148.

power, had produced change in all the dependent variables in the predicted direction.

Of course, the magnitude of the change was perhaps not so great as Brezhnev and his comrades had wished. Certainly, final agreements were a long way from Moscow's original proposals on all major issues. The West stayed in Berlin. The price for Gromyko's cherished Conference on Security and Cooperation in Europe was a nettlesome human rights clause in the Helsinki Final Act. Western "meddling" in human rights never ceased completely. The Soviets were denied their desired role in the Middle East conflict. They had to stand by while key clients were humiliated by Israel and stolen by the United States. The United States still seemed to apply double standards. In short, there was no superpower "equality." But Brezhnev and Gromyko, so proud of their "realism," knew very well that politics is an imperfect business. One can't always get what one wants. On balance, the policy no doubt appeared largely successful to them well into the 1970s.

Having learned from Khrushchev's experience in Berlin, the Brezhnev leadership avoided the tactic of provoking crises to resolve outstanding issues and lever up prestige. Unlike previous cold war cycles, the 1970s witnessed no decisive crisis signifying U.S. rejection of a change in international status for the Soviet Union. Instead, evidence of the Americans' rejection of superpower "equality" trickled in throughout the decade. Washington's real stance was apparently not clear to the Soviet leaders until the Americans, Western Europeans, Japanese, and Chinese shifted their security policy after 1979 and moved toward a much tigher anti-Soviet alignment.

After nearly a decade of successful policy based on the updated, revised, and sophisticated version of the old correlation-of-forces model, the Soviet leadership responded to the "new cold war" after 1979 with incomprehension. For a generation the Americans had flouted their nuclear power. For a generation they had appeared to derive political benefits from their nuclear superiority. They and the Europeans had talked unceasingly of the profound effects Soviet nuclear parity would have. Washington had unsubtly brandished nuclear superiority to defeat Khrushchev's bid for parity in 1961. They had talked of "equality" and "parity." They had stressed the decline of U.S. power, the "new era," limits, constraints. Yet the moment the Soviets, after great sacrifice, achieved unquestioned parity, all of a sudden the Americans claimed that their world status was based not on nuclear weapons after all, but on a varied mix of resources.

In a nutshell, the Americans defined "power" and conceptualized the balance of power in any way necessary to justify their continued hegemony. The Soviets' efforts to manipulate the variables that their major adversaries appeared to value were doomed because Washington would try to change the rules whenever it found them inconvenient. So the task for postdétente foreign policy was to decide who, in the final analysis, was right about the correlation of forces. As the Soviet leaders saw things, by the logic the Americans themselves had articulated over the last ten years, they would eventually be forced to come around again to détente.

The languid pace of the Brezhnev-era Cold War cycle yields some important lessons. To the ambiguity of feedback about policy and power in world politics must be added another consideration: the slowness of feedback. In the forty years after World War II the superpowers went through only three major policy cycles, based on different strategic assumptions and perceived balances of power (1947–1951, 1957–1962, 1979–1985). Even within a cycle, feedback takes time. For Brezhnev, working without the benefit of risky crises, almost a decade was required to reveal the underlying contradictions between his and the Americans' policies.

Brezhnev's experience also demonstrates the essential soundness of Moscow's much-criticized foreign policy strategy. Military power did have considerable political utility in the 1970s. It helped Brezhnev and Gromyko get much of what they wanted to achieve internationally. The middle powers did show a measurable tendency to bandwagon with Soviet power. Again, no one was thinking about any change in alignment. The issues concerned the *attitudes* of certain governments toward certain policies favored by Moscow. In addition, the "dialectical interaction" between the unifying and disintegrating factors within imperialism played themselves out quite nicely during the period. The behavior of Germany in 1969–70 and the Americans' effort to trump European détente the next year fitted so exactly the Soviets' modified theory of imperialism that it is no wonder they stuck to it so doggedly later.

One way to increase the volume and velocity of feedback is to do something leaders of major powers rarely screw up the courage to do: experiment with radically altered policies. This is, of course, what M. S. Gorbachev did in the years after 1985. And the key factors that conditioned Gorbachev's new departure were the eventual perception of the failure of Brezhnev's policy, the reassessment of the correlation-of-forces model that underlay it, and the onset of apprehensions about the USSR's decline as a great power.

[8]

Lessons from the Cold War's
Last Battle, 1980–1985

Brezhnev's détente policy was not the final Soviet effort to engineer a substantial improvement in the country's international position. That honor belongs to the revolution in Soviet foreign policy set in motion by Mikhail Gorbachev and his reformist colleagues after 1987. The impulse behind Gorbachev's relentless drive to extricate the Soviet Union from the dire straits he perceived cannot be explained without reference to his personality and the internal situation of his country. But the nature of his effort, and especially the ideas underlying it, were also products of recent international experience. And that experience was the perceived failure of Brezhnev's policy, whose outstanding feature had been its reliance on military power.

The "new political thinking," which would play such a fateful role in the end of the Cold War, can be traced most reliably to the years between 1980 and 1985. The temptations of hindsight are particularly acute when one considers the period immediately preceding a time of revolutionary change, and care must be exercised to avoid a determinism that is not supported by the available evidence. It would be impossible to sustain the argument that new thinking was the only possible Soviet reaction to the events of the early 1980s. It did not emerge wholly formed from the late Brezhnev "era of stagnation." Its eventual features were doubtless shaped more by Gorbachev's experience in power than by that of the ailing Brezhnev, Andropov, or Chernenko. Old thinking was not decisively and inevitably discredited for all time by the travails of the "new cold war" after 1979. The Brezhnev "test" of the old thinking, however, and especially of the correlation-of-forces model, was the most extensive yet; and a perceived adverse shift in the balance of power rendered difficult any Soviet argument for staging a comeback within the confines of the old thinking. If one stayed even roughly true to the old model of world politics, it was hard to be optimistic about Soviet prospects.

THE QUANDARY OF THE GENERAL LINE

Not for the first time in its lengthy history, the party's general line on the international situation encountered some difficulties in the years after 1979. The problem was simple. The other major powers in world politics were not behaving the way the old thinking predicted they would. They backed away from détente, raised defense expenditures, heated up anti-Soviet rhetoric, seemed less willing than before to deal with Moscow as an equal, and energetically cooperated with each other against Soviet purposes the world around. The dependent variables in the correlation of-forces model were moving in disturbing directions.

The Soviets' first response to the worsening of the international situation after 1979 was to profess continued faith in the détente policy. As late as 1980, with the United States' rejection of détente and attempts to "change the correlation of forces in its favor" clear to the Soviet leaders, they held on to the correlation-equals-détente formulation.[1] "Détente," Andropov reassured his Moscow "constituents" in early 1980, "reflects profound objective changes in the world arena, [and] has become too deeply rooted . . . to permit games to be played with it by any force."[2] This "deep roots" formulation was repeated by most other top leaders, appeared in a lead *Pravda* editorial, and was finally reaffirmed in the Central Committee's report on foreign policy to the June 1980 plenum.[3] It was only in his report to the Twenty-sixth Party Congress early in 1981 that Brezhnev finally jettisoned the correlation-equals-détente formula that had served him so well for so long.

Every general secretary after 1980 acknowledged the deterioration in the Soviet Union's international situation. Using language strikingly similar to that of the mid-1960s, Brezhnev's report to the Twenty-

---

[1] The quote is from Grigorii Romanov, *Pravda*, 7 February 1980, but it could as easily be that of any other top official.

[2] Iurii Andropov, *Izbrannye rechi i stat'i* (Moscow: Izdatel'stvo Politicheskoi Literatury, 1983), 188.

[3] *Pravda*, 4 February 1980, 1, and 24 June 1980, 1 (*CDSP* 32, no. 25: 7). See also Andrei Gromyko, "Za mir i sotsial'nyi progress," *Pravda*, 19 February 1980.

sixth Congress detailed the series of alarming trends in world affairs.[4] The Brezhnev team's heightened concern about the country's external situation was reflected in the final speech written for the aged Soviet leader, delivered to an impressive gathering of military brass in October 1982. In the most strident terms yet, Brezhnev portrayed a Soviet Union in dire international straits, assaulted by a rapidly arming and technologically sophisticated Western camp.[5] Not only were NATO countries and Japan all in cahoots against Soviet purposes, but China was energetically edging closer to them politically and even militarily.

After the Twenty-sixth congress, almost no speech by a top Soviet leader was complete without some reference to the darkened international horizon. Politburo members justified continued heavy defense spending, explained away poor economic performance, pleaded for greater internal and intersocialist unity and discipline, and explained their efforts to woo heretofore ostracized China all by reference to international difficulties. In a small but significant doctrinal move indicating less complaisance about Soviet prospects, a frail Andropov backed away from his predecessor's ideological claim that the Soviet Union had achieved "developed socialism."[6]

As it had done in 1947, 1951, and 1962, the general line beat a retreat from optimism. Sanctioned discourse on foreign policy in the country began a return to a 1960s-like circumspection and pessimism about the correlation of forces. Major political figures and lowly political commentators alike silenced or at least toned down considerably their heretofore ritual references to the shifting correlation of forces, and harped ever more insistently on the threat from the recklessly anti-Soviet Reagan administration. The old war-scare machinery was taken out of mothballs, oiled, and fired up yet again as the Soviet peoples were told of America's plans to "militarize space," achieve a first-strike capability, and seek victory in a sudden nuclear war against socialism. Worn but worrying refrains from earlier, similar phases of the general line made their reappearance, from xenophobic laws against mixing with foreigners to thinly veiled anti-Semitic propaganda against "Zionist" influences in Soviet life.

All this alarm created a quandary for those who worked within the

---

[4] *Leninskim kursom: Rechi i stat'i*, 9 vols. (Moscow: Izdatel'stvo Politicheskoi Literatury, 1970–1980), vol. 8, esp. p. 634.

[5] *Pravda*, 28 October 1982, 1.

[6] Andropov, *Izbrannye rechi i stat'i*, 145. For other speeches referred to in this paragraph, see *Pravda*, 7 November 1981, 3 (*CDSP* 33, no. 45: 4), 3 March 1982 (*CDSP* 33, no. 45: 4), 28 October 1982 (*CDSP* 34, no. 43: 1); Andropov, *Izbrannye rechi i stat'i*, 226; and Gorbachev, 2:86.

strictures of the official ideology. After all, the explicit premise behind Soviet foreign policy in the 1970s had been that the correlation of forces "objectively" necessitated détente. And now détente was a thing of the past. Had the correlation then taken a turn for the worse? Some official scholars and ideologists, in a backhanded and Aesopian way, suggested that it had. They stressed that the correlation had gone through "zigzags," "twists and turns," and "retrograde phases" in the past; that favorable shifts were inevitable only "in principle" rather than in practice; and that though the correlation continually improved at the level of basic productive and social forces, at the "decisive" interstate level it was by no means favorable and could actually worsen.[7]

But talk of Soviet decline was dangerous. If one believed the correlation-of-forces model, loose talk about adverse shifts in the balance of power could feed the ambitions of the adversary. Indeed, the collapse of détente must mean that the Americans had reassessed the correlation of forces in a sense favorable to themselves. And, true to form, the Reagan administration soon began touting the argument that its defense programs were intended to exhaust the weak Soviet economy and achieve arms control, or even victory in the Cold War, on Western terms. Confirmation of that assessment by responsible Soviet officials would be disastrous. Soviet leaders responded to this situation in typical fashion: they fudged the issue. They talked of the deterioration in the international situation without offering a consistent explanation for it.

The party's general line was no stranger to such inconsistency and ambiguity. During earlier retreats from optimism in 1947, 1951, and 1962, party propagandists had had to defend some weak briefs. In Stalin's day they trotted out the hostility thesis to explain imperialist enmity despite socialist strength. After the failure of the second Berlin ultimatum and the Cuban missile crisis, Khrushchev simply toned down the rhetoric and declared his mini-détente with Kennedy a victory, leaving hundreds of international affairs publicists to pick up the analytical pieces any way they might.

---

[7]For example, see Petr Fedoseev in *Pravda*, 13 November 1981, 2–3 (*CDSP* 33, no. 40: 19), and the discussion in V. I. Gantman, ed., *Sistema, struktura, i protsess razvitiia sovremennykh mezhdunarodnykh otnoshenii* (Moscow: Nauka, 1984), 122–23. For sober assessments of the correlation see Vadim V. Zagladin, "Sootnoshenie sil na mirovoi arene i razvitie mezhdunarodnykh otnoshenii," *Mezhdunarodnaia Zhizn'*, 1985, no. 2, 77, and his "Sootnoshenie sil na mezhdunarodnoi arene i bor'ba za mir," in *Mir i razoruzhenie: Nauchnye issledovaniia*, ed. P. N. Fedoseev, 140–53 (Moscow: Nauka, 1987), esp. 146–48.

But this time around the dissonance was greater. The intellectual inertia behind Brezhnev's policy and its supporting strategic analysis was many times more substantial than it had been in those earlier cases. In the decade after Brezhnev first articulated the correlation/détente argument, Soviet ideologists and international relations scholars built up an enormous semiofficial literature on the correlation of forces which dwarfed in complexity anything produced in the Khrushchev period.[8] Now weighing down upon those who created it, this literature presupposed the *inevitability* of favorable shifts in the correlation of forces. Socialism represented a higher form than capitalism. The world was in the epoch of the transition from capitalism to socialism. In principle, then, the overall correlation of forces between capitalism and socialism must shift in the latter's favor over time. Of course, this teleological inevitability thesis had always been part of official Marxism-Leninism, but international relations ideologists made more of it in the 1970s than they had before. For anyone who took it seriously, this ponderous intellectual edifice claimed that détente, which reflected profound and irreversible objective changes, was itself irreversible.

As arcane as this literature might seem, it was indicative of an important fact. The deterioration of the Soviet Union's position after 1980 presented a greater challenge to the old thinking than any earlier setback had done. The Brezhnev détente policy had been the most extensive test of the correlation-of-forces model in the postwar years, for the Soviet achievement of military parity was as unambiguous as things in international politics could be. Nuclear parity had eluded Stalin and Khrushchev, except in the barest sense of the term. The Brezhnev/Gromyko policy had been a qualified success for nearly a decade, so the reverses it suffered after 1979 were particularly jarring. Because it had appeared successful for so long, the intellectual, bureaucratic, and political investment in the policy was much higher than it had been in Stalin's and Khrushchev's efforts. The ramified intellectual and ideological edifice that had been built up around the policy and the correlation-of-forces model was a reflection of the posi-

---

[8] For excellent analyses of this literature, see Charles A. Lynch, *The Soviet Study of International Relations* (Cambridge: Cambridge University Press, 1987); R. J. Mitchell, *Ideology of a Superpower: Contemporary Soviet Doctrine on International Relations* (Stanford: Hoover Institution, 1982); Margot Light, *The Soviet Theory of International Relations* (New York: St. Martin's Press, 1988). A more abstract but also useful analysis is Julian Lider, *Correlation of Forces: An Analysis of Marxist-Leninist Concepts* (New York: St. Martin's Press, 1986). Soviet treatments are multitudinous. In English, see Dmitrii Tomashevskii, *Lenin's Ideas and Modern International Relations*, trans. Jim Riordan (Moscow: Progress, 1974), esp. 64–103.

tive feedback it had generated over so many years. The policy developed extraordinary inertia now not just because the Brezhnev government was bureaucratic or because its leaders were old and ill disposed to change but because it had been better thought out, more skillfully implemented, and backed up by more material resources.

This is where the new political thinking began. American intransigence, European's continued deference to Washington's strategic preferences, the eventual deployment of U.S. intermediate-range nuclear forces in Europe, the political and strategic costs of the Afghanistan intervention, and the continued existence of the anti-Soviet alignment of the world's major power centers were all international-political facts that did not sit well with the expectations generated by the old thinking. The 1980–1985 experience of hunkering down in the face of what must have seemed to the Soviet leaders a cynical and hostile assault by the United States did not, of course, predetermine the demise of old thinking. But it led many experts to one or both of two conclusions: either the old model was wrong or the Soviet Union was in decline. Neither reflected well on the Soviet leadership. Both played well with reformist sentiments among the elite.

The conflicted general line left the door ajar for members of the foreign policy intelligentsia to engage in more substantial rethinking than they had been able or inclined to do earlier. They still were hemmed in by external and internal restrictions. A large number, it must be acknowledged, mechanically pumped out articles propounding studied ambiguity or offering niggling amendments to safe dogmas simply in order to retain their status and privileges in the system. Nevertheless, an analysis of their output from 1980 to 1985 reveals another distinction between Brezhnev retreat from optimism and earlier similar episodes: a widespread sense of substantial deterioration in the Soviet Union's internal and external positions.

In the wake of the collapse of Khrushchev's prestige policy after the Cuban missile crisis, for example, a few reformist experts and intellectuals did fault the Soviet system on numerous grounds and favored some form of "market socialism."[9] But they did not doubt the existing system's ability to compete with the West at the state level. Though no one expressed the kind of optimism that Khrushchev's party program had projected, there appeared to be little doubt that the relative position of socialism on military and raw economic scales would improve. Arguments for reform therefore had to rest on the

---

[9] For a description of some of these currents, see Boris Kagarlitsky, *The Thinking Reed* (New York: Verso, 1988), chap. 5.

existing system's failure to live up to the humanistic ideals of socialism rather than on hardheaded realpolitik concerns about great-power competition on the international scene.

The contrast with the pessimistic postdétente period could not be greater. Members of the Soviet elite questioned their country's capacity to perform at every level of the rivalry, from the military balance to the economy and the Third World. The international situation had worsened, the correlation of forces had taken a turn for the worse, and from institutes, universities, General Staff organs, and even Central Committee departments came analyses raising doubts about the Soviet Union's ability to stage a comeback in the absence of some measure of domestic change. Reading the open literature closely and supplementing it with interviews, one can piece together a rough outline of the multifarious intellectual tendencies at large within the Soviet elite. Their platforms were amorphous and variegated, and even had they been well worked out, they were impossible to articulate clearly in the pages of the censored press. But most noteworthy is the apparent agreement among representatives of so many of these tendencies, whether broadly reformist or conservative in outlook, that new initiatives were needed.[10]

It is important to distinguish between decline and deterioration. For the vast majority of politically active citizens in what we now know to have been the twilight years of the Soviet system, the problem was a relative deterioration in the country's internal and external position as a result of inept or corrupt leadership. New policies, whether centralizing or decentralizing, authoritarian or liberal, would restore vigor to Soviet socialism internally and prestige internationally.

DISTRIBUTION AND MECHANICS OF POWER

"The course of world history, in all its complexity and contradictoriness, has convincingly confirmed the veracity of Lenin's theory of imperialism."[11] With these words Leonid Abalkin, soon to be hailed as an "architect" of Mikhail Gorbachev's economic reforms, concluded his article "Lenin's Theory of Imperialism in Light of Contemporary

---

[10] On intellectual currents in this period, in the political elite as well as among intellectuals, see Vladimir Shlapentokh, *Soviet Intellectuals and Political Power: The Post-Stalin Era* (Princeton: Princeton University Press, 1990), chaps. 6–8.

[11] L. Abalkin, "Leninskaia teoriia imperializma v svete sovremennykh real'nosti," *MEiMO*, 1985, no. 5, 73.

Realities," published in May 1985, two months after Gorbachev assumed the post of general secretary. Abalkin's conclusion suggests the tenacity of the theory's grip on Soviet discourse about the international economy and world politics. The inertia behind the Leninist theory was such that it still served as the basic international relations text for students in 1988. Not until 1990 did the journal that had carried Abalkin's piece publish an article directly questioning the adequacy of the theory and its central term, "imperialism."[12]

Since Lenin's theory still called the official tune, the debate among experts on American decline and world alignments followed more or less familiar lines. Most Soviet Westernologists continued along intellectual paths well worn during the détente years of the 1970s. The questions concerned which lever to pull, which contradiction to play, and how to balance security, economic, and political goals. Soviet diplomacy on the issue of intermediate-range nuclear forces (INF) in Europe reflected the traditional approach of seeking to exploit evident political and especially security contradictions within the Western alliance.[13] The deployment of multiple-warhead mobile SS-20 missiles produced a typically contradictory reaction in the West: on the one hand, NATO banded together in December 1979 and agreed to a "counterdeployment" of American missiles; but on the other hand, it simultaneously expressed a commitment to negotiate with Moscow on the issue. This old combination of opposition and conciliation was by now classic Cold War fare for Moscow. Would Soviet firmness yield confrontation or détente? Only time would tell.

In hindsight, what stands out in the history of the INF issue in the early 1980s is the leading role taken by the Europeans, and especially the Germans, in engaging the United States to oppose the threatening Soviet deployment. At the time, that development competed for attention with other events: the growing peace movements opposed to the U.S. missiles, the hesitation of NATO governments to adopt decisions to deploy them, and, most intriguing for Moscow, the development of alternative security platforms by all the key opposition parties in Europe. In the eyes of NATO watchers in Moscow, those platforms were direct manifestations of the basic security contradiction Soviet policy had so long sought to exploit. American "extended deterrence" in Western Europe simultaneously lacked credibility (would Washington trade Chicago for Cologne?) and appeared to

---

[12] P. Khvoinik, "Imperializm: Termin i soderzhanie," *MEiMO*, 1990, no. 1, 5–19.
[13] An excellent analysis is Jonathan Haslam, *The Soviet Union and the Politics of Nuclear Weapons in Europe, 1969–1987* (Ithaca: Cornell University Press, 1990).

place Europe under threat of nuclear annihilation. European civilization could be ended by a war in whose onset it had no interest, no stake, and no voice.

Well after the U.S. deployment got under way, and even after Moscow agreed to reverse the SS-20 decision in the 1987 INF treaty with the United States, sophisticated Soviet analysts could claim that the original deployment was "objectively" a success. The INF battle, they argued, was the crucial precondition for pan-European rethinking of security policy. And that rethinking, in turn, made possible Gorbachev's hope for a new, demilitarized and denuclearized security system in Europe. Equally sophisticated Western analysts, fearing precisely such an outcome, criticized the INF treaty for the same reasons.[14]

Soviet officials insistently played upon Europeans' nuclear fears, seeking to bring the essential contradictions surrounding extended deterrence to light. Brezhnev, for example, reminded a German magazine in 1981 that "Europe is our common home." The "American militarists," however, think of Europe as "if it were a little box of tin dolls that deserve no better fate than to be melted down in the flames of nuclear explosions."[15] Defense Minister Dmitrii Ustinov warned of "retaliatory strikes against West European countries" if Washington ever used its NATO missiles. Andropov told Chancellor Helmut Kohl in 1983 that East and West Germans would "have to look at each other through a thick palisade of missiles."[16] Meanwhile, the Central Committee's International Department geared up to galvanize Western European peace movements, funneling financial and organizational support through fraternal communist parties and front organizations such as the World Peace Council.

With time, and particularly after the Americans began to deploy intermediate-range nuclear missiles in 1983, Soviet observers admitted that the policy was not succeeding in its immediate objectives. Intrawestern cooperation had increased and the West's inclination to defer to Moscow had decreased in the face of increased Soviet military

---

[14]Examples include Sergei Karaganov, "The Common European Home: The Military Angle," *International Affairs*, 1988, no. 8, 71–78; Jeffrey Record and David B. Rivkin, Jr., "Defending Post-INF Europe," *Foreign Affairs* 66 (Spring 1988): 735–54; William Odom, "Soviet Military Doctrine," *Foreign Affairs* 67 (Winter 1988–1989): 114–34.

[15]*Der Spiegel,* 3 November 1981 (*CDSP* 33, no. 44: 1–7).

[16]*Pravda*, 25 October 1979, 1 (*CDSP* 31, no. 47: 3); 27 August 1983 (*CDSP* 35, no. 31: 2). Earlier Andropov made the incredible claim that at present Soviet missiles "are not aimed against the FRG's armed forces. But that situation will change if American missiles are deployed on West German soil. Then the military threat to the FRG will increase manifold": *Pravda,* 5 July 1983, 1 (*CDSP* 35, no. 27: 2).

power. This set of responses was the exact opposite of what had occurred in the 1970s. The key question for Russian Westernologists was how to interpret these responses. As the decade progressed, analysts of all stripes acknowledged that the "centripetal," unifying tendency now predominated in interwestern relations. The question was: Why? For some observers the coming to power of conservative leaders (Margaret Thatcher, Helmut Kohl, Ronald Reagan, even the "pseudosocialist" François Mitterrand) was enough to explain Western harmony. But most recognized deeper explanations, many of which implied an even more profound appreciation of the fundamental stability of the bipolar arrangement.

Many Soviet onlookers reacted to the events of the 1980s by concluding that they had overrated the extent of American decline in the 1970s, or had underrated the extent of decline necessary to produce significant political effects in the Western alliance and on the world scene generally. Even those who favored a traditional Leninist approach could agree that in the early 1980s the United States had succeeded in recovering some of the territory in the world capitalist political economy it had lost in the preceding decade. In a departure from their writings in the 1970s, many Soviets now began to remind their readers of remaining American strengths, including a continued lead in high technology and "science-intensive" production; the United States' unquestioned military hegemony; its unchallenged hegemonic role in the NATO bloc; its lead in military technology; its lead in expenditures for research and development; and its rapid restructuring away from the old smokestack industries to more promising areas.[17]

In addition to the apparent U.S. resurgence, the economic growth of the Western European "power center" in the early 1980s looked less robust than it had earlier.[18] America's apparent reversal of the law of uneven development, though small and perhaps temporary, highlighted yet again the fundamental stability of postwar power and alliance relationships, even for those who operated within the traditional modified Leninist framework. In retrospect, neither the United States' fall from its "hypertrophied" dominance in 1947 to "normalcy"

[17] N. Volkov and N. Shmelev, "Strukturnye sdvigi v ekonomike kapitalizma," *MEiMO*, 1985, no. 8, 33; E. Kirichenko, "On Certain Specific Features of the Inter-imperialist Rivalry," *International Affairs*, 1985, no. 6, 78–86; Iu. Stoliarov and E. Khesin, "Tri tsentra sily v ekonomike sovremennogo kapitalizma," *MEiMO*, 1984, no. 1, 40.

[18] On U.S. resurgence, see Stoliarov and Khesin, "Tri tsentra sily." On "Eurosclerosis" see Valentin Kudrov, "Tri tsentra imperializma: Novye aspekty protivorechii," *Kommunist*, 1985, no. 13, 107; and Volkov and Shmelev, "Strukturnye sdvigi," 36.

in the 1960s nor the relative U.S. decline coupled with Soviet strategic parity in the 1970s had produced major effects on the basic alignment structure. Now, in a mild repeat of post-Suez perceptions, America's relative power was increasing. After iron laws and inevitable trends, Soviets now were dealing with cycles, which spoke convincingly of stability.

On a more conceptual level, there were three essential Soviet reactions to the apparent increase in Western cooperation in the early 1980s. For a small group of innovative Soviet analysts, the sources of stability within the Western political and economic system were even deeper than mere changes in the intrawestern balance of power. These scholars began to question the extent to which intrawestern cooperation required American hegemony at all, given the highly interdependent character of the modern capitalist economies. The implications of their writings, though not always spelled out in so many words, ran directly counter to those suggested by the theory of imperialism. Where *Imperialism* portrayed intrawestern relations as a zero-sum game, the new approach saw the sum as positive. Where *Imperialism* focused on the military sources of American dominance, the new approach highlighted economic factors. The old view expected international change to follow from American decline; the new view projected robust stability. The new approach reflected the reformers' vision of world capitalism: it was stable, successful, and challenging, but not militarily threatening.

Retrospective Soviet accounts date the origins of the revised view of world capitalism to the 1970s, when the Institute of World Economy and International Relations (IMEMO) and particularly its director, Nikolai Inozemtsev, tried unsuccessfully to get the political leadership to take cognizance of the "scientific-technological revolution" and the increasing "internationalization" of capitalism.[19] The increase in apparent intrawestern cooperation in the 1980s played very well with this nascent intellectual movement. The new argument, expressed prominently in the writings of the reform-minded

---

[19] See Georgii Arbatov's accounts of his and Inozemtsev's efforts in his *Zatianuvsheesia vyzdorovlenie (1953–1985 gg.): Svidetel'stvo sovremnnika* (Moscow: Mezhdunarodnye Otnosheniia, 1991), 171–73; and two articles by other former colleagues of Inozemtsev's, on the occasion of his seventieth birthday: E. M. Primakov, "Uchenyi, rukovoditel', chelovek," *MEiMO*, 1991, no. 4, 104–10; and Oleg Bykov, "Sovremennye problemy mirovoi ekonomiki i mezhdunarodnykh otnoshenii," *MEiMO*, 1991, no. 6, 113–19. An important Western analysis of Soviet views of capitalism in this period is Franklyn Griffiths, "Attempted Learning: Soviet Policy toward the United States in the Brezhnev Years," in *Learning in U.S. and Soviet Foreign Policy*, ed. George Breslauer and Philip Tetlock (Boulder, Colo.: Westview, 1991).

economist Nikolai Shmelev as well as in those of many IMEMO analysts, questioned traditional Soviet ways of thinking about American
hegemony and the world capitalist economy in general. Shmelev attributed intrawestern cooperation to the "socialization of production
on a world scale," under which "the state-monopoly capitalism of
individual countries gradually evolves into interstate-monopoly capitalism."[20] The old methodology of comparing the raw economic output of various countries, dating from the pre–World War I treatises
of Lenin, Rudolf Hilferding, and Rosa Luxemburg, had become
anachronistic. The Western economies were so complex and interdependent that shifts in the correlation of aggregate GNP against the
United States might not lead to a decline in America's political predominance.

Shmelev and some of his colleagues bought wholesale the neoclassical analysis of mutual gains from international trade. Consequently,
in their view, all major partners had an interest in furtherance of
trade and the amicable resolution of any trade "contradictions" that
might arise.[21] Shmelev tacked dangerously close to Karl Kautsky's old
"ultra-imperialism" position by stressing the "internationalization of
production." Since productive processes were becoming internation-
alized, the world capitalist system was unifying at the level of the
"base," in the Marxist understanding of that word. This process led
to contradictions whose resolution required synchronization at the
level of the superstructure—that is, policy.[22] Contradictions existed,
of course, but their political effect might be the opposite of what
Leninism predicted.[23] The writings of this school exhibit Kautsky-like
fascination with the various "imperialist coordinating centers," most
prominently including the annual G-7 meetings, the International
Monetary Fund, and the General Agreement on Tariffs and Trade.

What was novel in these arguments, something even Varga had not
considered, was their implication that the law of uneven development
of capitalism does not lead to significant conflicts among the Western
powers. As Shmelev observed, "the exploitation of the resources of
other countries in the epoch of highly developed monopoly capital-

[20]N. P. Shmelev, "Interstate Regulation of the World Capitalist Economy: New Tendencies," *International Affairs*, 1985, no. 9, 62.
[21]Volkov and Shmelev, "Strukturnye sdvigi," 35.
[22]Kirichenko, "On Certain Specific Features," stresses this point.
[23]Shmelev, "Interstate Regulation," 63; Kudrov, "Tri tsentra imperializma," 114. This
was the dominant position at IMEMO, as it was endorsed in a basic institute study:
O. S. Bogdanov and V. V. Azovtsev, *Mezhimperialisticheskoe sopernichestvo: Tendentsii
80-kh godov* (Moscow: Mezhdunarodnye Otnosheniia, 1985), 4.

ism requires ever less noneconomic, forceful methods, which had such wide application in the epoch of colonialism, particularly at its earlier stages."[24] The implications, though Shmelev could not draw them out explicitly, were profound. Capitalism led not to aggressive behavior but to cooperation. Political and economic arrangements among the Western countries were stable. Soviet efforts to play on economically generated contradictions would in all likelihood be counterproductive.

These nearly "neoclassical" scholars had no influence on official opinion. Their ideas would come to the fore later, under Gorbachev. When the new ideas were expressed in the early 1980s, they were vigorously resisted by traditional thinkers within academic circles. Indeed, IMEMO officials later recalled that their institute came under political pressure from higher authorities just for trying to express such ideas in fairly mild forms.[25] The majority of published materials in this period adhered to the basic revised Leninist theory, under careful adjustment since Khrushchev's time. Many analysts believed that underneath the surface solidarity of the conservative Western governments, opposition parties lay in waiting with security programs much more amenable to Moscow. For them it was too early to declare Soviet contradictions-based diplomacy in Europe a failure. On the contrary, a well-known official scholar claimed at a conference on this question held in 1987, Moscow had not yet done enough to exploit interimperialist contradictions.[26]

The scholarly argument on the salience of interimperialist contradictions continued throughout the first two-thirds of the decade.[27] Lying between the reformist "neoclassical" analysis of Shmelev and more traditional Leninist views lay a third group of approaches that could fairly be described as "realist." Several scholars began to develop the concept of "power centers" in international relations. Their

[24] N. P. Shmelev, "SShA v mirovom kapitalisticheskom khoziaistve," *MEiMO*, 1984, no. 4, 44; and "Nastoiashchee i budushchee kapitalisticheskoi ekonomiki," *SShA: Politika, ekonomika, ideologiia*, 1985, no. 7, 115.

[25] The former IMEMO director Aleksandr Iakovlev recalls some of these travails in *Ce que nous voulons faire de l'Union Soviétique* (Paris: Seuil, 1991). See the review by S. Churgov in *MEiMO*, 1991, no. 12, 138–42.

[26] Comments of Vadim V. Zagladin in "Sovremennye osobennosti obshchego krizisa kapitalizma," *MEiMO*, 1987, no. 6, 72. For classical critiques of Shmelev and treatments of this issue, see Iu. Shishkov, "V labirinte protivorechii i krizisov," *MEiMO*, 1983, no. 11, 71; and the editorial "Aktual'nye voprosy analiza kapitalizma," in *Kommunist*, 1984, no. 8, 11.

[27] For an argument on the centrifugal vs. centripetal debate, see "Mezhdunarodnaia konferentsiia: Zapadnaia Evropa i politika imperializma," *MEiMO*, 1985, no. 11, 80–97, esp. 96.

prime objective was to retain Leninism's focus on maneuvering among great powers but escape from its economic determinism. While struggling to remain within the formal confines of the general line, they sought to portray great powers and regionally active Third World states pursuing prestige, aggrandizement, or security on the world scene.[28] Other Soviet international relations scholars advanced equilibrium models of international politics quite close to Western realist theories. Though limited in circulation and even more limited in influence, these articles and monographs ran directly counter to the general line's propositions about the correlation of forces.[29]

Soviet realists, like their Western counterparts, were not so sanguine about international peace and prosperity as the liberal Shmelev school. By dispensing with the class-struggle notions that lingered in the official line, however, they portrayed a more stable world where the external threat was much more manageable than it appeared in the traditional approach. States, after all, can reach agreements much more easily than classes can. These Soviet writers, like the Western equilibrium theorists, suggested that no state, neither the Soviet Union or the United States, could hope to achieve dominance, and thus the most prudent course would be cooperation to preserve the existing balance of power. Soviet scholars of both the realist and neoclassical persuasions would feel vindicated later in the decade when some of their ideas were reflected in Gorbachev's new political thinking.

The general line maintained a studied ambiguity on interimperialist relations well into the first years of Gorbachev's tenure. Official statements continued to analyze contradictions among the "three centers of imperialism," but also incorporated power-centers terminology. Experts in key Moscow institutes and officials on the Central Committee managed to introduce language into the new party pro-

---

[28]See, e.g., V. P. Lukin, "'Tsentry sily': Kontseptsii i real'nost' (Moscow: Mezhdunarodnye Otnosheniia, 1983), and Lukin's discussion with Aleksandr Bovin, "'Tsentry sily'—doktrina i real'nost'," *Rabochii Klass i Sovremennyi mir*, 1985, no. 2 (March–April), 83. For the application of "power centers" thinking to the Third World, see Evgenii Primakov, "Zakon neravnomernosti razvitiia i istoricheskie sud'by osvobodivshikhsia stran," *MEiMO*, 1980, no. 2, 28–47. For Western analyses, see Lynch, *Soviet Study of International Relations*, and Jerry Hough, *The Struggle for the Third World* (Washington, D.C.: Brookings Institution, 1985), esp. 255.

[29]E. A. Pozdniakov, *Sistemnyi podkhod i mezhdunarodnye otnosheniia* (Moscow: Nauka, 1976). See also Pozdniakov's *Vneshnepoliticheskaia deiatel'nost' i mezhgosudarstvennye otnosheniia* (Moscow: Nauka, 1986), esp. chap. 3; Fedor Burlatskii, "Nekotorye voprosy teorii mezhdunarodnykh otnoshenii," *Voprosy Filosofii*, 1983, no. 9, 36–48. By 1984 a collective IMEMO study on international relations theory absorbed much of this kind of thinking: Gantman, *Sistema, struktura, i protsess*.

gram, adopted at the Twenty-seventh Party Congress in January 1986, about the development of "subimperialist power centers" in the Third World. The mid-1980s orthodoxy that reigned supreme among hard-headed policy makers at all levels, from institutes to the Foreign Ministry's Stalin-era skyscraper on Smolenskaia Square and the Politburo itself, acknowledged the stability of the existing American-dominated international structure more forthrightly than ever before. Over the long run, however, the Western European and Japanese power centers would become more independent, and other such centers would emerge in the Third World early in the next century. For the time being, there were many useful interwestern contradictions to exploit.

The outlines of this view were evident in Gorbachev's report to the Twenty-seventh Party Congress in early 1986. American pressure, he claimed, relying on its remaining strengths, was responsible for whatever intrawestern agreement had been achieved. "That leads, in turn, not to a dampening but to an intensification of contradictions." The centripetal/centrifugal dynamic will go on, Gorbachev said, but within the context of the existing (America dominant) correlation of forces: "It is difficult to expect that the complex of economic, military-political, and other common interests of the three power centers that has taken shape in real conditions of today's world can be dismantled. But within the limits of that complex, Washington cannot expect submissive obedience to American dictates by its allies/competitors."[30]

THE ELEMENTS OF POWER

The story was much the same in respect to Soviet consideration of the elements of power. Two central revisions of the attitudes popular in the mid-1970s stand out: an across-the-board recognition of a stalemate in most areas of East-West competition, and a related careful retreat from some of the assessments underlying the 1970s optimism. Most important here was the Soviets' markedly reduced infatuation with the impact of nuclear parity. The importance of this careful reassessment is due to the fact that it not only concerned nuclear weapons, which had been so central to the argumentation behind Brezhnev's détente policy, but took place at the highest levels of the Soviet political system.

During the first part of the 1980s, the top leadership and the military reduced the salience of nuclear weapons in the calculation of

---

[30] *Izvestiia*, 26 February 1986, 3.

military power and embraced ideas of stable deterrence. Though acceptance of robust deterrence ought to lead to a more sanguine view of the security situation, this intellectual route was partially blocked by both groups' deep concern about the high-technology threat from the West. Politicians and military professionals alike harped on the future threat posed by "smart" conventional weapons, stealth technology, and strategic defense.[31] The KGB's Foreign Intelligence Directorate sent out "priority" requests to stations abroad to collect all available information regarding possible technological breakthroughs.[32] Under the assumption that vigorous military competition would continue, the reduced salience of nuclear arms devalued a major Soviet asset. The Soviet economy could continue to churn out any number of nuclear missiles but its capacity to deploy high-technology weapons was subject to doubt.

In response to the foreign policy and domestic troubles the country began to experience at the end of the 1970s, Brezhnev engineered a change in official Soviet military doctrine. Change on the military doctrinal front, like everything else in the Brezhnev era, was gradual and incremental. Between 1977 and 1982 the general secretary crept toward officially accepting the existence of mutual nuclear deterrence and pledging that the Soviet Union would never use nuclear weapons first.[33]

The Soviet doctrinal shift was at least partly a result of the ongoing "perceptual struggle" with the United States. Stalin had denied the importance of nuclear weapons when the Americans enjoyed a monopoly. Khrushchev endeavored to counter the Kennedy administration's "limited war" strategy by asserting that any local war would inevitably escalate. When the Americans touted deterrence and "mutual assured destruction" (MAD) in the 1960s, the Soviets countered

---

[31] See Brezhnev's speech to the General Staff Academy in *Pravda*, 28 October 1982 (*CDSP* 34, no. 43: 1); Nikolai Ogarkov "Na strazhe mirnogo truda," *Kommunist*, 1981, no. 10, 85; Makhmut A. Gareev, *M. V. Frunze—voennyi teoretik* (Moscow: Voenizdat, 1985), 425, and "Tvorcheskii kharakter sovetskoi voennoi nauki," in *40 let velikoi pobedy*, ed. P. N. Fedoseev (Moscow: Nauka, 1987), 175. Western analysts suggested a mutually perceived confluence of interests in this period between military modernizers and reformers such as Gorbachev, who stressed the need for "intensive" growth. See Russell Bova, "The Soviet Military and Economic Reform," *Soviet Studies* 40 (July 1988): 394; and Dale Herspring, *The Soviet High Command, 1967–1989: Personalities and Politics* (Princeton: Princeton University Press, 1990), chaps. 5 and 6.

[32] See Christopher Andrew and Oleg Gordievsky, "More 'Instructions from the Centre': Top Secret Files on KGB Global Operations, 1978–1985," *Intelligence and National Security* 7 (1992) (special issue).

[33] Jeremy R. Azreal, *The Soviet Civilian Leadership and the High Command, 1976–1986*, R-3521-AF (Santa Monica, Calif.: Rand, June 29, 1987).

with blood-curdling talk of fighting a nuclear war. And now, in the late 1970s and early 1980s, Moscow countered Washington's talk of "prevailing" in a nuclear war by rejecting the possibility of such a war and embracing deterrence.[34] Even as a purely rhetorical ploy, the doctrinal shift had consequences, for it served to rehabilitate intellectual advocates of the antinuclear war-fighting view and thus shape the perceptions and options considered by the Soviet system as a whole.[35]

Change in Soviet perspectives on nuclear weapons went beyond the level of propaganda struggles with the West, important as that element was. As the political leadership was engineering this change in Soviet public doctrine, military professionals were rethinking the centrality of nuclear weapons. Increasingly they considered the possibility of prolonged, major conventional war and questioned the usefulness of strategic nuclear weapons.[36] Long before Brezhnev's 1977 Tula speech a secular trend had been under way toward military consideration of an ever-larger conventional phase and denigration of the military utility of nuclear weapons. In 1981 the General Staff staged its first all-conventional exercises in decades, and the next year it formally downgraded the Strategic Rocket Forces in the hierarchy of military services from the primary place they were assigned under Khrushchev.

Of less importance but still notable was Soviet disillusionment with "revolutionary" regimes and movements in the Third World, a shift aided by the death of the ideology tsar, Mikhail Suslov, in 1982.[37] At

[34] For arguments along these lines about the "doctrinal interaction" between the United States and the USSR, see George H. Quester, "On the Identification of Real and Pretended Communist Military Doctrine," *Journal of Conflict Resolution* 10 (June 1966): 172–79; James M. McConnell, "Shifts in Soviet Views on the Proper Focus of Military Development," *World Politics* 37 (April 1985): 317–43; and Robert Jervis, *The Logic of Images in International Relations* (New York: Columbia University Presss, 1989), 232–37.

[35] See Stephen Shenfield, *The Nuclear Predicament: Explorations in Soviet Ideology* (London: Routledge & Kegan Paul, 1987).

[36] An immense Western literature analyzes Soviet consideration of the "conventional option." See, e.g., Mary C. Fitzgerald, "Marshall Ogarkov and the New Revolution in Soviet Military Affairs," *Defense Analysis* 3 (1987): 3–19; Christopher Donnelly, "Soviet Operational Concepts in the 1980s," in *Strengthening Conventional Deterrence in the 1980s*, Report of the European Security Study (London: Macmillan, 1983), 105–35.

[37] For accounts of reassessments in the Politburo and the military and among economic and party specialists, see, respectively, Rajan Menon, *Soviet Power and the Third World* (New Haven: Yale University Press, 1986), 242–48; Hough, *Struggle for the Third World*; Mark Katz, *The Third World in Soviet Military Thought* (Baltimore: Johns Hopkins University Press, 1982), 115–17; E. K. Valkenier, *The Soviet Union and the Third World: An Economic Bind* (New York: Praeger, 1983), 27, 56–57; Francis Fukuyama, "Soviet Strategy in the Third World," in *The Soviet Union and the Third World: The Last Three*

the Twenty-sixth Party Congress, Brezhnev demoted the radical parties from "Marxist-Leninist" to the lowly status of "revolutionary democratic." Andropov was even more disdainful, observing somewhat acidly at a party plenum, "It is one thing to proclaim socialism as one's aim and quite another to build it."[38] Increasingly, Soviets concluded that even the modest optimism of the 1970s had been ill founded. "Vanguard" parties and pseudosocialist regimes in the Third World proved unreliable foundations for support; they drained resources from a strapped Soviet economy and they damaged other, higher foreign policy goals.

The reassessment was so rapid in part because optimism about the Third World had never been so widely shared and deeply held in the 1970s as it had been in the Khrushchev years. Many members of the scholarly community had never been enthusiastic about Soviet support for vanguardist movements and regimes. As evidence accumulated late in the 1970s about the poor performance of these regimes and the seemingly low returns to Soviet policy toward them, skeptical analysts could advance their alternative approaches in scholarly journals and in memoranda prepared for the Central Committee. Unlike other aspects of the postdétente reassessment, revisionist views of the Third World appeared to get a sympathetic hearing from the higher echelons of Soviet power.

At one level, the Soviet reassessment was a straightforward reaction to American activism in the Third World, which culminated in the "Reagan doctrine" of military assistance to anticommunist rebels around the globe. Increased Soviet military capabilities, it turned out, not only did not prevent the West from inhibiting pro-Soviet change, in some cases it was insufficient to stop American-armed movements from rolling back "revolutionary gains."[39] But the reassessment went deeper than merely questioning the utility of reliance on revolutionary as opposed to "bourgeois nationalist" regimes. It was more than a recognition of the effectiveness of American military power in the Third World. It was the beginning of a serious revision of the salience

---

Decades, ed. Andrzej Korbonski and Francis Fukuyama (Ithaca: Cornell University Press, 1990). For an overall review of this literature, see George Breslauer, "Ideology and Learning in Soviet Third World Policy," *World Politics* 39 (April 1987): 429–48.

[38] Quoted in Fukuyama, "Soviet Strategy," 41.

[39] Note Aleksandr Bovin's comments on "rollback": *FBIS-SOV*, 11 March 1986, A9. See also I. Gurb'ev, "Osobennosti uglubleniia obshchego krizisa kapitalizma v sovremennykh usloviiakh," *MEiMO*, 1981, no. 2, 16. Many specialists, however, agreed with "dovish" Americans that the costs of military intervention will always exceed the gains: V. Gantman, ed., *Mezhdunarodnye konflikty sovremennosti* (Moscow: Mezhdunarodnye Otnosheniia, 1983), 200.

of the West-South antagonism. As early as 1980 another very well-connected Soviet scholar, Evgenii Primakov, concluded that the era of major gains in the Third World at the expense of the West was over.[40]

The portrait was a grim one from the perspective of the classical old thinkers. Decolonization, which contributed to optimism about trends in the 1950s, and the national liberation movements that seemed so promising in the 1970s were things of the past. Nothing similar was in the offing. Moreover, upon reflection it appeared that even those momentous upheavals had failed to damage the West in any serious way or improve the Soviet Union's position substantially. As Primakov laconically put it, as a rule "the conditions that developed as a result of the downfall of the colonial system favored the growth of capitalism in the liberated countries."[41]

Implicit in the new view was an appreciation of the pervasive interdependence of the capitalist economic system as well as the inherent complexity of trends in the developing world.[42] The United States was successful not just because of military or even economic coercion but because it relied on its significant economic advantages to exploit South-South contradictions and North-South interdependence.[43] Further, in its dealings with the developing world the West capitalized on the development of a "statist bourgeoisie" interested in playing power politics on the regional scene and on the rise of a large group of economically important and successful states, such as the oil exporters, Brazil, and the newly industrialized countries of Southeast Asia. U.S. policy could play off objective and subjective differences of interest among developing countries and create "subimperialist centers" to take over the regional burdens of anticommunism.

Public Soviet writings about the economic performance of the Soviet bloc and the industrialized market countries in the late Brezhnev and transition years also followed a predictable pattern. They focused on the worldwide recession of the mid-1970s, followed by the late-1970s oil shock and inflation-unemployment problem. Their attention then turned to the 1980–1982 recession, the continued high unem-

[40] Evgenii Primakov, "Zakon neravnomernosti razvitiia i istoricheskie sud'by osvobodivshikhsia stran," *MEiMO*, 1980, no. 12, esp. 27, 39.

[41] Evgenii Primakov, "Nekotorye problemy razvivaiushchikhsia stran," *Kommunist*, 1978, no. 11 (July), 87.

[42] Even Chernenko allowed a statement to this effect to be included in one of his speeches: *Izbrannye rechi i stat'i* (Moscow: Izdatel'stvo Politicheskoi Litertatury, 1984), 20.

[43] Karen Brutents, "Neokolonializm na poroge 80-kh godov, 'modernizatsiia' strategii," *MEiMO*, 1979, no. 6, 72–74, and no. 7, 87–94.

ployment, the rise in protectionism, and the United States' fiscal and foreign trade difficulties. But then Soviet analysts also noted the strong Western recovery, the fast pace of technological innovation and adjustment to new, high-technology production techniques, and, with some surprise, the success of anti-inflationary policies. The trend line of repeating cyclical crises of increasing intensity which called forth Soviet doomsaying from the early 1970s to the early 1980s moderated considerably.[44]

Though official statistics on the performance of Soviet-style economies were fictional, practiced consumers could read even in them a tale of stagnation. The problem for the Soviet government's Central Statistical Administration was that it had inflated Soviet economic performance from the very outset, so it became increasingly difficult to claim relative gains vis-à-vis the United States as time went by and maintain any credibility. Having stated authoritatively in 1960 that Soviet national income was 60 percent of America's, it had to admit that by 1982 that figure had grown only to 67 percent, while the Soviet growth-rate advantage had declined.[45] Capitalism had weathered the storms of the 1970s and early 1980s, while socialism was muddling through. Even viewed through traditional Soviet conceptual lenses, the picture was not encouraging, for comparisons of the two systems continued to acknowledge that socialism still lagged behind capitalism in almost all key indices. Given capitalism's lead, socialism would have to perform much more vigorously to close the gap. This imperative lent a certain urgency to official pronouncements about the domestic economic situation.

Beneath the highest official level, experts were coming to even more gloomy conclusions about the prospects of Brezhnev-style socialism. The new view of capitalism contained implications not just for balancing mechanics and the struggle for the Third World but also for comparisons of the economic performances of the two systems. In the early 1980s, reform-minded economists sought to change the ways economic performance had been measured in the Soviet Union. They argued that rough comparisons of industrial strength could be misleading. Instead of the traditional concentration on raw industrial output, they attempted to draw attention to competitiveness, techno-

[44]Indeed, in 1984 Vadim Zagladin contradicted his boss, the old-liner Boris Ponomarev, who had discussed a "qualitative shift" in the general crisis of capitalism, branding as "premature" the talk of "some Marxist scholars that the general crisis of capitalism has entered a new stage": "Sovremennyi mezhdunarodnyi krizis v svete leninskogo ucheniia," *MEiMO*, 1984, no. 4, 9.

[45]See Valentin M. Kudrov, "Sovetskii Soiuz–SShA: K sravneniiu ekonomicheskoi moshchi," *Svobodnaia Mysl'*, 1991, no. 17, 88–96. For a contemporary analysis of the

logical innovation, flexibility, the internationalization of production and finance, and agricultural productivity.[46] Old measures, such as steel production and resources consumed, obscured the Soviet economy's inefficiency in comparison with the market economies of its competitors.

The new-thinking economists were seeking measures of the "scientific-technical revolution," and by these criteria socialism's status looked dramatically worse than it did according to the old methodology. In addition, military analyses placed increased importance on high technology as a fundamental determinant of the military power of the state. The result was that the analyses of traditional thinkers concerned about the state-military competition between the two systems and those produced by reformist intellectuals who thought primarily about humanizing the statist Soviet system were mutually supporting. For different reasons, people of both frames of mind began to see a more dynamic and challenging capitalism, which threw a new light on the performance of the socialist system.

And the travails of the "world socialist system" were the other side of the coin. If the split with China and the invasion of Czechoslovakia in the 1960s had compelled official Soviet spokesmen to acknowledge the international contradictions of socialism, the events in Poland in the 1980s led to admission of socialism's internal contradictions.[47] Reform Communists lodged at Oleg Bogomolov's Institute of the Economics of the World Socialist System in Moscow, who had analyzed reform in Czechoslovakia in 1968 and later in Hungary and China, were deeply impressed by the Polish crisis of the early 1980s. Even in open publications they described the existence within Soviet-style societies of profound conflicts of interests between workers and managers.

The essence of their analysis was that socialism faced a classic contradiction between the forces and relations of production. The archaic and authoritarian system of economic (and, usually by implication,

---

economic competition at the turn of the decade, see "Kapitalizm kontsa 70-kh—nachala 80-kh godov," *MEiMO*, 1980, no. 5, 85–109.

[46] See, e.g., Volkov and Shmelev, "Strukturnye sdvigi"; Shmelev, "Interstate Regulation"; Kudrov, "Tri tsentra imperializma." For more explicit Gorbachev-era analyses along the same lines, see E. M. Primakov, "Kapitalizm vo vzaimosviazannom mire," *Kommunist*, 1987, no. 13 (September) 109–10; R. Simonyan, "Where We Stand—The USSR in the World System of Economic Coordinates," *Izvestiia*, 8 July 1988, 3 (*CDSP* 40, no. 27: 15).

[47] Anatolii Butenko, "Nekotorye teoreticheskie problemy razvitiia mirovoi sistemy sotsializma," *MEiMO*, 1971, no. 9, 99–108; "Protivorechiia razvitiia sotsializma kak obshchestvennogo stroia," *Voprosy Filosofii*, 1982, no. 10, 16–29. For more on the early-1980s debate on socialist contradictions, see Stephen White, "Ideology and Soviet Poli-

political) management imposed in the Stalin era had become manifestly inappropriate to the requirements of the present stage of economic development, captured under the rubric "the scientific-technical revolution." The result was an alienated work force overseen by a cowed and unimaginative managerial class. The system not only failed to tap the creative impulses of society but actively suppressed them. Institutes forwarded analyses containing essentially these arguments to the Central Committee and other "appropriate" bodies, where they were officially ignored.[48] According to Aleksandr Iakovlev, for example, in 1984 IMEMO sent the Soviet Central Planning Agency a ninety-page assessment of the economy's prospects which concluded that in the absence of major changes the Soviet economy would sink to "second-class" or even "Third World status" by 2000. The shocked planners returned the document with a sharply worded request for more optimistic conclusions.[49]

The limited character of these early 1980s analyses must be kept in mind. All were very carefully worded and seem extremely mild and even conservative today. All assumed that socialism was reformable and possessed immense internal reserves that had only to be released through a more enlightened policy. All suffered from a lack of reliable information about the Soviet economy and society. And the early new thinkers' access to the corridors of power was limited. Retrospective accounts cite only one member of the ruling group who listened, who seemed open to new ideas, and whose safe was "stuffed" with reform proposals by 1985. That, of course, was Mikhail Sergeevich Gorbachev, who later dated the intellectual origins of perestroika precisely to the years between 1980 and 1985.[50]

AMERICAN PERSPECTIVES: THE 1983 Shift

A certain dualism characterized American perspectives on the superpower balance from the very early years of the Cold War. Ameri-

---

tics," *Ideology and Soviet Politics*, ed. Stephen White and Alex Pravda (London: Macmillan, 1988).

[48] See, in addition to the Butenko articles cited in n. 47, Viacheslav Dashichev's account of and excerpts from his 1978 memo in "Iz istorii stalinskoi diplomatii," in *Istoriia i Stalinizm*, ed. A. N. Mertsalov (Moscow: Politizdat, 1991), 238–40; Stanlislav Shatalin's recollections, "'500 dnei' i drugie dni moei zhizni," *Nezavisimaia Gazeta*, 31 March 1992, 1, 5; and Taliana Zaslavskaia's famous "Novosibirsk Report," *Survey* 28 (Spring 1984): 89–90.

[49] Churgov's review of Iakovlev's recollections, *MEiMO*, 1991, no. 12, 139.

[50] In conversations with American officials, he dated its origins to 1982. See John Gooding, "Perestroika as a Revolution from Within," *Russian Review* 51 (January 1992): 46, n. 29.

can officials were generally alarmed and concerned by the growth of Soviet military power, fearful of its potential political effects, but at the same time confident of the United States' economic superiority. In the early years of the Cold War, and especially during the 1950s and early 1960s, Americans even worried about future economic trends, believing in the superior growth potential of Soviet-style socialism. Even as relative Soviet nuclear capabilities increased in the 1960s and 1970s, however, U.S. officials grew more confident in their country's economic and technological superiority and more disdainful of Soviet economic performance.

The "Soviet military threat" was the dominant refrain of the late Carter and early Reagan years. The USSR was portrayed in public and in internal documents as a dynamically expanding military power, continually adding to its capabilities.[51] In 1982 President Reagan claimed that "on balance the Soviet Union does have a definite margin of [military] superiority."[52] Defense Secretary Caspar Weinberger made numerous such statements, publicly and in private briefings for the president.[53] Though claims of Soviet superiority were controversial, the vast majority of official Washington shared the administration's basic concern. And it was not only the United States that perceived increased Soviet military power in the late 1970s and early 1980s; so did the major Western European countries, Japan, and China.

But the alarmist focus on Soviet military power concealed another strain in American thinking which was present all along. The Reagan administration was perhaps more confident in capitalism's superiority and most disdainful of socialism's prospects than any other in the Cold War period. As a former Reagan adviser, Martin Anderson reconstructs them, the basic postulates of the administration's "grand strategy" included the conviction "that the productive power of the United States economy was vastly superior to the Soviet economy, [and] that if we began a drive to upgrade the power and scope of our military forces, the Soviets would not be able to keep pace." Reagan claimed in June 1980 that "the Soviet Union cannot increase its production of arms . . . we're hearing of strikes and labor disputes be-

---

[51] Cf. Thomas Banchoff, "Official Threat Perceptions in the 1980s: The United States," and Michael Jochum, "The United States in the 1980s: Internal Estimates," both in *The Changing Western Analysis of the Soviet Threat*, ed. Carl-Christoph Schweitzer (New York: St. Martin's Press, 1990).

[52] Quoted in Keith L. Shimko, *Images and Arms Control: Perceptions of the Soviet Union in the Reagan Administration* (Ann Arbor: University of Michigan Press, 1991), 111.

[53] Caspar W. Weinberger, *Fighting for Peace; Seven Critical Years in the Pentagon* (New York: Warner, 1990), 30, 34.

cause people aren't getting enough to eat." He repeatedly expressed the idea that the United States had the power to drive the Soviets to a more forthcoming attitude in arms negotiations.[54] As the former secretary of state Alexander Haig put it in his memoirs (published before Gorbachev's ascent to power): "The Soviet Union, as Reagan came into office, was in an expansionist period, but already, as the Russians themselves would suggest, the point of excess had been reached. . . . The United States and its friends had enough assets to be able to deal with the Soviets and their proxies with confidence. No one knew this better than the Soviets."[55]

This more confident strain in U.S. thinking found its way into public statements even during the early phase of the Reagan administration, when it was all but swamped by "Soviet threat" concerns. In June 1982 Reagan delivered a sweeping address to British members of Parliament in the Palace of Westminster, in which he claimed that the Soviet Union, the "home of Marxism-Leninism," was gripped by a "great revolutionary crisis, . . . where the demands of the economic order are conflicting with those of the political order." Consequently, the USSR was "in deep economic difficulty," and the communist experiment was destined for "the ash heap of history. . . . The constant shrinkage of economic growth combined with the growth of military production is putting a heavy strain on the Soviet people. What we see here is a political structure that no longer corresponds to its economic base, a society where productive forces are hampered by political ones."[56] These last two sentences could almost have been penned at exactly the same time by such Soviet new thinkers as Tatiana Zaslavskaia, Anatolii Butenko, and Viacheslav Dashichev.

Secretary of State George Shultz developed this argument into a lengthy and nuanced philosophical treatise on the intellectual premises of the "Reagan Doctrine." Consciously turning Marxism-Leninism's teleological economic determinism on its head, Shultz argued that the present, postindustrial stage of economic development required political democracy. The unfettered sharing and transfer of information over open and ramified networks was the key to the new age. Soviet-style command methods and ultracentralization consequently contradicted the essential dictates of the present epoch. The American policy of going "beyond containment" and supporting

[54] Quotes in the paragraph are in Lou Cannon, *President Reagan: The Role of a Lifetime* (New York: Simon & Shuster, 1991), 296–97.

[55] Alexander Haig, *Caveat: Realism, Reagan, and Foreign Policy* (New York: Macmillan, 1984), 107, 96.

[56] *Department of State Bulletin* 82 (July 1982): 24–28.

"freedom fighters" reflected the underlying trend of global development at its most basic level. Schultz appeared to be well informed on the Soviet correlation-of-forces model and took delight in undercutting its arguments publicly. Not only were the classical determinants of state power moving in America's favor, he claimed, but the fundamental economic and intellectual trends worked to strengthen liberal ideas globally.[57]

The more confident strain in U.S. perspectives came to the fore after 1983, when the Reagan team shifted its approach from confrontation to a willingness to engage Moscow seriously in arms negotiations. Reasons for the 1983 shift are numerous: pressure from allies had built up since 1980; terrifying Reagan rhetoric about winning a nuclear war had scared publics and energized peace movements; the Soviets had reacted extremely negatively; the balance of forces within the administration had shifted in favor of the moderates, led by Shultz; Reagan had always had strong antinuclear proclivities; and the sober talk of Soviet superiority did not sit well with the upbeat "morning in America" theme of the upcoming presidential election.[58] The reason the administration itself gave, however, was a shift in the balance of power in favor of the United States and the West. Major military programs were under way, the missile deployments in Europe were proceeding, and officials claimed they now had confidence that they possessed a stronger negotiating hand. From the summer of 1983 onward, a consensus emerged and strengthened that the United States had reversed the adverse trends of the 1970s and was ready for bargaining.[59]

However prophetic Reagan's Westminster speech and Shultz's anticommunist manifesto now seem, all evidence suggests that bargaining with the existing Soviet regime was the real issue. Those statements about capitalism's superiority and socialism's fatal weaknesses were less precise guides to policy than indicators of basic American confidence. Reagan, Shultz, and their fellow officials in the U.S. government were consciously contrasting their present mood with the doom-and-gloom declinism they felt had characterized the previous decade. The notion that the balance of power had really shifted between 1980 and 1983 might be regarded as opportunistic in the extreme. But it was far from the first time the Americans had

---

[57] *Department of State Bulletin* 84 (December 1984): 1–5 and 85 (March 1985): 13–20.

[58] The best source on the 1983 shift is Don Oberdorfer, *The Turn: From the Cold War to a New Era* (New York: Poseidon, 1991). See also Cannon, *President Reagan*, and Banchoff, "Official Threat Perceptions."

[59] Oberdorfer, *The Turn*, esp. 36–37.

suddenly shifted emphasis on power relationships. Two differences distinguished this episode from earlier sudden shifts. First, despite talk of the changed military balance, Americans were more forthright than ever in stressing the economic sources of their world status. And second, for the first time they possessed solid evidence that the Soviets themselves were reassessing the balance of power in a direction unfavorable to themselves. As Shultz put it in 1984: "Some in Moscow wonder if the 'correlation of forces' is not shifting against them."[60]

THE COLD WAR'S LAST CYCLE

The détente of the 1970s, based on an apparent convergence of Soviet and American views on the balance of power, unraveled as diplomatic interaction suggested to each side that its conception of that balance and of the prestige hierarchy was not shared by the other. Between 1979 and 1983 Washington and Moscow stuck to their guns as each waited for the other to come around. The result was the lowest ebb in relations since the Berlin and Cuban missile crises, almost two decades earlier. The last Cold War cycle was not punctuated by one clarifying crisis but dragged on for years, manifesting itself in disputes over Afghanistan, Poland, and the INF battle in Europe. Soviet policy makers clung to their positions, expecting first the Americans (until 1981) and then the Europeans to return to the détente relationship, as Moscow understood it. The Western powers squabbled among themselves, occasionally seemed to waiver (especially on the issue of trade with the Soviet bloc), but in the end coupled all talk of negotiations with commitments to increase military forces.

After reaching a high point in 1983, tensions began to subside, and the superpowers began a slow stumble back into a mini-détente. As of 1985, however, the terms of that détente had not yet been decided. In 1985, of course, no one knew that the recent cycle of tensions had been the Cold War's last. All available evidence at that time pointed toward a new round of negotiations based on the status quo. That is, the Soviet Union would yet again temporarily settle for less than parity in prestige and the West would proceed on the basis of a divided Europe with Soviet influence limited to approximately its level of 1970, perhaps even less. People on both sides of the iron curtain

---

[60] *Department of State Bulletin* 84 (December 1984): 4, cited in Banchoff, "Official Threat Perceptions," 90.

were thinking in terms of cycles. No one saw an endgame on the horizon. The languid pace of the postdétente cycle, the similarity of so much rhetoric and policy with what had come before, the absence of a decisive crisis—all suggested stability and continuity. The one new element was the depth and character of the Soviet Union's third Cold War retreat from optimism.

In his study of Britain's experience of relative decline around the turn of the century, Aaron Friedberg concludes that "external shocks are a necessary but not sufficient condition for downward adjustments in assessments. The presence of individual 'change agents' ready to capitalize on sudden developments is critical to the process through which such shifts occur." Another of his conclusions is that "changes in assessments are likely to proceed more quickly in some sectors than in others. The entire process of movement from overall optimism to collective pessimism may take a long time to complete, even if accelerated by a series of shocks."[61] With all due reservations about a comparison between such dissimilar countries and situations, these conclusions appear to apply to the post-Brezhnev Soviet Union. One could add the argument often made in the literature on political psychology: a change in assessments within a given strategic framework is more likely and easier than a change of strategic frameworks.

No one external shock defined the unraveling of Brezhnev's strategy or provoked the onset of official pessimism. Instead, a series of "setbacks" and "difficulties," as Soviet leaders dutifully noted, led to a deterioration of the country's foreign relations. It would be impossible to fix a precise date on which responsible Soviet officials should have concluded or did conclude that things were steadily worsening. Nineteen-eighty-one was the year they began to adjust their public line to the new circumstances. For some, alarm probably set in much earlier, as far back as the end of détente's golden era in the mid-1970s. In some areas, such as the Third World, significant reassessments were already under way in the 1970s. Other areas of concern, such as the economy, were slower to attract official attention.

Although often and justly accused of complaisance and corruption, the late Brezhnev regime and the transition leaderships of Andropov and Chernenko did take cognizance of the situation and make some effort to alter it or adjust to it. They publicly acknowledged most of the basic problems: declining economic performance, low efficiency, a low rate of technical innovation, the high-technology threat from the West, the anti-Soviet encirclement of great powers. They adjusted

---

[61] Aaron Friedberg, *The Weary Titan* (Princeton: Princeton University Press, 1988), 291.

official nuclear doctrine to remove some of its scarier aspects and facilitate a much more effective propaganda line; they made some effort to improve relations with China; they showed new flexibility in various negotiations. Even in the absence of a major shock, the Soviet government was able to perceive unfavorable trends in political relationships and potentially dangerous adverse shifts in the distribution of capabilities, both economic and military. Before Gorbachev took the helm in March 1985, the anti-Soviet alignment of all the other major power centers looked less solid than it had in 1982; the limits on China's collaboration with the West were clearer; and some movement toward negotiations was detectable on the Western front.

But the external evidence was clearly insufficient to compel such old party warhorses as Chernenko and Gromyko to consider altering their fundamental strategic approach to world politics. There is no evidence to suggest that had they lived longer they would not have carried on with policies compatible with the old correlation-of-forces approach. And "change agents" in the Soviet Union faced rather different circumstances than those in nineteenth-century Britain. Institute analysts could forward memoranda to the appropriate Central Committee department. They could meet with KGB colleagues. They could write articles subtly suggesting new approaches. Critics of past Soviet Third World policy, mildly nonconformist political scientists, and critical economists and sociologists actually worked in the Central Committee apparatus or had access to some Politburo members in the early 1980s. Access to governmental circles, however, was problematical. Access demanded respectability. Respectability presupposed that one operated in or near the official ideology.

But the basic pattern of adjustment described by Friedberg does fit the Soviet case, if roughly. Evidence of significant setbacks accumulates. It is seen as such even within the confines of the old model. Individuals within and around the government, by dint of their positions or intellectual proclivities, seize the new evidence to support their reassessments. Reassessments of various kinds proceed at different paces and intensities in the various sectors of the regime, each concerned with its own aspect of the country's politics. A leadership transition brings a new government to the fore. In its effort to break from past policies now seen to have failed, the new leadership uses and develops some of the alternative approaches.

The ideas floating in and around the Soviet corridors of power during this period were new in three main senses. First, they suggested not just a temporary reversal but a secular adverse trend in the correlation of forces, in its broadest and narrowest definitions, and across its economic and military dimensions. Most important here were new ways of *measuring* the economic and military correlations, with the new measures according much greater importance to technological and "software" capabilities obscured by previous indexes. Second was an increased appreciation for the robust and stable character of modern capitalism and its international arrangements. To many Soviets the international order imposed by the Americans seemed more stable in 1985 than it had in 1975, despite continued shifts in the intrawestern power balance. And finally, many of the new ideas and concepts at large in these years suggested a diminished role for military power in the Soviet intellectual approach to world affairs. This was evident from the highest official level, where public military doctrine accepted a deterrence-only role for nuclear weapons, to institute analysts who argued that interdependence rather than coercion was the glue that held the capitalist world together.

[9]

Power, Ideas, and the
Cold War's End

The Cold War's end will generate as many competing explanations as its beginning. A truly satisfying account would pay heed to a multiplicity of causes, from personalities to sheer luck. My focus here is inevitably narrower. States may have a multitude of reasons to compete, but one necessary condition is their perception that they have the capabilities to do so. Soviet leaders had many reasons for trying to change the terms of the struggle and eventually giving up the very idea of struggle with the United States, but a necessary condition for their reappraisal was a perceived decline in capabilities. The *nature* of the intellectual change and policy experimentation of the Gorbachev years had to do with recent experience, the domestic political conjuncture, personalities, the liberal-capitalist nature of the other major states, and doubtless other factors as well. But the *compulsion* to change is difficult to imagine without reference to the perception of decline within the terms of the old approach to international politics.

Any account of the Soviets' withdrawal from the Cold War which focuses on the classical issue of great-power decline must confront the most striking feature of the whole story: the absence of war. Realist thinking gives rise to the expectation that precipitous decline and thoroughgoing international change will either cause or result from large-scale war. There are numerous analytical reasons for this association of war and change, but the most important reason, as always, is history. As Jack Levy put it, "History provides few examples of states' non-violent acceptance of their national decline."[1] Here

[1] Jack Levy, "Declining Power and the Preventive Motivation for War," *World Politics* 40 (1987): 97.

[252]

again it would be foolish and indeed unfair to rule out the influence of ruling personalities, the existence of nuclear weapons, and the democratic nature of the Soviet Union's major adversaries. But, in keeping with the analysis so far, the focus here is on the peculiarities of perceived power. The nature of the Soviet reaction to decline obscured the depth and consequences of that decline until very late in the game. With hindsight, much of the new political thinking and perestroika appear illusory. But they were constructive illusions, for they delayed the agony of the Soviet reappraisal until the consequences of a violent reaction were posed in unusually stark terms.

My approach to the course of events after 1985 is simple and admittedly incomplete.[2] Decline leads to extremely unsettling conclusions within the confines of the old model. That dilemma generates experimentation with new ideas, mainly Western in origin, and new policies. The new ideas and policies generate positive feedback until suddenly the strategy begins to collapse, followed quickly by the Soviet Union's international position and then the Soviet Union itself.

THE LAST GENERAL LINE: NEW POLITICAL THINKING

To the extent that the new thinking resulted from the earlier post-Brezhnev reassessment, it could be described as an episode of learning from past failure. However, one must not confuse learning from Brezhnev's failures with learning from Gorbachev's successes. Sovietologists debate whether Gorbachev came to the leading party post in 1985 already fully armed with radical ideas for domestic reform and new thinking fully worked out. Gorbachev did introduce the new thinking very slowly. Old-thinking rhetoric, notably on the issue of "the aggressive nature of imperialism," lingered in some of Gorbachev's presentations, particularly programmatic speeches to major party gatherings. Gorbachev sold "new political thinking" as the best way to counter imperialism's aggressive impulses—a modernized variant of the argument first propounded by Malenkov in 1953.[3] In the 1985–87 period, however, his less formal speeches contained more new thinking than his official reports to major party gatherings. In private or unreported discussions the general secretary was yet more revisionist.

---

[2] Some of the ideas in this chapter first appeared in W. C. Wohlforth, "Gorbachev's Foreign Policy: From 'New Thinking' to Decline," in *Emerging Dimensions of European Security Policy*, ed. W. F. Danspeckgruber (Boulder, Colo.: Westview, 1991).

[3] Gorbachev, 4:442.

Several reasons for the slow introduction of new thinking suggest themselves. Resistance to the new ideas on the part of old cadres accustomed to the class approach clearly played a role in it. Having expounded old thinking for decades, many veteran diplomatic, propaganda, scholarly, and military cadres were now required to tout the advantages of "interdependence" and "common human values." For some the transition proved easy, for others it was impossible. It took the Gorbachev leadership some years to pension off large numbers of old thinkers in the foreign policy apparatus. Some had too much invested in the old thinking to change; some resisted on policy grounds, truly believing the new policies to be disastrous; others felt their roles threatened by the new approach. Major programmatic documents, such as Gorbachev's report to the Twenty-seventh Party Congress, the new party program, and his speech on the seventieth anniversary of the Revolution in November 1987, were compromises to appease the old thinkers.

The Gorbachev leadership's need to proceed carefully with the introduction of the new line should not be underestimated. This need is especially clear when one recognizes the fateful role eventually played by the new thinking, which was nothing short of the elimination of the Leninist legacy in Soviet perspectives on international relations, and indirectly the elimination of Leninism as an organized international force. The Soviet Union's experience with new thinking, however, is also a story of on-the-job leadership for the Gorbachev team. All ideas contain ambiguity, and new thinking had perhaps more than its share. Ideas may permit or facilitate actions, but actions give ideas substance. The ambiguity inherent in much of the new thinking was removed only when the course of events forced it aside, when implicit trade-offs became explicit, when choices became stark. In every area, from the new thinking considered as a whole through its application to various regions and issues to actual policy, the patterns of change suggest an intensified trial-and-error learning process in the years after 1985. What is most remarkable about Gorbachev is not the newness or intellectual power of the ideas he sought to introduce but the relentless way he went about trying to extricate his country from the dilemma he thought it was in.

The new general line contained three interrelated elements: a reassessment of basic relationships on the world scene; a revision of fundamental assumptions; and an associated series of new policy concepts.[4] All of these changes reflected intellectual currents long on

---

[4]This dissection follows roughly Robert Legvold's approach in "Revolution in Soviet Foreign Policy," *Foreign Affairs* 68 (1988–1989): 82–98. Analyses of "new thinking" are

the rise among the Soviet elite. What was new was that they were becoming, fitfully and always with reservations, the general line of the Communist Party.

The Gorbachev leadership intensified public pessimism about the correlation of forces. Gone were the Aesopian references to "zigzags" in the correlation and delicate Brezhenevian allusions to "problems" and "complications" in international life. Now Gorbachev framed this issue starkly: "the country's historical destiny," the prospects for remaining a "mighty, prosperous power," and the "preservation of our positions on the world scene" were all threatened unless the political elite agreed to increasingly radical reforms.[5] Though they never entirely abandoned that argument, Gorbachev and Foreign Minister Edward Shevardnadze began in 1987 to articulate its reverse side: foreign policy must be made to serve domestic reform.[6] Either way, the passage of time saw increased official recognition that adverse trends had set in at least by the late 1970s and the time had come to reverse them.

At a deeper level, the new line contained an effort to revise fundamental assumptions that had long lain at the very heart of official Marxism-Leninism. The party's Central Committee and the Institute of Marx, Engels, and Lenin formed commissions, each naturally with numerous subcommissions, to review and revise official ideology.[7] The revision that perhaps attracted most attention was the devaluation of the class struggle. The Gorbachev team decided to exclude from the new party program the old line that peaceful coexistence "is a specific form of the class struggle." The new argument was that the overarching danger of nuclear weapons and the general threat posed by global problems in an interdependent world set up a contradiction between pursuing the class struggle and addressing the problems of humanity as a whole. A Gorbachev aide found a convenient, if obscure, Lenin quote to support the view that humanity's interests must take precedence over those of the proletariat.[8] Shevardnadze clearly

legion. A good example is Stephen Kull, *Burying Lenin: The Revolution in Soviet Ideology and Foreign Policy* (Boulder, Colo.: Westview, 1992).

[5] *Vestnik MID SSSR*, 1987, no. 1 (August 5), 4; *Pravda*, 24 April 1985 (*CDSP* 37, no. 17: 3); 12 June 1985 (*CDSP* 37, no. 23: 2), 17 April 1987 (*CDSP* 39, no. 16: 11).

[6] See Shevardnadze's speech in *Vestnik MID SSSR*, 1987, no. 2 (26 August), 31.

[7] For progress reports on the work of these commissions, see V. A. Medvedev, "Velikii Oktiabr' i sovremennyi mir," *Kommunist*, 1988, no. 2 (February), esp. 5; "Sotsial'nyi progress v sovremennom mire." ibid., no. 7 (May), 80; Evgenii Primakov, "Kapitalizm vo vzaimosviazanom mire," ibid., 1987, no. 13 (September), 109.

[8] See Stephen Shenfield, *The Nuclear Predicament: Explorations in Soviet Ideology* (London: Routledge & Kegan Paul, 1987), 46, for a derivation of the relevant Lenin quotation.

stated the corollary, that the struggle between the two opposing systems should no longer be considered the taproot of world politics. This revision of such a hallowed concept naturally called forth opposition from conservatives, but it also cleared the intellectual decks for scholars and diplomatic professionals to articulate much more forthrightly views based on national interest, political realism, or interdependence.[9]

The old-thinking rampart Gorbachev found most difficult to storm was the "aggressive nature of imperialism." That Leninist tenet was in many ways the linchpin of the classical Soviet approach to world politics. It was the underlying justification for the militarization of Soviet society for the Soviet approach to the correlation of forces. An attack on this basic assumption was virtually required by Gorbachev's effort to reduce the role of the military factor in domestic and foreign policy. In unreported discussions, Gorbachev did allow that the West posed no immediate military threat.[10] Yet in public the general secretary advanced very slowly on this front. At the Twenty-seventh Party Congress early in 1986, he suggested that growing interdependence might put a brake on imperialism's aggressive tendency. A year and a half later Gorbachev delicately suggested that capitalism could develop without militarism, citing the examples of postwar Germany and Japan.[11] Over the perestroika years, Gorbachev and the intellectual heavy hitters on his reform team focused on the argument that interdependence and "general human values" constrained imperialism's aggressive impulses, rather than make a direct assault on the old Leninist equation of monopoly capitalism with aggression.[12] Meanwhile, the general secretary continued to rail against imperialism's military-industrial complex and occasionally allowed himself to slip back into Brezhnevesque statements to the effect that only Soviet power restrained the imperialists.[13]

---

[9]Shevardnadze statement in *Pravda*, 26 July 1988, 4; an attack from Ligachev: ibid., 6 August 1988, 3; a defense from Iaklovlev: ibid., 13 August 1988, 2.

[10]See, e.g., *L'Unità*, 7 October 1986, cited in Gerhard Wettig, "Soviet Threat Perceptions in the 1980's," in *The Changing Western Analysis of the Soviet Threat*, ed. Carl-Christoph Schweitzer (New York: St. Martin's Press, 1990), 280.

[11]See Gorbachev, 3:197–99; "Revoliutsionnoi perestroike-ideologiiu obnovleniia," *Kommunist*, 1988, no. 4 (March), 29.

[12]See Shevardnadze's elaboration of these points in *Vestnik MID SSSR*, 1987, no. 1 (5 August) 18; and Anatolii Dobrynin, "Za beziadernyi mir, navstrechu XXI veku," *Kommuist*, 1986, 9 (June), no. 18–31.

[13]As he stated after a visit to Khabarovsk: "The Soviet Union—its power and our well-organized and strong-willed people—is the chief obstacle to the imperialists": *Pravda*, 30 July 1986, 1 (*CDSP* 38, no. 31: 6). See also his post-Reykjavik appearance on Soviet television; Gorbachev, 4:169–71.

Many assumptions fundamental to the old thinking were implicit, and in the perestroika years they underwent implicit rather than formal revision. Most important here was the concept of stability. Naturally the word *stabil'nost'* had appeared in the Soviet political lexicon before, but its use was carefully limited to particular diplomatic communications. Since official ideology claimed that the present epoch was one of transition from capitalism to socialism, and since policy supported a revision of the bloc structure in Europe as well as major changes in West-South relations, Soviet representatives had to be careful with talk about "preserving international stability." The term was often portrayed as a bourgeois cloak for preserving ill-gotten international privileges. In the Gorbachev years the concept made slow but steady gains. Affection for stability increased as fears of instability in the Soviet outer and inner empires grew. As we shall see, it was only in 1989 that the word "stability" attained as hallowed a place in Soviet discourse as it had long occupied in the Western lexicon.

All these changes had long been fermenting within the Soviet political elite. The class struggle had been downplayed, shunted aside, or temporarily abandoned since Chicherin's day. Revising the assessment of capitalism was also an old Soviet tradition, beginning in the postwar years with Eugen Varga. What was new about the new thinking was the comprehensiveness of the assault on old approaches, as well as the similarity of many of the new official views to typical Western thinking. Both of these factors came particularly to the fore in the Gorbachev team's new set of policy concepts. The new concepts had not only an official ring but a Western one as well.

The "mutuality of security" was one of the first and most important concepts. Gorbachev began touting it even before his first party congress in February 1986, and over the years it became a new-thinking article of faith.[14] The Soviet Union's official endorsement of the concept aroused great excitement among Western academics because it implied recognition of one of their favorite notions: the security dilemma. One state's defensive efforts can threaten other states, calling forth countermeasures and an unending spiral. Some new thinkers acknowledged that they had first encountered the idea in meetings

---

[14] After the Geneva summit with Reagan in the fall of 1985, Gorbachev claimed that the USSR "would not want a shift in the strategic balance in our favor . . . because that situation would strengthen suspicion on the other side and increase the instability of the overall situation": Gorbachev, 3:100.

with Western intellectuals.[15] The Soviet leadership at long last acknowledged that others could legitimately perceive its military programs as threatening. Western hostility was not always a cynical ploy; sometimes it reflected genuine fears. The task for diplomacy now was to erase the West's image of the Soviet Union as the enemy, an image that Soviet actions had encouraged.[16]

The Gorbachev leadership's sensitivity to the security dilemma manifested itself in other key policy concepts of the perestroika period. As Robert Jervis had written over a decade earlier, the security dilemma is exacerbated when a state seeks offensive solutions to defense problems.[17] Since they are particularly threatening, postures of offensive force call forth particularly strong reactions on the part of other states, intensifying the spiral. As if trying to prove that they had read American international relations literature on cooperation under anarchy, Gorbachev and his comrades introduced the concepts of "defensive defense" and "reasonable [or defensive] sufficiency." As Gorbachev construed it, the aim was "such a structure for the armed forces of a state as would make these forces sufficient for repulsing any possible aggression but inadequate for conducting offensive operations."[18] Military professionals and civilian intellectuals naturally disagreed about the precise meanings of these concepts, but they were nonetheless adopted as the Warsaw Pact's official military doctrine in 1987.

Other important policy concepts included "freedom of choice," which meant that neither the Soviet Union nor the West should interfere in the internal affairs of Eastern European states.[19] Another catchphrase was "the balance of interests," which was supposed to replace the balance of power as a principle of policy. This concept, together with the "primacy of law in international affairs," captured Moscow's new affection for multilateral diplomacy and working

---

[15] Arbatov, for example, picked up the notion of the security dilemma ("mutual security") from his association with the Palme Commission in the early 1980s. See Georgii Arbatov, *Zatianuvsheesia vyzdorovlenie* (Moscow: Mezhdunarodnye Otnosheniia, 1991), 204–41.

[16] See, e.g., Andrei Mel'vil', "'Obraz vraga' i novoe politicheskoe myshlenie," *SShA*, 1988, no. 1, 29–39.

[17] Robert Jervis, "Cooperation under the Security Dilemma," *World Politics* 30 (January 1978): 167–86.

[18] Mikhail Gorbachev, "Reality and Guarantees for a Secure World," *International Affairs*, 1987, no. 11, 6.

[19] Mikhail Gorbachev, *Perestroika: New Thinking for Our Country and the World* (New York: Harper & Row, 1987), 165; Gorbachev, 7:188.

through the United Nations. The meaning of every concept was debatable. If the West intervened in a Warsaw Pact state, would Moscow intervene too? What actually constituted intervention? Did reasonable sufficiency mean minimal deterrence or the minimum necessary to prevail? Did Gorbachev really mean to say that the USSR could defend the Warsaw Pact against a coalition with three or four times more economic weight if it lacked the capacity for attack? Or were the concepts directed as much against the NATO militaries as the Soviet one? Only events, and Soviet reactions to them, dispelled the ambiguity surrounding the new thinking.

Two fundamental and ultimately fateful premises underlay Gorbachev's innovative diplomacy. Both of these premises ran directly counter to their old-thinking predecessors. The new thinking held that balancing, rather than bandwagoning, governed the alignment of states on the world scene. And it maintained that military power was no longer so important either for achieving security or for pursuing political goals. What the new approach did not address directly was the question of prestige. Could the country reduce its reliance on military power without grave risk to its prestige? The answer appeared to be yes. While devaluing the country's major international asset and focusing ever more insistently on economic and social problems, the rhetoric about world politics still contained a strong expansive and globalist element. Despite all its inadequacies, the Soviet Union once again held the keys to the world's major problems. It would thus play a major role in the creation of a new and better global order. This new Soviet universalism obscured the old question of decline. The public debate on decline in the "restructuring" Soviet Union was but a pale shadow of the agonizing reappraisals endured by earlier declining great powers, such as late nineteenth-century Britain and even post-Vietnam America.

New thinking's new universalism was tactically useful. A leadership that assaulted so many Leninist sacred cows clearly preferred not to be saddled with international decline as well. Conservative critics could be disarmed by the argument that new thinking posed a major challenge to such old and disliked Western institutions as NATO and their policies, such as deterrence, "Star Wars," and anti-Soviet trade restrictions. But the new expansiveness was not without intellectual support and confirming evidence from abroad. The key here was the belief in balancing. Just as the old correlation-of-forces belief had been useful for an ambitious elite with growing military capabilities, the balancing belief provided comfort to an elite used to world prestige but now compelled to reduce its reliance on military power.

THE DISTRIBUTION AND MECHANICS OF POWER

On the eve of the collapse of the postwar alliance system in Europe, Soviet foreign policy intellectuals and practitioners were well aware of the potential threats to that system's stability. They had come of age in the postwar world, were accustomed to its ambiguities and trade-offs, and were sensitive to its many weaknesses. They saw that Western Europe was entering a new phase of unification that promised fundamentally to alter the relationship of the USSR and the United States to Europe. Closer to home, they were aware that their allies in Eastern Europe were almost as inefficient economically as the Soviet Union itself, and, in the cases of Poland and Hungary, subject to greater societal pressures for change. Even after four decades, many Soviets questioned the long-term stability of the German division. They believed that change in the postwar arrangement was inevitable, and discussed the likely nature of that change with optimistic anticipation, ambivalence, or foreboding, depending on their philosophical and political convictions.

So, as has often been argued, some members of the Soviet political elite did anticipate the general direction of events in 1989, but not the speed or the timing.[20] Although that formulation is accurate, it is misleading. Timing is no small detail. It is true that people anticipated the collapse of bipolarity in Europe in 1988 or even in 1987. But people anticipated its end in 1949, 1952, and 1956 as well. If the postwar arrangements had come to an end two or three decades before they did, paper trails could no doubt be unearthed to show that individuals foresaw precisely such an event. The postwar system was always widely viewed as more or less unstable, but change was always a matter for the unspecified future. Meanwhile, practical politicians and diplomats had to deal with existing realities. And those realities seemed even more permanent after 1985 than they had looked a generation earlier precisely because accumulated experience had shown how resilient they were. One did not have to be a "structural realist"

---

[20]For accounts that highlight Soviet foresight, see Jonathan Haslam, "Soviet Policy toward Western Europe since World War II," in *Learning in U.S. and Soviet Foreign Policy*, ed. George Breslauer and Philip Tetlock (Boulder, Colo.: Westview, 1991); and Hannes Adomeit, "Gorbachev and German Reunification: Revision of Thinking, Realignment of Power," *Problems of Communism*, July–August 1990, 1–23.

or even be familiar with the term to think that the existing alliances reflected underlying geopolitical imperatives. That assumption, it turns out, underlay much thinking about balancing mechanics on both sides of the old East-West divide. But it became manifest only when events forced it into the open.

The Case for Revision

It is hardly surprising that Soviets would anticipate change in the bloc structure since their country had officially supported its revision throughout almost the whole of the Cold War. Formally, Moscow always professed a pro-Europe policy, favoring the dissolution of both blocs and their replacement by a pan-European security system, which in Soviet proposals always had a negligible or nonexistent role for the Americans. But if a policy envisions big changes, such as reengineering the security arrangements of a whole continent, it must accept big trade-offs and at least some risks. Khrushchev and Brezhnev had been willing to accept neither, so the offer to dissolve the blocs had always been regarded as a propagandistic effort to play on Western contradictions. It was in this spirit that Brezhnev and Gromyko had first employed the term "common European home" in the early 1980s.[21]

After 1985, however, the intellectual impetus for major change in world security arrangements picked up considerable steam, abetted by an official climate more open to a genuine Europe-first policy than at any time since the early postwar years. From 1985 onward, Gorbachev and his diplomats made much of the "common European home" slogan, which was suggestive of a pro-European orientation. Analysts in Moscow and in the West noted the prominence on Gorbachev's team of Aleksandr Iakovlev, an official with a long vita indicating animosity toward Washington and fondness for the idea of Europe as an independent "power center."[22] A new Institute of Europe was opened under the auspices of the Academy of Sciences. Experts pre-

---

[21] See Hannes Adomeit, "Gorbachows Westpolitik: 'Gemeinsames europäisches Haus' odor atlantische Orientierung," *Osteuropa* 6 (1988): 423.

[22] As Iakovlev told *La Republica* in 1985: "The distancing of Western Europe, Japan, and other capitalist countries from U.S. strategic military plans in the near future is neither an excessively rash fantasy nor a nebulous prospect. It is dictated by objective factors having to do with their political and economic interests, including security": *FBIS-SOV*, 24 May 1985, CC1. See also his anti-American treatise *Ot Trumena do Reigana* (Moscow: Molodaia Gvardiia, 1984); and his analysis of interimperialist contradictions: "Mezhimperialisticheskie protivorechiia: Sovremenyi kontekst," *Kommunist* 1986, no. 17.

dicted a new and innovative "turn toward Europe" and an anti-American shift in policy.[23]

In principle, everyone was in favor of dissolving the blocs and ending bipolarity. The issue was the terms. Numerous Moscow intellectuals had long believed, and now began to argue more insistently, that the traditional Soviet preference for "status quo plus" (or "What's mine is mine, what's yours is negotiable") was no longer acceptable. That approach was comforting to conservatives, for if it had little chance of success, it also entailed little risk to Soviet positions. Critics of past government policy now suggested that the time had come to run risks and accept some potentially unpalatable trade-offs in exchange for the possibility of achieving fundamental breakthroughs: the end of NATO and the Warsaw Pact; a commensurate reduction in the American role; the demilitarization of Europe; inclusion of the Soviet Union in the new Europe and the inclusion of Europe in Soviet reform. The radical credentials of a Soviet new thinker could be easily ascertained by reference to the terms he or she was willing to consider when contemplating the ideal Soviet European policy. No one, naturally, was sufficiently radical to propose that the country accept the terms it eventually agreed to in 1990.

For many Soviet Westernologists, the main route to the agreed goal of the "gradual demilitarization of the bloc structure including its eventual liquidation" was paradoxically a greater openness to Western European integration. The analysis was based on an old Soviet supposition: that Europe and the Soviet Union had many common interests and that the United States was the primary cause of the West's unconstructive and militarized posture toward Moscow.[24] European independence, therefore, was always desirable and to be encouraged even at the risk of reduced cohesion in the Soviet bloc. After the European Community member states signed the Single European Act in 1986, envisioning a single market by 1992, Soviet enthusiasts for power-centers diplomacy had new arguments to deploy. The Western European drive for unity simultaneously held out the promise of a real continental counterweight to American influence and the threat of relegating the Soviet Union and its Warsaw Pact allies to Europe's sidelines. To minimize the threat and maximize the promise, some Soviet Europeanists called for a policy of maximum accommodation toward Western European unity.[25] A completely constructive and

[23]See, e.g., Jerry Hough, *Russia and the West* (New York: Simon & Shuster, 1988), chap. 9.

[24]D. Proektor, "O evropeiskoi idee," *Kommunist*, 1988, no. 17 (November), esp. 127.

[25]See, e.g., "The 19th All-Union CPSU Conference: Foreign Policy and Diplomacy," *International Affairs*, 1988, no. 10, 37; "Posledstviia formirovaniia edinogo rynka Evro-

supportive posture toward Western Europe would ensure that the increased Western strength brought about by the drive to unity would be compensated for by reductions in American influence.

A very small contingent of radical new thinkers believed that a real breakthrough on the western front would require a much more decisive departure on Moscow's part. According to his own retrospective account, Viacheslav Dashichev, of the Institute of the Economics of the World Socialist System, advanced such proposals at meetings of diplomats and of the International Department of the Central Committee in late 1987, 1988, and the spring of 1989.[26] He argued that the Soviet Union ought to adopt a policy of gradual withdrawals of U.S. and Soviet troops from Europe and confederation and neutralization of the two German states. To get things moving, he maintained, Moscow should be prepared to begin the process with unilateral measures. The Soviet Union might lose some of the control it now enjoyed in the Warsaw Pact states, but in exchange it would reduce immensely the costs of its foreign policy while gaining the kind of major opening in Western Europe that Soviets could only dream about in the past. Strictures against insulting loyal allies, especially the German Democratic Republic, prevented people from expressing such notions openly, though there were hints of such sentiments in the press and scholarly journals.[27] Later, however, Dashichev maintained that even in reliably closed gatherings he was virtually alone in supporting such a radical proposal.[28]

The Impetus for Revision

Though the overwhelmingly majority of the Soviet establishment refused to consider going as far as Dashichev, it did exhibit a measur-

---

peiskogo soobshchestva," *MEiMO*, 1988, no. 4, 38–44, esp. 43; S. Vybornov, A. Gusenko, and V. Leontiev, "Nothing Is Simple in Europe," *International Affairs*, 1988, no. 3, esp. 35. A bellwether issue was European cooperation in defense, which Euroenthusiasts supported and the official line opposed. See L. Spirodonov, "Vremia novykh otsenok," *MEiMO*, 1989, no. 3, 142; A. V. Rassadin, "Zapadnoevropeiskaia voennaia integratsiia—perspektivy i vozmozhnye posledstviia," ibid., no. 2, 104–15, and "Evropeiskoe soobshchestvo segodnia: Tezsisy Instituta mirovoi ekonomiki i mezhdunarodnykh otnoshenii AN SSSR," ibid., 1988, no. 12, 17–18; V. Stupishin, "Indeed, Nothing Is Simple in Europe," *International Affairs*, 1988, no. 5, 73.
[26] See his interview "Dann Erhebt sich das Volk," *Der Spiegel*, 21 January 1991, 136–43.
[27] See, e.g., Iu. Borko and B. Orlov, "Razmyshleniia o sud'bakh Evropy," *MEiMO*, 1988, no. 9, 54, 58.
[28] In 1991 Dashichev claimed that at the December 1987 meeting only one other analyst, Iurii Davydov of the Institute of the U.S.A. and Canada, agreed with him openly; at the 1988 gathering of the International Department, he was isolated. See *Der Spiegel*, 21 January 1991, 137, 140. In a 1988 interview Dashichev was much more

able compulsion to change the external environment rather than simply adjust to it. On the surface, this compulsion to change represents something of a puzzle. Why should a great power ostensibly in decline consider major international projects? One answer is that the problem of decline presents no obvious solution: a declining state may reasonably decide to retreat to more defensible positions, expand to the detriment of challenger states, unleash preventive war, doggedly hold on to the status quo, or rearrange commitments and seek new allies to reduce the costs of external policy.[29] Like many earlier great powers, the Soviet Union considered the latter option, and just as many predecessors had done, it eventually found that choice, like all others on the menu of decline, to be unpalatable.

The late-1980s Soviet Union was not a declining hegemon but a declining challenger. Much of the Soviet political elite had always regarded the existing system of alliances as an American creation; the United States had pieced it together only by exploiting extraordinary postwar circumstances, and the system had redounded unfairly to Washington's advantage ever since. Revisionism perhaps spared the Soviet political elite some of the sentimental attachment to and identification with the status quo which bedeviled the elites of more thoroughly conservative powers in the past. For many Soviet foreign policy intellectuals, even those of a completely reformist cast, the existing bloc system was the product of America's containment policy, whose aim was to bleed the Soviet Union into submission by exhausting it in military competition. The bloc system fostered this militarization of security. If new thinkers wished to demilitarize security, they were led naturally to oppose the bloc system. The Soviet Union's economic problems were partly the result of external commitments imposed on it by the United States. The last thing the Soviet Union should do was to secure the status quo that was bleeding it white. That course would represent a victory for the plans of Western Cold Warriors. Instead, Moscow should break the encirclement through decisive unilateral measures. Why was such a policy considered possible? The answer lay in part in the reasoning behind the Soviet response to decline: the increasingly widespread belief in the prevalence of balancing in world politics.

---

guarded: "History," not immediate Soviet policy, would resolve the German issue; the West must not interfere in Eastern Europe and should assist in reforms there; Germans might live together in one state *after* Europe's division was overcome and the "two systems" had "grown together": "So stand der Wagen vor dem Pferd," ibid., 4 July 1988, 123–27.

[29] Robert Gilpin, *War and Change in World Politics* (New York: Cambridge University Press, 1981), 187–98.

Taken together, the old-thinking postulates had served as supports for the correlation-of-forces model. The aggressiveness of imperialism meant that increments to Soviet military power would be interpreted as balancing against a threat. The primacy of coercive means in inter-imperialist and West-South relations meant that Soviet military power would produce political effects by negating the influence of Western military capabilities. Taken together, the new-thinking postulates constituted the first comprehensive assault on the correlation-of-forces model in Soviet history. If all states, regardless of social system, balance the military efforts of other states, then efforts to achieve political gains by exploiting military advantages are doomed. If mutual interest and interdependence explain capitalist cohesion, then American prestige must have sources other than military power. If military capabilities are not the key to America's dominance of world affairs, then its role must be explained by other factors: its economic and cultural influence or, most intriguingly, ill-advised Soviet policy itself.

On the surface, the shift to belief in balancing might appear to represent a sobering reduction in expectations about what might be achieved internationally. Gone was the correlation-of-forces model's optimistic confidence that increases in Moscow's main international asset, military capabilities, would translate into valuable political and security goods. The Soviet Union's formerly ebullient elite had finally had its wings clipped by the punishing realities of international life. But the transition was by no means so simple. The old bandwagoning notions were, after all, partially founded on fears of the West's aggressiveness and Eastern Europe's vulnerability to capitalist blandishments. They suggested not just opportunity but also vulnerability. Balancing beliefs, on the other hand, conceal an almost mechanistic optimism. While other states may not climb on our bandwagon, our allies are unlikely to jump on theirs. Indeed, if one believes in balancing, many policies designed to thwart incipient bandwagons are unnecessary and even counterproductive. Such policies are likely to threaten other states and cause them to counterbalance ever more tightly. Writers who stress the prevalence of balancing behavior, from David Hume to Stephen Walt, tend to be foreign policy minimalists.[30] They warn against overestimation of the value of allies and overreaction to potential shifts in their alignment.

[30] Hume maintained that the "passionate ardour" with which Britons have defended the balance of power "seems rather to require some moderation; and they have oftener erred from a laudable excess than from a blameable deficiency": "Of the Balance of Power," in *The Philosophical Works of David Hume*, 4 vols. (Edinburgh: Adam Black, Wm. and Charles Tait, 1826), 3:380; Stephen M. Walt, *The Origins of Alliances* (Ithaca: Cornell University Press, 1987), 282–85.

Balancing beliefs provided more than just assurance that Soviet world positions were not so tenuous as the old thinking suggested. They actually contributed to confidence that Soviet positions could be improved at little cost. The key was the growing conviction that Soviet policy had in the past violated the basic law of balancing in world politics and had consequently helped to create the opposing alignment of states on the world scene. The more convinced one was that balancing dominated international alignments, the more mistaken past Soviet policy, based on the opposite belief, appeared to be. The more mistaken past Soviet policy was, the greater potential current Soviet policy possessed. If the anti-Soviet alignment of the other power centers was primarily a result of the Soviet Union's own over-reliance on a threatening military posture, then it lay within Moscow's power to decouple that alignment by reducing other states' sense of threat. The more revisionist one was about past policy, the more optimistic one became about present prospects. The more past Soviet leaderships were thought to have overestimated the threat from the West, the more surplus military power Moscow could unilaterally reduce in exchange for political and security gains.

Positions on the balancing issue naturally varied among personalities and groups and over time. At one extreme, old thinkers held to the view that the anti-Soviet alignment was a reflection of imperialism's internal dynamics and had nothing to do with Soviet actions. At the other extreme lay the revisionist view that NATO was entirely the result of balancing against the Soviet Union rather than bandwagoning with the United States. Not surprisingly, this was Dashichev's view, which he first expressed publicly in 1988.[31] He held that Stalin's Khrushchev's, and Brezhnev's military-focused race for hegemony, instead of creating the prerequisites for détente, ended up pushing the middle powers even more firmly into America's embrace. Not only did the Soviets focus too much on military power, but their military adopted an overly threatening posture. New-thinking revisionists of Dashichev's stripe essentially shared a belief common among Western scholars, that the pre-Gorbachev Soviet Union had "encircled itself" by pursuing overaggressive strategies that threatened other powers and drove them into an anti-Soviet alignment. And the key to their proposals was that if the Soviet Union had created its own encircle-

---

[31] See Viacheslav Dashichev, "Dorogi, kotorye nam vybiraiut," *Komsoml'skaia Pravda*, 19 June 1988, 3; "O prioritetakh vneshnei politiki Sovetskogo gosudarstva," *Literaturnaia Gazeta*, 18 May 1988, 14.

ment, it had the power to dissolve it. All the risks and concessions Dashichev suggested Moscow ought to bear were supposed to yield a major dividend: the end of NATO, a reduction in the United States' military commitment to Europe, the return of a benign multipolarity.

Gorbachev, Shevardnadze, and other top officials never endorsed the revisionist view unreservedly, but they inched toward it over time. By 1988 their expressed position was that the achievement of nuclear parity had been a historically necessary precondition for the détente that followed. They therefore excused much of Stalin's and Khrushchev's bellicose behavior as an unavoidable response to Soviet weakness and Western aggressiveness. Furthermore, official new thinking claimed that capitalism had begun to change in a more peaceable direction only comparatively recently. Interdependence, the scientific-technical revolution, and other developments that tamed capitalism and changed world dynamics were also of relatively recent vintage. So until 1989 the top leadership limited its revisionism to the late Brezhnev era of stagnation. In Gorbachev's and Shevardnadze's version, Soviet foreign policy went awry mainly after 1975, as it permitted détente to collapse and contributed to the anti-Soviet alignment of the world's power centers after 1979.[32] It was only in 1989, when the disintegration of Eastern Europe and the Baltic republics broke into the open, that official Moscow was compelled to extend its revisionism to Stalin's foreign policy.

Despite variations in views among individuals, the hesitations and reservations of Gorbachev's public position, and continued expressions of faith in some form of the old correlation-of-forces model, the Soviet foreign policy discourse reflected a secular increase in balancing assumptions in the years after 1985. Balancing assumptions, in turn, helped create a situation redolent of the immediate post-Stalin period: a widespread conviction that the previous leadership's policy had been rigid and self-defeating, and consequently a sense that much could be done merely through a new, more flexible diplomacy. Even Gorbachev's limited revisionism suggested that many of the setbacks Moscow had suffered in world affairs after 1979 were at least partly the fault of Gromyko's unimaginative approach to foreign policy. A new course could at the very least undo the damage done since the demise of détente by beginning to decouple the anti-Soviet alignment of all the other power centers on the world scene.

---

[32] See, e.g., Gorbachev's speech in *XIX vsesoiuznaia konferentsiia Komunisticheskoi Partii Sovetskogo Soiuza: Stenograficheskii otchet* (Moscow: Izdatel'stvo Politicheskoi Literatury, 1988), 1:40; "The 19th All-Union CPSU Conference: Foreign Policy and Diplomacy," *International Affairs*, 1988, no. 10, 19–20.

Despite the official line's bias against the existing bloc structure, an element of the Soviet foreign policy community did perceive its virtues and argued that for the time being Soviet interests required its maintenance, and even further institutionalization. Taboos against discussing Eastern Europe forthrightly inhibited not only those who argued for a relaxation of Soviet hegemony over the region, such as Dashichev, but also those who advocated a more managed bipolar condominium. Bipolar advocates, mainly lodged at the Foreign Ministry, were the apostles of stability. With the Soviet Union undergoing deep reform and Eastern Europe facing potentially destabilizing crises, they argued, it was time to jettison the four-decade-old official revisionism, to accept the U.S. presence in Europe, the division of Germany, and even nuclear deterrence as stabilizing, while expecting from the West restraint in exploiting potential upheavals in the Warsaw Pact states and even assistance for communist reformers there.[33] The superpowers had common interests in Europe, mainly in maintaining stability, and they should not allow fealty to allies' sensibilities or their own past positions to stop them from rational coordination of their policies. The argument was old hat in the West, where in the 1970s it had been known as the "Sonnenfeldt doctrine," and where it enjoyed a brief revival in 1989 when it was vetted by former Secretary of State Henry Kissinger.

The top leadership and the majority of the elite retained their wariness of "bipolar management" until late in the perestroika game. The shift in official policy came only when the issue of declining prestige and loss of influence over external developments was posed in stark reality, rather than in policy memoranda or analysts' polemics.

ELEMENTS OF POWER AND PRESTIGE

Military versus Other Elements of Power

By the time new thinking reached full flower 1988 and 1989, it had become, as its name implied, a nearly complete negation of the old

[33]These points were made forthrightly by two Foreign Ministry officials, Mikhail Amirdzhanov and Mikhail Cherkasov, in "Our Common European Home," *International Affairs*, 1988, no. 12, 26–36, esp. 29–30. Bogomolov's Institute of the Economics of the World Socialist System, always cognizant of socialism's weaknesses, also expressed this view in 1988; see "East-West Relations and Eastern Europe (An American-Soviet Dialogue)," *Problems of Communism*, May–August 1988, 55–70, esp. 66. For a discussion of and further citations relating to the Soviet polarity debate in this period, see A. Bovin and V. Lukin, "Perestroika mezhdunarodnykh otnoshenii-puti i podkhody," *MEiMO*, 1989, no. 1, 58–70.

thinking. The lodestar of the old thinking was the primacy of military power for security and foreign policy. The lodestar of the new thinking was deemphasis of the importance of military power. Each proposition of the system of ideas that constituted old thinking had its own Leninist origins and its own post-Lenin intellectual history. But they all led to the same conclusion: that military power was the main key to major security and political problems. Each proposition of the new thinking had its origins in the West or in the pre-Gorbachev Soviet Union. But they all served to support the same argument: military power is no longer as important as it used to be.

Gorbachev began his attack on the utility of military power immediately upon his accession to the general secretaryship and sustained it steadfastly throughout his years in power.[34] He and his intellectual legions advanced numerous arguments in support of these basic propositions: interdependence vitiates the utility of military power because states have an economic stake in peace; common human values transcend and supersede the class struggle and create basic incentives for socialist and capitalist states to cooperate; "mutuality of security" means that any effort to increase military capabilities is inevitably offset by the countervailing actions of other powers; the proliferation of weapons of mass destruction renders absurd any cost/benefit rationale for resort to arms; and the proposition Gorbachev found hardest to state clearly and publicly, that, "imperialism" has changed and is no longer so threatening.[35] Where Gorbachev feared to tread, however, intellectuals strode confidently, arguing that Western democratic institutions themselves put a reliable brake on whatever aggressive impulses remained in those societies.[36]

The proposition that capitalism could develop without militarism was the key indicator of new thinking, just as the opposite view had been most central to the old. The equation of monopoly with aggression was so central to Lenin's thinking that it resided almost below the level of conscious expression. It came to the fore only when the Social Democrats under the "renegade" Kautsky and the "opportunist" Eduard Bernstein dared to differ with Lenin on exactly this point. After World War I and the Russian Revolution proved Lenin so dramatically right, no Bolshevik, not even Bukharin, dreamed of revising Lenin on this issue. Even Varga skirted the question in the

[34]See, e.g., his speech at The twenty-seventh Party Congress in Gorbachev, 3:245.
[35]Gorbachev's ideas on many of these issues can be found in his speech to the U.N. in ibid., 7:183–202.
[36]V. Zhurkin, S. Karaganov, and A. Kortunov, "Vyzovy bezopasnosti—starye i novye," *Kommunist*, 1988, no. 1 (January), 42–50.

postwar years with his sophisticated correlation-of-forces reasoning. For Khrushchev and Brezhnev, the proposition that the American adversary relied to a great extent on military power was axiomatic. From this proposition followed their own military-centered drive for prestige. For Gorbachev, the notion that the West was not incurably addicted to military power was central, for from it followed his whole foreign policy revolution.

The proposition that military power was the linchpin of America's relations with its own allies and the Soviet Union, as well as of relations between the capitalist West and the developing South, was the intellectual bulwark of Soviet competitive foreign policy throughout the Cold War. The idea reflects a classic combination of offensive and defensive concerns. The West was dangerous not mainly because it was going to attack the Soviet Union but because it would seek to exploit its military power to contain and even undermine the international positions of socialism. Since the West's policy of containment and intimidation was based mainly on military capabilities, Soviet military power could defeat it. This was the logic behind Moscow's military-centered reactive policy, in which each perceived American move was countered by the Soviet Union, almost regardless of cost. The more the new thinking progressed, the more intensely this old Soviet policy was criticized.

By 1988, two essential critiques of past Soviet foreign policy became commonplace. One was that earlier leaderships, though essentially well intentioned, had blundered into responding symmetrically to the West's military challenge. Achieving military parity with America had been absolutely necessary, Gorbachev maintained, but "having concentrated enormous resources on the military aspect of countering imperialism, we did not always take advantage of political means of maintaining the country's security and reducing tensions."[37] The blunder turned out to be a costly one, for Gorbachev blamed the military rivalry for the parlous state of the Soviet economy. The implication was that a lower-cost method of achieving Moscow's goals existed and was now being implemented by the leadership. The second critique of past policy was really a corollary of the first: that earlier Soviet leaderships overestimated the political utility of military power. Gorbachev himself trod carefully here, usually making the point by implication, but other leadership figures were quite clear on the issue. For example, the head of the Central Committee's International Department, Valentin Falin, who was no one's candidate for

[37] *XIX vsesoiuznaia konferentsiia*, 1:40.

ideal new thinker, declared in 1988 that "it is naive to believe that military might can automatically be transformed into political strength and influence. . . . We simplified a good deal here and found ourselves trapped by our own delusions."[38]

Deemphasis of the utility of military power naturally entailed emphasisis on the utility of other elements, primarily economic power. It was almost an axiom of the Gorbachev era that in the long run a state's place in the society of nations would be determined by its economic performance and the attractiveness of its social system. For Gorbachev, economic power was often the functional equivalent of military power in the old-thinking framework. He claimed not only that improved economic performance would enhance Soviet positions worldwide and lead to genuine détente but that Soviet socioeconomic weaknesses had tempted the West to jettison détente in the late 1970s and unleash a new round of the Cold War.[39] Khrushchev had also tried, at least rhetorically, to increase the relative importance of economic performance in the competition with the West at the expense of military capabilities. But Khrushchev and the Soviet political elite of his time were optimistic about the existing system's capacity to compete with capitalism economically. The Gorbachev years witnessed a steady crescendo of criticism of past and present Soviet economic performance coupled with admiring portrayals of the Western and Japanese economic systems.

The leadership first talked of "negative phenomena" in the Soviet economy, then acknowledged a "precrisis" situation, "absolute stagnation," and "forgoing one position after another in comparison with the more developed countries." At the Nineteenth Party Conference in 1988, Gorbachev confessed that he had earlier underestimated the depth of the economy's travails. What growth there had been in the last two decades, he claimed at a party plenum that year, had resulted from the domestic sale of vodka and the export of oil at high world prices.[40] Experts published analyses showing Soviet per capita income at 20 to 30 percent of the American figure, labor productivity less than one-third, and agricultural productivity less than one-fifth.[41]

[38] *Studio* 9 TV broadcast (*FBIS-SOV*, 1988, no. 201: 84–85).

[39] See, e.g., Gorbachev, 4:20, 442.

[40] See resolution of the Twenty-seventh Party Congress, *Pravda*, 6 March 1986, 2, and the June 1987 Party Plenum: "O zadachakh partii po korennoi perestroike upravleniia ekonomikoi," *Kommunist*, 1987, no. 10 (July), 22; *XIX vsesoiuznaia konferentsiia*, 1:22; and Gorbachev's report to the February plenum, "Revoliutsionnoi perestroike," 24–27.

[41] S. Nikitin and M. Gel'vanovskii, "Gde zhe my? (Ekonomika SSSR s pozitsii mezhdunarodnykh sopostavlenii)," *MEiMO*, 1990, no. 1, 20–34. For more, see Alec Nove, *Glasnost in Action: Cultural Renaissance in Russia* (London: Unwin-Hyman, 1989), chap.

Poverty, inefficiency, and corruption were all on the rise, as was frank reporting on such matters, which magnified the impact on the public and elite mind. And every critical article, every sober analysis of each troubled aspect of the Soviet economy and society made stark and unfavorable comparisons with the way things were under capitalism.

New Thinking and the Lippmann Gap

The implications of deemphasizing the military element, stressing the importance of economic power, and simultaneously advertising socialism's economic failings were obvious and devastating for the Soviet elite's traditional portrayal of their country as a world power. They implied an immediate downgrading of the Soviet Union's power and prestige status far more dramatic than any calculation of measurable trends after 1985 would suggest. Only in comparisons of military forces could the Soviets claim parity with the United States or between socialism and capitalism. If overall economic capabilities were truly to be taken as the main determinant of a state's global position, then Moscow would have to accept a world political status on a par with Japan. If, however, the new thinkers were right when they claimed that raw industrial output was less important than economic dynamism, flexibility, technological level, and integration into the international economy, then Soviet Russia had a very long road to travel to reach Japan's present status.

Gorbachev dealt with the prestige problem in a delicate and contradictory way. He cherished his country's great-power status, claiming that it was one of the party's main achievements in seven decades of rule.[42] Naturally he refrained from suggesting that Soviet prestige had declined during his tenure. For him, major threats to the country's prestige lay in the future, usually around the turn of the century, and then only if the political elite and the people rejected his reforms.[43] But Gorbachev and Shevardnadze did try to address what Samuel Huntington called the "Lippmann gap," after Walter Lippmann, the influential commentator who had pointed out the require-

---

8; Isaac J. Tarasulo, *Gorbachev and Glasnost: Viewpoints from the Soviet Press* (Wilmington, Del.: Scholarly Resources, 1989), chap. 5.

[42] "We cannot say the revolution fulfilled everything it promised. . . . But it is also true that as a result of the revolutionary transformations over these seven decades the Soviet Union has today become one of the states in the world that determines the historical destiny of mankind": *Pravda*, 16 November 1989 (*FBIS-SOV*, 1989, no. 220: 67). See also Gorbachev, 4:448.

[43] See, e.g., Gorbachev, 2:86, 154–55; 5:14; and *Vestnik MID SSSR*, 1987, no. 1 (5 August), 4.

ment of "bringing into balance, with a comfortable surplus of power in reserve, the nation's commitments and the nation's power."[44] They provided two essential solutions to the dilemma: reduce the costs of foreign policy and increase the degree of vital economic cooperation with the world's major powers.[45]

The question was whether these moves could be implemented without a substantial reduction in the Soviet Union's present status as a global power. What the Soviet leaders thought privately on this score may never be known. Publicly, they expressed confidence that perestroika and new thinking would close the Lippmann gap *and* improve the country's international standing. The reasons why that confidence may not have been entirely the result of wishful thinking and posturing before domestic and international audiences will be discussed presently.

Foreign affairs commentators and intellectuals were understandably more forthright in addressing the prestige issue. They stated clearly that though the Soviet Union had achieved military parity with the United States, its "possibilities for nonmilitary influence on the world scene have narrowed." They drew attention to the "disquieting" discrepnacy "between our country's immense foreign policy role and its comparative economic and scientific-technical strength."[46] They recognized that the problem was particular acute in Europe, where Soviet positions had previously been thought to be strongest.[47] By 1988 and 1989, it was commonplace for analysts to state forthrightly not only that the United States topped the prestige hierarchy but that its economic power and cultural attractiveness made its position natural and inevitable.[48] Many drew the conclusion that, in the words of Fedor Burlatskii, "it was impossible to continue with the crazy race for hegemony with the United States."[49] Lippmann would doubtless have appluaded the straight talk on this score from Aleksei Iziumov and Andrei Kortunov in 1988:

[44] Quoted in Samuel P. Huntington, "Coping with the Lippmann Gap," *Foreign Affairs* 66 (1987–1988): 453–77.

[45] Shevardnadze's speech to diplomatic professionals is an early and good example of this type of analysis: "Vystuplenie E. A. Shevardnadze," *Vestnik MID SSSR*, 1987, no. 2 (28 August).

[46] Vladimir Lukin and Aleksandr Bovin, "Na poroge novogo veka," *MEiMO*, 1987, no. 12, 53; Zhurkin et al., "Vyzovy bezopasnosti," 48.

[47] See Bovin's comments in "Perestroika mezhdunarodnykh otnoshenii—puti i podkhody," *MEiMO*, 1989, no. 1, 66.

[48] See, e.g., "Gosudarstvennye, natsional'nye i klassovye interesy vo vneshnei politiki i mezhdunarodnykh otnosheniiakh," *MEiMO*, 1989, no. 2, 68; S. Blagovolin, "Voennaia moshch'—skol'ko, kakaia, zachem?" *MEiMO*, 1989, no. 8, 5–19, esp. 8.

[49] Interview with *L'Unità*, 2 November 1988 (*FBIS-SOV*, 1988, no. 212: 2).

. . . a new international strategy would have a solid economic foundation based on a sober-minded appraisal of the present state of, and prospects for, our economy, as well as the economies of our rivals and allies. We should display more selectivity in identifying our goals and commitments abroad. In particular, it would be expedient to gradually abandon our global rivalry with the USA and refrain from the costly support of unpopular regimes, political movements, parties, etc.[50]

In no area were Soviet intellectuals more ready to close the Lippmann gap than in the Third World. The struggle for the Third World, already heavily devalued during the old-thinking early 1980s, was now widely regarded as an absurd diversion from which the Soviet Union should withdraw as quickly as possible. All the ideas about the competition for the Third World under development since the late 1970s now found ringing expression in the pages of the international relations press: Third World "socialism" was a cloak for brutal dictatorships and a tactic for wheedling money out of an ideologically gullible Soviet Union; Marxist-Leninist vanguard parties, far from being the reliable partners of the Central Committee's International Department had hoped, were actually politically unstable and inclined to cut deals with the West as soon as the "liberation" phase of the struggle was over and Soviet weaponry no longer so vital; Moscow not only harmed its larger policy aims with the West by supporting unpopular leftist regimes, it drained its own treasury in the process, for it lacked intrinsic ties of economic interdependence with most developing countries (India was an important exception).[51] The leadership's withdrawal from Afghanistan and sponsorship of regional settlements there and in southern Africa and Kampuchea, while ap-

---

[50] Aleksei Iziumov and Andrei Kortunov, "The Soviet Union in a Changing World," *International Affairs*, 1988, no. 8, 54. Other contributions to the Soviet grand strategy debate in these years which were widely discussed in Moscow at the time include Zhurkin et al., "Vyzovy bezopasnosti," and Igor Malashenko, "Interesy strany: Mnimye i real'nye," *Kommunist*, 1989, no. 13 (September), 113–23, both of which also argue for giving up the struggle for hegemony with the United States; G. Kunadze, "Ob oboronnoi dostatochnosti voennogo potentsiala SSSR," *MEiMO*, 1989, no. 10, 68–83; S. Blagovolin, "Geopoliticheskie aspekty oboronitel'noi dostatochnosti," *Kommunist*, 1990, no. 4 (March), 114–23. See also Kull, *Burying Lenin*, esp. chap. 5.

[51] Representative examples include Andrei Kolosov, "Reappraisal of USSR Third World Policy," *International Affairs*, 1990, no. 5; Georgii Mirskii, "The USSR and the Third World," *International Affairs*, 1988, no. 12; A Solonitskii, "Tsentr i periferiia mirovogo kapitalisticheskogo khoziaistva," *MEiMO*, 1989, no. 4. See also Kull, *Burying Lenin*, chap. 6.

plauded, were often not enough for the intellectuals, who wanted rapid and drastic cuts in subsidies, especially to Cuba.[52]

The problem of the Lippmann gap and the potential solution of outright retrenchment and retreat were in the air in Gorbachev's Moscow. The staler air of Soviet corridors of power doubtless contained even more sharply worded critiques of past and present policy, penned by diplomatic professionals proud of their realism. But an account of the twilight days of Soviet power that portrayed an elite gloomily pondering retreat and capitulation would bear little resemblance to the actual mood of the time. For those authors who spoke in such dramatic tones about retrenchment were arguing against the globalist and revisionist aspects of the new-thinking general line that then dominated the discourse. Drawing heavily on the works and traditions of their Western counterparts, these self-styled Soviet realists thought of themselves as an embattled minority crying out in a wilderness of utopian new thinkers. Arrayed against them were the top leadership and its large contingent of intellectual well-wishers, who laid before the Soviet people and the world a strong analytical case for optimism about present prospects. The diplomacy of new thinking, they argued, could more than compensate for revealed Soviet shortcomings in the classical scales of power.

It is true that the Soviet leadership had numerous incentives to mask any private convictions about the inevitability of decline. All the factors that encouraged some elites in the past to avoid frank discussion of decline and project optimism applied to Gorbachev. No leader wants to acknowledge international decline on his watch. None wishes to feed arguments to his political opponents. No statesman entering a negotiation wants to signal the other side that his hand is weak and he must retrench in any case. Some official cheeriness of the Gorbachev era was no doubt attributable to these classic concerns. But the intellectual roots of Soviet confidence were deeper, and much of the optimism was genuine, just as was the disquiet that Gorbachev's innovative diplomacy created in conservative Western foreign offices.

A reform project requires a certain measure of confidence.[53] Conservatives typically are at once proud of their polity's accomplish-

---

[52] See, e.g., Andrei Kortunov, "Generosity or Wastefulness?" *Moskovskie Novosti*, 3 December 1989 (*CDSP* 42, no. 2: 15).

[53] Shevardnadze told a session of the Supreme Soviet in October 1989 that before perestroika could begin "we had to have confidence and eschew our weakness complex, if you will, so we could assess the situation objectively": *Pravda*, 24 October 1989 (*FBIS-SOV*, 1989, no. 204: 45).

ments and worried about its fragility. They fret about slippery slopes at home and falling dominoes abroad. Reformers are more critical of their polity's accomplishments but more confident of its potential. They dismiss the conservatives' worries as transparent defenses of their own privileges and an inequitable status quo. A belief in inevitable balancing is more suitable to them, for it engenders a sense of security about the state's external positions and highlights the dangers of costly overreaction to foreign events. Not surprisingly, old thinking and new fitted perfectly into this reformer/conservative dichotomy.[54] Many of the most central new-thinking concepts were the brainchildren of Western reformers critical of their own governments' militarized overcommitment to the Cold War. Understandably, these concepts resonated for Soviet reformers.

The fundamental source of new thinking's confidence was its redefinition of the threat. New thinkers worked assiduously to dispel the old threat portrayal, which held that the two social systems were existential threats to each other and consequently that if imperialism gained a military advantage, its more aggressive representatives would be tempted to exploit it to socialism's detriment. From his early years in power, Gorbachev was at pains to argue that military power did not serve political goals, that both sides were *equally* threatened, and that the threat emanated more from the nature of the weapons and their associated security arrangements than from the nature of the two socioeconomic systems.[55]

An altered assessment of threat, a clear perception of the security dilemma, and the belief in balancing constituted the new thinking's recipe for confidence. The essence of the new-thinking argument was that in the past the Soviet Union had overestimated the threat it faced, and consequently built up a surplus of military power, which drove the other power centers on the international scene (Europe, the United States, Japan, China) to increase their defense efforts and coalesce into a worldwide anti-Soviet alignment. In its first years, and particularly between 1987 and 1989, the new Soviet policy endeavored to exploit the *reverse side* of this security dilemma. By unilateral measures—most spectacularly Gorbachev's announcement in December 1988 of a reduction of half a million troops in Europe—Moscow could

---

[54]For a further taxonomy of reform and conservative world views in the Soviet context, see Stephen F. Cohen, *Rethinking the Soviet Experience* (New York: Oxford University Press, 1985), chap. 5.

[55]See Gorbachev, 3:246, 4:449. While Gorbachev saw the system of nuclear deterrence as inherently threatening, many scholars bought Western arguments about its stability. Cf. Gorbachev, "Reality and Guarantees for a Secure World," *International Affairs*, 1987, no. 11, 4, with Zurkin et al., "Vyzovy bezopasnosti," 47.

reduce the other great powers' sense of threat, and thus engender a reduction in their defense expenditures, a decoupling of their anti-Soviet alignment in world politics, and mutually beneficial cooperation on a wide range of issues. Arms control, further Soviet defense reductions, the transfer of defense resources to the civilian economy, a more secure and predictable external environment, and joint ventures with rich Western partners—all this could flow from the new policy.

According to these lights, concessions on arms control did not represent capitulation to the West. Instead, they were calculated catalyzing moves, which would spark a benign spiral of arms reductions and security negotiations—the exact opposite of the arms race and Cold War. The existing security system was unfavorable to current Soviet interests but highly stable, mainly as a result of decades of inertia. Gorbachev's policy faced the same problem Stalin's and Khrushchev's had faced: How do you nudge into action a West that in the absence of some prodding will muddle along indefinitely as before? Feeling too vulnerable to make major concessions, the two earlier leaders tried exacerbating crises in Berlin. Now Gorbachev was prepared to make serious concessions in the expectation of reciprocal shifts from the other side. These were precisely the arguments Gorbachev deployed against his domestic military, and by using them he was able to win over important converts, such as Chief of Staff (and later presidential military adviser) Marshal Sergei Akhromeev.[56]

An analogous set of propositions governed Soviet policy toward regional conflicts. The goal of policy was not to reduce or replace Western influence but to serve as a catalyst for regional settlements agreeable to all parties. To achieve such settlements the USSR would sometimes have to twist regional allies' arms or build their sense of security by increasing weapons deliveries. But Gorbachev, Shevardnadze, and their intellectual allies steadfastly maintained that the policy was not a retreat. Rather, it would remove obstacles to other goals, mainly cooperation with the rich West, while enhancing the Soviet Union's influence by including it in major regional settlements. The policy generated positive feedback, as Soviet diplomats sat on great-power councils settling conflicts in Central and Southeast Asia and Africa. Even Soviet support for the American-led U.N. coalition against Iraq in the Gulf War brought relations with rich Gulf states and inclusion in the Middle East peace process. At the Helsinki summit, President Bush formally reversed three decades of U.S. policy

[56] See Don Oberdorfer, *The Turn: From the Cold War to a New Era* (New York: Poseidon, 1991), 320.

and welcomed the Soviets into the Arab-Israeli peace negotiations—
an objective that thirty years of costly competitive policy had failed
to deliver. Western analysts argued convincingly that the new course
was not a retreat but reflected a conceptual reordering that was bringing Moscow more influence in numerous reasons.[57] The policy also
generated domestic opposition, but conservatives who accused the
leadership of capitulation were balanced by more radical new thinkers
who accused it of clinging to Soviet imperial ways.[58]

The new thinking did appear to obscure the decline issue for a
number of years. It faced a major contradiction, however—one that
perhaps became evident only in hindsight. Even as it decried past
Soviet reliance on military power, even as it steadfastly rejected the
political utility of military power, the new thinking in fact continued
to use arms control to drive foreign policy. It was in effect cashing in
on surplus military capabilities left over from the previous leadership.
It was Soviet overall parity and conventional superiority that allowed
Moscow to drive for a "common European home." It was massive
Soviet arms transfers and longstanding client relationships in the
Third World that gave Moscow a voice there. Gorbachev was using
military capabilities to drive a policy of demilitarizing security.[59] The
old-thinking policy had relied on the image of an implacable, mono-
lithically powerful Soviet bloc. The new-thinking policy relied on the
image of a reasonable partner revising security arrangements the
world round via arms control. Both policies were based on Soviet
military capabilities. The problem with the new one, however, was
that, unlike the earlier policy, it was finite: once the arms-control deal
was signed, once the regional dispute was settled, the Soviet role was
reduced. In the end, there was no escape from the unidimensional
nature of Soviet power.

NEW THINKING AND THE END OF BIPOLARITY

The year 1989 began superbly for Soviet foreign policy. No contemporary journalistic treatment of Soviet affairs was complete without

[57] See Richard K. Herrmann, "Soviet Behavior in Regional Conflicts: Old Questions,
New Strategies, and Important Lessons," *World Politics* 44 (April 1992): 432–65.

[58] Before the Gulf War, radical critiques of Gorbachev's Third World policy actually
far outweighed conservative attacks in the public realm. Conservative attacks were
stronger during the Gulf episode, but still balanced (weakly) by the radicals. See Su-
zanne Crow, "The Gulf Conflict and Debate over Soviet National Interests," *Radio
Liberty Report on the USSR* 3 (18 February 1991): 15–17.

[59] For an article that recognizes this situation, though not the irony of it, see Sergei
Karaganov, "The Common European Home: The Military Angle," *International Affairs*,
1988, no. 8, 71–78.

the already shopworn contrast between success abroad and failure at home. Internationally, the reverse side of the security dilemma appeared to be delivering the goods: major reductions in conventional forces looked probable; relations with key Western European powers, especially West Germany, were better than ever; NATO was struggling to redefine itself as the uniting glue of the "Soviet threat" weakened, and as the year begin it had fallen into disarray over Germany's opposition to the "modernization" of short-range nuclear forces. As Gorbachev summed up the situation in a speech in Kiev in February:

> The threat of war has been weakened. The security of the Soviet Union has increased. The prestige of our policies has generally grown in the community of states. For the first time in the postwar years and maybe in all history our country's security has been strengthened not because of the escalation of military power and not because of the increase in the already huge defense expenditure.[60]

Those words were quite credible when he spoke them. Intelligent observers within the country and around the world agreed with them. Critics of Gorbachev's policy and the new thinking as a whole expressed themselves in early 1989, but they appeared to cause the leadership only mild discomfort. Much of the struggle, of course, was hidden. In more open political circumstances, more strident critiques and more organized opposition would probably have made themselves felt. But some of the leadership's confidence was the result of the positive feedback its policy had generated over the previous years.

As the new-thinking model predicted, positive feedback was generated mainly by manipulation of one variable: the perceived Soviet threat. The more Soviet diplomacy succeeded in reducing this variable, the more positive feedback flowed back to Moscow. Nuclear arms reductions, open inspection regimes, concessions on conventional weapons, domestic Soviet democratization—each step down the perceived threat ladder led to closer relations with the West on acceptable terms. "Freedom of choice" for Eastern Europe was an integral plank in the threat-reduction platform. Gorbachev had begun to articulate the policy in 1987, and he decreased the ambiguity of his statements over the succeeding two years.[61] The policy may have

---

[60] Moscow domestic radio, 23 February 1989, *FBIS-SOV*, 1989, no. 036: 54–55.

[61] For exhaustive analyses of official statements on nonintervention, see Ronald D. Asmus, J. F. Brown, and Keith Crane, *Soviet Foreign Policy and the Revolutions of 1989 in Eastern Europe*, R-3903-USDP (Santa Monica: Rand, 1991); and the chapters by Robert G. Livingston and Christopher Jones in *East-Central Europe and the USSR*, ed. R. F. Starr (New York: St. Martin's Press, 1991).

reflected personal convictions or even complacency. Why take on the Eastern European nomenklaturas when things seemed under control (at least until 1989)? The new line certainly reflected an assessment of the high costs of intervention: the end of positive feedback from the West, the assumption of Eastern European debt and the responsibility for perestroika in a foreign country, the rise of domestic conservatives. And announcing the policy in such forums as the United Nations and the European Parliament in Strasbourg produced immediately salutary effects on the image the Soviet leadership was cultivating.

Dispelling the Soviet Union's reputation as the enemy in the West implied demolishing its reputation as the hegemon in the East. As Eastern Europe began to stir politically, eyes trained by Cold War experience focused on Moscow to discern signals and ascertain the limits of change. At each stage of the process, confirmation of nonintervention was forthcoming: through the strikes in Poland in 1988, the "round table" talks there in April 1989, on to the communists' thrashing at the hands of Solidarity in the June election and the reform-communist leadership coup in Budapest the same month; though the formation of the noncommunist Mazowiecki government in Warsaw and the beginning of the East German exodus in August, the Hungarians' removal of the barbed wire along their western border in September and their reincarnation as Socialists in October, on to the mass demonstrations in Leipzig and Berlin that month, and November's opening of the Berlin Wall.

The events along the road to bipolarity's end were cumulative and reinforcing. After each event it was impossible to know where developments would lead. With the passage of time, the collapse of the postwar system moved from the realm of the potential to that of the possible, the probable, and eventually the inevitable. Determining precisely where each government's assessments were on that spectrum will have to await better evidence than that now available. What available records do indicate is that for the Soviet Union, as well as for its Western counterparts, the impact of each event and each decision was attenuated by two expectations: that reform Communists might succeed in stabilizing the situation; and that even if regimes changed in Eastern Europe, geopolitical imperatives would create strong incentives to preserve existing international alignments, at least for a reasonable time. Soviet, American, and European officials expressed both of these expectations, privately and in public, throughout the year.[62]

---

[62]See quotations in Bill Keller, Bernard Gwertzman, and Michael T. Kaufman, *The Collapse of Communism* (New York: Times Books, 1990), 164, 181, 213, 272–73; Ober-

As change gathered momentum in Eastern Europe, Gorbachev engineered what analysts later laconically called a "correction" in Soviet foreign policy.[63] For the first time in its history, the Soviet Union became a status quo power. Official policy shifted from revision to securing the bipolar arrangements in Europe. The shift requires a brief explanation.

Because his foreign policy focused so intently on arms control, from the outset Gorbachev found himself according practical primacy to relations with Washington, which held most of NATO's military keys.[64] Gorbachev the visionary thought about overcoming Europe's division and establishing a demilitarized security system based on military forces capable only of defense. Gorbachev the practical statesman sought concrete agreements: on intermediate-range nuclear forces, strategic weapons, conventional forces, trade restrictions. Though these immediate objectives could be connected conceptually to more visionary goals, the practical need to deal with existing realities inevitably pushed policy into familiar paths.

In addition to facing the practical need to work with the Americans, Gorbachev was well aware of Western suspiciousness about Soviet splitting tactics, and sought to reassure audiences abroad that Moscow entertained no such intentions and recognized the depth of America's ties to Europe.[65] Nevertheless, until 1989 he and his diplomatic machine retained classical Soviet caginess about the bipolar arrangements in Europe. Official policy still supported the dissolu-

---

dorfer, *The Turn,* 361; and the interviews in Kull, *Burying Lenin,* chap. 7, esp. 136, 142. The value of all these interviews lies in the fact that they were conducted before the outcome was known. My own interviews in Moscow after the fact corroborate these findings. Read closely, Shevardnadze's recollections are also revealing on this score: *Moi vybor: V zashchitu demokratii i svobody* (Moscow: Novosti, 1991), chaps. 6–7. Cf., e.g., 223 with 243–45. For more evidence on the "perestroika illusion" and Eastern Europe, see Asmus et al., *Eastern European Revolutions.*

[63] See O. N. Bykov, ed., *Mezhdunarodnyi ezhegodnik: Politika i ekonomika, 1990* (Moscow: Politizdat, 1990), 73–75; Iu. A. Borko, A. V. Zagorskii, and S. A. Karaganov, *Obshchii evropeiskii dom: Chto my o nem dumaem?* (Moscow: Mezhdunarodnye Otnosheniia, 1991), 105–10.

[64] See Hannes Adomeit,"Gorbatchows Westpolitik," *Osteuropa,* 1988, no. 6, 419–34; no. 9, 816–34; no. 12, 1091–1105. At a policy review conference at the Foreign Ministry in 1988, numerous diplomats expressed dissatisfaction with the focus on Washington, though the "majority" expressed the view that it reflected "objective reality," and that "no attempt to dissociate Western Europe from the United States could bear fruit": "The 19th All-Union CPSU Conference: Foreign Policy and Diplomacy," *International Affairs,* 1988, no. 10, 35–36. The official momentum for a push toward Europe had gathered more steam a year later: "The Foreign Policy and Diplomatic Activity of the USSR," *International Affairs,* 1990, no. 1, 46–47.

[65] Gorbachev, *Perestroika,* chap. 6. Here Gorbachev combines such assurances with classical Eurocentric jibes about European countries' "National interests" being "carried across the ocean," and the "onslaught of 'mass culture' from across the Atlantic."

tion of both blocs. Despite disclaimers from Gorbachev, rhetoric and policy initiatives emanating from Moscow continued to take advantage of endemic Western contradictions, especially between Germany and the rest of NATO, but also between Europe as a whole and the United States. For four years Soviet officials danced around the question whether Washington would receive an apartment in the imagined European home, and if so, how long its lease would run.

The incentives for deliberate ambiguity about bipolarity were numerous: the genuine desire of many official and semiofficial Soviets to overcome Europe's division, either in a benign, demilitarized common home or in a more sinister "status quo plus" version (since both were distant goals, it was hard to tell the two apart in their rhetorical manifestations); the pull of earlier official positions; and, by no means least, the utility of pro-Europe statements in the classic game of playing on NATO contradictions in pursuit of immediate policy objectives. Soviet elite and official statements about new openings to Europe fed intense speculation, especially in West Germany, that Moscow was preparing a new and enticing reunification offer. When they came from the mouths of such conservative diplomatic veterans and known opponents of unification as Valentin Falin and Nikolai Portugalov, these statements were clearly designed to manipulate German attitudes toward current Soviet policy objectives, particularly surrounding Bonn's decisions to participate in the Strategic Defense Initiative and withdraw intermediate-range nuclear weapons.[66] Falin was playing this game with gusto as late as the spring of 1989, when, in an effort to influence the controversial German decision to go along with NATO's modernization of short-range nuclear forces, he hinted that Moscow might view unification and neutralization with equanimity. In internal discussions before and after this event, when unification began to be seen as a real possibility. Falin and his protégés stood sternly against any change in Moscow's two-Germanys policy.[67]

Soon after Falin's gambit, however, the policy "correction" began to work its way through the Soviet foreign policy machinery. It con-

---

[66]See, e.g., Portugalov's article in *New Times*, 1987, no. 22, suggesting withdrawal of all foreign troops from the two Germanys. Speculation about a change in Soviet German policy got so far out of hand that Gorbachev, who had already made his opposition to unification clear in 1987, had to issue several more strongly worded antiunification statements in 1988. See *Pravda*, 8 July 1987, 2, and 15 October 1988, 2; Gorbachev, *Perestroika*, 199–202.

[67]Based on Dashichev's interview "Dann erhebt sich das Volk," *Der Spiegel*, 21 January 1991, 136–43; and my interviews in Moscow with members of the staff of the International Department and other participants at the department's meetings on the issue in 1988 and 1989.

sisted of two shifts: explicit endorsement of the American role in Europe, and support for the continuance of the Warsaw Pact and NATO and their transformation into "political" institutions. The reason was obvious: stability. The explicitness, and indeed urgency, of official statements on both matters correlated exactly with the mounting crisis in Eastern Europe. Gorbachev began to introduce the "correction" in March 1989, and it flourished into a full-blown reversal by December.[68] At the Malta summit that month, Gorbachev startled President Bush by stating emphatically: "We want you in Europe. You need to be in Europe. It's important for the future of Europe that you are in Europe, so we don't want to see you out of there."[69] Shevardnadze later added credibility to the new Soviet position by saying, "Not very long ago our objective was to force the Americans out of Europe at any cost."[70] At their gathering in July 1989 the Warsaw Pact states retained the dissolve-the-blocs line, but when they met the following January Gorbachev told the closed meeting: "NATO and the Warsaw Pact should be maintained despite their shortcomings because they are elements of stability."[71]

Until 1989, the stability of the postwar settlement had been bothersome to a restless Gorbachev trying to refashion his country's external relations. During the spring and summer of that year, the system's nettlesome stability gradually turned into a virtue as the unhinging of Russia's alies moved from potential to possible to probable. In a matter of months, the short-term need to secure international stability began to take precedence over the long-term desire to replace the existing structure of security. Tactical manipulation of NATO contradictions also now had to take a back seat to the urgent need to clarify Soviet support for stability and measured change.

By introducing his policy "correction," Gorbachev did what "realistic" Western analysts such as Zbigniew Brzezinski and Henry Kissinger had long wished him and his predecessors to do: he transformed the Soviet Union into a status quo power not only in

---

[68] See Heinz Timmermann, "Begegnungen mit Gorbatschow: Interne Aufzeichnungen über sieben Spitzentreffen den Führenden von KPdSU und KPI," *Osteuropa* 41 (July 1991): 695–700 (review of Antonio Rubbi, *Incontri con Gorbaciov* [Rome, 1990]); and Gorbachev, 7:395.

[69] Quoted in Oberdorfer, *The Turn*, 381. See also U.S. House of Representatives, Committee on Foreign Affairs, *Soviet Diplomacy and Negotiating Behavior, 1988–1990*, vol. 3, *Gorbachev-Reagan-Bush Meetings at the Summit* (Washington: U.S. Government Printing Office, 1991), chap. 5.

[70] *Izvestiia*, 19 February 1990 (*CDSP* 42, no. 7: 17).

[71] Quoted in Oberdorfer, *The Turn*, 385.

deed but also in word.[72] In the summer and fall of 1989 the Soviet Union formally became a "sensible duopolist," ready to cooperate with the other superpower to maintain stability. It assiduously removed all uncertainty regarding its intentions in Europe—something it had studiously avoided through the rulerships of Stalin, Khrushchev, Brezhnev, and all the phases of Gorbachev's perestroika up to that point. By the Malta summit in December 1989, Presidents Bush and Gorbachev talked like managers of the international system.[73] The irony is that by then the events that compelled them to speak the language of management had gone beyond their control.

From November 1989 to January 1990 Soviet policy opposed unification and supported maintenance of the blocs. The leadership and the Foreign Ministry placed great hopes in the mere existence of a confluence of U.S. and Soviet (as well as British and French) interests on the German question. However, the Soviet Union's grasp for bipolarity was brief. By early 1990 its futility became evident, and it was not because of a lack of support on the part of the American manger. In November and December, Washington made every sort of promise not to exploit Eastern European developments and even gave East German reform Communists symbolic support.[74] Events on the ground, especially in Germany, outran the initiative, and in 1990 Washington and then London, Paris, and Moscow adjusted to what appeared now to be inevitable. The next phase for Soviet policy was the long bargaining over the terms of German unification. From February until June the Soviets accepted unification in principle, but pushed for it to be preceded by the creation of a new security order in Europe. Finally they acceded to unification and the new Germany's membership in NATO, bargaining only over the terms of troop withdrawal.

---

[72]For Brzezinski's recommendations in 1988, see "East-West Relations and Eastern Europe (An American-Soviet Dialogue)," *Problems of Communism*, May–August 1988, 67–70; on Kissinger's January 1989 proposal, see Oberdorfer, *The Turn*, 342; on Soviet views on bipolar stability, see Amirdzhanov and Cherkasov, "Our Common European Home," 29–30.

[73]In preparation for the Malta summit, the National Security Council's Soviet expert, Robert Blackwill, consulted the classified minutes of all previous U.S.-Soviet summits and concluded that Malta was the first at which the drive for cooperation outweighed competitive impulses: Oberdorfer, *The Turn*, 379.

[74]For a brief period when the GDR was under the leadership of Hans Modrow, top U.S. officials, including the president and secretary of state, actually called it the "German Democratic Republic" rather than "East Germany." In November, Secretary of State James Baker paid a call on Modrow in Berlin. On support from the U.S. "manager," see U.S. House of Representatives, Committee on Foreign Affairs, *Soviet Diplomacy and Negotiating Behavior*, chaps. 5–6.

The grasp for bipolarity took place in an intellectual climate dramatically different from the one that had surrounded the heady days of new thinking. It was only then that Soviet discourse assumed the classic lines of a declining power: emotive appeals, agonizing reappraisals, spirited, emotional defenses of intensely contested policies. Only then did the leadership face squarely and publicly the issue of declining prestige. In a memorable defense of his and Gorbachev's decision not to intervene in Eastern Europe, Shevardnadze made reference to a famous speech of his predecessor Andrei Gromyko, in 1971. Then a confident Gromyko had declared, "Today there is no question of any significance that can be decided without the Soviet Union or in opposition to it."[75]

> I recall the storm of applause evoked by the words of one politician, whom I highly respect, to the effect that currently not a single question in the world can be resolved without the participation of the Soviet Union, or even less contrary to its interests. . . . But the whole point is how it is decided and at what price for the Soviet Union itself. . . .
>
> I can understand [great-power sentiments] because the belief that we are a great power and that we should be respected is deeply ingrained in me, as in everyone. But, great in what? Territory? Population? Quantity of arms? Or the people's troubles? The individual's lack of rights? Life's disorderliness? In what do we, who have virtually the highest infant mortality rate on the planet, take pride? It is not easy answering these questions: Who are you and what do you wish to be? A country of power or a country of kindness? . . . The time has come to recognize that there can be no parity between the two countries unless they are backed by comparable amounts of national product and comparable levels of scientific and technical development.[76]

The first reaction to these words might well be thankfulness that a man who thought like this happened to head the foreign ministry of one of the world's most powerful states as it entered a phase of rapid decline. But upon reflection, an additional peculiarity comes to mind: by the time those compelling words were spoken in April 1990, there was virtualy no question of reversing the flow of events in Eastern Europe. The Soviet political elite began publicly to grapple seriously with decline only after the fact. The nature of policy feedback, elite discourse, even the terms and issues of foreign policy shifted with

[75] *XXIV s"ezd Kommunisticheskoi Partii Sovetskogo Soiuza: Stenograficheskii otchet* (Moscow: Izdatel'stvo Politicheskoi Literatury, 1971), 1:482.
[76] *FBIS-SOV*, 1990, no. 081: 9–10.

unprecedented suddeness. There was, in short, a lag between what in retrospect appears to have been the Soviet Union's prestige position and the way it was perceived at the time.

The language with which the Soviet leadership addressed its great-power partners also underwent a rapid and radical shift. Once hailed as "the angel and instrument or change," the potential architect of a new security order, Gorbachev was now the conservative apostle of stability. He began to deploy what might be called the Ottoman Empire plea, suggesting to Western interlocutors that a Soviet Union of a certain stature was necessary to preserve international stability. It can be regarded as the fourth stage in Soviet power assessments, following the "status quo plus" notions of the 1970s, the "common Europe home" slogan of the perestroika years, and the effort to secure bipolarity in 1989. Gorbachev began using the argument in a domestic context. At the party plenum on 25 December 1989 he lectured the breakaway Lithuanian party: "The existence of a unitary, stable, and powerful Soviet Union is an urgent requirement of the epoch, of the entire existing complex system of international security. . . . And in contacts with us this is definitely and unambiguously confirmed by the leaders of all the major countries of the world, including those whose support our internal separatists would clearly like."[77] He then transferred the argument to the international scene, claiming that the inclusion of a united Germany in NATO would represent an unacceptable "shift in the balance."[78]

A second new tactic indicative of the new power assessment might be called the Versailles warning: the suggestion that any move to humiliate the Soviet Union when it was down could backfire by unleashing national sentiments that would cause the Soviet government to harden its policy stance in world affairs. "If attempts are made to put us in a constrained situation in affairs affecting our security," Shevardnadze warned in May 1990, "then this will lead to a situation—I say this frankly—where the degree of our political flexibility will be severely restricted, for emotions will come to a boil within the country, specters of the past will come to the fore, the national complexes rooted in the tragic pages of our history will be revived."[79]

Efforts to retain influence on European matters by explicit reference to internal vulnerability failed to bear fruit. A unified Germany was

---

[77] *Pravda*, 26 December 1989, 2.
[78] See his news conference with François Mitterrand on Moscow Central Television, 25 May 1990: *FBIS-SOV*, 1990, no. 103: 42.
[79] *Izvestiia*, 7 May 1990, 3 (*FBIS-SOV*, 1990, no. 088: 5).

included in NATO, which became Europe's premier security structure at least for the medium term. Soviet foreign policy professionals consequently settled on the Ottoman strategy. A unified Soviet Union, they argued, fulfilled a vital international function in preserving stability the world around. Its collapse would be an unmitigated international disaster. Even after the attempted coup in August 1991 Gorbachev continued to spell out a vision of a "great Eurasian democracy [that] will become one of the bulwarks of the new world, its security, and the rapprochement between the two continents in the building of a just world order."[80] And in pursuing this strategy, Gorbachev had powerful allies abroad, including the United States, France, Britain, and Germany, all of whose leaders openly expressed their preference for a unified state on Soviet territory with one foreign policy voice.[81]

As successful as the Foreign Ministry's prestige policy was in foreign capitals, it failed closer to home. Eastern European allies moved out of Russia's orbit and refused to pledge not to join other alliances. The constituent republics of the old Soviet Union continued their flight from the center. And at each stage of the process the same cognitive lag is observable. Adjustment to each new diminution of Soviet or Russian power appears to occur after the fact. Even the formal dissolution of the Soviet Union in December 1991 was accompanied by startlingly little imperial anguish. Only after the passage of several months, as the weaknesses of the Commonwealth of Independent States revealed themselves, did nationalist and great-power anxiety reach proportions even roughly corresponding to the magnitude of the changes.[82]

The superpowers' futile grasp at bipolarity and equally futile effort to retain the Soviet Union as a unitary great power for stability's sake mark the truest end of the Cold War. The Ottoman phase of superpower diplomacy was the last faint gasp of the Cold War agenda, signified by the Malta and Helsinki superpower summits and the Madrid conference on the Middle East, chaired by Presidents Bush and Gorbachev. The Cold War was mainly about competition with the United States. The Cold War agenda was determined largely by that competition. Now that Moscow had neither the capability nor the inclination to compete with Washington, its postcommunist prestige

---

[80] Moscow Central Television, 10 September 1991: *FBIS-SOV*, 1991, no. 175: 5.

[81] An example is Gorbachev's account of Bush's and Mitterrand's support: *Izvestiia*, 16 November 1991 (*FBIS-SOV*, 1991, no. 223: 27).

[82] See Vera Tolz and Elizabeth Teague, "Russian Intellectuals Adjust to the Loss of Empire," *RFFE/RL Research Report* 1 (21 February 1992).

policy was a hollow shell. The desiderata of Russian foreign policy had shifted utterly. They now had almost nothing to do with the issues that had defined Soviet policy for four decades. Several months were required, however, for this fact to become evident to most of Moscow's foreign policy community. Only then was it clear that foreign support was no more effective at holding the Soviet Union together than it was at keeping Germany apart.

THE IRONY OF BIPOLARITY'S END

The Elusive Balance and Gorbachev's Foreign Policy

The Gorbachev foreign policy story was not one of decline or conceptual revolution. It was a story of both. Their combination helps explain the peculiarities of the Soviet Union's end as a superpower. Perceived decline discredited the old conceptual framework. The new-thinking framework that replaced it obscured the trade-offs implicit in Gorbachev's foreign strategy. Gorbachev, Shevardnadze, and some of the Soviet foreign policy community were prepared intellectually for changes in the security structure, but on better terms than those they were eventually compelled to accept.[83] They thought they could reduce the image of their country as a threat without reducing its power. Feedback suggested success until the autumn of 1989. The strategy collapsed along with the idea of reform communism. The suddenness of that collapse, difficult to foresee and doubtless complex in causation, helps explain the Soviet decision not to intervene. But the bloodlessness of Soviet decline is also attributable to the new thinking itself, a body of ideas that refused to see dominoes in any of the series of events that led to the dissolution of Soviet power.

The temptation arises to subject the oft-praised team of Gorbachev and Shevardnadze to the kind of withering criticism scholars have been leveling against their dour predecessors for years. After all, the very same theories that postulate the prevalence of balancing behavior in world politics—the rule Molotov and Gromyko are accused of breaking—explain that law mainly by reference to the assumption that states desire survival above all else. To the extent that Gorbachev's foreign policy abetted the fall and collapse of Soviet power, it would appear to deserve some critical analysis. The same can be said for the new thinking, which embodied concepts long dear to Western

[83]See, e.g., Shevardnadze, *Moi vybor*, chaps. 6–7.

scholars. To the extent that those concepts blinded the Soviet leadership to the true consequences of decline, they might reasonably be accused of having been misleading and illusory. To the extent that they obscured the Soviet Union's ultimate and acute dependence on military power, they may well have been less accurate renderings of reality than the old-thinking postulates were. Hindsight suggests that capitalism and "socialism" were antithetical after all.

Had Gorbachev and Shevardnadze been less ardent new thinkers, they might have pushed for a deal on Germany earlier and gotten better terms for their country. They might have sent the signals required to slow the dissolution of the Warsaw Pact and negotiated a slower withdrawal of Soviet power that salvaged prestige and had a less dramatic impact on the armed forces. They might thereby have slowed the demonstration effect whereby East European independence fed immediately back into the center-periphery struggle within the Soviet Union itself. They might at least have postponed the day when their country was transformed from a subject of international politics to its object. Counterfactual surmises such as these might be useful counterpoints to those spun against Stalin, Khrushchev, and Brezhnev.

These criticisms, however, would be as unfair as those levied against Gorbachev's predecessors. They reflect the fact that evaluating foreign policy is always a subjective business. Much depends on how one values the prestige and perquisites of great power and the integrity of a great and oppressive state. The criticisms obscure the extent to which the Gorbachev team and its new thinking may have been responsible for the comparative peacefulness of the Soviet Union's decline and collapse. Further, they ignore the fact that the collapse was due largely to the nature of the hand Stalin had dealt the new thinkers. The brittleness of Soviet-style "socialism" and its utter dependence on military power were not the products of Gorbachev's policy. They were realities he inherited, and the fact that he, like the vast majority of observers east and west, did not accurately perceive them before 1990 was perhaps all to the historical good. Had Gorbachev and his fellow storm petrels of prestroika not believed in new thinking, they might have hesitated to embark on their reform course in the first place.

But the main reality such criticism ignores is the elusiveness of power and the consequent capriciousness of feedback, which foiled the expectations generated by old and new thinking alike. Like the expanding policies of Stalin, Khrushchev, and Brezhnev earlier, Gorbachev's innovative policy generated positive feedback for a prolonged period before facing a sudden and unexpected shift. For five years the new thinking delivered the goods in the form of cooperation, arms reduction, and retained prestige. And it did so in a way that appeared to complement the leadership's domestic agenda. But just as earlier expanding leaders had seen dominoes fall before them until a counterbalancing coalition suddenly stopped and reversed them, so Gorbachev saw an international position robust enough for reform and rescue until the dominoes suddenly began toppling backward too quickly to stop.

The Elusive Balance and Bipolarity's End

The balance of power has been described as elusive rather than as irrelevant or wholly ambiguous because people do try to capture it, though they rarely succeed. Unless one recognizes that those who make decisions on behalf of states care about power in world politics, one will not understand their actions. But evidence about the distribution of power and the adequacy of policies based on particular assumptions about the operation of the balance is often subject to multiple, equally plausible interpretations. Perceptions shift rapidly in the wake of events that generate new and compelling evidence about the relationships or composition of power on the world scene. Perceptions are always seeking to catch up to what in retrospect seems to have been the "real" distribution of power. Change in world politics thus often comes in spurts, as a result of catalyzing events—crises, wars, revolutions—that generate new evidence about power while simultaneously altering its distribution.

Nothing better illustrates these contentions than the Soviet Union's experience after 1985. When Mikhail Gorbachev took the helm of the Communist Party in March of that year, his country was seen from within and without as a formidable but troubled superpower that under energetic leadership was likely to emerge as a more capable competitor of the United States (itself widely thought to be in decline). Five years later the same observers saw the Soviet Union as a pitiful, disintegrating, anachronistic giant that could pose no threat to the great powers save the aftershock of its own collapse. Even more striking is the comparison between Soviet power and prestige as they were perceived in the spring of 1989 and as they appeared a year later. The shift in that year alone rivaled in magnitude the kinds of changes induced by great wars. And the consequent change in world politics was of equal significance.

The new perspective gained from knowledge of the outcome of

1989 casts an ironic glow on many earlier truisms. Over four decades of the Cold War, a great many Americans and Soviets feared or anticipated much more dramatic change in global alignments than actually was in the offing. Both sides concentrated their expectations for large-scale change on the West (and American decline) rather than on the East (and Soviet decline). Overestimation of potential change and fixation with American decline were particularly acute for the Soviets, who were influenced by the official status of the updated Leninist theory of imperialism. That way of thinking highlighted contradictions among the imperialists, not among the socialists. It saw markets, not planning, as creating centrifugal forces. It portrayed the United States, not the Soviet Union, as a state uniquely dependent on military power.

But arguably the greatest irony is captured by the flow of events after 1987. When at last Moscow rid itself of its Leninist "class" understanding of world politics and began to adjust to the bipolar international structure, that structure began to unravel. The Soviet Union's final and unambiguous transformation into a status quo power occurred only as the status quo was crumbling beneath its feet. In the 1970s, after three decades of more or less stable bipolar competition, American theorists, notably Kenneth Waltz, articulated a sophisticated structural argument for the stability, and hence desirability and likely durability, of bipolarity. Bipolarity's end had been declared so often that no one who suggested the likelihood of such a thing was taken seriously. The present international arrangements, it was now thought, reflected the underlying and quite stable structure of power. It became fashionable to view the two superpowers as "sensible duopolists," who had largely given up their ideologically induced struggle for hegemony and now would cooperate to manage the international system. Nixon's America had put a formal end to idealistic dreams of an American global hegemony, and Brezhnev's Russia had jettisoned Leninism for all but propagandistic purposes.

The Soviets were thought to have accepted this logic of stability and to have been prevented from saying so only by their official attachment to Leninist rhetoric. But the Soviet leaders finally and unambiguously embraced stability only when international politics entered its most unstable period since World War II. The Soviets' adjustment to bipolarity was called forth only by the end of bipolarity. Their convergence with Western views of international reality, captured under the rubric of "new political thinking," changed that reality fundamentally. Soviet-American cooperation to manage the international system was a contradiction in terms, since the system was mainly a result of their rivalry.

The bipolar structure took shape in the wake of World War II largely as a result of an argument about the distribution of power and prestige on the world scene. It was reinforced by every subsequent intensification of that struggle. The fear or the hope that the structure might not be stable was the glue that held it together. The vigor with which the structure was challenged or defended derived both from the degree to which the parties disagreed about power and prestige and from the extent to which they thought basic revisions were possible. Thus each cycle of the Cold War decreased in intensity as these variables decreased. Each cycle left a greater appreciation of the structure's stability in its wake. But differences over power and prestige as well as anxieties or hopes about revision were staples of the Cold War and never disappeared entirely. The bipolarization of international alignments, so typical of prewar periods, consequently remained intact. Born of and sustained by competing views of power, the bipolar structure collapsed when those views at last converged.

[10]

The Elusive
Balance of Power

This inquiry has sought to understand the ways the distribution of power influences world politics over lengthy spans of time. By concentrating on contemporary perceptions during the Cold War I hoped to remove some of the clarity that theory and hindsight impose on the role of power in history. I wished to explore the balance-of-power concept rather than to disconfirm it by showing that it misses important factors. We do not need another case study concluding that reality is more complicated than theory—everyone knows it is. The question is: What is gained by a careful analysis of the uncertainty rife in the situations we try to understand? Can we generalize about the elusiveness of the balance of power? Will further work along these lines contribute to our understanding of international politics or will it simply yield a few niggling footnotes to the discipline?

The experience of the Soviet Union and the United States in the Cold War suggests that perceptions of power may indeed follow definable patterns and that knowledge about them will add something beyond the bounds of each case study. Most of the lessons, it is true, are about the limits to our knowledge and the limitations of general concepts. Those lessons in themselves may be useful correctives. But this kind of research yields positive dividends, too. They do not constitute every scholar's dream: a paradigm shift, a debate-defining conceptual reordering. Instead, they suggest a workaday way to help resolve old questions and generate interesting new ones.

The nature of the superpowers' perceptions of power during the Cold War revealed by this investigation corresponds to the findings of earlier conceptual and empirical work, and consequently requires little elaboration here.[1]

First, perceptions of power are more dynamic than measurements of material relationships. Rapid shifts in behavior may be related to perceived shifts in the distribution of power which are not captured by typical measures of capabilities. The relationship of perceptions to measurable resources can be capricious and unfortunately discovered only through historical research. More research on perceived power will in all likelihood fail to produce a single, reliable conversion rule for translating measurable resources into operative perceptions. Arguably the best that can be expected is a set of general guidelines. On the other hand, changes in perceptions, as troublesome as they are for building and testing theory, do expand the explanatory utility of the distribution of power by accounting for a greater variation in behavior and outcomes.

Three versions of the resources-perceptions theme emerge from the Cold War experience. Major outcomes, such as World War II, churn up changes in material distributions which any measure would capture. Examination of distributions of measurable resources would yield the expectation that perceptions also shifted markedly. But no one could devise a measure that predicted the general *nature* of those perceptions without consulting the historical record in detail. Minor outcomes, such as Vietnam, produce disproportionate alterations in perceived power which are not reflected in material balances. And cumulative change, such as increasing Soviet capabilities in Khrushchev's day, can generate dramatic shifts in power assessments widely at variance with the measurable magnitude of the change.

Second, relational assessments (assessments of the values of variables within a given conceptual framework) change more frequently than conceptual frameworks. When a conceptual framework, such as

[1]See in general Robert Jervis, *Perception and Misperception in International Politics* (Princeton: Princeton University Press, 1976); and in particular Aaron Friedberg, *The Weary Titan* (Princeton: Princeton University Press, 1987), esp. chap. 6.

the theory of imperialism, leads to expectations that turn out to be inaccurate, adherents to the framework are more likely to conclude that the discrepancy is due to a measurement problem than to attribute it to some flaw in the conceptual framework itself. Soviets accounted for any number of unexpected interimperialist outcomes in this manner. While such dogged loyalty to a conceptual framework can strike the observer as bias or opportunism, there are often sound reasons for it. If the framework has accounted for important events in the past, it would be imprudent to discard it cavalierly. Even more relevant, though, is the virtual impossibility of testing any framework satisfactorily. Since power cannot be measured, a power-based framework cannot be conclusively tested, and its user has no objective standard for assessing it.

Third, conceptual change can lead to rapid and large change in relational assessments. Post-Stalin revisions of nuclear doctrine appear to have contributed to rapid shifts in power assessments: first, between 1953 and 1955, in an extremely pessimistic direction, and then, after 1957, toward optimism. Khrushchev's revisions of Third World doctrine also led to vastly increased confidence about competing in that area. Post-Brezhnev revisions of the methodology for measuring economic power, from raw quantitative to more qualitative indexes, produced drastically different conclusions about Soviet economic capabilities. Reduction of the relative salience of military power led to significant revisions of the Soviet Union's overall standing.

Fourth, change in relational assessments can contribute to conceptual change. It is more likely to do so when relational trends are adverse and unsettling within the terms of the prevailing concept than as a result of some scientific testing process. If, according to the reigning conceptual framework, adverse shifts in a particular category of power will inexorably lead to politically troublesome effects, decision makers may grope for new concepts to avoid having to face uncomfortable trade-offs. The Soviet correlation-of-forces model suffered its worst setback when its implications for Soviet prospects became particularly grim. The Americans changed strategic concepts whenever the existing one implied an unavoidable threat to their hegemony.

Fifth, expectations about trends feed into present assessments.[2] This was most evident during the Khrushchev years, when the Soviet

---

[2]For earlier Rand research corroborating this finding, see Herbert Goldhammer, "The U.S.-Soviet Strategic Balance as Seen from London and Paris," *Survival* 19 (September–October 1977): 202–7.

Union was widely perceived to be increasing its capabilities very rapidly. This dynamic rise in power and the assumption that it would continue magnified the Soviets' impact on the world. It not only fed Khrushchev's drive for parity but contributed to the seriousness with which the Americans treated it.

Sixth, expectations are more capricious than assessments, yet they influence policy. This generalization applies especially to expectations about the mechanics of power and alliance, alignment, and, most commonly, what has here been termed "attitude" (the tendency of one government to defer to the diplomatic or strategic concerns of another). Expectations of favorable or unfavorable attitude changes among the middle powers were constant Cold War fare on both sides. Yet the veracity of such expectations was rarely examined. Politicians on both sides appeared ill disposed to devote much effort to examining them.

More important, policies were often *preclusive,* meant to forestall some unexpected unfavorable development. Once a preclusive policy is implemented, there is no way to test the veracity of the expectation that sparked the policy. Such a test requires an extremely bold counterfactual history of what would have happened had the policy not been adopted. The situation is paradoxical. Would equilibria form if states believed balancing was inevitable? Some preclusive policies must have been necessary. Some states may not have been preclusive enough. Preclusive policies are the hallmark of conservative powers that wish to nip potential problems in the bud. They render testing of strategic propositions nearly impossible. The result is yet one more explanation for the long lives of Cold War strategic concepts: they seemed to be wonderfully successful at averting *potential* disasters.

LEARNING DIFFICULTIES

We cannot pronounce judgment on the quality of the Soviet Union's or the United States' adaptation to the international environment in which it found itself during the Cold War without establishing at least in very general terms the nature of that environment. Learning not to touch a hot stove, for example, is different from learning how to be popular and successful socially. In the first instance, feedback is instantaneous and unequivocal. In the second, it accumulates more slowly and is more ambiguous. Strategies that seem to work wonderfully when you are six years old backfire a few years later. Even at a given age, there always seem to be many potentially successful strategies for success, rather than a single obvious one. But you may find that a strategy that works well for someone else fails when you try it.

The nature of the environment should determine the standards we use to assess learning.[3] A child who repeatedly touches hot stoves despite the great pain this practice causes him surely alarms his parents more than one who has trouble getting along with playmates at school. The slowness or unevenness of Soviets' or Americans' adjustment to changes in the external environment may result from some internal problem or from the ambiguity of the external situation itself. To reach a clinical judgment about a historical actor's learning capacity we need some understanding of the nature of the environment it was supposed to learn about. The more ambiguous the environment, the more forgiving our standard of assessment must be.

Several problems make learning about the influence and exercise of power in world politics an especially complicated process. The first is the ambiguity of feedback, a problem faced time and again on both sides of the Cold War. The feedback generated by policies based on a particular strategic concept is almost always subject to multiple interpretations. Consequently, the adequacy of a given strategic concept is extraordinarily hard to judge, by actors on the scene or by analysts in retrospect.

Second is the capriciousness of feedback. Incoming evidence may support a strategic framework and its associated policy consistently for prolonged periods, only to shift suddenly. The prudent policy maker clings to the tried-and-true framework in the face of initial stormclouds on the strategic horizon. Sometimes this steadfastness is rewarded; at other times it is punished harshly. The major source of feedback is the behavior of other states on the world scene. Behavior, as every foreign policy analyst knows, is usually subject to numerous interpretations. The policy maker, like the scholar, wants to know the thinking behind the behavior. So the second major source of feedback is intelligence about other governments' assessments. That intelligence is often obtained through secret channels, but public statements of other governments' officials are important sources as well.

The Cold War experience shows repeatedly how each side's statements fed the other's expectations and reinforced reigning strategic

---

[3]See Kenneth Boulding, "The Learning and Reality Testing Process in the International System," in *Image and Reality in World Politics*, ed. John C. Farrell and Asa P. Smith (New York: Columbia University Press, 1967).

concepts, until suddenly statements and behavior lurched in the opposite direction. The feedback supplied by public statements opens an immense can of worms. Domestic politics may intrude, as it did in the case of Kennedy's and Khrushchev's exaggeration of Soviet capabilities. Governments can employ image-control strategies that introduce all sorts of noise in incoming feedback signals.[4]

The nature of each side's political institutions can produce mixed signals. Of particular note here is the asymmetry between the closed and dictatorial nature of the Soviet Union, where political communication at all levels was subject to careful management, and the more free-wheeling political discourse typical of the United States and its main allies. The Kremlin could carefully craft its message to influence Washington's perceptions. It had other ways of communicating with its allies, whereas the White House had to exert inordinate efforts in sending signals to its allies. For the allies, bargaining with Washington outweighed in importance any negotiations with the USSR. That bargaining often contained hints of pro-Soviet attitude shifts on issues important to the Americans. At times one gets the impression that American foreign policy was four-fifths about alliance management and one-fifth about the Soviet Union. Consequently, communication among the allies continually generated signals that suggested to Moscow the utility of manipulating NATO contradictions.

The third problem complicating learning is that conclusive tests of power relationships are impossible, and such inconclusive tests as exist are rare. Even a major war, as I argued in Chapter 5, provides but an imperfect test of the distribution of military power. The power relationship changes during the conflict and the relative power of the victors is not obvious from the results. A localized war, such as Vietnam, may have a disproportionate impact on perceptions without leading to clarification of the power distribution or even a convergence of assessments among the major powers. Other "tests," such as crises, are resolved on the basis of perceptions of power.

Fourth, the cumulation of evidence about feedback over prolonged periods is complicated by the fact that nothing stays the same. The world is a poor place to conduct experiments. If a policy based on a strategic concept is perceived to have failed in one period, decision makers may still have good reason to hope for its success in a different period. It is difficult to know whether lessons derived from previous

---

[4]For a general discussion, see Robert Jervis, *The Logic of Images in International Relations* (New York: Columbia University Press, 1989).

policies still apply to present circumstances. Conversely, a concept widely thought to have brought success in one period may lead to failure in new circumstances.

The problem of change intersects a fifth issue: the slowness of feedback. World politics does not move along a graceful line, curve, or spiral like some celestial body. It changes chaotically, in fits and starts, separated by long calm spells. In those doldrums, statesmen receive little or no feedback. Ministries and executive agencies dutifully monitor what comes in and base their expectations on it. Since the feedback is meager, it is easy to conclude that it supports the existing policy and its associated strategic analyses. Thus the stage is set for the capriciousness mentioned earlier, for a war or a major crisis will generate more feedback of a higher quality that may contradict the evidence of the previous years.

Sixth, general tendencies concerning the distribution of power are weak. If the balance of power has laws, then they are laws with loopholes big enough to drive a superpower through. If states show a tendency to balance against power, it is a weak one. For a good portion of its life, most notably in its formative years as a state, the Soviet Union arguably had the opposite experience. In addition, the categories we often use to assess the policies of statesmen past and present impose dichotomies that obscure shades of distinction important to decision makers. Do states balance or bandwagon? They may do both. If A increases its military capabilities, B may do the same, but also compensate A with long-sought diplomatic favors. If bandwagoning is defined as "a tendency to ally with," then the proposition that balancing prevails may hold. If bandwagoning is defined as "a tendency to defer to" or "a tendency to take seriously," we may get a different result. But these latter two definitions capture much of what statesmen fear or anticipate when they use bandwagoning terminology.

Further, any consideration of international-political laws must also issue a judgment on what the penalties and rewards for violation are. The mere fact of violating a law does not constitute evidence of irrational or suboptimal behavior. Many of the Soviet policies that may have broken the balancing law, such as Brezhnev's détente policy, also brought the country vastly increased prestige and other valued goods. Whether the trade-off made sense is a hard question to answer without reference to one's own preferences and values.

This last issue is particularly acute when one attempts to assess whether a state exhibited a systematic propensity to violate certain laws. Both superpowers are often accused of "overexpansion."[5] To determine whether a systematic propensity to overexpand actually obtained, it is not enough to find likely cases of overexpansion. One must search with equal analytical energy for cases of underexpansion. Both endeavors, of course, require bold counterfactual reasoning to arrive at a conclusion about what would have happened had different policies been adopted. Now that the Soviet Union has collapsed, many people may wonder why the Americans took it so seriously as an opponent, and indeed why they did not dispatch it much earlier through a more aggressive policy. Doubtless fewer analysts will be inclined to speculate about potential Soviet cases of underexpansion, but numerous candidates come to mind: Stalin's missed revolutionary opportunities after the war, Khrushchev's unwillingness to push harder in Berlin, Gorbachev's reluctance to make a bold, destabilizing German reunification offer earlier in the game.

The weakness of general tendencies concerning power in world politics removes much of the mystery about the long lives of various strategic beliefs. People believe in bandwagoning because it often happens. People think military power is fungible because it often is. People adopt expansionary policies because they can succeed. Two states can act in world politics according to radically different strategic frameworks for long periods because both frameworks can be equally right (and equally wrong). Lenin's theory of imperialism and the correlation-of-forces model lived not only a long life but a productive one. They accounted for the Russian Civil War years, the interwar period, and World War II brilliantly. The concepts underwent creative revision after the war, but so did competing Western notions. Neither Soviet concept was as rigorously or parsimoniously formulated as recent social science scholarship might prefer. But it is open to question whether Lenin and Stalin would have fared much better in world politics if Waltz's *Theory of International Politics* rather than Lenin's *Imperialism* had lain on their Kremlin desks.

Statesmen, in short, are much like international relations scholars. They often appear to care most about things that are not subject to scientific testing. To establish whether a strategic concept concerning the distribution of power, such as the Soviets' venerable correlation-of-forces model, reflects bias is impossible in most cases. The only imaginable standard for assessing learning in this realm of politics is

---

[5] A strong case in favor of this proposition is made by Jack Snyder, *Myths of Empire* (Ithaca: Cornell University Press, 1991).

one's own subjective preferences.[6] For preserving and expanding the world positions of Leninism, Leninist ideas about world politics were effective. For destroying Leninism as an international force, new political thinking was effective. For anticommunists, the Soviet move from Leninist to Western conceptions was learning. For Communists, it was political suicide.

DIFFERENCES IN PERCEPTIONS OF POWER

Rapid change in perceptions, the ambiguity of feedback, and the rarity and inadequacy of tests all translate into the prevalence of differences in perceptions of power among the major actors in world politics. The fact that even world war may fail to clarify fully the distribution of power suggests that differences in perceptions of power must be regarded as the rule rather than the exception. Differences in perceptions of power cannot be captured by the numerical indicators often favored by scholars, but they affect diplomatic intercourse in important ways. Obviously, perceived power is only one among numerous variables bearing on diplomacy, crisis, and war. But U.S.-Soviet arguments about the distribution of power appear to have been an important factor in the ebb and flow of the Cold War.

The evidence presented here concurs with numerous secondary accounts in identifying four crisis phases in the Cold War: the origins in the immediate postwar period of 1945–1947; the intensification in 1949–1951; the series of intense crises between 1959–1962; and the final phase of high tension between 1979 and 1985. Each was shaped by a change in the power relationship differently interpreted by the two sides: the concentration of capabilities in American and Soviet hands revealed by the war; the Soviet atom bomb test and the Chinese Revolution; the Soviets' acquisition of a nuclear capability against the

[6]See Jervis, *Perception and Misperception,* chap. 7; Robert Jervis, Richard Ned Lebow, and Janice Gross Stein, *Psychology and Deterrence* (Baltimore: Johns Hopkins University Press, 1985), chap. 1; and Jack Snyder *Ideology of the Offensive* (Ithaca: Cornell University Press, 1984), 35–38, for analyses of ways to analyze bias in historical cases. On the difficulties of establishing the case for bias in uncertain circumstances, see George W. Downs, "The Lessons of Intervention Failure: Bias or Uncertainty?" in A. Levite et al., *Protracted Military Interventions: From Commitments to Disengagement* (New York: Columbia University Press, 1991). And for a critique, along these and other lines, of learning theory as applied to the study of change in Soviet security policy, see Matthew Evangelista, "Sources of Moderation in Soviet Security Policy," in *Behavior, Society, and Nuclear War,* ed. Robert Jervis et al. (New York: Oxford University Press, 1991), esp. 266–75.

United States; the Soviets' achievement of nuclear parity. In the wake of each shift, each side tried to maximize its own position. Unwilling to go to war to test the power distribution, they reached temporary stalemates after crises, posturing and signaling until a new perceived shift led to another round.

Each phase naturally differed from the others, but all had common features. The phases in 1945–1947 and 1979–1985 (as well as, to a lesser extent, the 1959–1962 phase) followed periods of amicable relations that deteriorated as the flow of diplomatic evidence revealed the contradictions between the two sides' views of the power relationship and its implications for the distribution of political influence. The Khrushchev and, most dramatically, the post-Brezhnev phases of tension were followed by détente as the two views of power converged for a time.

During each phase, familiar sets of arguments, perceptions, and public and private communications came to the fore. Bandwagoning fears, credibility concerns, "will to resist" worries. Circumstances changed but the same symbols and postures kept coming back. On the Soviet side, each instance saw repeated reference to World War II and the immediate postwar period, when Moscow was cheated out of its earned world role. Each instance was accompanied by the proclamation of a "new stage" by party ideologists. Certain key passages concerning the war-prestige issue from the speeches of Stalin, Molotov, Khrushchev, Gromyko, and Brezhnev could have been interchanged indiscriminately with no one the wiser. The same exercise could be performed with American national security memoranda from the three Berlin crises without catching any but the most meticulous historian's eye. One gets the impression that these same words, symbols, concepts, and policies would have continued on as long as there was a cold war.

ORIGINS OF CONTRADICTORY PERCEPTIONS

This analysis suggests that perceptions of power were not wholly capricious, but followed a broad pattern throughout the Cold War. The pattern was connected to changes in real capabilities, although it would be impossible to choose a single indicator or composite index that would predict the precise perceptual pattern without prior knowledge. In earlier periods of international relations that exhibited other diplomatic and power configurations, defined by the outcomes of other wars, similar perceptual patterns with somewhat different contours doubtless prevailed. To what extent these patterns are regular and subject to generalization is a matter for further research. On the basis of such research, it might be possible to generate productive hypotheses about the pattern that is emerging in the wake of the Cold War.

The Cold War experience suggests that differences in perceptions of power are not random, but are related to the mix of resources available to a given state's leadership and the state's position in the international hierarchy. What "power" is is determined in part by how given material distributions are interpreted. Since many interpretations are always possible, state leaderships in a competitive situation will tend to interpret particular changes opportunistically. A state with a comparative advantage in the production of sea power may stress naval balances, while one with advantages in land power may highlight its geographical position and large army.

During the Cold War, Soviet definitions of "power" predictably zeroed in on military capabilities. Shifts in the basic distribution were magnified to support Moscow's claim of diplomatic parity with the United States. The Soviet authorities engineered shifts in declaratory military doctrine in ways that usually sought to undercut the premises of existing U.S. doctrine and that would support the current prestige policy. The Americans, in turn, stressed economic and organizational resources, then nuclear forces, followed again by economic and technical resources as needed to explain continued U.S. hegemony. During each Cold War cycle, each side cited various material shifts to justify its efforts to alter or maintain the existing hierarchy of influence.

The frustrating reality for the dissatisfied challenger, in this case the Soviet Union, is that while the distribution of power remains a matter of dispute, the existing hierarchy of prestige does not. Everyone is always acutely aware of the relative rank ordering of states by diplomatic position. This reality is a hegemon's delight, or perhaps temptation. The ambiguity of power permits the leaders of the dominant state to indulge in endless opportunism in order to justify the continuance of their rightful place under the sun. And while they sometimes fail in this endeavor, we must recognize that they often succeed. That fact, in turn, is not lost on the powers contending for leadership.

HIERARCHY AND EQUILIBRIUM

Conflicting perceptions of power and concepts for comprehending power in world politics are arguably, at least in part, epiphenomena, reflections of other causes. The timing of the emergence of perceptual contradictions is doubtless determined by a host of personal and domestic political factors. But the timing cannot be explained without reference to actual changes in material balances. And the nature of perceptual contradictions is heavily influenced by the resource endowments of particular states, their geographical positions, and their rank within the diplomatic hierarchy.

If the leadership of a state perceives that the capabilities at its disposal have increased, it will usually desire more control over its external environment. To what extent this desire results from a security motivation, as opposed to emotion or ideology, will always be disputed in each case. Some Soviet resentment at American hegemony had to do with the concrete security problems U.S. expansion created for Soviet planners. Americans usually saw their expansion as a reaction to the Soviet threat, and portrayed the maintenance of hegemony as a prerequisite for U.S. security. But each side was also motivated by its attitude toward capitalism and "socialism." And the intensity of each country's compulsion to defend or expand its system cannot be separated from its capability to do so.

The relation between hierarchy and equilibrium can be fully understood only by reference to the elusive nature of the balance of power. The following generalizations emerge from the Cold War experience:

First, the Cold War struggle over hegemony created and reinforced the bipolar equilibrium. Each cycle of struggle reinforced this bipolarity until the challenger state, the Soviet Union, exhausted itself and bipolarity collapsed. The fact that the challenger state rather than the defending dominant power bankrupted itself in the rivalry bodes well for great-power stability, in terms of the hierarchical framework, for it ratifies rather than contradicts the existing hierarchy.[7] No one will feel compelled to challenge the hierarchy until the prolonged operation of the law of uneven development. Thus, even if we set aside such important factors as nuclear deterrence and the spread of liberal values, the immediate future of great-power politics may be regarded optimistically, from the perspective of (nonstructural) realism.

Second, uncertainty surrounding balancing mechanics reinforces hegemonic rivalry. Challenger and defender may have equally plausible expectations that the existing alignment system can be altered or defended.

Third, the coexistence of hegemonic rivalry with the balancing of

---

[7] Geoffrey Blainey, *The Causes of War* (New York: Free Press, 1973), 81–82; Robert Gilpin, *War and Change in World Politics* (Cambridge: Cambridge University Press, 1981).

military potentials complicates the distinction between the deterrence and the spiral model and between offense and defense. The struggle to create, maintain, and oppose hegemony on the part of the Soviet Union and the United States reflected a combination of offensive and defensive aims.

Fourth, the elusiveness of the balance of power is intensified by the differences in states' resources. This was the case in the Cold War, and characterized earlier periods of international relations as well. Centrally located land powers, such as the Soviet Union and Germany, enjoy a natural comparative advantage in the production of military power. For each unit of economic resources consumed they received a greater increment of perceived military power. Balancing the military efforts of such states requires a coalition possessing vastly superior aggregate economic resources, most spectacularly evidenced by the two coalitions that emerged to defeat Germany.[8] Given states' propensity to interpret "power" opportunistically, it is easy to see how hegemonic rivalries linked with spiral-model security dilemmas emerge together and reinforce each other. The dominant coalition believes its grasp on security is tenuous despite its economic preponderance. The land-power challenger feels constrained and even threatened by the opposing coalition and tries various strategies for breaking it.

Fifth, the salience of different sets of capabilities is not constant. The proposition appears almost commonsensical that the distribution of military power is most salient in systemic war and yet declines after the war, when the immediate renewal of hostilities is unlikely. This observation suggests that "soft," nonmilitary resources come into play precisely at the creation of an international order after a major war. A state can both establish and maintain a dominant political position in the international system without achieving a dominant military position. This situation puts in place the prerequisites for all sorts of conflicts and dynamics. The state that dictated terms in the war may be deprived of much of its influence in the war's wake. An

---

[8] Note Stephen Walt's argument that states balance against the most *threatening* state rather than the most powerful one: "Alliance Formation and the Balance of World Power," *International Security* 4 (Spring 1985): 3–41. Perhaps they do, but it is difficult to be sure. Walt measures power by aggregate resources, yet threat is inherently a perceptual phenomenon. Thus he assesses threat in terms of perceptions but power in terms of measured aggregate resources. It is likely that perceived threat and perceived military power covary. Independent influence may be hard to sort out.

enduring contradiction exists between the structure of military power and the structure of influence.

The balance-of-power concept emerges from this analysis as a useful but limited tool for analyzing lengthy spans of international-political history. The large-scale historical forces identified by equilibrium and hierarchical interpretations of the balance of power left their mark on the Cold War years. States do seek security and that search does appear to lead to a very rough balancing of military potentials over the long haul. States also seek control over the international system and struggle over their relative status. The complex interaction between hierarchy and equilibrium goes a long way toward accounting for the onset, cycles, and end of the Cold War. The temptation is powerful to create out of the Cold War experience a pseudo-deductive model of the elusive balance, covering the interaction between equilibrium and hierarchy, and then to apply the model to past and imagined future international systems. But the interaction is too complex for simple modeling. And the nature of the interaction between hegemonic rivalry and balancing behavior which typified the Cold War may be untypical of other periods of international history.

The good news is that there is more to the venerable balance-of-power concept than many analysts imagined. It is still capable of generating useful hypotheses for research. The issues it highlights turn out to be important in every states system of which we have record. They arise in each of the various configurations the modern states system has assumed. It would be intellectually imprudent to think that suddenly these factors will cease to matter. The bad news is that the issues of power, prestige, and security appear to arise in different ways, in different mixtures and intensities at different times.

We can capture the ways power influences history only by studying perceptions and ideas. The elusiveness of power becomes clear only when the clarity of hindsight is removed by careful historical research. That research reveals the multitudinous ambiguities surrounding power in world politics. Only by understanding those ambiguities can we understand how power really works.

The sources of ambiguity identified here are almost too many to name. Power cannot be tested; different elements of power possess different utilities at different times; the relation of perceived power to material resources can be capricious; the mechanics of power are surrounded by uncertainty; states possess different conversion ratios and comparative advantages; the perceived prestige hierarchy and the military distribution may not coincide for prolonged periods; states adopt asymmetrical strategies to maximize their positions and undercut rivals; signals get confused among allies, rivals, and domestic audiences. Drawing boxes and circles around these various sources of ambiguity and connecting them with lines and arrows will not make their interrelation any clearer. For all we know, the nature of their interaction uncovered here was peculiar to the Cold War. Only further research on the sources of ambiguity surrounding power in world politics can determine whether the interaction between hierarchy and equilibrium and between security and prestige is subject to useful generalization.

What this investigation does give us is pause; pause before we issue oracle-like judgments on the performances of past statesmen, before we assess the behavior of actors on the world scene according to deceptively clear theoretically derived laws, and before we apply such laws in confident predictions.

Index

Abalkin, Leonid, 229, 230
Acheson, Dean, 106, 127
Adomeit, Hannes, 261n, 281n
Afghanistan, 217, 218, 248, 274
Africa, 217, 218, 274
Akhromeev, Sergei, 277
Aksiutin, Iu. V., 142n
Aleksandrov, A., 108n
Alignment, 42, 43, 167. *See also* Alliances; Balancing; Bandwagoning; Bipolarity; Multipolarity; Polarity
—views of: postwar Soviet, 65–77; postwar U.S., 87–94; prewar Soviet, 54–61
Alliances, 54–56; Soviet desire to revise, 262–67, 276–77. *See also* Alignment; Balancing; Bandwagoning; Bipolarity
Ambiguity: of balance of power, 3, 13, 16, 26, 100, 138; of feedback, 55–57, 75, 96–97, 138; of power calculations, 9–10, 61; of Soviet leadership pronouncements, 61–62, 77, 195, 236–37, 254, 259, 281–82
Ambrose, Stephen E., 169n
American hegemony, 25, 59, 142; perceived decline of, 199–200; Soviet views of, 72, 75, 80, 85–88, 138, 152–56, 195–96, 233; U.S. explanations of, 222, 303–4
Amirdzhanov, Mikhail, 268n, 284n
Anderson, Martin, 245
Andrew, Christopher, 238n
Andropov, Iurii V., 225, 231, 240, 249
Angola, 206, 217
Aron, Raymond, 6
Arzumanian, Anushavan, 161

Asmus, Ronald, D., 279n
Atlantic Alliance. *See* North Atlantic Treaty Organization
Atomic bombs. *See* Nuclear weapons
Attlee, Clement, 70, 150
Arbatov, Georgii A., 140n, 188n, 207, 233n, 258n; and Soviet détente policy, 189–91
Attitude vs. alignment or alliance, 27, 222, 296

Bacon, Francis, 9, 10
Balance of power, 1, 10–17, 20; defined, 3, 5, 26–28; and equilibrium, 8, 23, 54, 59; equilibrium vs. hierarchical understanding of, 11–14, 24–25, 135–36, 138, 179–83, 220, 304–6; utility of, 2, 24, 182, 306
Balancing: and reformist ideology, 276; and Soviet hostility thesis, 52, 56; as systemic imperative, 23, 288, 296
—vs. bandwagoning: in superpower perspectives, 52, 55–57, 95, 259–68; in theory, 27–28, 138, 299, 305–6
Baldwin, David A., 4n, 5n, 9n
Banchoff, Thomas, 245n
Bandwagoning: and hierarchy, 24
—perceptions of: Soviet, 51–52, 73, 80, 98, 114, 151–57, 182–83, 188, 198–99, 259–60, 264–68; superpower, 95, 148, 300, 302; U.S., 88, 92–93, 145, 167, 170–72, 216. *See also* Balancing
Barker, Elisabeth, 70n, 89n, 90n, 121n
Baz', I. S., 108n
Bazhanov, E. P., 113n

Index

Index

Index

Power (*cont.*) 298–303; economic vs. military, 26, 32, 57–58, 92–93, 115, 117–18, 120–21, 126–28, 132, 143, 244–48, 268–72; measures of, 5–10, 59–61; structure of, 8, 237–44. *See also* Economic performance; Military power; Perceptions; Polarity

"Power centers," 117, 155, 197, 200, 214, 232, 235, 237, 261, 276

Pozdniakov, El'giz A., 236n

Presidential Review Memorandum 10 (PRM-10, 218–20

Prestige: and bipolarity, 295; defined, 28; and Gorbachev's foreign policy, 259–60, 268–69, 272; impact of World War II on, 102, 129, 131, 135–36; Khrushchev's policy of, 156–60, 180; vs. security as behavioral motivation, 11, 25, 138, 306; and superpower relations, 175–76, 211, 221, 265, 272

Primakov, Evgenii M., 206n, 236n, 241, 243n

Quester, George H., 239n

Ra'anan, Gavriel, 65n
Ra'anan, Uri, 142n
Radek, Karl, 42, 48
Rapallo Treaty, 39, 43, 45, 50, 194
Ray, James Lee, 59n
Reagan, Ronald, 232, 245–47
Reagan Doctrine, 240, 246
Realism, 11, 13, 14, 24, 26, 59, 94, 100, 131, 236, 252, 260, 275; and cooperation, 13–14; and perceptions of power, 1–10. *See also names of individual authors*
Realpolitik, 41
Record, Jeffrey, 231n
Revisionism, 10, 264, 266, 267
Revolution, 39, 111–15, 125, 126, 203; Soviet expectations of, 44–45, 111–15; U.S. fears of, 124–27; and war, 35–36, 38, 49, 145
Rice, Condoleeza, 42n
Richter, James Gerard, 141n
Rivkin, David B., Jr., 231n
"Rollback," 165, 240n
Ropponen, Risto, 2n
Rosecrance, Richard, 11n, 21
Rosenberg, David Allen, 169n
Ross, Graham, 121n
Rothwell, Victor, 70n, 121n
Rousseau, Jean-Jacques, 6
Rush, Myron, 144n, 158n, 165n
Russett, Bruce, 4n, 6n
Rybkin, E., 191n

Sanakoev, Shalva P., 190n
Schapiro, Leonard, 37n
Scott, Harriet and William F., 202n
Security dilemma, concept of, 257–58
Security vs. prestige as behavioral motivation, 11, 25, 138, 306
Shakhnazarov, Georgii, 166
Shaposhnikov, Boris, 48
Shatalin, Stanislav, 244n
Shenfield, Stephen, 239n, 255n
Shepilov, Dmitrii, 151
Shevardnadze, Eduard, 255, 267, 272, 277, 283, 285, 288, 289
Shevchenko, Arkady, 188
Shishkov, Iu., 235
Shlapentokh, Vladimir, 229n
Shmelev, Nikolai, 232n, 234–36
Shneerson, A., 116n
Shulman, Marshall, 19n, 65n, 85n
Shultz, George, 246–48
Signaling, 135, 143, 175, 176, 275, 289, 298, 307
Simonian, R., 191n
Simonyan, R., 243n
Singer, J. D., 8n., 21, 59n
Siverson, Randolph, 3n
Slavin, N.V., 156n
Smith, Walter Bedell, 88, 93, 102n, 125n, 126
Snyder, Glenn H., 27n, 143
Snyder, Jack, 24, 25n, 300n, 301n
Socialism, 81, 106, 139–40, 227–28, 304; and alignment, 199–200; contradictions of, 200, 243–45, 289; vs. imperialism, 145–49, 205; in Third World, 274–75
Sodaro, Michael J., 192n, 196n
Sokolov, I., 187n
Solodovnik, N., 151n
Solonitskii, A., 274n
"Sonnenfeldt doctrine," 268
Sontag, John P., 47n
Spiral model, 305
Spirin, L. M., 107n
Stability: Brezhnev-era views of, 190–93; Gorbachev and, 283, 286; of postwar international system, 182–83, 197, 232, 233, 260, 291
Stabilization: of capitalism, 40–41, 43–44; of postwar Europe, 88–94
Stalin, Iosif: and Berlin blockade, 75; vs. Bukharin, 49–50; on capitalist crises, 50–53, 62–63, 76; death of, 76, 137, 141; on interimperialist contradictions, 42, 45, 53, 62–63; military doctrine of, 107–11, 238; model of world politics

Index

CORNELL STUDIES IN SECURITY AFFAIRS

edited by Robert J. Art *and* Robert Jervis

Nuclear Crisis Management: A Dangerous Illusion, by Richard Ned Lebow

The Search for Security in Space, edited by Kenneth N. Luongo and W. Thomas Wander

The Nuclear Future, by Michael Mandelbaum

Conventional Deterrence, by John J. Mearsheimer

Liddell Hart and the Weight of History, by John J. Mearsheimer

The Sacred Cause: Civil-Military Conflict over Soviet National Security, 1917–1992, by Thomas M. Nichols

Inadvertent Escalation: Conventional War and Nuclear Risks, by Barry R. Posen

The Sources of Military Doctrine: France, Britain, and Germany between the World Wars, by Barry R. Posen

Dilemmas of Appeasement: British Deterrence and Defense, 1934–1937, by Gaines Post, Jr.

Winning the Next War: Innovation and the Modern Military, by Stephen Peter Rosen

Israel and Conventional Deterrence: Border Warfare from 1953 to 1970, by Jonathan Shimshoni

Fighting to a Finish: The Politics of War Termination in the United States and Japan, 1945, by Leon V. Sigal

The Ideology of the Offensive: Military Decision Making and the Disasters of 1914, by Jack Snyder

Myths of Empire: Domestic Politics and International Ambition, by Jack Snyder

The Militarization of Space: U.S. Policy, 1945–1984, by Paul B. Stares

Making the Alliance Work: The United States and Western Europe, by Gregory F. Treverton

The Origins of Alliances, by Stephen M. Walt

The Ultimate Enemy: British Intelligence and Nazi Germany, 1933–1939, by Wesley K. Wark

The Tet Offensive: Intelligence Failure in War, by James J. Wirtz

The Elusive Balance: Power and Perceptions during the Cold War, William Curti Wohlforth

Deterrence and Strategic Culture: Chinese-American Confrontations, 1949–1958, by Shu Guang Zhang

Library of Congress Cataloging-in-Publication Data

Wohlforth, William Curti, 1959–
  The elusive balance : power and perceptions during the Cold War /
William Curti Wohlforth.
      p.   cm. —(Cornell studies in security affairs)
    Includes bibliographical references and index.
    ISBN 0-8014-2822-X (cloth)—0-8014-8149-X (pbk.)
    1. World politics—1945–   2. Balance of power.   3. Cold War.
I. Title.   II. Series.
D842.W64   1993
320.9'04—dc20   93-6857